ISRAEL IN EGYPT:

A Poem.

BY
EDWIN ATHERSTONE,
AUTHOR OF
"THE FALL OF NINEVEH," "THE HANDWRITING ON THE WALL," &c. &c. &c.

"The children of Israel sighed, by reason of their bondage: and they cried; and their cry came up unto God."

ISBN: 978-1-63923-957-3

All Rights reserved. No part of this book maybe reproduced without written permission from the publishers, except by a reviewer who may quote brief passages in a review to be printed in a newspaper or magazine.

Printed: March 2023

Published and Distributed By:
Lushena Books
607 Country Club Drive, Unit E
Bensenville, IL 60106
www.lushenabks.com

ISBN: 978-1-63923-957-3

MARY ELIZABETH ATHERSTONE,

HIS BELOVED DAUGHTER,

AND MOST FAITHFUL FRIEND,

THE AUTHOR INSCRIBES THIS POEM.

PREFACE.

WITH the desire, apparently, to render more easily credible those extraordinary events, the Plagues of Egypt,—some of the commentators on the Book of Exodus have laid much stress on the fact, that they are all, *in kind*, such phenomena only as have not unfrequently been known in that country. They say, for example, that, at certain seasons, the Nile assumes a reddish color, resembling blood : that the rivers, at times, produce immense numbers of frogs: that the Egyptians have frequently been afflicted with small vermin on their bodies: that immense swarms of flies occasionally pester them, filling the houses, and the air : that a murrain among cattle has often destroyed thousands; and grievous boils have been equally fatal among men : that most violent storms of hail have caused great destruction : that clouds of locusts have wrought havoc through the land : that, at certain times, during a peculiar wind, the air has become fearfully dark ; and that pestilences have suddenly carried off numbers who, up to the hour of attack, had been in full vigor.

In this way are the ten plagues represented as *natural* events merely ; and, so far, easily credible. The *preter*natural, and *super*natural differences from those, are—

that, whereas, in the usual course of events, such a train of visitations would have extended over many years,—*these* scourges occurred within the space of a few months; or even, as some say,—and as it is assumed in the present work,—within less than one month;—many of them, therefore, at a season of the year in which, except in this instance, they have never been known;—that they were awful, and destructive, in a degree to which there is no parallel in other history;—and, furthermore, and chiefly,—that nearly all of them were predicted by Moses; and many of them were removed at his intercession with the God of Israel.

This is not a fit place to enter into argument on the subject,—even if the author were disposed to argue upon it at all,—which he is not. To those who doubt, or wholly disbelieve, the narrative of these wonderful occurrences, it might, *so far as the following poem is concerned*, be sufficient to cite the indisputable maxim, stated by Southey in the first note appended to his Roderic,— "FOR THE PURPOSES OF POETRY, IT IS IMMATERIAL WHETHER THE STORY BE TRUE OR FALSE."

In the present work, however, the Plagues of Egypt are treated as truths; but, truths wholly, and *in the highest degree*, MIRACULOUS.

Much uncertainty exists as to the precise nature of some of the animals which constituted three of the Plagues. The Hebrew word which, in our Bible, is translated *frogs,*—is, by some scholars, understood to mean an Egyptian fish; while, by others, it is supposed to signify, a crocodile. The word which, in our Bible, is rendered *lice,* is, in the great work of Kalisch, rendered *gnats.* The word which, in our version, is translated *flies,*—is, by Kalisch, and other critics, rendered *beetles.*

By several writers of antiquity, however, that word was believed to mean, "*all kinds of noxious animals, and serpents, and scorpions, mixed together;*" while, by others, it was supposed to signify, "*wild beasts in crowds; as lions, and wolves, and bears, and leopards.*"

Josephus, again, says: " *God filled that country full of various sorts of pestilential creatures, with their various properties,* SUCH, INDEED, AS HAD NEVER COME INTO THE SIGHT OF MAN BEFORE."

This uncertainty will, he hopes, be sufficient to justify the present writer for having, in two instances, depicted animals differing considerably from those which are commouly indicated by the names. The poor frog of our streams, and ditches, could not easily be represented as a scourge sufficiently fearful to hold rank in that series which included the Plagues of Hail,—Darkness,—and Death of the first-born: nor, without supernatural properties imparted, could it have accomplished that which was threatened, and brought about. The frogs of the Plague *covered the land;* filled the houses, the bedchambers, the troughs, the ovens, &c. In its *natural* state, the common frog *could* not have accomplished these things: and it is, therefore, a no unfair inference, that the animals in question were supernatural in their *qualities,* as well as in their birth.

The fourth Plague, again,—if the word "*flies*" is understood to designate merely the little animals that somewhat unpleasantly infest our rooms in hot weather,—could not, any more than that of the common frog, have been an affliction so severe, and terrible, as to bow the pride of that Pharaoh who had, just before, defied two torments far more annoying, and detestable; and who, afterwards, till the evening of the third day, bore up against all the horrors of a *darkness that might be felt.*

Even without the authority of Josephus, therefore, a writer in verse may surely be allowed to represent animals, " SUCH AS HAD NEVER COME INTO THE SIGHT OF MAN BEFORE ;" provided that, in doing this, he presents an agent more fit to the accomplishment of the effect produced; a scourge more like a real and terrible infliction from Supernal Power; and that, at the same time, he disturbs no important truth.

Except in these two instances, the author has differed little from the narrative of Moses, as to the general nature of the Plagues: but, in filling up the outline of Scripture, he has felt himself at liberty to give full scope to imagination (such as he may possess) in the attempt to depict events, which, as proceeding from direct supernatural command,—whether for warning, or for punishment,—may justly be supposed to have been grand, and terrific, in a degree far surpassing aught that history has recorded, as having occurred in the established course of Nature.

To render it more probable, and credible,—many sincerely pious persons have sought for *natural* means by which the last great event of the Exodus, the passage of the Red Sea, may have been accomplished. Some have thought that,—on account of its great width, it must have been *impossible* for the Israelites to pass it in one night: others have objected, that it was far too deep for the waters to be piled up on each hand; and to *stand like walls:* and they suggest, therefore, that it was not through the Red Sea that the Hebrews passed; but through the gulf of Suez,—a water much less broad, and, comparatively, shallow.

Now,—if this parting of the water was *not* the work of Supernatural Power,—the most remarkable part of the narrative must be regarded as fable; since there are no *natural* causes by which it *could* have been effected. It is, indeed, related, that there was a strong east wind at the time: but no wind could possibly cut a dry channel through even the narrowest brook, or pond; and heap up the waters on each hand, *like walls*. If, on the contrary, Supernatural Power is admitted as the agent,— why should we trouble ourselves to seek for *natural* causes;

in order to render the act, and event, probable, and credible? If Omnipotence was engaged in the work,—what could be the difficulty? Would the parting of the Red Sea,—or of the Atlantic,—be a miracle greater than the *creation* of those waters? Nay—would the channelling of the Great Pacific, and the walling up of its waves, leagues in height, be, in reality, more truly a *miracle*, than the walling-up of the water in a mill-pond? These acts would be alike *miraculous*, as being alike interruptions of the established Law of Nature: and, for Almighty Power, the one act would be as easy as the other.

One learned modern traveller says that, had the Israelites passed through the Red Sea,—instead of *walls*, there must have been *mountains* of water piled up to the right hand, and to the left, as they journeyed over its bed. What then? Was this too hard a task for the God of Israel? and must the narrow gulf of Suez, therefore, be assigned for the scene of the exploit; as being better suited to His power? The event was wholly miraculous, or the narrative is not wholly true.

The gulf of Suez has been passed several times, when the tide has been low, and the wind favorable; and no one dreamed that a miracle was thereby wrought. On the last recorded occasion, the passage was made by one as unlike to Moses, as Moloch to the Archangel Michael, —Napoleon Bonaparte. But, of the passage of the RED SEA, there is no record, except that of the Israelites, under Moses. The Bible states clearly, that it was through the RED SEA that they went; that "THE CHILDREN OF ISRAEL WALKED UPON DRY LAND IN THE MIDST OF THE SEA; AND THE WATERS WERE A WALL UNTO THEM ON THEIR RIGHT HAND, AND ON THEIR LEFT."

Through that RED SEA, accordingly, are they, in the following poem, conducted: and the "*mountains*" of water, upright as walls, on their right hand, and on their left, are presented as the natural phenomena.

To follow strictly the Scripture narrative,—and have, thus, the opportunity to attempt the picturing of scenes so grand, and terrible,—was, it is hoped, a wiser—as, to the writer, it was certainly a more tempting course,—than,—for the sake of preserving an appearance of *rational probability*,—to depart from the Bible history, and conduct the Israelites over the gulf of Suez,—BECAUSE, forsooth,—"*the sea there is only* 757 *double paces broad: and the Hebrew army could well journey it within* 6 *or* 7 *hours :*" BECAUSE,—"*the water is here free from sea-weeds, which, in more southern sections, considerably aggravate the passage, and render a quick march impossible.*"

Why,—what have these, and such like considerations, to do with an event conducted by Omnipotence! And, even had they been of weight,—who can know, from appearances at the present day, what may have been the state of the Red Sea, or the gulf of Suez, in the time of the Exodus? Within 4000 years, hills may have sunk down to plains; plains may have arisen, and become hills. In our own country, houses and farms are now upon ground which, within a far less period of time, was the bed of the sea: and lands whereon man built his dwelling-places,—lived, married, feasted, died, and was buried, century after century,—are now swept over by shoals of ocean fish.

As before said,—if Omnipotence commanded,—the Pacific might have been channelled; and the waters walled up, leagues high. Those who sincerely believe that the Omnipotent, and the God of Israel, are one and the same,—and that by His power were all those wonderful things done, for the deliverance of His people,—should not too anxiously measure the width of the sea, the depth of its water, and the condition of its bed, in order to make it credible that the work was not too great for Him.

Of the exact place at which the Israelites crossed the Red Sea, nothing whatever is known: and conjecture has been vain. As before mentioned,—some points are discarded because the sea is too wide; and the Hebrews could not have crossed it in one night! Other points are objected to, because "the mountains of the wilderness," which shut in the Israelites, are not found in the neighbourhood. Should that sea ever be dried up,—and should the bones of the Egyptians, and of their horses; the iron wheels of the chariots, and the mail of the warriors, be dug up from its bed,—then, indeed, may it with some certainty be pronounced,—" by this way passed the Israelites; and here was the host of Pharaoh overwhelmed:"—but, till then, it is most probable that no sure knowledge of the precise spot will be obtained.

It will scarcely be questioned that the subject of the poem is sufficiently great to justify the use of Poetical Machinery. The author has, however, restricted this to Angels only, "both those who stood, and those who fell." Except so far as the text of Scripture compelled him, he has not presumed to represent Deity. The Bible says repeatedly, "the Lord spake unto Moses." A Voice, therefore, is introduced; but a personal God never.

In adopting a portion of that Machinery which was so magnificently treated by Milton, the present writer had, assuredly, no thought of imitating,—far less of vying with, that sublimest of all poets. Perhaps, on the contrary, he may be thought more justly liable to the charge of audacity, for having, in so many important points, presumed to differ from him. In one simile will be found the only image which he has, *consciously*, borrowed from him, or from any other poet: and even in that instance, the variation is so considerable, that the theft will not, he hopes, be regarded as a very serious crime.

In the Paradise Lost, that Machinery was an all important *element;* and both demanded, and excited, the very highest power of the poet : in the present work, it is an *adjunct* only; and, as such, in even Milton's hands, would not have stimulated to the like excess of imagination; nor demanded the like almost superhuman strength. It was resorted to, chiefly, for the purpose of preventing a too probable monotony, by coupling with the main interest of the Poem, another of a nature wholly different from that, yet not discordant with it. The subject did not *require* the aid of Machinery; but neither did it forbid its use : and, in one respect, it seemed to offer a no inconsiderable advantage, by affording a means for overgetting that terrible stumbling-block to theologians,— the hardening of Pharaoh's heart *by God himself*. That so evil a deed should be done by the great originator of evil, is, at least, quite consistent with his character. He who tempted Eve to sin, might harden Pharaoh to disobey : but, that the ALL JUST should have compelled the man to crime, and then punished him for having done that which He Himself had *forced* him to do,—is utterly incredible. Surely it is better to suppose error in a transcriber, or a translator, than to impute to the ALL GOOD and ALL MERCIFUL, conduct for which even the worst of men would appear yet worse, and more odious.

In one passage of the grand address of Satan to the Sun, Milton makes the Fallen Angel express a belief that, by a sincere repentance, and submission, he might obtain pardon for his sins, and be restored to heaven.

> "Oh then at last relent! Is there no place
> Left for repentance ; none for pardon left ?
> None left *but by submission?* . . . . .
> * * *

"But say I could repent, and could obtain,
By act of grace, my former state; how soon
Would height recall high thoughts; how soon unsay
What feigned submission swore. . . . . .

* * * * *

"Which would but lead me to a *worse relapse*,
And *heavier fall;* so should I purchase dear
Short *intermission*, bought with double smart."

Milton, who was well versed in the works of the Fathers, knew, of course, that such a doctrine had been propounded even so early as in the time of Origen. The present writer has no intention to argue the matter. If a fable, it is, at least, a very beautiful one; and perfectly consistent with the character of that Deity who is, at once, Almighty, All Just, and All Merciful. Redemption was offered to *man*, because he had been *seduced* to disobedience. Among the host of Fallen Angels, may it not be supposed that there were myriads of the weaker Spirits, who, in like way, had been seduced by those who were the strongest, and the highest in glory? On behalf of such feebler spirits, might not, then, the same plea for mercy be urged? The doctrine may be frowned at by the stern Calvinist; but may surely, without blame, be cherished by the poet. No one is called upon to believe it: but they who feel assured that God must be All Merciful, as well as Almighty, will, at least, *wish* it to be a truth. Be it, however, a verity, or be it a pleasing fancy only,—the author has, in the following poem, assumed it to be a truth; and, in the instance of one of the humblest of the Fallen Angels, has attempted to show how,—after repentance the most deep, and the firmest resolve to endure all that hell could inflict upon him, rather than continue in its bad service,—he had been pardoned by the All Merciful, and restored to happiness in Heaven. This is not, however, the first occasion on which, in our own day, the above doctrine has been a subject for the poet. In that extraordinary production of genius, Festus,

Mr. P. J. Bailey has represented the final restoration to God of *the whole host of Fallen Angels*.

Dante has conceived his own hell: has gorged it with abominations,—and has been applauded for the choice music of verse, in which he has blasphemed God, by attributing to Him the infliction, — through demoniac agency,—of torments, at once the most horrific, and the most disgusting. Milton, also, has depicted his own hell; and, though with an imagination incomparably grander than that of the savage Italian, has, like him, dwelt too much upon terrific torments in fire and in ice. The present writer,—notwithstanding such great authorities for what a hell ought to be,—has felt himself at liberty to imagine a far different place, and kind, of punishment for the rebellious Angels : and, if he has thus deprived himself of the aid of all those splendid horrors which, for the majority of minds, render the descriptions of hell so fearfully fascinating and sublime,—he trusts that he has, at least, represented a mode of retribution for sin, more in harmony with all the undisputed attributes of Deity.

The reader is entreated to correct the following misprints:
P. 15, line 18, for "exstinction," read "extinction."
P. 214, line 11, for "franctically," read "franticly."
P. 374, line 1, for "ook," read "look."
P. 388, line 4 from bottom, for "stars-points," read "star-points."

ISRAEL IN EGYPT.

BOOK FIRST.

Tombed in the solid night of starless space;
From nearest living orb so far removed,
That light, of all material things most swift,
Myriads on myriads of earth's years must speed,
Ere the mere outskirts of that Stygian gloom,
If ever, it might reach,—at rest eterne,
Lies the cold wreck of an extinguished sun.
Prime glory once of all heaven's radiant host;
Body, for soul of purest light most fit—
'Tween its first darkening, and eclipse complete,
Streamed years which might eternity appear;
While into ether, like the particles,
Invisible, which are the breath of flowers,
The mighty bulk its softer elements
Still ever was exhaling. As when flesh
And sinew of earth's monster Mastodon,
By the slow wasting of the elements,
All are dissolved, and hard, enduring bones
Alone remain,—even so, of this immense,—
When, by the ocean waves of centuries,
Millions succeeding millions, worn away,—
The adamantine skeleton alone,
In darkness, silence, utter solitude,
A ruin for eternity, was left.

From glory of heaven, from eye of God, so far
Remote was this, that even His own work,
Omniscience had forgotten? that no more
Was Omnipresence there? that Power Supreme
No longer, like a beacon-flame to mark
Confines of Night, its once vast fires upheld?

Forgetteth not Omniscience; faileth not
Omnipotence: the Omnipresent still
There present is; though, to even angel's ken,
Invisible, as, to weaker eye of man,
Earth's centre.   In the depth of ages past,
Over heaven's brightness,—nay, within the courts
Nighest the Throne, a shadow had there come:
Sin, like a foul mist charged with pestilence,
Had risen portentous; and in Beings pure
And happy, entered; gendering envy, wrath,
Discord, and mad revolt against the Power
By Whom alone they lived. A little while,
Frenzied they thus had stood; as gods with God
Hoping to rule; and, on the spirits true,
Words of contempt, and looks of high disdain,
Proudly outpouring: but, no sign of wrath
Forewarning; no dread voice, doom-speaking, heard,—
Throughout his whole Essential, suddenly,
Felt every tainted angel that, for him,
No longer were God's mansions fit abode!
As by dark lightning-blast, so, by a Power
Unseen, resistless, sheer o'er face of heaven,
Like clouds of dust before the hurricane,
Deep down into the void were they borne off,
All terror-struck, strengthless, dumb. Away—away—
Swifter than speed of light-beam flew they on:
Stars gleamed before them;—swelled to suns—died out
As stars again behind them, and were lost;—
Yet still on—on—by the invisible Might
Urged through the infinite—on still they shot:
Mid constellations vast and numberless,
Above—below—before—to right, and left,—
All seeming, in the speed of that dread flight,

Like fire-sparks on the wind, to stream the sky:
Strange forms, unknown to man,—far, far past ken
Of telescopic eye, though myriad-fold
Space-piercing more than his of the emerald isle,
The astronomer's glory;—yet still on,—on,—on,—
Through regions darkening,—darker,—darker still,—
As though the confines of the universe
They had approached; where few, and fewer yet,
Dimmer, and more remote the shining points,—
Till, far beyond even glimpse of living orb,
Deep in the ocean of eternal night,
On that huge sun-anatomy, at length,
Scattered like sand-grains flung upon the wind,
Down fell they,—and their perilous flight was done.

Here then, alas! their future place they knew!
For heaven's all-glorious beams, a solid dark!
For heaven's seraphic music, a dead load
Of silence, crushing! for unspeakable joy,
Gloom evermore! and, for the presence of God,
Death, universal death!—such their new home
They felt; and such, throughout eternity,
Dreaded would be their doom.
                          A thousand years,
As mortals measure time,—even as at first,
Wide scattered, on the sun-wreck they had fallen,—
Silent, and motionless, by terror fixed,
The outcast spirits remained. But then, at length,—
By the All Merciful permitted so,—
From torpor waked, their leader's mighty voice
Once more they heard; throughout all Essences
Piercing, as light through darkness; and from death,
To a new life uprousing. In the heart
Of that dead sun, vacuous and huge, where, erst,
With light intensest had the heaven-fire blazed,
He bade them gather. At the welcome call,
From their long trance all started. Down at once,
Mid utter darkness, through the adamant bones
Of the great skeleton, as through air, they pierced:
And lo! within the void—though as of flame,

Blood-red and gloomy—light! light! once more light!
The long lost, glorious light!
                          As, to the eye
Of lonely shepherd, on some tall hill's brow
Watching by night, seems heaven's stupendous round,—
So vast to these astonished, in mid way
Pausing to gaze, on every side alike,
Showed that immense rotund. A solid sphere
Of lurid fire—an atmosphere of fire,
All seemed; yet only seemed; for heat was none;
But, from the genial beams of living sun
So inconceivably far, a cold intense,
That earth's thin air to solid had congealed,
Made flesh as granite.
                          Yet nor cold, nor heat,
In Spiritual Natures, as in bodily nerves,
Shoots the sharp sting of pain. Bad dream of man,
Which, in the All Wise, All Just, All Merciful,
Sees but the worst Inquisitor's prototype,
The avenger, the tormentor infinite!
All love is God: Heaven but His Presence is;
Hell, banishment from Heaven; and dread remorse,—
"THE WORM THAT NEVER DIES, THE FIRE NE'ER
    QUENCHED,"—
Which, like the ravening tiger o'er his prey,
Mangles and gnaws the spirit ceaselessly,
Though undestroying; till,—the sin purged out,
By utmost penitence, submission full,
And prayer intense for pardon and for help,—
Again upon the erring spirit beams
The smile divine of God. Such the mild law
Of the All Merciful, Omnipotent,
To fallen angels; and to man, by them
Seduced. To those, at least, of men, whose day
Was, ere the Mediator, filled with love
And pity for lost creatures, came on earth,
An easier, swifter means of Grace to give.
And to those, surely, also, who, though born
After His wondrous advent, yet of Him,
His life, His teaching, nay His very name,

Nought hear; or, hearing, fail to understand:
Else, for one half mankind, His gracious scheme
Its end would fail to accomplish;—argument
Of insufficiency, with Power Supreme
Impossible!
         But nought, as yet, knew they
Of God's unbounded mercy. Sin they knew,
By them committed; wrath eternal feared,
And punishment unending; if themselves,
By victory, gained not freedom. Yet even then,
Like the first tinge of day on the dark night,
Was God's great goodness opening. Not for aye
Designed He that dead orb their prison-place;
Not to a blackness never ending, doomed
Spirits for Heaven create; to whom was light
Even as life; darkness a worse than death.

    Permitted then,—yet, in his own fond thought,
Originator sole,—on the blank night
Of the dead sun's great heart, the wretched chief
Of the fall'n host that dark red gleam had waked;—
Throughout the vast, even like an atmosphere
Of flame, pervading; whence, in one deep glow,
Gem-clear, the nigh, the distant, equally
Apparent stood; and shadow could be none.
Yet, after their long night of misery,
Silence unbroken, utter loneliness,—
Gladdening as sunrise to night-wandering man,
On the fall'n angels broke that dark red gleam:
Light, blessed light, not, then, for ever lost!
So that, with spirit thrilling, the great voice
Of their proud leader listened they,—wild hope
Stirring of progress sure; and victory yet,
Even o'er the Omnipotent! Despair, a crime
Against themselves, he taught. They had been foiled
By power more mighty, won from knowledge more
Of Nature's causes, workings, instruments.
But, with the ages, to themselves not less
Would wisdom come—to godhead lifting them;
Till, with power like his own, they might confront

Him who was now their victor; and, perchance,
Down from His Heaven-throne cast Him: or, at least,
Dominion equal gain; o'er one half Heaven
Ruling supreme, as, o'er the other, He.

   To such proud, foolish thoughts, a willing ear
Did the fallen Spirits give: and, after him,
Others, as proud and foolish,—though less strong,
And, in their former glory, lower far,—
Words of same madness spake; till, like the swell
Of some great sea, storm-vexed, the multitude
In dire commotion worked; impatient all
From that drear dungeon to go forth at once;
And in some better place, more nigh to Heaven,
New life begin, and their new course essay.

   But not, as yet, the pitying Deity
Their bonds thought fit to loose. From this terrene
Right up toward heaven, as easily might man
Ascend, and skirt the stars, as, from their place
Of banishment, might those fall'n Spirits depart.
Attempt they made; but,—by the Power withheld,—
Beyond the outside of their dungeon orb
No more could stir, than, from an iron mass,
Its grains could part, and, like winged insects, take
Their separate tracks through air. Dejection deep
Sank then on all. Again, through many an age,
Silent, and wandering lone, and dead to hope,
Mourned the fall'n angels;—Heaven for ever lost,
Weeping, as Spirits weep: of mercy none,
Less of forgiveness, thinking: and no more
Of growing strength expectant; such as, yet,
Might from their dungeon aid them to escape;
And, somewhere in the orbs of life and light,
New course begin; less dolorous, even though glimpse
Of brighter prospect, nigher to Heaven's bounds,
Never should gladden them. Remorse they felt;
Yet, less for sin, as wrong against their God,
Their Maker, the Great Fountain of all Good,—
Than as the source of their own misery;

Their loss of Heaven; their dread captivity
In that gaunt skeleton, that realm of death,
Mid everlasting night. Long ages, long,
Thus miserable they.
                         The time, at length,
By the All Merciful decreed, was come.
Somewhat had penitence the Spirits touched,
By misery bowed; and, though Omniscience knew,
How, greater freedom given, would pride arise;
How the plague-tainted Spirits, their disease,
Throughout a world yet uncreate; and man,
Its destined habitant, would haste to spread;—
Yet, all the depths of the eternal years
Clearly beholding, as the immediate Now;
And the great consummation—Evil made
To work out finally a greater good;
Fullness of joy throughout His Universe,—
Else, had Omnipotence failed, Omniscience erred;
The All Merciful, more than man been merciless,—
Beholding thus,—by pity moved, nay love
For even those rebellious, folly struck,—
Their great, their heaviest fetters He bade drop.

   As on earth's midnight sky the lightning gleams,
So suddenly through every Spirit shot
Sense of new freedom gained. As instantly,
For the dark ruby beam, burst splendor such,
As though, at last, from his long, death-like sleep,
To a new life the mighty orb had waked.
From floor to roof, from side to side, it burned;
Amid the bones of the sun-skeleton
Flashing and quivering with a thousand hues,
As on a round of ribbëd diamond.

   Intensest joy broke forth. The Spirits all
Sent up their voices till the concave rang;
Full freedom feeling; light of Heaven once more
Beholding: yet, to God's All Merciful Love,
Nothing attributing; but Nature—Fate—
Or their own growing strength, and excellence,

The cause misdeeming. Straightway gathering then,—
Ere through the solid darkness they should speed
Amid the suns and systems,—lofty words,
By Satan, and the Spirits next in power,
O'er all the assembly rolled; as, in a flood,
Earth's o'ergorged rivers thunder o'er its vales.

ORDER MUST EVER REIGN;—so taught their chiefs,—
Nor mocking, though all order had themselves
Madly o'erthrown; and into very Heaven
Foulest disorder brought: OBEDIENCE TRUE
TO THEIR GREAT LEADER, SATAN; though himself
The first to example disobedience
Toward Him, his greater, as eternity
Than Time's least moment greater. Through all space,
Wherever power opposing checked them not,
His own free course might every Spirit take:
Yet nighest to Heaven still best; so aught, perchance,
Of good might be espied; or hope of good,
Through their united powers attainable.
But, at fixed seasons,—then to be resolved,
When in the mid Creation they should pause,—
To that extinguished orb, their prison so long,
Must every Spirit return: in safety there,—
For, surely, to that utter depth of space,
Nor eye, nor ear of jealous God could pierce,—
Tidings from all the countless worlds to hear,
And tell; and conference hold, on what to do,
And what to shun; so working evermore
To victory at last.
 The Council o'er,—
For flight across the void immense of night,
Even to the heart of the great Universe,
In silence they prepared: then, all at once,
Right up through the ribbed arch of adamant,
As through thin ether, they sprang: through rock on rock,
Emerald, chrysolite, ruby; till, at last,
On the broad outside of the perished orb,—
Darkness eternal shrouding them,—they came,
And in deep silence paused.
 By spiritual sense,

To man unknown,—throughout the countless host
Their leader's will was felt; the place of each,
Mid uttermost dark, apparent was to all.
He, in the centre, gave the voiceless sign,
Their course directing; and,—no noise of flight
Creating,—instantly amid the void
The ardent legions shot. For, not on wings,
Laborious, slow, do Spirits take their way,
But at thought's speed; one moment on man's globe,
And, ere from cloud to earth lightning could leap,
Deep in the burning glory of the sun,
WILL urging, might they stand.
      So went they on,
In silence, yet rejoicing; glad to see
Again the light of countless living orbs;
To speed at pleasure through the infinite;
Yet feel themselves from eye of God secure,
And from his baffled vengeance: for,—so lost
In sin and folly were they,—all unknown
By the Omniscient, deemed they their escape;
All unpermitted by the Omnipotent:
And how to oppose Him; how His heaven invade;
How dim His glory, and decrease His power,
Insanely brooded; while the All Merciful
Their every thought, their every motion knew;
And, their own good, at last, through ill to work,
Their folly suffered.
     Through the universe
At length they scattered: but, the appointed times
Ever observing, to the perished orb
Duly repaired; from all the suns and worlds,
Tidings to tell, and hear.
      Long ages gone,—
Of man they heard; on a small globe, named Earth,
Newly created: like unto themselves,
But of inferior nature: yet, 'twas said,
Destined, no doubt, their vacant place in heaven,
At the due time, to fill. Then envy rose,
And hatred; and resolve, by force, or guile,
God's purpose to defeat; and man to bring,
Through disobedience, to their own fall'u state;

Or lower still; so most to exasperate
Him whom they deemed their foe; the God of love,
Of mercy; God Omnipotent, All Wise;
Who their vain pride, and boasted power,—so willed—
Might, even by feeblest thing, have utterly crushed:
Nay, their great selves,—immortal, as they deemed,—
Eternal, for the ages yet to come,
As Deity itself—might have sent back
To Nothingness, whence first to life they rose,
By His sole word called forth.   That God of love,
Of mercy, to incense, and thwart His ways,
Then man they tempted: and, through them, man fell!
Glory they deemed it; proof of growing strength,
Ere long to match them with Omnipotence:
Unknowing how—for their own sharper grief,
More dread remorse, and deeper penitence,
And for the greater good to injured man;
Nay, to themselves, when, in the infinite
Of ages should the time appointed come,
For everlasting peace, and perfect bliss,
Throughout the universe—their deed malign
Supernal power permitted.   Man thus fallen,
Earth as their own domain they boasted then;
Pleasantly living, save when thought of heaven,
Its glories, and its happiness—so far
Best joy of earth transcending,—a sharp pang,
As from a serpent's tooth in human flesh,
Through Spiritual being shot: in some, worse hate
'Gainst man and God arousing; but in some,
Remorse, repentance; sense of heaviest guilt,
Of black ingratitude toward Him, whom, once,
The source they knew of all their happiness.

Few, few, as yet, were these: and, when the sting
Had gone—by old proud thoughts again they strove
To thrust from memory all good forfeited;
And, in their new existence, find a joy
To balance loss of Heaven.   For, from the first,

Lost evermore they feared it; God incensed,
Inexorable for the eternity to come.
But, as the ages pass,—again, again,
The wholesome pangs are felt; and sharper still;
And longer-during the keen agony;
Till, even though hoping nought, a silent voice
Stirs in the spirit, and a prayer goes up:
A prayer, though supplication there be none
In act direct,—for, to offended God,
Prayer vain, they deem, as sure to be repulsed;—
Yet penitence is prayer: and, though unheard
By ear created, to the throne of heaven,
Distinct as on a thousand thunders borne,
Straightway ascends; and there is registered.

Thus, in long course of ages, one by one,
The fallen Spirits are raised: the heaven-outcast,
Penitent, humble, joyful; filled with awe,
But love as strong, toward the All Merciful,—
Again heaven enter; by the angels pure
Radiantly welcomed: and with them, once more,—
Joy every joy surpassing,—nigh the place
Of the Invisible their stations take,—
His Presence feeling: bliss that, all the worlds
To purchase, never would they lose again!

Man fallën, ages many there passed on;
And, for the rebel angels, triumph great
Accomplished seemed: for, even than themselves
More wicked, vile, as of a lower kind,
Earth's wretched race they deemed. In man they saw,
Part spirit, matter part; but, by the gross,
The higher nature ruled; the animal,
Such as with brutes the human nature shared,
Above the etherial,—man's peculiar,—
Rampantly lording; till the compound strange,
But a worse brute among the brutes might seem:
And even they, the outcasts from all good,
The first to sin, the tempters to his fall,
Looked on him loathing: yet rejoicing, too:

For, was not this fouled nature as a shout
Of victory, aye sounding to heaven's vault;
Telling to Him they once Almighty deemed,
How He had been defeated? Was not this,
This thing abhorred, the creature made so late,
So favored, loved; so with ripe wisdom formed,
That happiest, best—the appointed changes past—
Had been designed his lot? The Omnipotent, then,
Had not their guile o'ercome?
        Thus foolishly
Reasoned the proud rebellious: yet, with watch
Never remitting, marked the course of man;
His acts, and sufferings, hopes, and fears; his words
Attentive listened; if of heaven's designs
Aught should he learn: for sometimes—as they knew—
By shape celestial had a favored one
Been visited; and message from above
Within the heart had felt: nay, even words
Of human speech, with bodily ear had heard
From lips divine, as if to man spake man.

 Thus, sometimes, of the things by God designed,
Knowledge they gathered; subtly, as they thought,
And unsuspect: then, straightway,—summons spread
From sun to sun, throughout the universe,
Wherever Spirit might be,—to their lone orb
Their flight they took; assured therein to hold
Council unknown by even Him, once deemed
Omniscient; viewless even to eye of Him,
The All-Seeing named. There, how the best to o'erthrow,
Or turn aside to issue different,
The purpose known of their great enemy,
Debated they: nor ever deemed how plain
Before Him lay their every act, and word,
And thought most secret: and that, bent on ill,
Good final were they working; though by way
Most foul; as, from the loathsome ordure, springs,
Fragrant, and beautiful, and pure, the flower.

 From words of Noah, spoken to his sons,

Thus, though but half believing, some had learned
God's purpose, dread, strange, inconceivable,
The whole great globe with deluge to o'erwhelm:
Man's race entire—one family except—
To bury 'neath the waters. "Was, then, God
Mad in his anger? Could the wisest sink
To foolishness, pride-stung, that even His own,
His favorite work, He would in pieces break,
Like a vexed child?" So, in their secret thoughts,
Pondered the astonished Spirits.
                            But, at length,—
Beneath the dome of their great council-hall,
By summons gathered—through the general host
Spread the strange tidings; certain, now, as strange;
And with amazement smote them, that long time
Silent stood all; for every Spirit was lost,
Self-questioning, but answer finding none,—
Wherefore his own last work, the angry God
Thus ruthlessly should smite, as if in hate
'Gainst the whole kind,—yet one small family,
As plants from which the race should spring anew,
Mid the great wreck preserve! "From future man"—
So argued they—"what better may He hope,
Than from man past? Wherefore not all destroy,
Or none? For, if, in very nature, man
Is now to Him abhorrent,—the same taint,
Throughout all time to come will show itself,
Like a disease in blood, from sire to child
Transmitted; and the myriads yet to come,
Be loathsome to Him as the myriads gone."

   Thus they, unable to conceive design
Of the Omniscient, pondered, and were mute.
But their great leader's thunder-voice, at length,
Rolled through the silent concave.
                            How to foil
The scheme divine, he counselled. If their foe,
The race entire, save one small family,
By his own hand would slay,—their aim should be,
The worst to save; the favored to destroy;

So, of his hoped-for race of better men,
Defrauding him; and forcing to desist.
From his grand scheme of peopling earth for heaven,
Their vacant room to fill: or, else, compel,—
In first attempt defeated,—to essay
His power in new Creation; which their guile
Again might turn to mockery. Easy means,
Doubtless, would be, that foolish Ark to sink
Beneath the stifling waters: and himself,
In due time, would effect its overthrow.
Meanwhile—as nought had chanced, nought been foreknown,—
To earth would they return, and wait events:
There, all unseen themselves, would all things see;
Snatching occasion, whatsoe'er, God's schemes
To baffle,—their own purpose to work out.

As he, so other of the leaders spake:
And all were bold; all firmly resolute
Against their enemy ceaseless war to wage;
Sure of success. Far surer of defeat
Had been, if knowing how their utmost might,
Against the Almighty, would prove less than strength
Of gossamer-thread to poise the universe!

And vain found they the attempt. No living thing,
Doomed to destruction, had they power to save;
No thing, for life reserved, could they destroy.

In later days, conjectures dark they had
Touching God's final purpose with man's race,—
The earth again o'erspreading rapidly,
As herb and flower, amid the tropic climes,
Upshooting after rain.
      One man they saw,
Whom men named Abraham; agëd, and, as yet,
Childless; and she who should have borne him sons,
Old also, and past hope of progeny.
Yet, from his words, o'erheard, the Spirits learned,
How heavenly promise unto him had come,

That even from him, and from that barren wife,
Should spring a mighty nation; chosen of God,
His own peculiar people; and, through them,
Should all the earth be blessèd. And, behold!
Accomplished soon they saw one half the word—
Israel a numerous people! yet, most strange,
Not blessing earth; nay, even themselves not blest;
But slaves to cruel masters! Day by day,
Night following night, they saw their wretchedness;
Heard their loud cries of anguish, sobs, and groans;
And marvelled how of God they thus were left;
How from those fallen should kings of nations spring;
How to a mighty people they should grow;
Their glory filling earth: for one, at length,
A savage king, they saw, who, to their race,
Speedy destruction threatened; unto death
Their every male child dooming: whence must come
Exstinction certain, if prevented not.
And nought awhile prevented; as though God
Had left them, and His promise had withdrawn.

One infant, in a rushy cradle launched
On the broad river—as to death devote,—
Thence, by the virgin daughter of that king,
Rescued they had beheld; and with great love
Unceasing tended. And, in after years,
Still the same mother's heart upon him poured,
Marvelling they saw: how in man's deepest lore
He was instructed: how in fame he grew;
How rare in strength, and comeliness, and grace:
How, by his mien majestic, awe he raised
In loftiest men; how, by his mildness, love:
How unto him, as storm-beat seamen gaze
On a sure landmark, the down-trodden race
Of Israel 'gan to look, as to their help:
For then his name was glorious; and his might
In battle had from vanquished Egypt driven
Fierce Ethiop's scourge. But yet again they saw
How, pressed by enemies, his life to save,
Israel's great champion, to a far-off land

Hurriedly fled; lost evermore, as seemed,
To the now strengthless, joyless, hopeless race;
The deeper plunged in darkness, that, on him,
Thus gone from sight, as on their morning star,
Heralding happy day, they long had looked.

Yet not from sight of demons had he gone.
As one apart from all of human kind,
They knew him; and for some peculiar end,
Destined, had deemed him long: though *what* that end,
Vain their conjecture. Unremitting watch
Around him still they kept; nor ever once,
Unnoted, or unheard, moved he, or spake.
At length, in that great night on Horeb passed,
While hovering yet around him,—suddenly
Vanished they, terror-struck: no threatening arm
Thence scaring them; no word, no sign, no sound;
But irresistible Necessity
Making, for aught impure, existence there,
Impossible as silence in the swell
Of heaven's full choir, or midnight at mid-noon.

But when at length, by instinct sure, they knew
The Awful Power withdrawn,—once more on watch
The fallen Spirits went: and proof had soon
That for great purpose, though as yet unknown,
And mighty change to bring, that favored man,
Even by the Highest had been visited!
Words, tones, looks, motions, with intensest care,
All marked they: yet, awhile, could nothing gain,
Save that to Egypt, on some mission high,
By God commanded, straightway was he bound.

Him, and his family, ere long, they saw,
In lowly guise depart: and, day and night,
Close watched them, as the tiger on the fawn,
Nigh to his lair approaching heedlessly,
With burning eye keeps watch. Yet still went on
The meditative man; his soul with God

Alway communing; or, with words of love,
Or pious wisdom, to his family
Gently discoursing; or with hope of good
For Israel, through him destined to be wrought,
Their spirits cheering :—still, of that great night,
The secret speaking never.
                    But, at length,
The brothers, long years parted, they saw meet:
Their converse listened: heard the wondrous tale,
To Aaron told by Moses,—God's own words,
In human language spoken from the bush,
Burning, yet all unburnt: and instantly,
Through earth,—throughout the countless worlds, and suns,
To the fall'u host,—thus wide dispersed,—went forth
Summons to council prompt.
                        Nor time was long
Ere, past the region of all living orbs;
And far within the void of night and death,
The myriads flew; and in the blazing round,
The heart of that great sun-anatomy,—
A congregation numerous and bright
As ocean's sun-tipped waves, from lofty cliff
At morn beheld,—in deepest silence all,
The voice expecting of their leader, stood.

  He, with that towering form, and mien sublime,
Still glorious, though sin-shadowed, which in heaven
Had marked his high pre-eminence,—on a rock
Outblazing gem-like, full in view of all
The semicircle deep of ardent eyes,
His station took; looked round, and thus began.

ISRAEL IN EGYPT.

BOOK SECOND.

"Powers, erst of heaven; and, haply, yet again,
As, with the years, we wiser, mightier grow,
Thither, triumphant, destined to return;—
Not by permission; but in our own right,
And strength resistless: for, our past estate,
Our present, ponder; and thence clearly see
The inevitable future. How at first
To being came we,—who shall say! Time was
When we were not;—or, if at all we were,
Unconscious, embryotic,—or, perchance,
In dream, remembered not. Ye have seen, on earth,
The corn-grain, coffined with the human dead,
Through ages long he death-like: yet, to soil,
Air, rain, and light brought forth,—behold, the germ
Stirs in its husk,—the seeming dead shows life:
Expands,—bursts,—shoots out stem,—leaf,—flower, and
    fruit!
And even so with us may it have been,—
From the beginning, in a death-like trance
Lying, till waked.—By what?—By our own strength,
Throughout eternity waxing?—From the first,
Surely hath *something* been: why not ourselves? . . . .
Yet, not to know we live,—is dead to be:
And certain this—when we to life awoke,

The universe, and God, already were.
Of those, which first existed?—None can know.
The word in heaven was, that, by God alone,
The suns, and worlds, yea all things, had been made,—
Even we ourselves: but, which of us aught knew
Touching his own creation,—*if* create,
Not self-existent,—as still possible is,
Since rightly know we not: or who beheld,
When worlds were formed, the hand of God put forth
To fashion them? . . . . Fiction that rumour, then,
To bow us to his yoke: for if, in truth,
God had created,—surely not from heaven
Had he so cast us,—our slight, sole offence,
To have deemed our Natures kindred to his own,—
Spirit imperishable,—in time's infinite
Destined, like him, to godhead: thence, not bound
To yield him everlasting worship and praise,
Due to our greater only. Venial sin
Had this been held,—a truer knowledge given,—
Our ignorance pardoned. Clearly thus it seems
That not from God we are. . . . Whence then,—or how?
Nay—first,—whence God himself? for, whence *He* came,
Thence, doubtless, also we. *Some* Cause must be,—
Itself uncaused:—impossible, alike,
To comprehend, or doubt. . . . . Admitted then—
Uncomprehended,—from eternity,
What *is* that Cause, uncaused? . . . Answer is none,—
Ask midnight for noon sun. A name we make,—
Of the *thing* ignorant;—Nature, Fate, we say,—
Necessity,—or whatsoever else
May shadow meaning, meaningless,—*that* Power,—
If Power;—that Something—if such be—
Existent sole, ere Matter, Space, Time, God—
That, only, First Cause is,—Original
Of all else, named Original: and by That,
Doubtless, the Universe, ourselves, and God,
Were to existence brought. He, far the first;
Thence, far the wisest, mightiest: yet, we feel,
Not more eternal *now;*—nor mightier
Than, *sometime,* shall *we* be. If Hè yon earth,

And man, created,—and those other worlds,
Within our memory made,—from that First Cause,
Unknown, for ever inconceivable,
His power was: and to us, when time shall be,
Like power, be sure, will come: and we new worlds,
Yea, haply, suns,—and a new heaven, our own,
Outshining His, may make. . . . . Space is enough
For Him, and million gods. . . . . Vain dreaming this,
To weaker Spirits: nay, in truth, to all,
For this hour present, vain: though weighty still,
As food for ceaseless thought.
        "Time was," I said,
"When we were not; and, in that deep abyss
Of cycles, this great orb, now dark, had birth;
And, in long flight of ages, more and more,
Grew vast and glorious. But, the highest point
Of splendor reached,—decay, though slow, yet sure,
Its brightness 'gan to dim. Years numberless
Stole, ray by ray, its fires; till,—as when first
Our eyes beheld it,—roaming the infinite,—
Like but a dark red cinder did it hang,
Glooming, not lighting space. Ye know what length
Of ages followed ere, unwillingly,
By some strange power of our stern foe compelled,
Hither we came; and utter blackness found
Where, erst, had been sun-splendor; death, where life;
Where the great body,—this gaunt skeleton.
Such, of all things *material*, seems the doom:
A birth, a growth, decay, and final death.
But, to the things etherial, spirit all,—
Decay is none—death is impossible:
In power and wisdom wax they evermore;
Till, at the summit arrived,—all knowledge won,
All strength obtained,—omniscient they become,
Omnipotent. Thus, in procéss of years,
Be sure, our state will mount to Deity;
Gods shall we all become. Even since that time,—
Brief in the scope of ages,—when, first fallen
On this lone orb, in darkness and deep gloom
Of spirit we lay, as helpless for all good,—

What stretch enormous toward the godlike power
Have we not made! For that abhorrëd night
Whereto our enemy doomed us,—in full trust,
Doubtless, that here, to all eternity,
Would the black prison hold us, shorn of strength,
And opportunity, his schemes to vex,—
Lo! light we have, as in the courts of heaven;
And, from yon arch of gems that girds us round,
Colours more glorious than of choicest flowers
In fields celestial.

"Wherefore, think ye, sprang
Within the hollow heart of this dead sun
That wondrous glory of light? Had life again
Come to the mouldering skeleton? Nay; for death
Yet reigns throughout, save here, in this one vault,
Our council-hall. But wherefore here alone,—
The whole vast orb beside yet steeped in night—
Shines thus heaven's radiance, well may ye enquire
Haply because, at first, through art of mine,
Came the dark ruby glow that welcomed you,
Hither arriving, after your long trance,
Silent and dark as death,—to me again,
As being in art more potent, ye impute
That change far greater, likewise: yet not so;
For, more than even the least among you, nought
Of such bright coming knew I. Cause profound
For this new motion of life in midst of death,
Must be; perchance to us, at this our stage
Of being, far too deep for our best powers
Of vision, and clear reason to discern:
But, in the time to come, be sure, right plain,
This, and all other things mysterious most,—
THE ONE GREAT MYSTERY, CAUSE, UNCAUSED, except—
Will stand before us. In conjecture alone,
Lies all our wisdom now: but greatest things,
Distant, are by conjecture only known,
Till nearness gives them form. Thus, when, at first,
Piercing through space, on sight comes figure strange
In the far regions; and with curious ken
We scan it, marvelling what may be such patch

Of cloudy light; shapeless, or, haply, shaped
Grotesquely, like some thing that crawls on earth,
Or floats upon her seas: but lo! anon,
As through the space we cleave, the cloudy spot
Brightens to stars; the shapeless puts on form;
The crawling thing a constellation becomes,
Burning with countless suns! And even thus,
As, with the ages, will diminish space
'Twixt what we are, and what we shall become,
Speeding toward Godhead,—will all mysteries
Of hidden knowledge, dimly now beheld,
Or guessed at rather,—like that host of suns,
Shine forth in glory. Meantime, seeking cause
Wherefore that sudden radiance on us burst,
Thus I conjecture.
     " Matter, in all forms,
Contains most wondrous qualities, and powers;
Unthought of, latent sleeping, till aroused.
Thus, in even coldest things of earth, lies fire.
Ye have beheld, amid her frigid zones,
Huge crags, from rocky mountains, by fierce frost,
Rent, and hurled down. Scarce ice itself more cold;—
Yet, as they crash, and leap, and thunder on,
Lo, from their shivering sides, fire, sulphurous fire,
As from swift whirling torches!—fire, thus waked
From sleep of myriad years. Nay,—wondrous more,—
In earth's dark polar oceans, ye have seen
The storm-tossed hills of ice together clash,
And grind out streams of fire; yea, fire from ice;
Which ice is, solely that it lacketh fire:
For, fire imparted, ice it is no more;
But water! Yet, within those hills of ice,
Lies all the while, in slumber wonderful,
Fire that might parch a forest, or consume
Man's proudest city.
     " In ways numberless,
Matter on matter—lifeless seeming all—
Yet acts like thing of life: as friend, sometimes,
Sometimes as mortal foe. In one shape, fire,
As in fierce anger, seizing the green tree,

Turns it to ashes: yet that self-same fire,
In shape of summer warmth, the small seed aids,.
Till a great tree it waxes. . . . . One small grain
Slays the strong man in health,—another saves
From pain, or death, the weak. . . . . The sea hath gulped,
Of solid salt,—impervious to light's beam
.As granite—bulk to have formed a continent;
Yet fluid as ever remains, and crystal clear
As from spring-head. . . . . Water, now, quenches fire,—
Now, with some matter working, kindles it. . . . .
Some things there be, of so strange qualities,
That, brought together,—though, from earth's first day,
Until that instant, motionless,—yet, like foes
Deadliest, each on the other fixes hard,
As in a mortal conflict: but, at length,
Strife done,—as closest friends they join; and take
Form, aspect, quality, utterly unlike
Those to each, singly, native. Undisturbed,—
Thus, even for ever, might they quiet lie.
But, haply, will some other matter come,—
Stronger than these conjoined; and lo! at once,
Like a wild beast voracious,. tooth and claw
It fixes—rends asunder;—upon one
Seizes, and grapples it—and intertwines
Its own, and victim's substances,—till,—each
Mixed with, and lost in the other,—both appear,
As single things, annihilate—transformed
To a substance wholly new. The other thing,
Thus violently divorced—wondrous to see,—
Sometimes its primitive form resumes; and rests
Calm and content, though vanquished,—takes, sometimes,
Shape of a fume, and, hissing, as in wrath,
Flies off, and disappears. . . . . Most fluent tongue
Of Spirit the most eloquent, ages through,
Unpausing, might the marvellous powers rehearse,
And qualities of matter; yet, untold,
Leave work for cycles. All are mystery:
Nor, till beheld in the act, could we have known
The property of one atom. Wherefore, then,
Though yet unknown to us, may not Spirit, too,

Power have to influence Matter? Not more strange
That living Essence should dead Matter rule,
Than that the dead rule dead. . . . Yet more for thought:
What, if this Matter be *not* wholly dead?
What if some wondrous kind of life it have,
Surpassing our conception?—and, in truth,
Much of its ways *seem* lifelike. What if it have
With *Spirit* some mode inconceivable
Of commune, or sympathy—even as sound with sound,
Strange sympathy hath. Ye all remember yet,
How, when one string upon our heavenly harps,
Singly was stricken—from some other came
Sweet tone responsive. Nor with sound alone,
Doth sound hold commune, or sympathy: ponderous things,
Substantial most,—with sound *im*ponderable,
Viewless as Spirit,—have commune. Thunder speaks,
And the ground trembles. Mystery this, not less
Than the other mystery, conjectured now.
We guess in the dark: yet, till all possible powers,
And attributes of Matter, and Spirit, both,
Lie clear before us, who shall dare affirm
Of either the limits? or how each on each
May operate? *If* God, then he alone.
Meantime, conjecturing, once again I ask,—
As matter upon matter, in such ways
Mysterious acts,—wherefore,—not mystery more—
May not the mightier *Spirit* on it act,—
Even though unconsciously? Ye remember well
How—at that moment when the glory-flood
Suddenly fired this concave—we ourselves,
In our new splendor, had become as suns
Just risen, or freshly kindled. Strength to mount
From this our dungeon; and the universe,
From end to end,—the courts of heaven except,—
Freely to traverse,—sudden as the flash
Of lightning, in our spirits had arisen;
Sense waking of existence new begun;
New cycle opened in the eternity;
A mighty step in rank of being, gained;

A power, a glory, in our onward march
Toward Godhead. From ourselves, then, glorified thus—
Even though we knew it not,—as sun to earth
Gives light and warmth, unknowing of the gift—
May not some God-like influence have gone forth,
Which, like to breath of life, quickening the dead,
Within this mighty corpse-heart,—yea, well nigh
In all its wondrous glory original—
The Light-soul summoned back?
        " Truth may this be,—
Not wild imagining. Instance have we not?
Why is Heaven glorious—but from presence of God?
And why not, then, *this* mansion glorified,
From *our* inhabiting? . . . . But whate'er the cause,—
Whether a power from us, unconsciously
Transmitted;—or a power within itself,
By us but roused,—as fire from grinding rock,
Or clashing ice—alike must we conclude
That in ourselves sole cause immediate is
Of that new glory. For, what other thing
Can be imagined cause? Not He who holds,
As yet, heaven absolute; who drove us thence;
And here in blackness fixed us; confident
That in this void, beyond the bounds of life,
Prisoned we were for aye,—not He, be sure,
Freely would give to them whom most he hates,
And fears, aught that would gladden, or might aid
From durance to escape. And, if not He,
Who, or what else, ourselves alone except,
Can be conceived as cause? Though how ourselves
Cause *could* be, ignorant of the effect to come,
May wonder raise. But, through the universe,
Cause is not known, until effect appears;
Nor, known as cause, is ever understood
Why cause for such effect. A truth is seen,
And, by wise Spirit, registered for aye;
Though cause thereof a mystery ever be:
And every truth, so known, becomes a power
Unto the knower: truth on truth up-piled,
Is power on power upheaped: until at last,

All truths accomplished; all effect and cause,
In the infinitude of ages, known,—
Omniscience is the growth, Omnipotence;
The state of Godhead.
     " Hence, the Eldest of things,—
A Spirit, doubtless, even as ourselves,
In his first origin,—through the infinite years
For ever gathering truth on truth; and power
Thence heaping upon power—now sole God reigns:
Mightiest of all, because the wisest far;
Wisest, because, by half eternity,
Eldest of beings. Yet even He, perchance,
All causes knowing, all effects, knows not
Wherefore, from that which causes, should effect,
Such, and no *other* come: from fire, why heat,
Not cold; from all the living suns, why light,
Not darkness. Well may we, then, be content,
Effect beholding, to admit a cause,
Unknowing *how* the cause; since, this except,
None else seems possible.
     " As effect from cause,
Pronounce I, then, that sudden splendor of light,
From our own glory, as sudden, to have come:
Splendor most like to heaven's: and, or I err,
Plainly foreshowing how, with each access
Of power—to Spiritual Nature the sure growth
Of ages—will new lustres ever rise;
Till, with a glory, and might, and majesty,
Equal to His, we shall with Him divide
The rule of heaven; or, haply, a new heaven,
Solely our own, shall found; and therein reign,
Potential even as He in the heaven of old.

 " But ever, this to hinder, be ye sure,
His power will cross us; and, so vast the odds
Betwixt us now, 'twere madness to oppose
Might against might; for, even if alone
Against his angels striving,—strength from Him
To them would be transmitted; and our power,
Great of itself as theirs, would thus be foiled.

Direct affront of strength avoiding then,—
Still, not the less, wise caution fending us,
Unceasing, unremitting be our war.
His schemes to counteract; our own work out;
His glory dimming thus, ours lighting up;
His power curtailing, aggrandizing ours,—
Such be our rule of action, day by day,
And age by age, throughout eternity;
Or till, the time arrived, on thrones as high
As His we sit; and through the realms of space
With might as potent rule.
      " The one great blow
At His last, loved creation, man, we struck;
And deadly seemed the wound; though still lived on
The wretched race,—a mockery of His power;
A loathsomeness so hateful in his sight,
That, as ye know, by one great deluge-swoop,
All but annihilation absolute
He sent upon them. Hoped he, from the few
Whom he preserved, a loftier, purer race?
If so, the All-foreseeing, wrongly saw;
And ours the truer foresight,—from same tree
Predicting the same fruit; even though the axe
Close to the ground should hew it: for a brood
More vile and bestial never cumbered earth
In the old times of sin that brought the flood,
Than that which now, o'er nine parts of the globe,
Makes mockery of God's prescience. Yet one race,—
His own peculiar people, as they boast,—
For secret end, apart from all the rest
Long hath he kept; designing, it may be,
In way mysterious, through them to work out
Some good for general man. That end, once seen
Through the thick shade that still his purpose hides,—
To thwart, our everlasting aim must be;
Even though, all ignorant of the consequence,
In veriest night we toil: for this we know,
That, whatsoever his intent,—to us
Ill must it bring, successful; but great gain,
Being defeated; since power lost to him,

To us is power transferred. And, through the depth
Of the eternal ages striving thus,
And gaining still,—though but in such degree
As one small drop in twice a hundred years,
To drain earth's oceans taken,—yet, as that
Scant measure, through the cycles infinite
Pursued, would drain at length the final drop,
And leave the sea-bed but a sandy waste,—
So, atom after atom of his power
To us transferred, would bring us equal at length;
And, in the end, to such high state exalt,
That we, to him, should be as gods; to us,
He but a subject Spirit. Evermore
This, then, must be our aim,—seen, or not seen
The ultimate result,—his purposes,
Whate'er they be, to thwart.
                           " This old design,
Long known to us, through Israel to work out
Some good to all mankind, claims from us, then,
Action immediate; for the means at length,
Are set in motion; the beginning made
Of that which, haply, we, not he, may end,
If wise we prove, and diligent, and firm,
And strong in our persistence.
                           " For what cause,
This chosen people, during so long years,
In bondage miserable hath been left,—
As though of God the accurst, not favored most,—
Vain 'twere to guess: nor, for our purpose, aught
Importeth it: but now the time is come,
When from his thraldom, and from out the land
Of his oppressors, Israel shall go forth.
Such the design, at least,—by God's own voice
Announced: and tenfold, therefore, be our toil,
And subtlety, and never sleeping watch,
His word to render vain. A triumph that,
Greater than even the great original blow
Which struck down man; for, though God made him pure,
He promised not that he should never fall:
But now, in human words, as man to man,

Distinctly hath He promised, his own hand
To stretch o'er Egypt; working wonderments
And judgments on the people and their king;
Till he, and all, as with one voice, shall cry
On Israel to depart. This to prevent,
All diligence, all wisdom, and all power,—
Yet peaceably working still,—must we put forth.

"Through man His will performing,—as of yore
Oft have we seen,—the chosen instrument
Is now that Moses, whom, to some great end
Unknown intended, from his birth we judged;
And heedfully have marked: for other men,
In all rare gifts, of mind and body alike,
Surpasseth he, as the fleet desert steed
The slow-paced ox surpasseth. Marvel much
Hath held us, wherefore, to high power and fame,
As by heaven's special favor, having risen,—
Suddenly thence, as though by heaven accursed,
He fell; and, hastily flying, safety sought
In a far land; where, all unknown,—his power,
His wisdom all unused,—in labor mean
Long years he passed; as if, like lowliest men,
His doom it were to toil, and eat, and die,
And be forgotten. But the purpose firm,
Though seeming all abandoned,—as man's earth,
Myriads of centuries ere he was made,
For use of rational thing, abandoned seemed,—
Silently still advanced. Reserved, not lost,
Was Moses: the time fixed, not yet had come:
Not yet, perchance, to its full height of power,
Wisdom, and daring, had his spirit risen;
But, by long solitude, and abstinence,
Labor, and nightly watchings, must be trained,
And fitted for his task. But, be the cause
Whatso' it may, his time for rest is gone;
The time for action come. To him it was
That the voice spake,—deliverance promising
To wretched Israel. Face to face, the king
Who holdeth them in bonds must he confront;

Demanding that, for sacrifice to God,
A three days' journey in the wilderness
To Israel he should grant. But, known it is
That this will be refused. By marvellous signs,
And miracles, shall Moses then attest
That he from Heaven is sent: but yet the king
Will not believe; till, by strange wonderments,
And plagues unknown before, his haughty soul
Shall be brought down; and he shall bid them go;
Yea, hasten them by gifts. Such God's intent.
Accomplished, unto Canaan, a fair land,
Will Israel be led forth. In the after time,
What they shall do, what suffer; how work out
The final purpose,—whatsoe'er that be,—
As yet in darkness lies. Unceasing watch
On every motion must we keep; each word
Must hearken, and well weigh; for, out of these,
Glimpses may come of the design concealed;
Or intimation of the means most sure
Our foe to harass; and impede, at least,
If not foil wholly. To this great design,
Then bend we all our strength. The battle-field,
'Twixt us and our relentless enemy,
Egypt is now,—poor room for such great strife:
A petty land, by a small river alone
For man made habitable; else, a waste
For reptiles merely. Thither in force must go
Our subtlest, strongest Spirits: there must toil
By day, by night: in souls of men must pass,
And sway them to our will; Egyptians both,
And they of Israel; moulding all alike
To fashion of such thoughts and acts, as most
This God-announced deliverance shall oppose.
But, first and chief, the headstrong, fickle king
Our aim must be: his spirit so to rule,
His heart so harden, that, defying all,
Threats, miracles, plagues, the iron bonds he still
Shall keep on Israel, and not let them go.
Him, therefore, to myself I take: his soul
Will enter: every thought, and word, and act,
Will strive to rule. His priests, his ministers,

The women of his court, whose honied tongues
The hearts of all will sway,—to Spirits strong
And subtle shall be given. The general mass,
Women and men alike,—both of the race
Of Egypt, and of Israel,—to the care
Of Spirits less potential,—though not less
In ardour for the work, and diligence
Each in his proper labor,—must be left.
This the great law to all;—by every thought,
And every word, and act,—or of man's own,
Or to his heart suggested,—still to strive
Toward the one end,—prevention absolute
Of this, the God-announced deliverance
Of Israel from his bondage. That achieved,—
Glory, and triumph, and increase of strength,
To us will bring; to God, and all heaven's host,
Vexation, and discomfiture, and shame,
Never to be effaced.
     " As next in power
And wisdom to myself; and next in rank
Among archangels; and of subtlety
Not to be overcome,—to thy strict watch,
Beelzebub, that Israelite I give,—
Moses, the God-appointed instrument
In this new work. By whatsoever means
Man may be ruled, or led: by power, by wealth,
By thirst for knowledge, by desire to pry
In mysteries forbidden; or, best lure
To those frail things of flesh, by woman's love,—
By each, and all, occasion seize to tempt,
And draw him from allegiance. Next the king,—
Nay, haply, in this strife, like eminent,—
Is he, that humble tender upon sheep,
These two score years just passed. Fix all thy force
Of subtlety upon his human soul,
His fleshly nature. Lure him the sweet cup
Of sin to taste; and that one draught may raise
Thirst so unquenchable, that, with floods o'ergorged,
And drunken, he may perish.
     " In like way,
Ye Spirits all,—both ye of loftiest power,

And ye of humblest,—on the hearts of man,
And woman,—on their thoughts, hopes, fears, desires,—
Both waking, and in dreams,—work ceaselessly,
That Egypt still 'gainst Israel may stand firm,
And hold him in his bondage. Yet, by all,
Ever be this remembered; guile alone,
Temptation, cunning words, inflaming thoughts,—
Whate'er the spirit, or the flesh, can lure,—
These, solely, be your arms: for such, unseen
By Powers of heaven may be,—occasion fit
Seized wisely, and due caution alway kept,—
But, the strong hand on any mortal laid,
Would be a trumpet, sounding the alarm
To Spirits of heaven; that force by greater force
Soon would be quelled; and, haply, to such wrath
Power now Almighty wakened, that from earth,—
As once from heaven—the unseen lightning-blast
Might hurl us down the unfathomable deep,
Far, far beyond even this. For, space there is,
Wherein float shadowy ruins, once bright orbs
Of an old Universe which had passed away,
Ere this had birth. Wandering the Infinite,
With thee, Beelzebub, long cycles gone,
One such we found; its adamant soft as cloud,
Its mountains as thin air. Even this lone wreck,
To such, would be a heaven. All cautious heed,
All diligence, all wisdom, to your task
Take with you then. In secret ever work:
Heaven's angels shun; for sunbeams pierce not more
Through darkness, than their vision through best shows
That cunning can put on. All that ye need,
Now is made known: yet, if there be, whose thoughts
For public good weigh on him, let him speak."

He paused; but all were mute. With eyes that flashed
Sun-like, he looked around. No sound, no stir,
'Mong all those myriads was there. Then, at length,
The well known sign he gave; and instantly,—
Ere quickest eye of eagle could have glanced
From rock to plain,—the spirit-host was gone;
The dead sun's heart again was solitude.

ISRAEL IN EGYPT.

BOOK THIRD.

WHILE morning yet was young, within his hall
Of justice Pharaoh sat: his princes, priests,
Judges, and ministers, in costly robes
Of ceremony clad, on lower seats,
At either hand were placed; their task, to hear
The accuser, and the accused; and judgment give,
As by their law decreed. But, when the sun
To his fifth hour had reached, went forth a voice
Among the people, bidding them depart.

Then, presently, before the king, and all
The intently gazing court, a man there stood:
One among many; yet, as singly there,
Sole object of all eyes: for well 'twas known,
That he, illustrious once throughout the land;
But suddenly lost to sight, and long deemed dead;
As suddenly, and with some purpose high
Toward his own people, Israel, had returned;
And of the king craved hearing. At his left
Stood Aaron; and, behind them, closely grouped,
The Elders; anxious all, and pale of hue,
And inly trembling. But,—due reverence first
To that high presence made,—not firmer stands
The marble statue, than stood Moses there;

His eye upon the king, and all his court,
Placidly moving; in each form and face,
Seeking the known of old. As though his glance,
Had been a sunbeam, from it turned aside
All eyes on which it fell. Amazement strange
In silence held them; for the countenance,
In manly beauty eminent, grave, yet mild,
Scarce mortal wholly seemed; so pure a light
Beamed from it; radiance gentle as the touch
On thinnest cloud from yet unrisen moon.
In silence, therefore, long time, sat they all,
Gazing, and marvelling. Till the king should speak,
None dared presume: and not a word found he;
Strengthless, as men in dreams, when they would shape
In speech their thoughts confused, yet utterance lack.
At his own weakness wrathful, twice he strove
Silence to break; and, with the lofty tone,
Kinglike, his power and dignity make felt:
But the voice came not; the awe-fettered lips
Quivered,—but tongue was mute.
      That Satan saw,—
And in the spirit of the troubled man
Poured courage, and strength; and lifted him with pride
Of regal greatness; that his voice went forth,
Firm, and commanding,—as, to humble men,
Discourse the mighty.
     "Thou art he," he said,
"Of whom the sister of my father spake,
On the day past; imploring for thee speech
In presence of the king; because that thou,
In times long gone,—nay even from thy birth,—
Hadst favor in her sight; thy very name
From her receiving. What thou hast to say,
Speak freely then; Pharaoh inclines the ear."

Then Moses bent the head; and with calm voice,
Deep-toned and soft; yet such nice utterance,
That, on the ear most distant, fell each word,
Clear as the stroke upon a silver bell,
Thus made reply.
    "Not name alone, O king,

To that great princess owe I; life, and all
That makes man's life more worth than that of beast:
Knowledge of men, and things; the lore of books;
Of wisdom unrecorded; nature's laws;
And laws that govern men; the mysteries
Profound of your religion; of the stars
All that men know, or guess; of earth, and sea,
The magnitudes, and forms,—in brief, whate'er
Of wise and wondrous Egypt's priests could teach,
To her alone I owe."
      Upstarted then,
Self-prompted,—for no demon needed he,
Malice and wrath to waken—the chief priest,
Thamusin: with eye flashing, quivering lip,
He bowed before the king; then rose, and said.

"Will dread Sesostris, Splendor of the Sun,
Grant to his servant liberty to speak
With this long banished man; against the law
Hither returned; and, with shame-lacking face,
Daring before the king of kings to stand;
Doubtless, for his accursed race, some boon
To wheedle from the mercy of their lord;
When heavier tasks, and sharper stripes alone,
Should fall upon them."
     But the king, displeased,
Motioned the priest to silence; and himself
Thus questioned.
    "Thou hast heard," he said, "the words
Of the chief priest. Speak now to *me;* and say,
If just the accusation he hath brought.
Wert thou, in truth,—or by award of law,
Or by my royal father's will alone,—
From Egypt banished? and, against the law,
Or, 'gainst his doom, thy sentence unrepealed,
Hast thou come back?"
      Then Moses bowed, and spake.
"Nor by the law, nor by thy father's will,
Nor any other power of earth, was I
From Egypt banished. Wilt thou, Pharaoh, hear,

Wherefore this land I fled; wherefore again
Hither am come; and, so permitted, stand
To plead before thee,—in the briefest words
The plain truth will I speak."
                    " The king will hear,"
Said Pharaoh gently, " and thy words will weigh."

" Be it not thought I boast,"—then Moses said;
" For thousands, tens of thousands, yet there be,
Who could my words attest. Nay, in this court,
Some see I now, who knew me in the day
When, of thy father, king, the favored most
Of all in Egypt was I. For, when scourged,
And overrun, and plundered by the hosts
Of Ethiopia, was this fertile land;
And army after army, under rule
Of Egypt's chosen captains, had been driven
Before the invader, beaten and disgraced;
And when a cry from all the land went up,
Utter destruction dreading; and the king,
The princes, priests, and rulers, feared to see
The fall of empire; and the countless heaps
Of riches in the treasure-cities, seized
By hordes barbaric; and themselves enslaved,
Imprisoned, tortured, sent to shameful death,—
Then upon me,—already high in rank,
And favor of the king,—the people called:
The priests and rulers, also, raised the voice,
Me naming fittest leader of that host,
Egypt's last strength, which, rallying from defeat,
Though in despair, she had gathered. To that call
Answered the king; and, in my hands, sole rule
O'er all the army gave.
                    " Now, Pharaoh, list.
Four times a hundred years hath Israel dwelt
Within this Egypt; here with friendly love,
At first, received; and, as close friends, long time
By your forefathers cherished. Enmity
From us toward you, was none. No law brake we;
Offence gave not; no treason ever planned:

But, rich by honest labor had we grown;
And, living temperate and virtuous lives,
And for our children caring, had become
A strong and numerous people. This beheld
By the Egyptians,—prosperous less than we,
Because less diligent; observant less
Of God's, and nature's laws,—suspicion rose,
Lest Israel, waxing mighty, should become
Greater than they: and, with suspicion, grew
Hatred; and thirst, by ways iniquitous,
To injure whom they envied. Like a plague,
Throughout all Egypt ran this mind's disease;
People, and priests, and princes, women, and men,
All were infected; all in madness cried
Against unhappy Israel. Then the king
Frowned on our innocent people: of their wealth
Despoiled them oft: taskmasters o'er them placed;
Made them, as slaves, beneath the lash to toil;
Till all their life was bitterness.
                              "Now, O king,
Bethink thee. When the enemy had come;
Had vanquished all opposal: when last hope
Had gone from trembling Egypt;—when the foot
Of conqueror, on the morrow might have stamped
Thy father's throne-steps,—Pharaoh, what if then
The men of Israel, maddened by their wrongs;
Alike for freedom and revenge athirst,—
'Gainst their oppressors, as one man, had risen;
With Ethiopia joined their strength; and fought,
Their tyrants and taskmasters to o'erthrow;
Making, of masters, slaves,—of slaves, their lords,—
Who justly could have blamed them? Ever strive
The oppressëd to be free: and public praise
Goes with them. But, if Israel, on that day,
His wrongs alone had thought of; and his sword
For Ethiopia drawn; or even, unmoved,
Neutral had stood, leaving to chance of war
Decision of the strife,—sure as the sun
At eve declines, so surely had gone down
The day of Egypt's glory. But the land

Wherein their fathers, and forefathers, long
Had sojourned,—even though, in later years,
So bitterly oppressed,—as home they loved;
And when, prime leader of the shattered bands
Going to battle, I sent forth the call,
Then Israel answered; all his bravest men
Thronged to my standard; and the land was purged
From her fierce enemies.
      "Through them, in chief,
The valiant sons of Israel, was the field,
In many a bloody fight, for Egypt won.
Be this remembered, Pharaoh, when, at last,
Justice to them I ask: for bitter shame
To Egypt is it, that the noble men
Who her deliverance wrought, themselves are slaves,
To those whom they delivered. In the sight
Of man and God, iniquitous is this;
And must in evil end. But, of myself,
Now will I speak.
     "The contest o'er,—the land
Cleared of her enemies, and firm peace made,—
Into thy father's hands I rendered up
My rule in war; and to my former state,
Content, returned; reward demanding none
For that which, at the first, acknowledged all
Service most eminent,—save this sole boon,—
That Israel's bondage lighter should be made,
If freedom full not given him. Solemn word,
So promising, spake thy father: but, alas!
Bad counsels quickly poured into his ear;
Telling that Israel's good, was Egypt's ill:
That, Israel prosperous,—Egypt soon would fall;
That, Israel rich,—the king, the lords, the priests,
Soon would be poor; that Israel was the slave,
By right, to Egypt; and his labor owed
Unto his masters, as the ass, and horse,
To man owe labor; and content had been
In that long during servitude to stay;
Had not the turbulent tongue of factious men
Taught them to covet freedom.

"Then on me,
In chief, were flung malicious word; and threat,
Not doubtful, of a vengeance soon to fall;
Not loss of kingly countenance alone,
But even of life; if not by public hand,
Then by the private. Not one lord, one priest,
But scowled upon me. Even the king, at last,
Coldly received, and with suspicious eye
Lowered on me. Yet awhile I firmly stood,
Strong in mine innocence; and fearing nought
That lying tongue might charge.

"But, on a day,
As with a man I pleaded, who in rage
Smote cruelly a Hebrew, old and weak,
Me also did he strike; and struck again,
Nor would hear reason; but still, furiously,
Strove as to slay me. Backward then I drew,
As to desist: but this way looked, and that,
Hoping some man to espy, who *his* voice, too,
Might bring to stay the wrong: but Hebrew slaves
Alone I saw, and distant; and well knew
That neither hand nor foot would such dare stir
Against Egyptian master. Meantime, he,
As he were mad, the old man smote again,
Till his howling wrung my soul. I grasped his arm,
And bade him cease: but, thereat, on myself
With worse rage struck he. Him, then, to disarm,—
Not hurt,—with lifted staff, his staff to strike,
I aimed; with hope that either I might break,
Or cast it from his hand: but other end
God purposed; for, while mine too strongly fell,
His staff he shifted suddenly, and left
Defenceless his bare head. Alas! too late
I saw! my staff descended. Heavily
On the shorn crown it fell; and, without groan,
Or cry, or struggle, to the earth he dropped,
Dead! Bitterly I grieved; but help was none;
Tears useless.—That by accident he died,
Knew I, and God alone. If to the seat
Of justice I should go; and the plain truth

Tell in defence, well knew I that no man,
On whom the jealous priests and lords had sway,
Would dare acquit me. My own words would be
Death sentence: an Egyptian I had slain,
And therefore must I die. With sorrowing heart,
I scooped the sand; and decently the corpse,
From fowls and beasts protecting, covered up;
Then homeward sped: heavy of soul, in truth,
But not blood-guilty; for of God it was,
Not will of mine, that such had been the event.
On the next day, two Hebrew men I saw
In strife; and, unto him who did the wrong,
Said, 'Wherefore smitest thou thy fellow thus?'
With insolent tongue he answered—'Who made thee
A prince and judge o'er us? Intendest thou
To kill me, as the Egyptian thou didst kill?'
Then knew I that the thing was known; and saw
That I must flee, or die. So God's plain will
It seemed, that forth from Egypt I should go.
Wherefore, I asked not; but, submiss, obeyed;
And foodless, drinkless, with my staff alone,
Went onward toward the desert. How I fared,
Or wherefore so long years I made sojourn
In a far country, needs not here be told.
The truth, whole simple truth, I now have said;
Answering the charge most false, that banishment,
Or by the law, or by the king's decree,
Against me was pronounced."
       There Moses paused,
And stood, expecting that the king would speak.
But, when he saw that, with a thoughtful brow,
Sesostris silent sat,—then once more rose
Thamusin, the chief priest; his fierce dark eye,
Though bleared with age, flashing malicious fire;
And, lowly bending, with a thick, harsh voice,
Tremulous 'twixt hate and fear, his thoughts thus spake.

 "Light of the Sun, may now thy servant's voice
Be heard; not him, the murderer, self-convict,
To question,—but thyself, the fountain head

Of justice, to address.   That banishment,
After his flight, against this man was passed,
Boldly doth he deny: yet I affirm,
That, for his crime, when the king vainly sought
To slay him—being fled—doom spake he then
Against him—banishment for evermore.
That sentence heard he not perchance, because,
Knowing his guilt, self-banished.   Not the less,
O king, doth law award against him death,
As one, 'gainst law, from banishment returned,
His sentence unrepealed.   For such offence,
All men expect due punishment to fall,—
Thy mercy staying it not.   But, for that crime,
Full pardon granted,—still is there a deed
By this man wrought; a crime of blackest hue,
That no proof needeth,—since, with his own tongue,
Even in this court of Justice,—in the sight
Of thee, O king, the judge supreme of all,—
And in the face of these thy ministers,
Princes, and priests, his guilt hath he confessed.
Light of the Sun,—for crime like this, even thou,
No power to pardon hast.   Clear speaks the law,—
'*If any stranger an Egyptian slay,
That man shall surely die.*'   He slew; and fled;
Or had died instantly.   His long sojourn
In foreign land, hath not wiped out his guilt;
Fresh now as on the day when it was done:
And death, which on him should that day have fallen,
This day will fall; or old Egyptian law
Become a mockery."
                             Hurriedly stopped he there,
With spite and fury trembling; and with dread;
For on the countenance of the king he saw
Wrath, and disgust.   So hastily he paused,—
Not daring more to speak, yet 'shamed to stop
In mid career,—that o'er his wrinkled brow
Confusion settled,—as a wintry cloud
The hill top darkens: and, with quivering lips,
That seemed to mutter, yet nought said, at once
Down sat he; and, with furtive glance, peered round,

Marking men's looks; but, most of all, the face
Of him he hated, and whose death he sought;
Marvelling to see that, calm as breezeless lake
In summer sunshine, stood the Israelite;
His eye on Pharaoh fixed; yet not as one
For mercy mutely praying; not as one,
Or fearful, or incensed; nor as the man
Who doubts, and hopes, and trembles, while the word
Of judgment lingers; but as one assured;
In right, and potence confident; as one
Who rather stands superior, than abashed
Before superior; and with calmness waits
Progress toward certain good. To the fierce priest
The king spake not; but, with mild tone at first,
To Moses turning, thus.

"What thou hast said,
Touching that war of old, and thine own deeds
Against the Ethiop, know I to be truth;
For in our public records so doth stand
The story of that time; and from the mouths
Of those who witnessed, also have I heard,
That verily so thou didst. Thine own report
Of strife 'twixt thee and that Egyptian man
Whom thou didst slay, I, therefore, will receive
As also truth; acquitting thee of crime
Intended; and the punishment which, else,
On deed like that, even done unwittingly,
Law had awarded,—for thy services
Done in the day of trouble, I remit.
Wholly thou stand'st forgiven. Yet, beware,"
With lowering brow and stern tone he pursued,
"Beware—nor farther aggravate offence,
Which, in my royal father's mind, did blot
All service thou hadst done. Let not thy voice
Again be heard, stirring the Hebrews up
To hate their masters. Theirs it is to serve;
Ours to command. Old custom is as law:
They, and their fathers, long have been our slaves;
Our slaves they shall continue. From their birth,
Such have they been; such to the grave shall go.

That which our sires bequeathed us,—the clear right
To Israel's labor,—'twere a robber's hand
Would from us take; and, be thou sure, the attempt
A robber's meed should have. What though they stood
For *us* in battle,—for themselves not less
They fought; a slavery heavier tenfold, so
To 'scape from: gainers by the event, as we.
Be this enough. My will, the will of all,
Now hast thou heard. Within thy memory
Be it well treasured: and when, as thou saidst,
For justice unto Israel thou shalt plead,
Ask not the leave to rob us; for thy words
Vain were, as treasonous; and the heavy hand
Would fall upon thyself; and, on thy race,
A harder servitude. Thus warned, speak on,
And say,—why back to Egypt thou hast come;
By whom commanded, or by what impelled;
And to what end this audience thou hast craved."

Stirred by the demon, thus Sesostris spake;
Threatening his tone; his brow like gathering storm:
But Moses in the might of God stood firm;
And with clear voice, unmoved, thus answered him.

"Already, Pharaoh, hast thou given reply
To my most just request: nay, the harsh word
Of threat hast spoken; knowing in thy heart,
That what thou didst forbid my tongue to speak,
Is that it would have spoken. Said I not
That *justice* unto Israel I should ask?
And, for the wrongfully enslaved, what else
Than freedom *can* he ask, who justice asks!
From thee, O king,—as by wide-spread report
Instructed,—nobler things might I have hoped.
Men call thee clement, candid, generous, just;
Albeit, they whisper, sometimes iron-hard
Of will; sometimes, again, o'er apt to turn
With newest counsels;—is it generous, just,
The priceless benefits of old to slight,
As things unworthy? of the noblest deeds,

Self-sacrificing done, to make the mean,
The selfish only? Israel for the cause
Of Egypt, solely, in your battles stood;
His own clear rights, to a more peaceful day
Deferring: and the life-blood of his sons,
For Egypt purchased victory. But for them,
Ye now had been the slaves: thy throne, O king,
A clay-shed; and thy sceptre, it may be,
A spade, an axe, a shovel, or the tool
Of poor brickmaker. All thy power, thy state,
Thy riches, unto Israel dost thou owe;
Yet with contempt dost fling into his face
His noble deeds: and, for deliverance wrought
By him for you, dost the deliverer thank
With slavery on himself! Just, generous this?
Bethink thee, Pharaoh, how the tongues of men,
Throughout all countries, and throughout all times,
Will name thy deed; will picture of thyself,
If more to this abominable wrong
'Gainst your deliverers, thou dost lend thy power.
Nor sin alone for ever will it stand
Against thy name, but folly: for, be sure,
The days already, in the thoughts of God,
Are counted, ere the universal voice
Of Egypt, and thine own, shall bid us hence,
Free through the world to go."
      "Hold! hold! enough!"
Exclaimed Sesostris, starting on his throne,
Pale-faced, and fiery-eyed;—rage, and strange fear,
Conflicting in him;—for the countenance,
Heaven-kindled, that upon him looked; the voice
Potential more than man's, his very soul
Had shaken; till the watchful fiend again,
Suddenly entering, with old pride and ire,
To the height inflamed him. For a moment thus,
Upstanding, cried the king; his arm outstretched,
His foot advanced, as though irresolute
If to descend, and with the sceptre smite
The audacious speaker; or again to sit,
And with strong speech confound him. Down, at length,

As quickly sat he; for the calm clear eye
Strangely subdued him; but, with wrathful tone,
Thus spake he on.
     "My word of promise past,
That calmly I would hear, and weigh thy words,—
I punish not, bold man, thine insolence.
Nay, matter rather for my mirth it were,
From one most impotent, such mighty words
To listen. How the thoughts of God ye know,
And of days counted till your chains shall drop,
A marvel verily is. If not all fume,
Vain boasting, tell me, then, whence learn ye this?
Who hath revealed to you the thoughts of God?
Hath shown to you the future?"
       With low voice,
And solemn, Moses answered. "When I tell,
O Pharaoh, words of simple truth to thee,
Thou wilt a liar deem me! For, of things
I have to speak, passing belief of man;
Yet, not the less, sure as the steadfast earth,
The seas, the stars, the sun. The thoughts of God,—
With reverence hear me, king, nor let thy lip
Curl in derision,—even by the voice
Of God himself were spoken."
      "He is mad!"
Furiously starting up, the chief priest cried.
"Hear him no longer, Splendor of the Sun;
But send him to the straw, the chain, the scourge,
'Mong other madmen."
     "Be thou silent, priest,"
Said Pharaoh; "and thou, Moses, tell me more.
Where saw ye God? what said he? and how spake?
With thunder's voice? or sound of many seas?
What was his stature? and his countenance
How fashioned? like to face of man? or how?
And of what substance? flesh, or air, or flame?
Or like to sunbeams moulded? *that*, methinks,
Best would a God beseem."
     Silent, and stern,
An instant Moses stood; then briefly thus.

"Thy speech doth mock me. To the word of scorn
I answer not. Enough that I have said,
By Israel's God commanded, stand I now
Within thy presence: and His words I speak.
' Thus saith the Lord, the God of Israël;
Let thou my people go, that they may hold
A feast unto me in the wilderness.' "

Loudly at that laughed Pharaoh; and his court
Loudly laughed with him.
      "Who, then, *is* the Lord,"
Proudly he cried, "that him I should obey,
And let your Israel go? I know him not;
Nor will let Israel go."
     Then Moses thus:
"Truly O king thou speakest. Israel's God
Thou dost *not* know: yet God is He of thee,
As of the Hebrews; God of earth, and heaven;
Creator sole of all things. At His frown,
The earth, the seas, the stars, the sun, would fade
To nothing; like thin smoke upon the wind!
And He it is whose words I speak to thee,
As by His own voice spoken. Harden not
Thy heart against us, then: but let us go,
We pray thee, three days' journey in the desert,
That we may sacrifice unto our God."

"And when return,—those three days granted you?"
Cried Pharaoh, mocking. "And, for sacrifice,
Why to the desert should ye go at all?
Is not, in this great country, room enough?"

"Our sacrifices, Pharaoh, well thou knowest,"
Moses made answer, "by the Egyptian race
Are held abominable; for the flesh
Of animals we offer. At our rites,
They would make mock; our worship would molest,
And fling into confusion; that great wrath,
On both sides, would spring up; and blood, perchance,
Not meant for sacrifice, would stain the ground,—

Holy devotion changing to fierce strife;
And Deity incense, that pestilence,
Or sword, against both people might He send.
Far in the desert only, may our rites
Fitly be ministered. Once more, O king,
We pray thee let us go."
       Then, mockingly,
Cried Pharaoh, yet in wrath; "Ay, go; go hence;
And instantly: but, to the wilderness
Go not; or now, or ever. And look well,—
Thou, Moses,—and thou, Aaron,—and ye all,
Elders of Israel,—look ye well, I say,
That with your busy tongues ye hinder not
The people from their works; else may yourselves,
With clay and straw, the trowel, and the spade,
Your delicate palms make rough."
        "Thou art incensed,
O king," then Moses placidly replied;
"And wilt not this day hearken to our prayer.
With a new morn, new thoughts may visit thee;
More just, more wise. Till then, our God I pray,
That from thine eyes the blindness may pass off;
And from thy heart the hardness."
        Having said,
He bowed; then Aaron, and the Elders bent,
Due reverence yielding; and with solemn mien,
Patient and hopeful,—though the smothered laugh
They heard behind them,—from the hall went forth.

ISRAEL IN EGYPT.

BOOK FOURTH.

But, when they were alone,—and now no more
By that subduing presence overawed,—
With free tongue giving loose to wrath and hate,
Rulers and priests 'gainst Moses 'gan to rail,
And 'gainst rebellious Israel,—born their slaves,
Yet daring to ask freedom. Head to head
They turned, low talking; yet with burning eyes,
Flushed faces, quivering lips, and hands hard clenched,
Like men who long to strike.
                              But Sethos now,—
The first-born, and the favorite of the king,—
The throne-steps mounted; and, close standing, poured
Into his ear sharp words; inciting him
To wrath more bitter still against the man
Who so had dared affront him; and 'gainst all
The hateful race of Israel; heavier toil
And stripes advising, as best means to tame
Their hearts rebellious.
                         A too willing ear
Sesostris lent: and, when he looked around,
And saw, on every countenance, hate, and scorn;
And the deep tones of smothered anger heard,
Then, with like wrath inflamed, thus spake he out.

"Princes, and priests, and rulers; ye have heard
The bold words of that Israelite; and seen
His looks audacious, in the very court
Of Egypt's monarch. Shall we, then, obey
The mandate of his God; of Israel's God;
A God unknown,—and let this people go
Into the wilderness,—thence never more,
Be sure, to come again; unless with chains
And whips forced back? or, rather, at their God
Shall we not laugh; and them with heavier stripes
And burthens vex? better to make them know
That now they are, and evermore shall be,
Slaves wholly."

    At that word, new stir awoke
Among the priests and rulers: many rose,
And stood before the king; and many tongues
Hotly exclaimed, that slaves from birth were they,
The factious Israelites; and all their toil
Justly to Egypt owed: and by the scourge,
If they held back, like asses should be driven
To labor harder yet. Then once again
Spake Pharaoh.

    "With this contumacious brood,
Until this day too lenient have we been;
And pampered to rebellion: but, henceforth,
Wiser shall be our rule. They now are many;
And even but one hour's labor through each day,
Enforced upon them, difference vast will show
In sum of years. Our treasure-cities, roads,
Embankments, fosses,—whereon with slow hands
As yet these men have labored,—soon shall speed
Toward quicker ending: profit great to us;
To Israel greater toil: and, harder yet
To task them, henceforth shall they have no straw,
Wherewith to make them bricks: even let them go
And gather straw themselves. Yet, the same tale
Of bricks which heretofore they made, that same
Shall be laid on them: nought thereof at all
Shall be diminished: for they idle are;
And therefore do they cry, 'Let us go forth,

That we may sacrifice unto our God.'
Be, then, more heavy work laid on the men,
That therein may they labor; and vain words
Let them regard not. This sharp medicine
Quickly, methinks, will purge distempered thoughts,
By sloth begotten; and their rightful state
Teach these rebellious."
      Pausing there, arose
Sesostris from his throne; his sceptre waved,
In sign of council o'er; and left the hall.

 With willing haste his orders were obeyed.
To all the taskmasters, at utmost speed
Was sent the word: and they, as eagerly,
Went out among the people; with loud voice
Proclaiming, "Thus saith Pharaoh; 'from this time,
I will not give you straw: where ye can find,
Go ye, and get it; yet, of all your work,
Shall nought,—no, not one brick, diminished be.'"

 When that the children of Israel heard, again
Their cries went up to God. Throughout the land
Began they then to scatter all abroad,
Stubble to gather, where they found not straw;
Long hours consuming thus; yet, ere from toil
At night they might be freed, the self-same tale
Of bricks enforced to bring, as when the straw
Freely was given. Still Pharaoh's taskmasters
Hated them, saying; "all your works fulfil,
Your daily tasks, as when the straw ye had."
And those who underneath them held the rule,—
The officers of Israel, whom themselves
To overlook the laborers had set,—
The king's taskmasters scourged with rods, and said;
"Wherefore, ye idlers, have ye not fulfilled
Your tasks, enforcing from these men the tale
Of bricks as heretofore; both yesterday,
And this day also?"
      When these things they found,
And that deliverance, promised, had not come;

Nay, that their burthens heavier far had grown;
Louder and louder railed the Israelites
'Gainst Moses, and 'gainst Aaron, and 'gainst all
The Elders, who had taught them that the hour
Of freedom was at hand.
                         Then, when some days
Had passed, the officers of Israel went,
And stood before the king; and, weeping, said,
" Wherefore, O Pharaoh, with thy servants thus
Dost thou deal harshly! To the laborers now
No straw is given, wherewith the bricks to make;
Yet do thy taskmasters cry out to us,
' Make brick, make brick;' though well as we know they
That, lacking straw, brick never hath been made.
And yet, behold, thy servants do they beat;
Though not with us, O king, but all alone
With thine own people is the fault."
                                     To them
Sternly spake Pharaoh.
                      " Ye are idle all;
Idle ye are; and therefore do ye say,
' Let us go forth into the wilderness,
And sacrifice unto the Lord our God.'
Go therefore now, and work: no straw at all
Shall be given to you; yet the tale of bricks
Shall ye deliver."
                  Then the officers,
Beheld that in an evil case they were,
After the king had said, ' ye shall not aught
Diminish of your bricks, your daily task.'
And, as from Pharaoh they were coming back,
They met the sons of Amram in the way;
And with dark brow, and wrathful tone, thus spake.
" The Lord upon you look, and judge! for ye
Have made us hateful in the monarch's eyes,
And in his servants' also; so to put
A sword into their hands to slay us all."

  Then was the heart of Moses sorrowful,
And his thoughts were troubled. . Far beyond the walls,

Alone, on foot, and fasting from all food,
He went; in silence and in solitude
To meditate, and commune with his God.
All day, mid groves, or by the river's bank,
He wandered; slow his steps, his head depressed,
His heart weighed down with grieving; so that nought
Of beauty or of wonder, nigh his path,
Saw he, or heard at all: the Pelican,
Snow-white, the Bird of Paradise,
The huge, strange fish that wallowed in the deep;
The Eagle, and the Vulture, high in air,—
Unnoticed all, as sparrow on house-top,
By the lone city-muser. Till the sun
Far down heaven's arch had journeyed, wandered he,
Of hours regardless; all his thoughts on God,
And the deliverance promised; yet, as seemed,
In but worse bondage ending.
       Him thus sunk
In dark dejection, that fallen angel saw,—
Beelzebub, the never sleeping spy
O'er all his thoughts and motions,—and the time
Propitious deemed,—with prospect of high power,
Fame, wealth, and victory o'er all his foes,—
From that plain path, by God prescribed, to lure,
And draw him; and with pride of heart inflame,
That his own might and wisdom he should trust,
For the deliverance, promised, unachieved,—
Rather than doubtful word, by thing unseen
Spoken; or, haply, heard in dream alone;
A dream that he was waking.
       Instantly,
Legions of Spirits summoned he; and bade
That, in the guise of warriors, darkest hued
Of southern Ethiopia; large of limb;
Of stature more than man's; with sword, shield, spear,
Helmet, and armour shining like the sun;
And in the firm array of ordered hosts
Marching to battle,—with the speed of thought,
Should they appear.
      In a high car of war,

Splendid with gold and gems; a blazing crown
Upon his head; and with all regal pomp
Attended, he himself the foremost rode.
Behind him, twice a thousand brazen cars,
And warriors gleaming all in steel and gold;
Huge horses, fiery-eyed, in steel, and brass,
And gold resplendent; their high-lifted feet
Seeming to scorn the ground; their arching necks,
And wide-spread nostrils, speaking fierce contempt
Of all opposal,—lightened o'er the plain.
A hundred ranked abreast, the chariots went:
Behind them, clouds of horse that shook the ground
With their hot trampling; all in shining mail,
Rider and steed, attired: and, after them,
The infantry unnumbered: all at once
Planting the foot; together all at once
Uprising on the toe; that their bright helms
Of burnished brass, like sun-fired ripples seemed
On a great rushing river. Like the beat
Of battering rams against an earthen mound,
Their firm tread sounded.
                         From a shady grove,
Wherein he long had wandered, going forth,—
This wondrous sight saw Moses; and drew back,
Gazing and marvelling; for at once he knew
That not of Egypt was this armament;
But, as it seemed, of those whom Egypt most
Of all her enemies dreaded; that fierce race
Of Ethiopia, whom himself in war
Had fronted, and with labor hard subdued;
With labor, blood, and life of Israel's sons
Had vanquished—thanked by heavier slavery.

Yet, of a war at hand, had no report
Gone forth: of such an inroad prompt, far less.
Till better he bethought him, instant doom
On the oppressors seemed he to behold:
The tyrant king, the tyrannous lords and priests,
Scattered like chaff before a mighty wind;
Or like to dead leaves trampled underfoot,

Before that multitude enormous, strong,
Gigantic-statured all, both man and steed:
A sight like which, surely had mortal eye
Never till then beheld.
     With course oblique,
Toward the grove tending, moved they; and the van
Not distant now; though, far as eye could trace
That fiery torrent rolling o'er the plain,
No rear was visible. But passage none,
Through the close wood, to any ordered force,
Could be at all; and, therefore, great his hope
That, in the shade abiding, by no eye
Should he be seen: so that, when all had passed,—
Course more direct pursuing than could they,—
With utmost speed of foot might he return;
And in the city, and in Pharaoh's court,
Sound out the alarm; though, as he felt, all vain
Egypt's full strength, before such foe to stand
One moment in the battle.
     But keen eye
Was on him: and when, hearing sound of feet,
He turned to look,—behold, toward him there came
A multitude that seemed to fill the wood;
Dark men, of size prodigious. Chance to escape,
By mortal means, impossible now—he stood,
Their coming to await; yet dread felt none;
Protected ever by the hand of God,
Knowing his life to be.
     " What man art thou,
Here lurking like a spy upon our path?"
Said soon the voice of one who leader seemed.
" Thy name declare; thy purpose; and yet no,—
For see—the king approacheth: unto him
Be thy words spoken. Follow, and with speed."

So saying, on he moved. To right and left,
And thronging close behind, were mighty forms,
Mail-clad, with spear in hand, and sword on thigh:
No choice was left; and with them Moses went.

Soon to the dazzling chariot in the van
Nigh drew they; and a mighty voice came forth
From him who rode therein.
                       "Whom bring ye here?
Stand all; and I will question him."
                                    His arm,
Thus speaking, lifted he; and, van to rear,
At once the host stood still. Then answered one;

"A spy, O king, he seemeth; for, close hid
In the thick grove we found him, with sharp eye
Noting thy coming on."
                     "And well might note,"
Said he, as king addressed; "for sight like this,
Never, till now, saw man. Yet how a spy
He may be deemed, I know not. But fall back,
And let him stand alone; that, with free tongue,
He may reply to me."
                    Obedient moved
The soldiery; and half a bow-shot off
Retired; then stood; and, looking toward the king,
Farther command awaited.
                        "Lift thine eyes,
And look me in the face while we discourse,"
Said he, named king. "Ha! surely is that mien,
That eye, that lip, nay that whole countenance,
Familiar to me! Not as yesterday
Beheld; but as a face, in years far back,
Graven on memory, as a word on rock,
Never to be effaced.—Deny it not;
Thou art that Moses who my father foiled
So oft in battle; after half this land
He had o'errun, and conquered: but for thee,
Wholly had vanquished; and his rightful seat
On Egypt's throne had won. Now, answer not
With the false tongue, as one afraid; for, so,
Of guile convicted, surely shalt thou die:
But with true words, as one who scorns a lie,
Even death to 'scape, say, art thou he, or no."

Then Moses on the sable countenance,
Fierce and commanding, fixed his placid eye,
And calmly answered, " Whom thou say'st, I am;
Even that same Moses who from sword and spear
Of Ethiopia, rescued this fair land."

" And thy reward, what was it?" with the tone
Of mockery, said the phantom: " For his crown
And kingdom saved, what treasures gave thy king?
What honors, rank, and power? For wife, no doubt,
His fairest daughter gave he, most beloved;
And, as her dower, a kingdom. Tell me all;
That I may know his worth; and at what price,
Service like thine he valued."
                                A brief time
Moses stood silent; then in low tone said:
" No rank, power, honor, treasure, as reward,
Did I require : my sole petition this;
That Israel's bondage lighter should be made;
If freedom full not given them."
                                " Trifling boon,
For priceless good to ask;" still mockingly
The giant shape replied; " but freedom large,
Doubtless, to all he gave; and treasure much
Heaped on your people: for, remembered well
To this day is it 'mong our countrymen,
That by the men of Israel, foremost far,
Were done those deeds of valour, that amazed,
And overcame them. In this Egypt still
Sojourn they? for a rumour even then
Was rife, that toward some distant country, soon
Would all of Israel go: therein to dwell
For ever; and this Egypt see no more."

With tone of sorrow, Moses thus replied.

" For service done, no gratitude he showed
To our long suffering people: treasure none
He sent among them; nor their galling bonds

Slackened at all. Me,—some loud praises given,
While their first joy was flush,—the priests and lords
Soon 'gan to hate; and into Pharaoh's heart
Their venom poured, that also he, at length,
Turned on me the cold face."

"But he is dead,
Resumed the questioner: "this present king,
Sesostris, haply, hath with juster hand
Dealt toward thy people: five years hath he now
Filled Egypt's throne; and, if not *all* your bonds
He hath cast from you, yet, what most did gall,
Doubtless he hath struck off. In few words tell,
What acts of justice, or of gratitude,
Hath he shown toward them."

"I am ignorant
If such have been at all," with look deject,
Then Moses answered: "for, these two score years,
In a far distant country have I dwelt;
And but at sunset of the tenth day past,
Hither returned: nor of one righteous act,
By Pharaoh to our suffering people done,
As yet have heard report. Nay, heavier bonds
Of late hath he cast on them; in his rage
That, by commandment from on high, I craved,
A three days' journey in the wilderness
That we might go; and offer sacrifice
Unto the Lord our God."

"A savage deed!"
Exclaimed the dark-hued phantom of a king;
"And vengeance on him, surely will ye all
Laugh out to see. But, absent so long years,
Of Ethiopia's wondrous history
Perchance thou nought hast heard; nor what the might
Unequalled she hath gained. No power of earth
Before her now could stand. In me behold
Her king, Amosis,—for my father sleeps
These ten years in his tomb: in these behold,—
Ay, Moses—for a warrior's ken is thine—
Look on them,—hence, to where in distance lost;

Though, then, not half their numbers dost thou see,—
What think'st thou of such arms, such steeds, such men?
Is there on earth a power 'gainst these to brave
One stroke in battle? And, for Egypt's king,
With all his legions, dare he a moment bide
The sun-flash of their swords?"
               " Beyond compare
With aught mine eyes have seen, is this great force,"
Moses made answer—" as by look adjudged;
By seeming strength, stature, and multitude.
But, not to strength, and multitude, alone,
Is victory alway given: the soldier's heart,
The leader's wisdom, yet a greater might
Than number, and the bulk of body give.
Small hosts, well led, and ardent for their cause,
Have vanquished greater far, when cold the heart,
Or dim the eye, of soldier, or of chief,—
As slender steel more strong than bulky wood,
Unsound within."
               A moment, thoughtful sat
The seeming king; then lightly from his car,
Leaped to the ground; close unto Moses went;
And, his gigantic form down bending, thus,
With voice suppressed, began.
               " Thy words are gold,
To whoso' right receives them. Best of strength,
Truly, in bulk, or multitude, is not;
But in the spirit, and wisdom. Hear me now,
Moses—for thou, I know, of living men,
Far wisest, bravest art: and of this land,
By merit, king shouldst be, in place of him,
The ingrate, who therein had never ruled,—
Thine aid withheld. And, haply, even yet,—
Thy wonted wisdom failing not,—his throne
May have more fit possessor. Hearken now;
And weigh what thou shalt hear. Thou see'st this force
'Gainst Egypt come; giants of iron frame,
And numberless as sands on ocean's shore.
Nought, surely, can resist us. Yet, thy words
Thoughts have awaked, that else perchance had slept.

Not might alone, how vast soe'er the odds,
Gives alway victory. The eagle eye
Of a wise leader must the arm direct,
Or even oak-splitting blow may cleave but air.
Myself, though king, the warrior's wisdom lack:
And he, the unconquered captain of our host,
This morn by death was smitten. 'Mongst us all,
No chief like him,—wise, subtle; in the arts
Of war accomplished perfectly,—remains.
Not less, doubt can be none, beneath such force
Must all opposal sink, as, 'neath the foot
Of Mammoth,—even though blind, and running wild,—
Sheep, wolves, nay, lions, if before his path,
A moment they should stand. But, yet more sure
The sure to make,—keen eye, and wisdom deep,
Even Mammoth force should guide. Now, Moses, mark:
The wisdom, warlike lore, which so we need,
Thou, more than all men, hast. Bethink thee, then,
How with thy people is it; with thyself;
What ye have suffered; what ye suffer still;
What more will suffer, if that heartless king,
That cruel race of Egypt, still shall hold
The mastery o'er you. Pictured all these woes,—
Paint next in fancy, what ye shall become,
If thou, even thou alone, wilt aid to wrench
The sceptre from his grasp; and on *them* put
The chains which wrongfully on you they flung.
I ask not, of your people, that one man,
Thyself except, draw sword. Thy single deed,
Merit for all shall stand: and every man,
Woman, and child of Israel, shall be free:
Not from slave-bondage only, but, to go
Whereso' they will; to any land on earth,
Whither they would. Thy guidance in the war
Is all I ask. Of this unequalled host,
The captain would I name thee. To thy rule,
Sole, irresponsible, would all submit.
What recompense thou wouldst,—that boldly name,
And hold it granted. Yet, lest over-nice,
And diffident thou be, reward to ask,

Hear now my own resolve. The victory won,—
As won it must be, strength by wisdom led,—
To thee the throne of Egypt will I give;
Subject to Ethiopia though it be,
Yet great and wealthy still, most lands beyond;—
And, with it, treasure that might rear a pile
More vast than proudest pyramid,—thy name
To blazon through the world. Yet, more than this;
My youngest daughter, fairer than the flowers
Of spring-time, will I give thee for a wife;
Her dower, a mine of gold. This to refuse,
Thy wisdom, world-wide famed, would bring in doubt;
Thy justice also; for, toward Egypt, nought,
Save enmity, can thou, and Israel feel:
Nought owe, save retribution for foul wrongs;
Which not to punish, power within your hands,
Would be to approve, and make the guilt your own.
This also weighed must be: if obstinate
Thou stand; to Egypt, rather than to us,
Intent thine aid to give,—then, both thyself,
And all thy people, enemies must we hold;
And so deal with you. Honor, on one side,
Advantage great, and freedom to thy race;—
Unto thyself a kingdom, and a queen,
Glory and riches, and a deathless fame,—
All cry aloud upon thee to be ours:
While, on the other side, a hideous voice
Croaks strange allurements; memory of deep wrongs;
Of burthens, scourges, hunger, thirst, and toil,
And chains,—sole thanks as yet from Egypt, saved,
To Israel, his saviour; and sole thanks
For all the years to come. Th' alternate such,
Useless thy choice to ask; for wise thou art,
And canst not,—gold, and dirt, for preference placed
Within thy reach,—take filth, and gold refuse.
My captain therefore art thou; leader sole
Of this all-conquering host; and, few days hence,
King destined to become. My car then mount:
As king with king, beside me take thy seat;
And, while we move, thy counsels in mine ear

Freely pour forth."
      There paused the phantom shape;
And, as though answer he expected not,
And doubt impossible were,—with lordly grace,
His hand extending, as to honored guest
Yielding precedence,—toward the chariot signed.

 But motionless and silent Moses stood;
His eyes upon the ground, as one whose thoughts
Sorely perplex him: and, when this he saw,—
His huge form rearing, with an aspect proud,
And tone of cold displeasure, the dark king
Him thus addressed.
     "When monarchs deign to speak,
Quick ear they look for, and a nimble tongue
In answer. Have my words inaudible been,
That thou repliest not? for, in thing like this,
To hear, is to resolve; since doubt of choice
'Twixt offered life, or death,—conditions none,—
Not more impossible were, than thought of doubt
'Twixt opposites like these. . . . Or, with long care,
Is thy brain crazed; so that of best, or worst,
Thou know'st not which to chuse? . . . Be't how it may,
At least give answer: let me know thy thoughts,—
If thought thou hast at all."
      "Amazement strange
O'ercometh me," with low and solemn voice,
At length said Moses. "With the bodily eye,
A force I see, that Egypt's utmost strength
Surely might overwhelm, as a great rock
Would crush a molehill: with the bodily ear,
Thy words I note, telling that even so
The immediate purpose is; and my poor aid
Inviting to the work: yet, not more sure
That here I live, and breathe, and with thee speak,
Am I, or can be, than that never thus
Will Egypt fall, or Israel be set free:
For, from Heaven know I that, by other power,
God's purpose is it, Pharaoh to subdue;
From his long bondage to lead Israel forth."

"Thou dreamëst, Moses; stir thy senses up,
And look about on firm realities,
Not on mist-visions," said the great, deep voice,
Each word as 'twere a blow,—" How knowëst thou,
How can'st thou know God's purpose! Hidden deep
As the earth's centre, evermore from man
Are all His counsels kept. The crazy brain
Alone, affects the invisible to see;
The blind alone, sees not the visible,
Glaring before the eye. Crazed, then, thou art,—
Thin air for substance taking; or, else, blind,—
The mountain piled before thee seeing not.
That which thou call'st God's purpose, is thy dream;
Less than a shadow; for a shadow still
From substance comes; yet, solid as the earth
Thou seem'st to hold it; while this mighty strength
Of men, and arms, and steeds, invincible,—
Real, substantial as the eternal rocks,—
Either thine eye beholds not, or thy sense
For shadow taketh; else impossible
The thought, that of its purpose it can fail.
Say,—art thou wakened now? Wilt thou the head
To this vast body be? or, traitor-like,
Aid Pharaoh to hold Israel yet his slave?
Answer at once: but yet the alternate weigh:
For, as toward us, or Egypt, thou shalt lean,
So, on thyself, and Israel, wilt thou bring
Good, or worse evil."
                    " Choice is left me none,"
Firmly him Moses answered. " All I see,
All hear, with absolute voice declares aloud
Egypt must fall before thee. Yet, best vouch
Of eye, ear, reason, light as shadow is,
Poised 'gainst the words of God, which to my soul
On Horeb's mount were spoken. Nought of thee,
Amosis; nought of this o'erwhelming power
On Egypt coming, spake the awful Voice:
But of a hand Almighty, to be stretched
O'er Pharaoh and his people; smiting them
With plagues unheard of; till, with one acclaim,

They should cry out on Israel to depart.
Such, then, *God's* means, *thy* purpose is as nought ;
In nought will end. Like dew-drops in the sun,
Thy myriads may exhale; like rain-drops, sink
In thirsty earth; like corn unreaped, may fall,
And rot upon the ground; like clouds may pass,
And fire and thunder pour on other lands,—
But, for this Pharaoh, this Egyptian race,
No power of thine may touch them. Useless, then,
My aid to give; nay, sinful, knowing well,
That in far other fashion am I called,
From bondage to take Israel. So assured,—
Power, kingdom, riches, beauty,—all combined
To lure me in thy service,—light would be
My heart to bend, as feather from dove's wing,
To bow the oak it drops on."
                    " Thou art fixed,
Plainly I see; but madness fixed," exclaimed
The phantom monarch; fury in his looks,
His voice like tempest: " take, then, thine own course
But, mark the end. Dream not that, hence to go,
And, fool-like, to your tyrant Pharaoh take
News of our coming, I shall leave thee free.
Us if thou aid not, him thou shalt not aid ;
Nor Israel; though ten thousand gods like thine
Had sworn the promise to thee. Yet, once more
I bid thee think. The moment now is come
When life, with honor, or immediate death,
Must be thy choice. I waste no longer words
On madness, or perverseness iron-hard."

   He signed; and instantly by Moses stood,
At either hand, a form of giant bulk,
Flame-visaged; high above each towering head,
A lightning sword uplifting.
                    " With thyself
Solely rests now thy fate," in tone severe
Pursued the phantom: " Not on me the blame,
If here thou perish; for thyself it is
Thy doom shall speak. Worse folly than the fool's

Were ours if, having thee beneath the foot,
We let thee rise to foil us as before.
Not to another Pharaoh shalt thou lend
Thy cunning in war. To me, and to this host,
Thy service must thou swear; else, 'neath that sod
Whereon thou standest, surely is thy grave.
This all thy choice; nor power of earth, or heaven,
The doom can alter. Life, or instant death,
At once then chuse."
       " Already have I chosen,"
Said Moses, on the wrathful countenance
Placidly looking; "in the hand of God
Am I; and as He willeth, be my fate.
That which is right, I know; and that will do,
Come life, come death. To other work am I
By heaven commanded; therefore, thee to serve,
Were God to disobey. Thou threaten'st death;
God's bidding, life assures. I see the swords,
As thunderbolts; yet know that greater Power
Back holds them, as in chains. They cannot slay
Whom God wills live. Thy strength is impotence;
Thy purpose nought; thy conquest all a dream.
Though armed with might of all the world thou came,
To Pharaoh couldst thou not bring punishment;
To Israel freedom; for in other guise
These hath the Almighty ordered. Ere too late,
Toward Ethiopia, then, thy steps tread back:
Else, as a billow broken on a rock,
Will all thy force be shattered."
         " Madman, fool!"
With voice that shook the ground, more terrible
Than roar of banded lions, in the night,
Roaming for prey, exclaimed the giant king:
"*This* sword, at least, no unseen power can chain!
Look on it! it is death! Unsay thy words,
Or perish."
     While he spake, from his great eyes,
As from two torches shaken, shot forth fire.
His sword, high lifted, quivered angrily,

As lightning on the edge of thunder cloud,
Straining to fly. The vast Titanic form
More huge became,—even as a burning hill,
To a mountain swollen: and, as from crater's mouth
Gush smoke and flame, so, from the demon-face,
Fury past aught by man conceivable,
Like torrents of fire burst forth.
      Yet, fearing nought,
In heaven's protection confident, his hands
The meek man lifted; and to Israel's God
A silent prayer began.
     The blazing sword
Higher went up, as if for feller swoop
Rising to strike; yet still, with calm, clear eye,
Praying, toward Heaven looked Moses; when, behold!
A Radiance as of present Deity,—
Splendor, 'gainst which noon-sunbeams, interposed,
Shadow had cast,—fell round him. Earth and sky
Were blotted out with brightness!
      As though life
Had been extinguished—senseless, to the earth,
By that great glory, as by lightning, struck,
Yet all unharmed, he dropped.
      A voice at length,
Not by the ear, but in the spirit heard,
Awaked him, saying: "Faithful hast thou been,
And art of God approved."
     With holy joy,
The meaning felt he. Firm the worst to abide,
Uprising, he looked round; the Ethiop king,
Mad in his rage, expecting still to see;
Still resolute to defy: but lo! the plain,
So lately with that gorgeous pageant fired;
Chariots, and steeds, and men of giant mould,
Glorious in sunbright arms, and numberless,—
Void was, and silent as the wilderness!

ISRAEL IN EGYPT.

BOOK FIFTH.

ON the next morning,—so by heavenly Voice
Instructed,—unto Pharaoh went again
Moses and Aaron; craving to be heard,
Because of wretched Israel. Soon they stood
Before him, and before the frowning priests,
Princes, and rulers: then at once outspake
The ill-pleased monarch.
                         "What ye have to say,
I doubt not, still the old dull tune will harp,—
Ye would go forth into the wilderness,
Your God to worship; as though room enough
In Egypt were not. Ye my thoughts have heard;
Nor likely are to change them: yet, speak out;
For still my father's sister,—who to thee,
Moses, though leader of this discontent,
Strange favor showeth, even as of yore,—
With earnest prayer hath moved me to give ear:
And, though all vain, I know, will be your words,
Yet, promise given, I listen. Briefly, then,
Say wherefore come ye."
                       As by Voice Divine
Commanded, Aaron for his brother spake.

"How strong thine anger 'gainst us, mighty king,
Too well we know: and how the tongues of men

Are loosed against us; so that, though thyself
Justice and truth wouldst listen, yet, with din
Of enemies hating us, thine ears are deaf.
But now the time is nigh, when hear thou must;
Or, on thyself and Egypt, will the hand
Of Israel's God be put forth heavily;
Plagues sending, that in terror ye shall cry
On Israel to depart. By God Himself
Commanded, to thy presence did we come:
His words we spake to thee; his warning gave.
But, when, to worship in the wilderness,
We did entreat that Israel might go forth,
Our prayer thou scornedst; at our God didst mock;
And, for the freedom we did beg of thee,
Bonds heavier, and worse scourgings didst inflict.
Yet still, again commanded, have we come;
Once more to pray of thee that we may go
A three days' journey in the wilderness,
And sacrifice unto the Lord our God."

With harsh voice, darkly frowning, thus the king;
"And still again do I demand of you,
How prove ye that from God ye hither come,
And His words utter? Show to me a sign,
A miracle, that of surety I may know
Ye speak the truth."
"That so thou wouldst demand,
Forewarned were we," said Aaron; "and a sign
Instructed were to show thee."
From the hand
Of Moses taking then the staff, in midst
Of all the assembly, where large space was left,
Firmly he walked till to the throne-steps near;
Then paused; and, full in view of all,—but, chief,
Of the much wondering king,—the travel-staff
Uplifted, and thus spake.
"This simple rod,
O Pharaoh, shall a sign sufficient be
That from our God we come. Behold it well:
Take it, O king, within thy royal hand:

Weigh it; the floor strike with it; what thou wilt,
That do, or bid be done; ring, bend, or cut,
Or thrust within the fire,—so thou, and all,
Assurance firm as the fixed earth may feel,
That but dead wood it is, dead, solid wood;
And, of itself, no quality, or power,
Of life can have, more than the crumbling bones
From oldest grave pit; or the eternal rock."

Smiling, that humble staff within his hand
Took Pharaoh; and from crook to point surveyed:
Then to his eldest son, still smiling, gave:
He to his brethren: they unto the priests;
But, frowning, these drew back. To Aaron then
Was it returned: and he, in the open space,
Fronting the king, but distant, taking stand,
Spear-fashion lifted it, and lightly cast.

Wonder and terror then! for, lo! the staff,
Which, ere it left his hand, two fingers' breadth,
At most, had been,—to even a dragon's bulk
Suddenly swelled: the crook a head became,
With quivering, flame-like tongue, and fiery eyes,
And jaws wide gaping, and terrific fangs;
The point, a bony tail that lashed the air.
Down to the floor it fell, a heavy weight;
Its horny talons stamping, like the hoofs
Of a war-steed. King, princes, priests, yelled out,
And sprang upon their feet.
                           But instantly,
The watchful demons in their spirits passed;
And therein courage inspired; and confidence
That even the like could Egypt's sorcerers do;
And so disprove that, aided by his God,
Aaron this wonder had done. Then went command;
And speedily into the presence came
Pharaoh's magicians,—each with rod in hand;
Each by his demon taught, both what had been,
And what was yet to be. But Mascron, first,
Mightiest among them, toward the throne went straight;

Brief reverence made; then, on the ringing floor
Striking vehemently his staff, cried out;

"Vile juggle all! O, Splendor of the Sun,
Heed not this paltry fellow. The poor trick
Of boy-magician is it he hath done;
First lesson in the art."
      While yet he spake,
Cried other sorcerers also, a like note
Of mockery sounding: and, their words to prove,
At once they cast their staffs upon the floor;
And lo! a serpent every staff became,
Writhing and hissing. Then went up a laugh
Of triumph; and the priests on Pharaoh called,
Emboldening him; and for swift punishment
On Aaron and on Moses, crying out.
But, with cadaverous hue gazed now the king
On sight more strange; for, fearful to behold!
Aaron's huge dragon on the serpents fell,
And swallowed them. Speechless awhile he looked
On the vast scaly monster, quiet now,
As snake full gorged: and, with much troubled thoughts,
Then all the assembly looked; silent and awed;
So great the marvel.
     But in Pharaoh's heart
The arch fiend entered,—body, sense, and soul,
Possessing fully,—so by Power Supreme,
For its own ends, permitted,—and, his tongue
Controlling, proudly thus.
      "More cunning skill,
Aaron, hast thou, than have my sorcerers:
Since they, snakes only from their staffs have brought,
Thou, yon huge dragon: yet the same your art;
Thine but the more accomplished: and like power,
Doubtless, could they, as practised, have attained:
No sign, then, may we hold this magic feat,
That, God-instructed, or from God ye come.
Take hence your dragon, therefore, and be gone:
For, while the sun lights Egypt, shall your race,
Be servants to us: ye shall not go forth

To worship in the desert. If true God,
Your God Jehovah,—nigh the city as well
May he be found, as in the wilderness.
The slaves are idle, and would leave their work.
Look to it; for I warn you that their toils
Shall yet be harder, and the whips more keen,
If all their tasks they do not, day by day,
As they are bidden. Hence then; and speak not;
For now my heart is hardened as a stone
Against you; and your words would all be vain."

Then Aaron silently advanced, and put
His hand upon the dragon, while it lay
As if asleep, one half the open space
Its huge bulk covering; by the bony tail
He grasped it,—and, behold, it was a rod!

Inwardly marvelling, yet with show of mirth,
And laughter, as at some surpassing feat
Of magic cunning, all the assembly looked;
Then freer drew their breath.
                              But Moses now,
Nigher to Pharaoh went; and, undeterred
By his harsh speech, thus calmly him addressed.

"Truly, O king, thou sayëst, that thy heart
Hardened against us is, as even the stone:
Else had this miracle been proof to thee
That of a verity from God we come,
And his command have spoken. By what power
Thy sorcerers wrought, but darkly can I guess;
For, in the secret lore of Egypt, I,
Deeper than they, was taught: and in the face
Of all I look, and challenge give, to tell
How this they did; or if at all they know
Why, or whence, came the marvel they have done. . . .
Spirits there be, O king, who, for bad ends,
Sights most prodigious, either by themselves,
Or through man's hand, exhibit. Such, myself,
But yester-eve, did witness; wonderments

Surpassing all belief; and which to tell,
Were madman to be reckoned. Of like sort,
Though in degree far less, even now, methinks,
By Spirits were wrought; these men, unconsciously,
Their ministers; else would they answer me,
Saying, by rule of magic they had worked;
And reasons had, *why* so this thing had been,
And still again would be,—same means pursued.
But they are silent all; for nought they know
How from their staffs came serpents; why not wolves,
Lynxes, or bears; or any monstrous thing,
In the old times fabled."

" And how knowëst thou,
Bold Israelite," cried Mascron, irefully,
" Wherefore from that man's staff a dragon came;
And not a bull, a dog, a crocodile,
Or a poor rat? or why came aught at all?"

In haste then toward the throne his wrath-pale face
Turning, with trembling lips, he thus pursued.
" Light of the Sun, thy servant pardon now,
That to this insolent he answer gives:
For never, sure, in memory of man,
Before a king, so spake a bold-faced slave."

The bowing head, and smile, approval signed.
Then, upon Moses turning, with a voice
Angry and harsh as hungry leopard's growl,
"Answer," cried Mascron, " man of impudence!
How knowëst *thou* why from that juggler's staff
A seeming dragon came? *Thy* magic rules
Explain to us; *thy* reasons give why thus
The issue was; and, the same means pursued,
For ever still must be; thy reasons too,
Why wolf, or bear, or any monstrous thing,
In the old times fabled, came not. All the force
Of thy keen argument, more upon yourselves
Than us doth fall: unless *indeed* ye know,—
What by no mortal else hath yet been known,—
How, from dead wood, to fashion living thing:

Nay, from the self-same block, a dragon, now,
And now a wolf, and now a lynx, or bear,
Or dog to make. If such in truth ye know,—
Your rules expound us first, your course of work;
Then from yon staff bring forth the River-Horse,
Or Elephant; so shall we honor much
Your deeper knowledge: but, if reasons none
Ye have to give; no rules by which to work;
Nought showing why a dragon, or a bear,
A wolf, a leopard, and no other thing,
Should, or could be the birth,—such spells in force,—
Then upon you same accusation falls,
Ye charge 'gainst us,—*ye* are by Spirits ruled,
To wicked ends; to them, ay willingly,
The ministers; for, even as ourselves,
No rules, no reasons have ye, why *this* thing,
Not *that* ye made. For us, boldly I say,
No law, no reason, cause, knew any man
Among us wherefore, when his staff he cast,
Should come a serpent: by the will alone
We wrought; we willed, and it was done.
Now give thine answer, Israelite: show proof
That thou,—if we be,—art not minister
To Spirit of Evil. But I warn thee first,
That bold assertion, even with oath on oath,
Will stead thee nought. Deny it as thou may,
Thine own words past will brand thee as the tool
Of Spirits Evil, if the reasons, rules,
Thou render not, why, from yon juggler's staff,
Came forth that dragon; wherefore, in its place,
Came not a wolf, or any thing beside;
And ne'er could come. The argument thine own;
Thyself thou judgest, if thou answer not."

A proud glance round the hall the sorcerer cast,
After he thus had spoken; and the king
Smiled on him; and the priests and princes smiled,
Approving all his words. Toward Pharaoh then
Looked Moses, and thus spake.
                    " Doth the king will

That I give answer?"
                    "Surely art thou bound,"
Said Pharaoh, the dark frown upon his brow,
"Proof manifest to give, that from a God,
This thing ye did; else will it nought avail.
That do, and we are silenced; for none here
A God's acts will dispute, because the mode
By which he worketh, may not be displayed.
If but by deeper magic ye have wrought,
God-sent ye are not: and your rules, and course
Of working must reveal; else on yourselves
Falls that same charge ye on my sorcerers cast,—
That unto Spirits of Evil have ye been
The ministers for evil. This to escape,
Cunning indeed thou wert."
                    Full on the king
His calm, clear eyes then Moses fixed, and thus.
"Proof have I none, O king. Proof none can be,
To him who truth rejects, when, nor through eye,
Ear, touch, nor supernatural aid, can man
Proof force upon him. What in secret thou
Didst yesterday, solely to thee is known:
Its truth thou knowëst, as that day is day;
Yet—couldst thou prove it? If thy solemn word,
Affirming it, be questioned,—in no mode
Couldst thou its truth demonstrate. Yet, not less
A truth it is, though proved not. Even thus
With me in this great matter doth it stand.
That, by the very voice of God Himself
Commanded, hither came we, and this sign
Before thee showed,—truth stronger is to me
Than aught which sense can warrant; for, not ear,
The bodily ear alone, but the inmost soul,
Heard it, and felt. 'Twas on the holy hill
Of Horeb, in the stillness of the night,
From a burning bush, unburnt; that came the Voice.
To Egypt was I bidden,—from his bonds
Israel to bring: and in thy presence, first,
This sign to show, as token that from God
My message was. How, from this humble staff,

Came forth the dragon,—ignorant I am,
As wherefore from the sun come light and heat.
That so 'twould be, from the Celestial Voice
Alone I knew. Yet also know I well,
That by no power of magic, in the schools
Of Egypt taught, from things inanimate,
Could man aught animate bring. Thy sorcerers all
This truth will grant. That, His own sign to mock,
And render vain, GOD would to them have given
Power the like thing to do,—impossible,
Monstrous; 'gainst reason of the veriest fool,
Plainly appeareth. If, then, nor from art
Of magic, nor from power by God bestowed,
Those wonders they performed,—what else remains,
Than that through might of Spirits Evil they wrought,—
Thereof albeit unconscious. Hearken not,
O Pharaoh, to their words; for false they are;
And judgments dire will come upon you all,
If thou by them be ruled. A harmless sign
That we by God are sent, we now have shown:
If thou reject it, and thy heart make hard,—
From God I warn thee,—other signs, even plagues
Unheard of through the earth, will He send forth;
Grievous afflictions over all this land;
Till ye, at last, shall feel that Israel's God
Is God indeed; and that, 'gainst Him to strive,
Perdition were, and madness. His decree
Saith, Israel from his bondage shall be freed;
From Egypt shall go out. Such the sure end,—
Now, or on day not distant. Yet, on thee,
On thy sole word approving, rests the hour:
We crave thee let us go,—nor, till thy voice
Permissive free us, may we hence depart.
But on thyself, and on this land, will fall
The punishment of refusal; for aye worse,
And worse will be the plagues that ye must feel;
Till all unbearable shall they become;
And thou, and all of Egypt, shall cry out,
Imploring us to go. These evil things
Wouldst thou prevent,—even on this day proclaim,

Saying to Israel, 'All your bonds are loosed;
Whither ye would, go freely; and no man
The hand shall lay upon you.'"
                              Like the burst
Of fire from naphtha kindled, was the cry
From prince, priest, lord, alike, when these bold words
Smote on their ears. The presence quite forgot,—
Upstarted many—hands clenched,—eyes on fire,
With fury of madness;—some, in chorus strange,
Screaming the bitter curse,—some, with black spite,
Pointing and mocking. But the king his voice
Uplifted angrily; and all were mute,
And to their seats went back. On Moses then
Looked Pharaoh, frowning; and with harsh tone thus.

" That thou art mad, is, for thine insolence,
Fondest excuse to make. A patient ear
I vowed to give thee, and have given; but, mark!
A point there is at which, with load opprest,
Even hardest rock must crack: and limit is,
Beyond which tried, patience more strong than steel,
Like glass must break. In ear of mortal king,
Surely were never yet such words as thine,
And with such boldness, uttered. Not again,—
I warn thee,—dare the threatenings of thy God
Before the king to speak: for, what is he?
A God of yesterday,—as ye yourselves
Of yesterday a people. Ages back,—
Long ere thine Israel, or that Israel's God,
Was known upon the earth,—this Egypt stood
Highest among the nations; and her Gods
Throughout all time were worshipped, even as now.
Our Gods, to thine, as oaks to mushrooms are;
Both in their might, and durance. If thy God
Us threaten, he may find, perchance, that Gods,
His greater far, will us protect; and strike
Even on himself. The Universal God,
God of all Gods,—with man, or things of earth,
Nought meddleth; unto Gods inferior
The rule deputing: of those lower Gods,

Your God, Jehovah, haply may be one;
One of the younger. Great ye boast his power;
But, with Osiris, Amun, on our side;
Pthah, Neph, Khem, Buto, Neith,—Jehovah's might,
Or anger, nought afears us. Then, no more
With message, or with threat from him, presume
To come before me: for the babbling wind
More vainly would not talk, than thou,—his threats,
As senseless, babbling."
      At those words, on high
Moses his arm uplifted, as to stay
The blasphemy, ere yet the thunder-stone
Should strike the speaker; and, with voice subdued,
Yet in authority terrible,—his eyes
Like living fire, his countenance like cloud
That brings the tempest, thus, reproving, spake.

" Knowëst thou, Pharaoh, of the fathomless sea
The secret bed, and what therein doth lie?
Couldst thou go down into the uttermost depth,
And bring up all its riches? Less, far less,
Of God aught knowëst thou; or of His ways
Aright can'st judge. There is no God but one;
That Universal God who,—as *ye* teach,—
With man and things of earth doth meddle not,—
O'er such to lower Gods deputing rule:—
Error pernicious! for all things from Him
First came; and by, and through Him, still exist:
Without Him, nought had been; nought still would be:
Sole ruler He o'er earth, and sea, and sky,
O'er stars, and sun; o'er man, and o'er each thing
That draweth breath of life. Of that One God,
Jehovah is the name,—I AM, the name,—
By His own voice thus spoken; and to Him
Doth Israel bow, adoring. Other gods,
None are there; fictions all! With shadows try
To throw down mountains; yet, the banded might
Of all your gods—Jehovah to o'erthrow,—
Shade of a shadow were! His words to speak

Again before thee, me thou dost forbid:
But, king of Egypt, from Heaven's king I come;
His messenger; and speak I must,—and thou
Must hear me: nor, as subject to a king,
May I speak humbly; but as greatest king
To humblest subject; for all earthly power
And grandeur,—to the majesty of Heaven,
Is dust, to sunbeams. By the Omnipotent sent,
Nought can I fear. Thy threats,—the hate and spite
Of those thy servants, such light pressure have,
As mist on Lebanon. Not as man I come
Before thee, my own thoughts, my own free will,
Alone impelling: a mere instrument I,
Sounding to thee His bidding. Be not deaf,
O king, to His command. My humble voice,
Rough, and offensive, galling to thy pride,
Though it may seem,—like but the small cloud is,
As messenger sent on from coming storm,
And warning thee to shelter. If thou bide,
Defying it,—as straws by whirlwind flung,
Will thou, and all, be scattered.
                              " I behold
Even now, Sesostris,"—and, while thus he spake,
Death-pale his countenance grew; his eyes were fixed,
As on far distance looking; and his voice,
From lips scarce moving, came, hollow and faint
As his who talks in slumber—" I behold
Even now, Sesostris, what the end will be,
If by repentance changed not. Realm, crown, life,
Are taken from thee! A great gulf I see;
And men, and steeds, and chariots, whelmed therein,
Amid a noise of thunder, and strong winds,
And roar of mighty waters! . . . . All are gone!"

Trembling, he suddenly ceased; and bowed the head;
And in his mantle covered up his face,
As one who mourneth.
                    Great the marvel was
Throughout the assembly: even the priestly rage

By wonder was borne down. But Pharaoh most
Awe-stricken sat: for scarcely human seemed
The form, the look, the words, the voice of him,
Speaking with power far greater than his own;
With grandeur more than mortal; so that mute
Upon his throne he sat; the threatened doom
Pondering darkly; doubt, and fear, and pride,
Perplexing him.
     But not to inward war
Long was he left: the great Arch Fiend again
His soul possessed; pride, anger, blowing up,
As winds, a sinking fire. To the height, at length,
Inflamed—thus spake he out.
       "That mad thou art,
Proof thou didst give before; but heap on heap
Thou pilëst it,—that chains and darkness now
Best physic for thee seem. Not crazed enough,
Fool that thou art, as messenger from God
To boast thyself,—but as a prophet too,
A seër of the things can ne'er be seen,
Thou'dst top all madness. Yet, the wind to stay,
As wisely might I talk, as thee to check
In thy wild raving. Get ye, therefore, hence,
And see my face no more: for, till the worm
Gnaw through a pyramid,—through my strong soul
Your threats shall pierce not. Israel shall *not* go,
Three days, or one, into the wilderness.
If sacrifice unto your God ye must,—
In Egypt be it done. Away, away,
I will not hear thee."
     Thus to Moses he,—
Seeing that he would speak: yet, not the less,
Undaunted all, the great law-giver thus.

 "King, with sad heart we leave thee; knowing well
How the dread storm is gathering over thee,
And over all thy people. But thy words
To obey, we dare not: still before thy face,
If God the message send, appear we must.

And send He will,—all merciful,—thee and thine
From guilt to warn; from punishment to save.
Let not thy mind be darkened. Thou hast seen
How Spirits of Evil through thy sorcerers wrought,
God's purpose to oppose: through thee still more,—
As being of power far greater,—will they strive
Evil to work: thy heart, by nature soft,
Will they make millstone hard; thy pride lash up
To very madness; as the hurricane
Lasheth the sea to madness: so that ills
Unspeakable will come upon you all,
And ruin everlasting. But, to God,
To Israel's God, wouldst thou incline thy heart,
And His command obey,—for *thee* then well,
For Israel well, for all of Egypt well,
Might be the issue. Yet alas! O king,
Not thus hath it been spoken! In the dust
Fall then, and pray; and haply, even yet,
The evil thou may 'scape."
       "Enough, enough,"
Cried Pharaoh,—from his throne upstarting quick,
And down the steps descending; "Let me now
Some music have, and cheering wine, and mirth,—
This Nightmare in broad daylight to shake off.
All they who will, come with me."
       Saying thus,
With rapid step, out from the hall he strode,—
By many followed. Moses, too, went forth,
And Aaron, grieving: but the elder priests,
And rulers,—restless as the rolling waves
After the storm hath passed,—with voices high,
Hot faces, flashing eyes, and gestures fierce,—
Their rage to vent, remained. 'Gainst Moses, chief,
Their hatred was: and how on him to glut
Vengeance most deep and swift, their thoughts they racked.
At last forth went they; eager in all hearts
To pour their malice; and with fury inflame
'Gainst Israel; and 'gainst him, the foremost, worst,

The hated of old days; who, on his throne,
The very Splendor of the Sun had dared
To insult and threaten; and with magic wrought,
Ruin to bring upon him; and sure loss
To universal Egypt, of her power,
Her fame, her riches.
     " Harder be the work,
Sharper the stripes, on that rebellious brood,"
Cried they aloud; "so surest shall we keep
The fetters on them, and their spirit break;
And make them know that, till the end of time,
Base Israel unto Egypt shall be slaves."

ISRAEL IN EGYPT.

BOOK SIXTH.

In the dead hush and darkness of the night,
While in the garden all alone he walked;
For Israel mourning, pleading with his God,—
To Moses came a Voice,—the words of man
Uttering distinct, but with no mortal tongue.
Calm as the sigh of eve through Lebanon's groves;
Yet vast as murmur of all seas in one;
Deeper than thunder of sky-cleaving world,—
Seeming all space to fill,—from highest heaven
Descending, thus the Voice Celestial spake.

"Israel is not forgotten of his God,
And surely shall be loosed. Against you now
Pharaoh is hard. At morning get thee forth.
Unto the water, lo! he goeth out.
Beside the river's brink, against he come,
Shalt thou stand waiting him; and in thine hand
The rod shalt take, that was to serpent turned.
And thou shalt say unto him, 'the Lord God
Of Israel me hath sent unto thee, saying;
Let thou my people go, that they may serve
Their God within the wilderness; for, behold,
Hitherto wouldst thou not. Thus saith the Lord;
In this shalt thou be taught that I am God;
Lo! with the rod which is within mine hand,

The waters of the river will I smite,
That they shall turn to blood. The fish shall die;
The river stink; and the Egyptians loathe
To drink the water.' . . . . But even yet his heart
Will hardened be; and yet again the hand
Of God must fall upon him."
                              Ceased the Voice;
And the earth trembled. Long time on his face,
Awe-stricken, yet in ecstacy divine,
Lay Moses,—man, and all the world, forgot,
In sense of that great Presence: but at length,
Loud choiring near at hand, the nightingales
From the deep trance awoke him: he arose;
And, with clasped hands, bowed head, and prayer-filled
    heart,
His chamber sought; and soon, in calm repose,
Dreaming of heaven, was wrapped.
                                  At early morn,
With Aaron toward the river he went forth,
And by its brink took stand; awaiting there
The coming of the king. Them, yet far off,
Saw Pharaoh, and was wrathful. O'er his face
A darkness gathered; and his angry eye,
Speechless, spake out, "Now get ye from my sight,
For I do loathe your aspect!"
                              But, serene
Stood they, expecting: till, when near them now
The frowning monarch drew,—bending the head,
With reverence meet, his right hand Moses raised,
Betokening wish to speak. Him, with the tone
Of harsh displeasure, Pharaoh thus addressed.

"Again? No day, no hour, may I be free
From thy vexation? What hast thou to say,
Which yesterday thou saidst not, and in vain?
By blow on blow the smith hard iron shapes;
And me, perchance, by ceaseless harassment,
Thou'dst hope to bend, till to thy prayer I yield,
And let you go: thou'lt find thy labor lost:
Or, if not lost, in your own loss to end:

In sharper scourgings, and in harder work,
On your obdúrate people. If aught new
Thou hast to say, speak quickly: else, depart."

Then Moses answered: "Not of mine own thoughts,
But as commanded, speak I. The Lord God
Of Israel me hath sent unto thee, saying;
'Let thou my people go, that they may serve
Their God within the wilderness; for, behold,
Hitherto wouldst thou not. Thus saith the Lord;
In this shalt thou be taught that I am God:
Lo! with the rod which is within mine hand,
The waters of the river will I smite,
That they shall turn to blood. The fish shall die;
The river stink; and the Egyptians loathe
To drink the water.' "
      When those words he heard,—
With a great utterance spoken; and with look
Majestic more than man's,—within his heart
Pharaoh was troubled, and awhile stood mute.
But they who with him were,—priests, sorcerers, lords,—
Mocked at the threatenings; and the spiteful laugh
One to the other passed,—though privily,
Because that Pharaoh yet had answered not,—
Hoping thus most to incense him. Well the king
Their smothered gibings heard; but secret dread
O'ermastered him, on those portentous words
Gloomily musing; and the fearful thing
Of the day past remembering. "Not more strange,"
So ran his thoughts, "of water to make blood,
Than of dead staff a living dragon make.
And that dread sequence,—death to all that lives
Within the river; and the sacred stream
With rottenness filled, and stench—that neither man
Nor beast thereof shall drink! What if such power,
Through Israel's God, to that mysterious man,
Truly be given; and the terrific threat
In act should end! how longer might I strive
Against that pestilent people! Blood to drink,
Or die of thirst! in blood to wash, or lie

Like swine in filthiness! on blood to gaze,
In place of those pure rivers, fountains, wells,
Bright springs, and sunny brooks!—abhorrëd thought!
The land would be one lazar-house; one den
Of beastlike madmen! one huge grave, at last,
Uncovered from the birds obscene, and beasts,
Where a whole people, rotten ere they died,
With stench would taint the sky! 'Gainst power like that,
All struggle vain! submit at once I must!
Ten thousand lands, at such price held enslaved,
Worthless would be as dirt; nay, all the gold
Of Egypt flung to Israel, would be gain,—
Their riddance buying, and so 'scaping Plague! . . . .
But, what if insolent boast alone that threat;—
How would the juggler laugh! and how, unproved,
Truth were it known, or falsehood? Plague itself
Scarce worse to bear, than sting of burning shame,
Too late to find, that bold-faced lies alone,
Egypt's great king had coward made, and fool.
Intolerable! All things will I dare,
Rather than such shame risk!"
       His eyes shot fire,
His face was flushed and anxious, as, at length,
Hastily turning,—with low, tremulous voice,
Thus to his priests and rulers he began.

 "What think ye? This strange summons should we heed?
This threat believe; and, the foul plague to escape,
At once let Israel go? . . . . Or, the man's words
Poor boasting shall we deem; or insolent lies,—
The king to scare, and mock? . . . . Who *is* this God
From whom he threateneth? Who hath heard of him
His birth, his dwelling place, his power, his rank
'Mong other Gods? . . . . Or is he but a dream,—
A fiction all, in whose pretended name,
This Moses hath wrought magic damnable;
Making from that dead staff,—as ye beheld,—
A living dragon, vast and terrible?
And now again, with that same staff, worse thing

He threateneth,—even with blood the land to drench,
That water shall be none; all fish shall die;
The river stink! Is this thing possible?
Or through his God,—if any such there is,—
Or through a magic mightier than all else
The earth hath known,—may he this horror work?"

   Then Sethos, stepping forward, on his arm
The troubled monarch touched, and softly thus;
"Father, thy soul for nought is now perplexed:
Thy priests, lords, rulers, at this threat make mock;
And thy magicians boldly challenge give,
All feats of sorcery which this man can work,
Themselves, in part, to do: and, for his God,
A shadow they esteem him; a pretence;
A name of nothing; a mere screen to hide
The cunning work of magic. Let him try
His spells upon the river: failing there,
Even to his grave the gibe will follow him;—
All his great blustering, like a bubble, burst;—
And, to his future threatenings, the great laugh
Best answer be. That, by some magic sleight,
Semblance of blood to water he may give,—
Thy sorcerers deny not; but, in *truth*,
A river to make blood,—impossible
They hold, as out of pebbles to make bread;
Or bring from heaven the stars; or, in the sea,
Plant the great mountains. But, come even the worst
Through his strong sorcery,—power that sends the plague,
As powerful is to stay it: time enough
For loosing Israel, when the profit more
From loosing, than from holding. But, at once,
Dismayed by insolent and lying boast,
The costliest jewel of thy crown to yield,—
Unworthy of thee, every voice would cry,—
A treason to thy people, and thyself!
Defy him then, O Splendor of the Sun:
Let him his worst essay: or, wiser course,
Arrest his juggling: try if his best spells,
Or links of steel, are stronger. Where he stands,

Let him be fettered; and his wizard staff
Be cast into the water,—there to work
Its best, or worst; while we look on, and laugh.
If now thou yield,—for aye is Israel lost;
Egypt for ever mocked: if now thou strike,—
For aye triumphant Egypt,—Israel bound!"

  Stirred by his demon, thus, with look inflamed,
The doomed prince spake: and him the admiring sire
In low tone answered.
      "Wisely, son beloved,
Hast thou given counsel. Yet, the nobler course,
Not to arrest, but to defy his power;
And so to prove it. If indeed his might
This Nile could turn to blood,—far easier 'twere,
Fetters of steel, and prison walls, to break.
That which he saith,—he *can*, or can *not* do:
Prove that he can,—and Israel must be loosed,
Or Egypt be a grave: prove that he fail,—
A pyramid of mocks will on him lie,
And Israel still be ours."
       Speaking aloud,
To Moses then he turned; and harshly thus.

  "Thy bold demand we have considered well;
And thus reply. We know not of thy God,
Nor of his power: but in our own gods trust;
And thine, and thee defy. Stretch then thy rod,
And work thy wonders: make thy boasting good;
And, afterwards, may we give ear to thee:
But, fail,—and by Osiris do I swear,
Such shall thy punishment be, as dread shall bring
On nations yet unborn."
       A moment, mute
Stood Moses,—on the angry-visaged king
Mournfully looking: then to Aaron turned,
And said; "Take thou the rod, and stretch thine hand,
And smite the river."
      Close unto the brink

Slowly walked Aaron; in his hand the staff.
Impatient to behold,—yet with the words
Of mockery on their tongues,—priests, sorcerers, lords,
Pressed forward: while the prince on Pharaoh's hand
Eagerly seized; and, laughing, drew him on.
" Sport shall we have, my father," whispered he;
"For, by old Aaron's trembling lip, I see
He knoweth the lie, and punishment doth fear.
Prithee now, father, give them to my hands:
Their sentence shall be light; for merriment,
Rather than vengeance. I would only fling
The conjurer and his wand into the stream;
So to prove which is mightier,—he, or Nile.
But haste; he lifts the rod."
       Two eager steps,
Close to the brink brought son and father both;
From Aaron so short distance, that the staff,
Thitherward stretched, had touched them. On each hand,
With heads out-thrust, and mocking look, and smile,
Thronged all the rest; now glancing at the rod;
Now at the water; now the lifted arm;
Now the pale countenance, quivering with the sense
Of the God-power within. Slowly, at length,
As loth to strike, Aaron stretched out the rod:
With large bright eyes upturned, and quivering lips,
On heaven a moment gazed; then downward looked,
And smote the water.
      As when fire breaks out
In a thick-peopled dwelling; cry and shriek
From all within are heard; the hurry of feet,
Pressings, and strugglings, who shall first escape,—
Even so, when on the river fell the rod,
Burst forth, from king, prince, rulers, sorcerers, lords,
A howl of frenzied terror: shuddering, sick,
Astounded nigh to madness, back they ran,
Thrusting and stumbling; covering each the eyes,
And the gorge heaving,—as from sight and stench
Of a foul grave-pit flying. For, behold!

To meet the rod, in a great wave arose
The water, as from fountain underneath,
With violence bursting,—but the wave was blood!
Had the great earth been living thing, even thus,
From her pierced heart, the torrent might have gushed.
Rolling and writhing, like a dying snake,
Water 'gainst blood made battle,—but soon sank,
O'ermastered; and one vast vermilion stream,
Like liquid fire, tossing and boiling, ran,
To affright the peaceful sea.
                            With death-spasm struck,
High from the gory flood great fish leaped up;
And smaller fry in shoals, all quivering;
Their gleaming sides,—silver, and pearl, and gold,—
In red slime quenched. The unwieldy river-horse,
Like a huge jelly of gore, came floundering out,
Blinded, and fearful; snorting hideously.
The crocodile, beside the bank asleep,
Or, with half opened eye, awaiting prey,—
By the dread wave o'erwhelmed, upstarted quick;
And, belly to the ground, in wild affright,
Like a great fiery lizard, open-jawed,
Fled the unnatural stream. The snow-white birds
That rode the crystal river,—screaming shrill,
Rose, crimson-breasted; and, with blood-tipped wings
Rapidly clanging, terror-stricken flew.

But, with calm spirit,—conscious that of God
The humble servants they,—beside the bank
Moses and Aaron stood; in wonder fixed,
And awe; yet fearing not; nay with strong hope
Uplifted, that now speedily must come
The day of Israel's freedom. The great hand
Of God thus visibly outstretched to save,—
Nor earth, nor hell the mighty work could stay.
Silent then stood they, marking how the flood,
Far as the eye could reach, both toward the sea,
And upward toward its source,—all blood rolled on,
Gurgling and frothing; small fish, numberless,
Like dead leaves floating; and the ocean-kind,

In the death-struggle, blind and suffocate,
Helplessly wallowing.
      Yet not quiet long
Thus stood they gazing; for, priests, sorcerers, lords,—
Like men from hideous dreams upstarting quick,
And the false terror spurning,—all at once,
All demon-fired together, round them came,
Fierce, open-mouthed, like wild dogs on their prey;
Alike all eager their sharp fangs to fix;
Alike with one false thought inspired; one hope,
The miracle to disprove; the king to arm,
As in a mail of adamant, 'gainst all shafts
Of truth from Israel's quiver. But their tongues,
Clamorously sounding, suddenly were checked:
For Pharaoh,—by the great arch fiend himself
Inflamed to madness,—toward the Israelites,
With threatening arm outstretched, and angry look,
Walked rapidly; and sending forth his voice
Storm-like, roared out,
      " Impostors are ye both!
By your vile art ye make us to see lies!
Ye have not changed the water into blood;
But, by black magic, have our sight bewitched,
To see what is not. Pure as ever runs
The sacred stream; and by all other men,
Not blinded by your spells, so would be seen:
Nay, at this very moment, so *is* seen
By thousands, far and near, whom your foul art
Hath reached not: and, ere long, even by ourselves,
Pure will be seen again; when from our eyes
Shall pass your mischief. But, though sight be fooled,
Our reason is not;—*that* ye cannot touch:
And, by that ruled, we know that falsehood all
Is this ye show us: proof of magic skill,
Incredible till now; but of nought else;
No proof that God-sent are ye; proof of nought,
Save your own cunning, falsehood, insolence:
And nought deserving, save such punishment
As should, throughout all ages yet to come,
Stagger the wicked. I command you now;

Undo your spell; and let our eyes again
See truth: or, if ye will not, look to feel
Ills that are real, and not cheats of sense;
Substance, not pictures; solid, crushing rocks;
Not shadows ye may walk through. Answer me:
But, first, bethink you: for, as men ye are,
Who stand before an earthquake's gaping jaws;
At the next step to turn,—or headlong go
Down to perdition."
     Trembling in his rage,
There ceased he; but his eyes shot living fire
Full in the face of Moses; and his hands,
Hard-clenched, hung quivering; as if blows, not words,
Best had his fury spoken. All unmoved
By such outrageous speech, and looks, then thus
Moses made answer.
     "That a great deceit
Is on thee, king, hereafter wilt thou know,
As now we know it: yet, deceit of sense,
Through any act of magic by us wrought,
None is it; but a cloud by passion raised;
Or foul delusion, by some Spirit of Ill
Whispered within thy heart. That which thine eye
Beholdeth, is a truth: your sacred stream,
Once crystal water, veritable blood
Now hath become. Taste, try it how you will;
Call your fair maidens; bid them in the stream
Wash their white garments; hither lead your flocks,
Your horses, or your mules, that they may drink:
All tests ye can devise, try heedfully;
And, where we stand, there slay us, if the proof
Gainsay that this is blood. Nor thy command,
A spell to undo, and thus to change again
The witness of your eyes,—can we obey;
For, not our own, but an Almighty hand,
Through ours, hath wrought;—we but the instruments,
As, to our hands, that rod was instrument.
Of its own will, might the dead wood as well,
Aught that we did, undo, as, of *our* will,
That which through us was done, might *we* undo.

Thy bidding, therefore, *can* we not obey:
Nor would we, if we could; for, God, and thou,
Diversely ordering,—less than sunbeam-mote
To the great sun, thy bidding against His.
And, though in verity before our feet
Earth to its centre gaped; yet, in the path
By God commanded, walking,—with firm heart
On should we still; for neither sea, nor fire,
Nor sword, nor bottomless pit, that man can harm
Who His work doeth."
                    When these words he heard,—
With great power spoken,—and the countenance
When he beheld, all shining, as with light
From its own substance issuing,—in the king
A new amazement rose; and silently,
On Moses gazing, stood he: but the prince,
Lords, priests, and sorcerers, 'mong themselves talked loud;
Wondering, yet angry. By his demon, at length,
Stirred, and instructed, Mascron, the sorcerer,
Forth stepping from the rest, before the king
Went boldly, bowed the head, and thus began.

"Light of the Sun! forgive thy servant now,
That other thought than thine he dares to speak.
Not a mere juggle to the eye is this,—
As to thee seemeth,—but, in verity,
A stroke of magic, that to blood hath changed
The water of the river: a great stroke,
Yea, wonderful; and more than power of spells,
Till now, hath done. But, nought of God is it;
No proof that these two Israelites, from heaven
To thee are sent, the will Divine to speak;—
For, even the self-same miracle, our art
Also can work,—though in a less degree;
Since in that craft is our experience less,
Our knowledge less;—for alway, from his birth,
In deepest mysteries was this Moses taught;
Alway for the dark knowledge did he thirst;
Alway did drink, and never was sufficed:

So that, in potency of magic, none,
Even from his youth, to him was equal found.
But, though *now* blood the river is,—true blood,—
Yet not for aye : the circle of the hours
Fulfilled, the power of sorcery will fade ;
The stream again be water: and the fish,
Thus floating dead, to life will come anew ;
And all things be, as this had never been.
Prove now, O king, our skill the like to do:
And, if we fail, then give to these belief
That by God-power, not magic, have they worked ;
And that, God-sent, they speak the will of God.
Two bow-shots hence is the great water-tank :—
Give the command, O king ; and, with our staffs,
That will we smite, as these the river smote ;
And, even as they, will water turn to blood."

To Moses then, and Aaron, spake the king.

"Ye hear what this man saith. Come with us now,
And see if this same miracle, by power
Of magic may be wrought. So prove it, ye
As but the mightier sorcerers must be held :
Yet rank impostors also ; since the act
Of cunning witchcraft only, ye hold forth
As very deed of God ; yourselves to avouch
His messengers, the speakers of His words,—
When your own insolence alone ye speak.
So if it prove, a stronger magic still
May fail you, seeking punishment to 'scape."

Frowning, he ceased ; then gave the sign ; and all
At once moved onward.
      By the first great tank
Arrived, on its broad wall of brick they stood,
Marking the deep still water, crystal clear,
By no air ruffled ; so that, in its depth,
Each separate brick, and every little stone,
As if in air, shone bright. Before him then
Pharaoh the chief magician called, and thus.

"Even in the faces of these Israelites,
Mascron, prove now thy cunning such as theirs.
Though but one bucketful of water pure
To blood thou turn, yet well might that suffice
To show their power thine also. But, the whole
If thou shouldst change,—supply full large, methinks,
For this vast city, through a moon, or more,—
Slight cause for envy hadst thou; since thy craft
Close upon theirs would press."

"No fear have I
Of what shall be the event,"—the sorcerer said,—
Emboldened by his demon; and full power
Feeling, the act to do. Without delay,
Then high his staff uplifted he, and smote:
And the bright water instantly was blood!

A joyous shout, from prince, priests, sorcerers, lords,
Welcomed the marvel: and with mock and laugh,
The Israelites they taunted.

"Not from God
Pretend *I* to be missioned," sneeringly
Cried Mascron then; "yet, your great magic trick,
Lo, have I also done! Wise men ye are;
But others, too, have wisdom of like sort,—
As ye behold; and, ere your impious lies
Ye tempt us to believe,—far greater thing
Than this must ye perform."

With lifted hand,
Pharaoh his vaunting checked; and briefly thus,
To Moses turning, spake.

"What say'st thou now,
Proud sorcerer? If your miracle, from God
Attest you for his messengers,—wherefore not
Also from God, he who the like hath wrought? . . . .
Yet not as you he counselleth,—to set free
Our rightful slaves; but evermore to keep;
Yea, on them heavier burthens still to lay,
And sharper stripes inflict. Why, then, to him
Should we not hearken, rather than to you;
Since the like witness of divine command

Bring both; and his the counsel pleasanter,
And profitable more? How answerest thou:
And how from falsehood may ye purge yourselves,
So punishment to escape?"
                         To him, with mien
August, and voice of high authority,
Moses thus made reply.
                       " No punishment
Fear we; for alway in the might of God
Our trust is: and His bidding we obey,
Unquestioning the event. If 'gainst deceit
Thy wrath is,—elsewhere turn it; for, with us,
Deceit is none. As, from his rod, this man
A serpent brought,—so, by that same dark power,
To blood hath he changed water; for no spell
Of sorcery so could work. That we, by art
Of magic, your great river turned to blood,
Boldly he saith: and that, by self-same art,
This water into blood hath *he* now turned:
Let him then show the rule by which he wrought.
For us,—the infant that this day was born,
Hath knowledge deep as we, of any cause
Occult, through which that miracle was done,
Save by the will of God. That so 'twould be,
Plainly I told thee,—even His very words,
As to me spoken, speaking unto thee.
Through me, His messenger, did Israel's God
Again require of thee to let us go,
That we might worship in the wilderness,—
For thitherto thou wouldst not; and this plague,
On disobedience threatened. Plain the words;
' Lo! with this staff which is within mine hand,
The waters of the river will I smite,
That they shall turn to blood: the fish shall die
The river stink; and the Egyptians loathe
To drink the water.' Such the words I spake,
Even as I AM had spoken. That the rod,
Smiting the stream, such wonder would perform,
From His word only knew we. His sole will
As cause we know. So know it thou, O king,

And his command obey,—then grievous ills,
Which else shall scourge you all, ye may escape.
For the great word is spoken: from this land
Shall Israel be brought out: or soon, or late,
As yet we know not. For this present time,
A three days' journey in the wilderness,
That we may sacrifice unto our God,
Is all of thee demanded. Yield thou that;
Then may obedience in the greater thing
Be easier; and heaven's judgments ye may 'scape."

"I will yield nought, bold sorcerer," cried the king,
Two steps advancing, with his arm uplift,
As if to strike: "thy God I do defy!
Thy magic I will stay; or prove the force
Of chain and dungeon on thee. Get thee hence;
Both of you hence: and let me see no more
Your rebel faces. In few hours, your spells,
Like to spent tempests, of themselves will cease;
And blood again be water,—even as this:
For, look! already hath the change begun:
Water and blood are here, where, ten breaths since,
Was nought but blood. . . . See! even while we gaze,
The wonder grows! the foul becomes the pure!
The blood-mist vanishes,—the sun comes out! . . . .
And, now,—lo! all is pure! So speedily
Shall pass *your* witchcraft also. Nay, perchance,
Already hath passed. Run quickly, some of you,
And look upon the river; and bring back
Report of that ye see. And, as I live,
Ye insolent! if also *there* hath died
The spell which, with blaspheming tongue, ye called
The very hand of God,—this earth no more
Shall ye pollute; but on the instant die!"

Foaming with rage, he ceased; and to and fro
Strode muttering: but, his anger heeding not,
With firm, calm voice thus Moses answered him.

"Not in *thy* hand, O Pharaoh, are our lives;—

For still the work of God have we to do.
This water,—by the Power of Evil changed
To blood, or semblance thereof,—soon again
To its original nature hath returned:
But that which by the will of God was changed,
Not till again He willeth, can return
To that it was before. Thy messengers
Will tell thee that the river yet is blood:
And now, O king,—*I* tell thee, that once more
This water will be blood; yea, all the streams,
The rivers, and the ponds, fountains and pools;
And water in all vessels, wood, or stone,
From which the people of this Egypt drink;—
All will be changed to blood! So shalt thou know
That Israel's God, on earth, and in the heavens,
Sole Lord and Ruler is. But yet, alas!
This wilt thou not believe! Thy heart is hard,
Proud and rebellious; and again the hand
Of God must fall upon thee."
       With stern tone
Of warning prophet having ended thus,
He tarried not; but,—unto king and lords
The customed reverence making,—with calm step,
By Aaron followed, forthwith went his way.

 Stiff with astonishment the king looked on,
Nor to restrain them, spake; by those dread words,
That voice and air portentous, overawed.
Mute also stood the sorcerers, priests, and lords,—
Awe-struck and troubled, when the king they saw,
As by a might superior stricken down,
And powerless to resist.
      But, in brief time,
Panting with haste, the messengers returned,
And said, "O king! the river yet is blood:
And thereon, numberless as autumn leaves,
The dead fish float!"
     In silence and dismay
Awhile stood all: but, demon-stirred, at length,
With wrath and pride Pharaoh again was filled.

"They shall *not* go," he cried, "though the whole land
Be soaked with blood. If, ere the sun go down,
The magic cease not: and, if other streams,
Fountains, and waters, as he threatened, change,—
Send ye command that, throughout all the land,
The people dig for water: but, in chief,
Upon those pestilent Israelites be the toil:
Till they pure water bring from out the ground,
Let the whips cease not; so their cries shall mount
And their magicians tell, that on themselves,
More than on those of Egypt, falls their plague. . . . .
But, haply, though blood seeming to the eye,
Unto the taste, still water all may be:
If so, the mischief less. Stoop, some of you,
And of this water drink; which real blood,
Even as the river, seemed; and then again
Water became. If to the palate sweet,
As though no change had been,—conclusion strong
Justly may follow, that to sight alone
The transformation was; and that small ill
The plague will bring upon us."
       While he spake,
Hastily kneeled the younger of the lords;
And also of the younger priests kneeled some;
And he who first into the brimming tank
Dipped hand, and therefrom tasted, cried aloud,
"Sweet is the water as from hill-side spring!
Cup-bearer,—hither bring the royal cup,
That Pharaoh, too, may taste it."
       To his hand
The crystal cup was given. He plunged it in;
Hurriedly laved, and filled it; then arose,
And with glad look the liquid diamond bore,
And to the king presented. A bright smile
Illumed the monarch's face, as in his hand
He took the cup, and held it to the light,
Its brilliance marking. 'Neath the nostril then
He placed it, and still smiled: once more upheld,
And gazed upon its sparkles; toward his mouth
Then drew it; and, with opening lips, prepared

H

To quaff the grateful drink. But, suddenly,
As by a serpent stung, he started back;
Shuddered, and shrieked; and, as it fire had been,
Flung from his hand the cup; for lo! 'twas red,
And thick as life-stream of the sacrifice!

From those who o'er the water bent, not less,
A great shriek rose; for, while, with hollowed palms,
They dipped, and drank,—joyously calling out,
That even as brightest desert spring 'twas sweet,—
Behold! in one same instant, all was blood!

ISRAEL IN EGYPT.

BOOK SEVENTH.

THROUGHOUT the realm of Egypt, a loud voice
Of lamentation rose; for everywhere,
In the same point of time, to blood was changed
The water of all rivers, fountains, pools;
All vessels, wood, or stone; so that to drink,
Though famishing of thirst, the people loathed:
Nor their soiled, heated bodies could they cleanse,
Or cool; for, of pure water, not one drop
Remained unto them. Consternation dire,
Even into madness growing, filled the land.
Men, women, children, wildly roamed about,
For water, water, clamoring. By the banks
Of the broad Nile, and of the smaller streams,
Thousands were gathered; with abhorrent looks,
On the great blood-flow gazing. Into wells
The deepest, greedily was bucket cast;
Yet still came nought but blood.
                              Then went command
From Pharaoh, that, beside the river-banks,
And nigh the margins of all running streams,
Both day and night the multitudes should dig,
Till the pure springs burst forth: but chiefly they,
The hated race of Israel, 'neath the whips
Incessantly should toil; so their loud cries

Might tell how, most of all, on them the curse,
For Egypt sent, had fallën.
                    Through the night,—
Through the next day,—and through the second night,—
Groaned the hard-toiling Hebrews. Also rose
Cries of the crowding multitudes, who, athirst,
Fevered, and panting, round about the wells
Were gathered, watching eagerly the work
Of those who dug; and, ever and anon,
Calling aloud, "No tokens see ye yet?
Dig, dig; for water must ye get for us,
Else shall we perish. Taskmasters, scourge on:
The slaves are idle: smite them till they bleed;
For we must drink, or die."
                    So everywhere,
Around each well, by day and night, the throngs
Stood crying ceaselessly; though parched all mouths,
All tongues though swollen, all bodies fever-fired.

But, toward the second morning,—Power Supreme
Permitting so; else universal death
Had fallen on Egypt,—from the deep-dug earth,
Both nigh the city, and in parts remote,—
Than gold more precious,—the pure water sprang.
Up then to Heaven were sent delirious shouts;
And everywhere, as burst the fountains forth,
Like madmen strove the crowds who first should drink;
Yea, in the water strove to cast themselves,
As though, from head to foot, all mouth they felt;
And throughout their whole bodies would drink in,
To slake the burning thirst.
                    But they who dug,—
The wretched Hebrew slaves,—regarding not
Boisterous command, or whip,—the foremost dropped,
Face-down within the stream: and many thus
Their death-stroke met; in the blood-boiling heat,
With the cold element gorging, till wellnigh
To suffocation filled.
                    To Pharaoh soon
Came the glad tidings. Through two days and nights,

Sleep had not closed his eyes,—wrath, fear, and pride,
So had distraught him. Man nor woman, yet,
Had dared beseech him to let Israel go:
Nor had his proud heart bent, to supplicate
The insolent wizards. Boldly, too, had spoken
His priests and sorcerers, saying that, ere long,
Sure as the coming day, the hateful spell
Would perish, and pass off; as shades of night
Before the sunrise. Exultation high
Came then on all, when in the presence rushed
Sethos, glad-eyed; and loudly made proclaim,
That from the wells, at length, in floods had burst
Water all diamond-clear, and pure to taste
As from hill-springs. Also, anon, came men,
Crying, "Joy, joy! again the sacred Nile
Crystal-bright runneth!"
      Proud were the sorcerers then,—
Of their foreknowledge boasting; prouder still
Was stubborn Pharaoh,—over Israel's God
Triumphant, as he thought: and harder yet
Than ever 'gainst that people, for whose sake,
O'er all the land had come such misery.

 But chiefly against Moses was his wrath;
And, if to death, or chains, to sentence him,
Darkly he pondered,—yet could nought resolve:
For, when a judgment 'gainst him he would speak,
Terror its utterance stopped: nor, though the voice
Of rulers, priests, and sorcerers, urged him on;
And the arch demon roused him at the heart,
That rebel, with high hand, to sweep away,—
Dared he the word pronounce.
      Worn out, and faint;
Thirsting for sleep,—at length the sign he gave
That he would be alone. Then instantly
All tongues were mute: along the cedar floor
Soft footsteps brushed; doors closed; and on his bed,
Heavily sighing, he sank; and, as a corpse,
All day lay motionless.
    But, on that morn,—

So in his heart instructed,—Moses took
His staff, and scrip; and o'er the spacious plain,
Toward Goshen bent his steps. Alone was he,
Save with his God: but, so accompanied,
No terror felt of king, or prince, or priest;
Or aught that man could do. For yet seven days,
Knew he,—by voice within,—that, his own heart
To question, must the proud, weak king be left,—
Ere, if still obdurate, again must he
Before him stand; and yet again the words
Of Israel's God pronounce. So, silent, calm,
In the fresh morn he walked; at crystal brook
Now drinking; now with any simple fruit
That by the wayside grew, wild, and yet sweet,
The palate cooling.
     In that happy vale
Of Goshen, knew he,—so by Aaron taught,—
That friends of his young days; and kindred, loved,
Though yet unseen,—in his long absence born,—
Would run to embrace him : and to them he longed,—
And to his people all,—the tidings great
To tell of their deliverance; as by voice,
Even of Jehovah, promised. With glad heart,
Thus he his way pursued; and, ere the sun
One half his course had journeyed,—on the mound,—
West verge of Goshen,—stood, and, joyfully
On that fair country gazed; with tree, shrub, flower,
Fruit of all kinds, sweet grass, and streamlets, rich,
And pure,—as it a spot had been, by heaven
Above all others blessëd.
     Wherefore, then,
By the oppressors spared,—much marvel was,
To them who knew not that, with policy
Like his who leaves untouched the hive,—nay, shields
From rain and storm, that so the luscious spoil
Richer may be,—long time had Egypt's kings,
The industrious Hebrews in full liberty left
Through all that happy land; thus, from their toil,
Tribute more large to gain. For, years had taught,
That the free workers in those fertile fields,

A tax might pay,—to the king's treasury
More worth, than would their labor all have been,
Compulsory; and, save by stripes, unpaid:
So that as jewel bright of Egypt's crown,
Was held that happy land; nor taskmaster,
Nor tyrant ruler, ever there was seen,
Darkening the spirit's heaven. Long time he stood,
Forth looking, as on second Paradise;
Far distant voices hearing, blithe and free;
And sounds melodious, on the gentle breeze,
Like dreams of music floating; light and faint
To sense, as gossamer swimming on the air
In sunshine; seen, and lost, and seen again,
Like a faint hope mid grief. Yet sighs, at last,
Breathed he, that bliss beholding; for, like one
Who, from the glory of the setting sun,
Suddenly eastward turning, the cold shade
Of gathering night beholds,—more deep and dread,
Following the gold and ruby of the west,—
So, from these happy, when in thought he turned
Toward those, their brethren, whom in slavery,
Toil-bowed, and spirit-broken, hopeless all,
That morning he had left,—by contrast gloomed
Yet deeper their sad state: and from his breast,
Sighs, groans of anguish burst.
                            But, in a while,
On God's great promise thought he; and at once
Strong was his heart; and from his countenance
All shadow passed. With firm foot, on he went
Down toward the happy valley; odorous airs
Fanning around him; sweet and sweeter still,
As nigh, and nigher to the spicy groves,
And flower-crowned fields he drew: till, at the last,
In the fair Eden entering, lo! the air,
Like to a fragrant bath invisible,
Around him floated; buoyant as the waves
Appearing,—for, so light seemed then his tread,—
The weight of flesh scarce felt,—that, 'neath his foot,
The very grass, he thought, would scantly bow,
More than to gentlest breeze: so was his heart

Uplifted, in that blissful spot arrived.
And now the sounds of cheerful toil; the voice,
From light heart singing; the soft-breathing tone
Of shepherd's pipe,—the mellow chords of harp,
Or psaltery, from garden, field, or grove,
Thickened around him; and desire awaked
With some of those, so blest, discourse to hold;
And of his kindred, and his friends enquire;
And his glad tidings speak. Yet living soul
None saw he nigh; and onward journeyed still;
Through field, and grove; and over singing brook,
Tree-bridged, or with stones dotted, that the foot
Dryshod might tread,—till now, at length, he spied,—
Midst of a garden, rich in choicest flowers,
And trees, with fruit and blossom both, full charged,—
A pleasant habitation. At the gate,
Wide open, he went in; and, by smooth path,—
Serpent-like winding,—and, to right and left,
By fragrant shrubs, and flowers of every hue,
Edged bounteously,—walked onward; and with staff
Struck on the open door. Then came a voice,
Gentle as dove's, than nightingale's more sweet,
Bidding him enter: and, without delay,—
Of welcome, though a stranger, doubting not,—
He entered; bared his head; the porch passed through;
And in a chamber paused. A maiden there,
Richly, yet simply clad, he saw; and bent,
With courteous salutation. From her couch,
With gentle dignity rose she; and bowed,
And modest welcome gave: then silent stood,
His words awaiting. O'er her countenance,
Serene and mild, nor blush, nor sign of fear,
Nor of surprise at stranger's entry, stole:
Still in her hand, the pale-green silken veil,
On which with golden needle she had wrought
Ere Moses came,—with fingers delicate,
And pearl-like chaste, in easy grasp she held.
Her eyes, as eastern midnight's cloudless heaven
Deep-hued, serene, and clear, on his she bent,—
Patiently waiting. He, astonished, stood,

And speechless; for, while mutely thus she gazed,
Her aspect holy, mild, and beautiful
Beyond all earthly beauty, on him came
Like music of a sacred hymn at night,
Afar off heard, from temple, field, or grove,
Or in mid air: and all around her head,—
Gilding the golden tresses,—purest light,
Yet faint, like spirit of the sunbeams glowed;
Or like reflected radiance from the face
Of angel bending o'er her. On him then
Assurance came that, for some purpose high,
Specially chosen was she; and he went
And took her hand, and reverently bowed,
And with his forehead touched it. Rising then,
On her meek head he laid his palm, and thus.

"Blessèd art thou, fair virgin! and, of God,
Above all women favored. Whatsoe'er
The end unknown designed,—through thee will come
Good unto thousands: to our people all,
Perchance, unspeakable blessing: for a voice,
Though wordless, telleth, that the present hand
Of the Most High is on thee; some great thing
Through thee to accomplish. Surely knowëst thou,—
Or from the tongue of angel, or from voice
Within thee speaking,—that select thou art
From all of woman-kind,—some special task
Divine to accomplish: or the instrument,
Though passive, it may be, by which will God
Some gracious wonder work. If, blamelessly,
I so may question, tell me, maiden blest,—
Of such high favor from our Israel's God
On thee vouchsafed, what know'st thou? and how taught?"

While thus he spake, she on him mildly looked,
Attentive listening, and with reverence meet:
For, in his countenance august, his voice
Tender, yet grand,—of strength, and dignity,
Of piety toward God, and love toward man,

Read she the witness; and with open heart,—
Surprise none feeling that a stranger's voice
Thus questioned,—made reply.
               "No angel tongue,
Shepherd of Israel,—for thy garb and mien
Such token thee,—within mine earthly ear
In word direct hath spoken, touching aught
Of great or good, through me by Heaven designed.
Nor craving feel I, in the eyes of men,
To have distinction,—or of power, or state;
For peace and holiness alone I love;
And in sweet silence evermore to live,
And meditate on God. Yet,—be it truth,
Or be it but sweet wandering of soul,—
Oft-times it seemeth that about me sound
Soft voices, like faint music heard from Heaven,—
Of blessings speaking, and of love divine,
And special dedication,—though to what,
Whisper they never. And, in dead of night,
Strains hear I oft, as of angelic bands
Choiring amid the stars, or nigh the throne:
And sometimes seemeth me, that round my bed
A presence feel I: and the still air, then,
Unearthly fragrance taketh; and is moved,
As by a gentle wing,—that slumber sweet
Falls on me; and, in dreams, the heaven of heavens
Is opened; and such glories I behold
As tongue may never tell. Nay, even in blaze
Of the mid-noon,—through garden, field, or grove,
Silently wandering,—doth my spirit feel,
Or mind imagine, that beside me moves,
Invisible, some dweller of the sky,
Murmuring in music; and celestial bliss
Transfusing through my being,—as, through air,
The sun his splendor. Nay, at times, hath seemed,
That faces all of light have looked on me
An instant, and then vanished. Waking dreams,
Perchance, all these; yet such the bliss they bring,
That, even the crown of all the world to wear,
Would I not lose them. But, of good to come

To our poor people,—or through word, or act,
Of so frail thing as I,—ne'er have I thought;
Nor couldst thou have imagined—hadst thou known
My weakness, and my simple ignorance,
In all that men esteem; in all that strength
To woman gives, o'er man to hold the sway.
No beauty have I to delight their eye;
No eloquence, no power of song, to move
Their reason, or their passion,—or to peace
Persuading, or to stir them up in war.
No learning have I; no accomplishment,
Such as oft steal men's hearts, in song, or dance:
Nor with gay raiment know I how to deck
My simple person,—of the humble grub,
So making the gay butterfly; that men,
Enamoured, may pursue. With God alone
Have alway been my thoughts: His holy ways
For ever meditating; and how best
Pure in His eye to live. For joys of earth,
Nought heed I: riches, honor, glory, power,
Unthought of, as the sands on which I walk:
Honey, and bread, and fruits, my only food;
Water my drink, or milk. Companion none,
Save my loved parents have I; and one more,
An upright youth,—when the due time shall be,
My husband to become. But, as myself,
Apart from all is he: ambition none
Renown to win, he hath; nor wealth, nor pomp,
Nor rule, desireth: in this lowly state,—
From poverty assured;—with flocks, and herds,
Vineyards, and fertile lands, our own,—content
With me to pass his life; God's blessed ways
For ever meditating; and how best
To glorify, and thank Him; and so live,
That evermore well pleasing in His sight
May be each act and thought. From such as I,—
Alone, or thus companioned,—aught of great,
Or good toward Israel, fantasy alone,
Methinks, could prospect see."
                              With grave, mild face,

Ceasing, upon her honored guest she looked,
Reply awaiting. He on her looked down,
With fatherly love, yet reverence; and thus spake.

"Maiden of Heaven elect,—for such mine eye,
And voice within, attest thee,—of God's ways,
Man knoweth not to judge. All human strength,
With Him, is weakness: greatest kings are motes
Before His breath; the feeblest, at His will,
Mightier than monarchs. Mountains, touched by Him,
Would sink to molehills; sand-grains swell to hills.
If chosen thou, thy weakness may become
A might to vanquish nations. But, for thee,
A work of love and peace for all mankind,
Haply God willeth: humbly wait we then
Till He withdraw the veil, and show distinct
The gracious purpose; now in darkness hid,
But certain as the glory of the sun,
Behind the cloud that veils it. Know thou this;
And, as a creature loved, and chosen of Heaven,
In every act and word still guard thyself:
For present evermore is God with thee,
And all beholdeth; even thy secret thoughts
Seeing distinct, as though with sunbeams writ.
So wilt thou, fear I not. And now, blest maid,
For thy free, gentle answer, take my thanks.
True innocence with open heart still speaks;
Guile fearing not, and seeking nought to hide.
But, lest o'erbold, intrusive, thou may deem
One, all a stranger, yet thy secret thoughts
Thus plainly asking,—somewhat of myself
Hear thou, in turn. A man I am, once known
To all of Israel; but, in far off land,
A two score years sojourning,—by the most
Forgotten now; or only as a thing
Of the old time remembered. Yet the name
Perchance hath reached thee. Moses am I called;
By the last Pharaoh, in his younger days,
Much honored for awhile; but, in the end,
Slightly esteemed; and, by his jealous chiefs,

Rulers and priests, so hated and traduced,
That . . . . ."
                    With a gentle start, and tone of joy,
His speech arresting, "Then the brother thou
Of our loved Aaron," said she,—a bright smile
O'er all her countenance playing, as the rays
Round diamonds, gently shaken,—" and thy name
Well known is here: from my first infancy
Oft have I heard it spoken; though, alas,
With sorrow; for my parents mourned thee lost;
Yea, all men deemed thee dead. Great joy indeed
Will fill them, knowing thee alive, and here.
At this hour, absent are they, on a work
Of mercy bound; but will anon return.
Meantime, for them entreating, do I pray,
If greater matters hurry not thy steps,
That thou awhile our honored guest wilt be.
Old friends, I doubt not, will my father bring
To welcome thee, and of old times discourse.
Nay, sure I am, that all of this fair land
Will haste to greet thee; so that pleasantly,
A moon, or twain, may pass; and yet new friends
New welcome bring. Now, may I speak for thee,
And answer 'yea'? Think me not overbold,
In my loved parents' name inviting thee;
For my weak prayer would they make tenfold strong;
Nay, with kind chains would bind thee to remain,
Honored, and honoring, their long-time guest.
Sincerely have I spoken; sure I am
Sincerely thou wilt answer."
                            A warm light
Of holy love and reverence from the face
Of Moses beamed, as thus he heard, and thus
Gently replied.
                "For this one day, blest maid,
And also for this night, thy bidding kind
Freely accept I, as 'twas freely given:
Nay, thankfully would longer be the guest,
Where I on thee might look, and with thee talk,
Communing of our God; and somewhat learn,

It may be, of His purpose, hidden yet,
Through thee to be accomplished: but not long
Here may I tarry; for throughout this land
Must I go quickly: not alone loved friends
Of the old time to embrace; but, unto all,
Proclaim to make of wondrous things at hand,—
Even of our full deliverance. Nay, the work
Already is begun. But not of this
More say I now. Thy father will, this day,
Gather his friends together,—such, at least,
Who briefly may be summoned; and to them
At large will I declare the marvels great
Our God will do; as by His very voice,
On Horeb spoken. Of these things to hear,
Canst thou, blest maiden, till the evening hour,
Patiently tarry? for thy face,—but late,
Pale as a pure white cloud of early dawn,—
At word of these glad tidings, gloweth bright
As that same cloud at coming of the sun."

Bowing her gentle head, "Oh great indeed,"
The virgin answered, "boundless is my joy,
Of such high things to hear, by God designed
For our long suffering Israel! but in peace
My soul shall rest; on Him relying all,
And on thy perfect truth. Till evening, then,
In blest hope will I wait: unmeet that I,
The lowliest, should find favor more than they,
The elder, and far worthier."
                              While she spake,
Softly the door was opened; and there stood
Upon the threshold, pausing suddenly,
As in surprise, or fearful to intrude,
A comely youth. Over his shoulders hung
Dark, waving locks: his chin, with down just touched,
Showed Spring on Summer entering. His fair brow
Capacious, the mild radiance of his eyes,
The tender, thoughtful mouth, the aspect all,—
Of spirit pure and lofty, wisdom ripe
Beyond his years, gave token. In attire,

Modest and plain he was: no ornament,
Save, on his finger, one small golden ring,
Pledge of affection, wearing. Standing thus,
As if in doubt to enter, or depart,
Kindly upon him smiled the beauteous maid;
And, lightly stepping, took him by the hand,
And welcome gave; then toward her honored guest
Gracefully led him; and, with radiant face,
Unblushing in her virgin innocence,
Open as day, on Moses looked, and said:

"He whom I spake of. On his gentle head
Lay thou thy hand, and bless him."
                                    At that word,—
Already by such presence spirit-bowed,—
On one knee sank the youth, and bent the head,
And, palm to palm, like one who utters prayer,
The blessing waited. But, while Moses stood,
Silently looking on him,—for, with joy,
Again he felt a chosen-one,—by the youth
Kneeled that fair virgin likewise; and her head
Bowed meekly; and her pure hands, palm to palm,
Pressed also. In a holy silence thus
The twain awaited. Mid that solemn hush,
With eyes uplift, in voiceless prayer awhile
Stood Moses; then, on each bowed head, a hand
Lightly imposed; and, with such utterance deep
As though before the very Throne he kneeled,
Thus spake the blessing. "On these chosen ones
Oh God of Israel look! I feel, I feel,
That Thine alone they are, in all their ways,
In life, in death! These temples pure, Oh God!
Hallow for ever: let no breath of sin
Enter within them; that, Thy purpose high
Through them accomplished here,—in robes of light,
At Thy right hand in glory may they sit,
Thee praising and adoring evermore!"

Awhile he stood in silence; then, with tone
Of love parental, thus. "My children, rise:

God's blessing is upon you; in you poured,
Even as your breath of life. By death alone,
The life-breath can ye lose; by sin alone,
The holier breath of blessing. Stand ye then
'Gainst sin for ever, as, against the winds,
Rocks stand unshaken; for, God's instruments,
Some gracious work to do, be sure ye are;
And pure as dropping snow your souls must keep,
Or from your high place fall: fall, worse than death!"

Thus having spoken, tenderly he raised
The twain, yet kneeling; and, when they stood up,
Upon the forehead kissed them. Silently,
Hand clasped in hand, in holy joy stood they;
And he, with love and admiration filled,
Silent stood likewise, gazing.
       All this while,—
To his bad office true,—unseen, he hoped,
By angel's ken,—or even the eye of God,—
Beelzebub, the spy and tempter, still
Nigh Moses watching, every word and look,
Heedfully marked; of every secret thought,
Subtle conjecture made: nor less on her,
That virgin pure, and on that spotless youth,
His burning Spirit-eye, exploring, fixed;
Hoping, of God's great purpose, undivulged,
Through them to be wrought out, that he might learn,—
All noting, and all weighing. Nor failed he,
Though thus intent, his more peculiar task
Also to ply,—from path of righteousness
Moses to lure; that so might God be foiled;
His chosen one cast down. By promise of wealth
Exhaustless,—Egypt's throne—Israel's release,—
Seductions strong,—already had he tried
The faithful servant; but had been repulsed,
Vanquished, and put to flight: yet stronger lure
Given to his hand, now thought he; that strange power
Of woman's beauty,—over heart of man
Oft irresistible proved: and when, before,
Had beauty like to that on which he gazed,—

Beauty, which even the loftiest Spirit of heaven
Might fix in wonder,—when, till now, on such,
Had eye of mortal looked! Intemperate thoughts,
Surely, thus on her gazing; her fair head
With spread palm touching; on her open brow
His lips impressing,—surely, carnal thoughts,
If human were he, must in Moses rise;
Though faint perchance, and with strong will subdued,—
Like fire down trodden, yet alive within,
And, breathed upon, of flame still capable.
Eagerly, therefore, in that righteous heart
Sought he to enter; that, if spark he found
Of love impure, to very ecstacy
Of madness he might blow it; and so bring
Destruction on him. But, as mail of steel
The pointless arrow laughs at,—even so,
The perfect panoply of holiness
That heart 'gainst entrance of foul thing made strong;
Nay, of attack insensible: for a thought
Toward that fair virgin, less than angel's pure,
None had he; on her gazing sinlessly,
As on the richest flower from plains of Heaven,
By seraph brought, sinless he might have gazed.

    Again defeated, the fallen Spirit lowered:
Yet, all undaunted, for a day to come,
New snares resolved: meantime, observance close
On every word and look would keep,—that scheme,
Yet hidden, to descry.
                  'Twixt earth and sun,
Hovering on watch, were angels, who each look,
And word, and thought,—so gifted specially—
Of that fallen Spirit, and the mortal three,
Clearly discerned. Silent and swift as light,
Are words of angels; felt, but uttered not.
In undistinguishable point of time,
Then thus,—in cumbrous language of mankind
Translated,—to his bright companion nigh,
The archangel Gabriel spake.
                      "Yon Evil One,—

Unseen, he thinks, by even the eye of Heaven,—
Hearkens, and looks; God's purpose through those twain,
Hoping to learn; that, by some subtlety,
Hell may prevent it. The I AM hath willed
That his bad wish be granted; so, at last,
Good out of ill to bring. Descend thou then:
In all thy glory before Moses stand;
In form and mien thine own; but, to the youth,
And virgin, viewless; and what thou dost know,
Declare unto him: so that Spirit Fallen,
Also, of their high destiny may hear;
In secret, as he thinks; and may repeat
In hell's full council; that their ill design
The lost ones may attempt: in time to come,
Thence keener pangs to feel; repentant tears
More largely to pour forth; and prayer, at last,
To the All Merciful;—from their fallën state,
So speedier to arise."
      Hand locked in hand,
Still stood that innocent pair; eye fixed on eye,
As reading speechless love: and Moses still,—
Though now some space removed, lest their free joy,
Too near, he should disturb,—in silence stood,
Gazing and wondering,—when, behold! a light,
As of heaven opened, suddenly filled the place;
And full before him the angelic shape
In all his glory stood. Down on his face
Fell Moses, by that wondrous splendor struck,
Even as by lightning: but a hand unseen
Upraised him; and a voice mellifluous,
Yet grand as thunderous music, to him thus,
Courage infusing, spake.
      "Servant of God,
Be thy heart strong: look on me; hear my words.
Chosen of Heaven art thou; and mighty things
For Israel wilt thou do. But, after thee,
In due time, will arise one greater far;
Born of a woman, yet the Son of God;
Messiah to be named; through whom shall be
Redemption universal to man's race.

From tribe of Levi hath it been ordained,
Shall come the Virgin Mother of that Son:
Yea, even from these shall spring; the maid and youth
Before thee standing,—so with upright heart,
Pure from all sin, in sight of God they live,
And pure they die. But, sinning, will they fall;
And Heaven's high favor forfeit. Look thou then
Heedfully on them: dangerous is their path,
And narrow: one false step, and they are lost!"

While thus he spake, Moses, with strengthened eye,
Looked on the glorious one; as on the sun,
Power given, he might have looked: and the great voice,
Humbly, yet firmly heard. One instant paused
The Radiance; while, with lambent hands outspread,
O'er that fair twain he bent, as blessing them;
One smile, like quivering lightning, his bright face
Brighter illumed; and then the glory fled;
Heaven vanished; and the common things of earth
Solely remained. Prone on the floor again
Sank Moses; and, in prayer and praise, his soul
To God poured out. Him seeing thus, the pair
Softly went forth, and in the garden walked;
Of that great guest discoursing.
                              But, with speed
That mocked light's course, exulting flew the fiend,
Where Satan he might find,—in Pharaoh's court
Plying his task; the hearts of king, and priests,
Princes, and rulers, iron hard to make
'Gainst Israel, and his God. A sign he gave,
Whither to speed, and how,—impossible so
That spy of Heaven could track them. Northward then
Flew he,—the ice-pole entered,—and shot down
Right to earth's core: but southward Satan glanced,—
The globe half rounded,—through the ocean flashed;
And in the centre stood: ere eye could wink,
Their wondrous journeys done. There, in mid fire,
Burning eternally, the Spirits met;
In that great light, to heaven's most piercing ken,
Invisible, as they deemed: and proudly then

Spake out Beelzebub; the marvellous tale,
So subtly learned, into the gladdened ear
Of his great leader pouring.   Up again
To air then flew they: and erelong, through earth,
And through the realms of space, a summons went,—
To their great council-hall each Spirit of hell
Instantly calling.   Through the universe
Of living orbs shot quickly then the hosts,
At such prompt summons marvelling; through the depths
Of the immeasurable darkness shot,
Right to the perished sun; and in its heart,—
Still dazzling bright as when the glory first,
By the Great Word commanded, had sprung forth,—
Gathered tumultuously,—each Spirit filled
With expectation of some great event,
Erelong to be proclaimed.   As, from the brow
Of lofty hill,—on forest, far outstretched
As eye can pierce,—what time, with slanting rays,
The sun on every tree-top pours his fire,—
Amazed the traveller looks, as on a sea
Of arborescent gold,—so wide outspread,
And congregated thick, to Satan seemed
The gathered millions, as, from his high throne
Of diamond rock, proudly around he looked,
Order, and silence waiting.   But, at length,
When every stir was hushed, and every eye
On him intently bent, his thunderous voice,
Mighty, yet calm, he lifted up, and spake.

ISRAEL IN EGYPT.

BOOK EIGHTH.

"Not with you to take counsel, Powers of heaven,—
For still that title ours,—in so great haste
Hither have I convoked you,"—thus began
The fallen Archangel,—"for rule absolute
Ye grant me still; both as, of right, mine own,
And for the good of all,—with justice used,
And wisdom,——not your counsel to invite,
I call you; but the speedier to make known
A mighty thing, that shall your spirits lift,
By showing progress on our certain way
Toward state of godhead. When Omnipotence,
Omniscience, shall be ours,—as, in due course
Of the eternal ages, they must be,—
Then shall our thrones lofty as His become;
He but our equal be; nay, haply, less;
For possible so I deem it. Then shall war
Of might 'gainst might, prove who for aye shall reign,
Monarch of heaven: and, haply, he, so long
Our tyrant, may our subject god become:
Or, to some perished orb, like this, retired,
Alone through all eternity may mourn,
His power and glory lost,—as now we mourn,
Though for a season only, our lost power
And glory in heaven. Time's cycles numberless

May seem, ere this can come: but every step
Makes less the journey: every slightest thing
Won from our adversary, him of strength
So far deprives; so far makes us more strong.
Time was, when from Omniscience nought was hid:
Nor act of ours, nor even thought most close,
From Him could we conceal; so far his power
Our power surpassed: and, stood we now, as then,
Inferior to him, powerless still were we
His watch to evade. Great, then, hath been our speed
Toward godhead, when, beneath his very eye,
Even in that Egypt, his own battle-field,
Our growing strength his watchfulness hath foiled.
Of his designs for earth, in ages past,
Oft, truly, have we learned; and, by our wiles,
Opposed them; nay, defeated: but, through all,
From mortal tongue alone the tidings came;
Never from habitant of heaven, by Him
Appointed to his work; for, as the grave
Its dead holds from the sight of living man,
So, in the bosom of his angels, close
God's counsel still was hidden. Not their strength,
Or deeper cunning, overmatching ours;
But strength from him, or keener subtlety,
To them imparted. Where they us o'ercame,
Never with their own power, but his, they wrought:
Else, with us equal merely; or, perchance,
Angel 'gainst angel measured, even far less.
With *them* comparing subtlety, or strength,
With *Him*, then, we compare: and, mastering *them*,
Him overcome. Rejoice then; for a day
Of victory is ours. The all-seeing eye
Dimmer hath waxed; or, seeing as before,
By our still growing potence hath been foiled,—
Striving our darkness to pierce. At last, close hid
From even the eye of God, may we expect
Power,—wheresoe'er we will,—to be, or act:
Whether, for our own purposes, to move
Through earth, and sky,—or, in deep secrecy,
Of *his* to learn; when, in our darkness wrapped,

We list his angels talking;—unto man
His message bearing,—or among themselves
Discoursing: for the ways of God toward men,
Be sure, is oft their theme,—that wretched race,
Which better were it to annihilate,
Foul as it is, and worthless, than, with strife
'Gainst strength like ours, to uphold awhile; then crush,
By deluge, as before; or, it may be,
By world-quake, pestilence, or fire. But thus
Deemeth not he; still resolute man to purge
From evil; and, to all the human race,
Redemption,—whatsoe'er that be,—to send.

" But, from the subtle Power who this hath learned,
Fittest it were *ye* learn it. Come thou, then,
Mightiest of all, save one, amid the hosts
That strive 'gainst Heaven; at my right hand come thou,
Beelzebub; and, of thy victory,
And of our enemy's purpose unto man,
To all aloud declare: so shall the voice
Of universal hell give honor and praise,
To him who first, beneath the all-seeing eye,
Unseen hath stood; and of his secrets heard,—
Himself all secret."
     Ere the word was done,
At the right hand of Satan,—suddenly
As bursts a flame volcanic,—stood the shape
High towering of the demon! As, through fumes,
Sulphurous, and pestilential,—the foul reek
From bed of smouldering earthquake;—or through clouds
Of fiery sand-storm, whirlwind-rapt, that sweep
O'er wastes of Afric, and whole caravans
'Neath a dry deluge bury,—the great sun,—
Though dimmed, and westering low,—still gloriously,—
Firing all round the dusky canopy,—
Flames on his throne sublime,—so, though by sin
Clouded and fouled, with half heaven's brightness yet
Lingering about him, the proud angel shone.
But, in his bowing form,—as greeted him
A loud acclaim which all the concave shook,—

Humble he seemed; or as by praise oppressed,
Conscious of undeserving; though, the while,
Worthy of all, self-deemed.   Long time he paused,
Like one who diffident feels; of words unsure;
Or fearful, when a vast assembly waits,
Lest he should fail: with downcast eyes he stood:
And in deep silence all the myriads gazed,
Great things expecting.   His huge form, at length,
Proudly he lifted; and his mighty voice
So loud sent forth, that past even farthest rank
Of listening spirits it rolled.
                              "Gods yet to be,—
Nay, gods already,—even as earth's small seed,
A flower, or even, perchance, a stately tree,
Essentially is,—the future in the *now*
Existent, though unseen,—would that my words,
To your expectance equal all might be!
But our great leader,—ever, as ye know,
Just, nay, o'er generous, merit to applaud,—
My humble triumph, with praise undeserved
So hath exalted, that the petty truth,
Seen in its nakedness,—like a poor stem,
Of branch, and leaf, and flower bereft,—may show
Mean, and unworthy.   Ne'ertheless, my speech
The truth shall fit: with words I will not gild,—
Like yonder miserable race of man,—
Mere lead, to show like gold.   *Perchance*, 'gainst Heaven
A great stroke hath been stricken; or, perchance,
Against a shadow: we from God have won;
Or have by him been mocked:—his watchful eye
We have evaded,—or, with cunning deep,
Seeing, he blind hath seemed; in hope, may be,
So to deceive, and harm us.   But, of this,
Judge ye when ye shall hear.
                              "My task on earth,—
As well ye know,—is, evermore to keep
Espial on that Moses, chosen by God
For the deliverance speedy of the race,
Whom, ages long, content he hath beheld,
Groaning in bondage;—such the government,

Incomprehensible, of him, All Wise,
By fawning angels named! Nigh that strange man,
No moment intermitted, have I watched;
Striving his thoughts to sway, his passions fire;
That, thus, from strict obedience to our foe,
Might he be lured; and, thence, unworthy found,
Might be cast off; and, falling, God's whole scheme
For Israel's freedom, through him to be wrought,
Might bring to nothing. Haply, not all vain
Hath been my striving; though, as yet, to the eye,
Unmoved he stands. 'Tis not the first storm-breath
That fells the oak; nor have temptations first,
Though strong, *him* shaken. But, by blast on blast,
The great tree is torn up; and wile on wile
Him luring evermore,—from God, at length,
In God's despite, may draw him. Victory great,
So we can win it! Meantime, other stroke,
And greater far, invites us.

" Through all earth,
Ye know how loathsome, in the sight of heaven,
This dust-race hath become: and some great burst
Of anger from their irritated God,
Long have ye looked for: second flood, perchance,
Or pestilence, or world-consuming fire;
Or other stroke, destruction absolute
Bringing on earth, and all that in it is.
So in our folly deemed we: but, behold!
For wrath, expected; and for vengeance, due,—
Love, and forgiveness, to the whole bad race,
God willeth; and REDEMPTION unto all!
What that redemption is, and how to come,
As yet we know not; but, of this be sure,—
Man's fall forgiven,—and man unto his God
Reconciled wholly,—by what means soe'er,—
To us will be defeat, and endless shame;
To our great foe, triumph for evermore;
And, even to that poor earth-seed, victory
O'er us, the sons of heaven! All conquests past,
'Neath this foul shame would be obliterate:
Hell's glories would go out, like trodden fire;

And that poor clod the trampler! To the last,
With all our strength, wisdom, and diligence,
'Gainst this new scheme, Redemption, must we fight.
Successful, it o'erwhelms us; baffled, lifts
Toward godhead, farther than in ages, else,
By due course, had we risen. Foreknowing, then,
Better our hope to cross it.
      " But, ye ask,
'*Who* knows? and *how*? and what the thing foreknown?
Plain words shall answer.
      " Constant at my task,
O'er Moses to keep watch,—from Pharaoh's court,
To Goshen, like his shadow followed I.
A house he entered; and therein beheld
A damsel, beautiful beyond compare
Of mortal beauty, else. Such charms, methought,
Might even an angel snare;—how, then, could he,
A thing of flesh, resist? Well as I might,—
For still some Spiritual armour fences him;
Its weak points viewless yet,—into his soul
Strove I hot love to shoot; but failed : for, lo!
As if in presence of a Being divine,
All holy rapture seemed he,—woman's charms
Unfelt, unlooked on,—so all thought and sense,
In feeling of some mystery seemed lost,
Touching that maiden, and design of God,
Through her to be accomplished. Well I guessed
The working of his spirit; and, erelong,
His voice, and act proclaimed it; for he went,
And, reverently bending, took her hand,
And to his forehead pressed it: rising then,
On her bowed head he laid his palm, and spake.
' Blessëd art thou, fair virgin! and, of God,
Above all women favored! Whatsoe'er
The end unknown designed,—through thee will come
Good unto thousands : to our people all,
Perchance, unspeakable blessing : for a voice,
Though wordless, telleth, that the present hand
Of the Most High is on thee; some great thing
Through thee to accomplish.'

"Other words he spake,
And she made answer,—needless to tell now.
Anon appeared a youth; in form and face,
Beauty of man exceeding, even as she
Exceeded all of woman. At the door
He stood, fearing to enter: but she went,
And took him by the hand, and led him in:
And, when to Moses she had brought him, said,
That he it was who, as already told;
In the due time, her husband would become.
Ev'n as on *her* with rapture he had looked,
So now on *him* gazed Moses, standing mute,
Again in wonder lost. But, on their knees,
His blessing craving, sank the twain; and thus
A blessing prayed he.
"'On these chosen ones,
Oh, God of Israel, look! I feel, I feel,
That Thine alone they are; in all their ways;
In life, in death! These Temples pure, Oh God,
Hallow for ever: let no breath of sin
Enter within them; that,—thy purpose high
Through them accomplished here,—in robes of light
At Thy right hand in glory may they sit,
Thee praising and adoring evermore!'

"That done, he paused; and silently, awhile,
Stood, as in prayer; then said; 'My children, rise;
God's blessing is upon you; in you poured,
Even as your breath of life. By death alone,
The life-breath can ye lose: by sin, alone,
The holier breath of blessing. Stand ye, then,
'Gainst sin for ever, as, against the winds,
Rocks stand unshaken: for, God's instruments,
Some gracious work to do, be sure ye are:
And pure as dropping snow your souls must keep;
Or from your high place fall: FALL WORSE THAN
  DEATH!'

"So Moses, little dreaming what ear heard.
Now, knowing the deep wisdom of that man;

And how, at times, by heavenly ministers,
Through dreams, nay, waking visions, secret things
Had been revealed to him,—some such, erelong,
Methought might come, of that great wonderment
Instructing him. In what profoundest night,
From eye of angel might I wrap me, then;
So that, myself unseen, all might I see,
All hear,—the thought perplexed me,—of new power
Within me risen, unconscious,—and I paused,
Dubious to stay, or go: for, not far off,
The coming of some heavenly thing I felt,
And his keen vision dreaded. But, behold!
While thus I stood,—thicker and thicker still
Heaping around me darkness,—suddenly,
Shining in heaven's full splendor he came in,
And stood before me! Well that Spirit ye know,
Zophiel, the sunbeam-eyed,—keen-sighted most
Of all God's spies; yet, with deep-volumed night
So had I girded me, that even he
The blackness pierced not. With the outstretched hand
Might he have touched me; yet he stood, and looked,
And saw me not! In all the glory of heaven
To Moses he appeared; so that to earth,
Covering his eyes, as blinded, fell the man,
And motionless lay, as dead. But, by the hand,
Zophiel upraised him, and thus spake. His words
Mark, and remember. 'Servant of God,' he said,
'Be thy heart strong: look on me; hear my words.
Chosen of Heaven art thou; and mighty things
For Israel wilt thou do. But, after thee,
In due time, will arise one greater far;
BORN OF A WOMAN,—YET THE SON OF GOD;
MESSIAH TO BE NAMED; THROUGH WHOM SHALL BE
REDEMPTION UNIVERSAL TO MAN'S RACE.
From tribe of Levi, hath it been ordained,
Shall come the virgin mother of that Son:
Yea, even from these shall spring,—the maid and youth
Before thee standing,—so with upright heart,
Pure from all sin, in sight of God they live,
And pure they die. But, sinning, will they fall,

And Heaven's high favor forfeit! Look thou, then,
Heedfully on them. Dangerous is their path,
And narrow. ONE FALSE STEP—AND THEY ARE LOST!'
Thus having spoken, over that fair twain,—
Unconscious of his presence,—with spread hands,
As blessing them, he bent; then heavenward flew:
And I, as quickly, to our leader hied,
Those wondrous things to tell. Now know ye all."

He ceased; and bowed the head. As when, on earth,
From deep foundation to its topmost tower,
Some mighty fortress, by the miner's fire,
Cloud-ward is blown,—the mighty thundering
Leagues round shakes air,—so, when the archangel ceased,
From the long silent, listening millions burst
Uproar of acclamation,—peal on peal
Rolling, like wave on wave, when ocean writhes,
Lashed by the hurricane. Silent once again,
All stood expectant: for the countenance
Of their dread leader, as around he looked,
'Tokened that he would speak. With hand outstretched,
Toward his great comrade,—now some space withdrawn,—
He pointed; and, in proud tone, thus began.

"Worthy, indeed, all honor and all praise
Is he, who first hath proved to us new power,
Godlike, arisen within us: for, as his,
So, doubtless, too, already, though untried,
The strength of each compeer: and such will be,—
Due time o'erpast,—the strength of even those,
Weakest among you now; such the sure growth
Of Spirit unto Godhead. 'Vantage great
Henceforth we have, into the hidden ways
Of God to pierce; and even his surest aim
To arrest, or turn aside. But ne'er, methinks,
Shall be, or can be, vantage such as now.
All, indeed, know we not; but yet enough
Our course to point. What this Redemption is;
How to be wrought; and when; and what its power
'Twixt man and God,—as yet, lies all in night.

Then, this strange thing, MESSIAH—SON OF GOD,
YET BORN OF WOMAN,—OF A VIRGIN, TOO!
What monster *that* may prove, we guess not yet.
But *this* we know,—and, knowing this, know all
Of instant moment,—on the gossamer thread
Of woman's life-long abstinence from sin,—
Her perfect holiness, both in act and thought;
From her now tender spring, throughout the years
Of glowing summer, and the ripening heat
Of autumn; when oft drops the fruit, that long
Had stood 'gainst roughest blast,—on such frail thread;
And on a second, scarce more strong perchance,—
The life-long holiness of man,—from youth,
Through headlong, scorching manhood, and old age;
Cold, but yet sensual oft, and prone to gripe
At riches, power, and honor; and all else
That in his stiffening clay may stir up life,—
On gossamer threads like these, on lines of mist,
Hangs this grand scheme, Redemption! Did we see
Man scheming, on the rainbow's arch to build
A tower to scale the Heavens,—less might we laugh,
At mortal folly, than at wisdom, now,
Of heaven's All Wise. Meantime, ye growing gods!
This aye remember. Never be the word
By Spirit uttered, which, of this great good,
This knowledge priceless,—may the secret tell,
To man, or aught of Heaven: else, down at once,
By our great enemy cast, our hopes will go:
And some new scheme, even from his angels hid,
Will be conceived, to baffle us; and work,—
As, unopposed, it will,—his end designed.

" Ye all have seen, in heart of earth's great rocks,
Firm-bedded shell, or reptile,—there encased
Myriads of ages past;—and there to lie
Prisoned through all the myriads yet to come,—
Even as those, in the rock's iron heart
Fast locked, be this great secret in *you* locked.
Whate'er may be the cause,—his dimmer sight,
Or slacker watchfulness,—or our new power

His eye to evade,—alike our victory.
But rather in our godhead-growing strength,
True cause I see : for, ne'er before hath slept
His vigilance; every act of ours, and thought,
Till now, plain shown, as, to inferior eye,
Mountains in sunshine: and still plain had been,
Not to Him only, but to that keen Power,
His messenger, that such a foe was nigh,
His secret listening,—had not new-born strength
Of hell's archangel baffled their sharp glance,
As mail of proof the sword-point.
                              "What saidst thou,
Beelzebub, as doubtful?—'*perhaps*, 'gainst Heaven
A great stroke hath been stricken; or, perhaps,
Against a shadow? we from God have won;
Or have by him been mocked? his watchful eye
We have evaded;—or, with cunning deep,
Seeing, he blind hath seemed; in hope, may be,
So to deceive, and harm us?' . . . . Yea, even thus,
Saidst thou, thy triumph questioning: but *I* say,
'Gainst heaven a great stroke *hath* been stricken: we
From God *have* won: his watchful eye *have* mocked:
Nor fear that, seeing, he hath blindness feigned,
So to deceive, and harm us. Be thou sure,
His thunder would he put within our power,
Freely as such great secret. Better guard
Than his, be ours; else, all that we have won,
And more, will soon be lost. What now remains,
Is, of this secret such wise use to make,
As surest, swiftest, will to ruin bring
This folly of Omniscience: topple down
That wondrous structure of Redemption,—based
On less than moonbeam's shadow, or the sound
Of a past wind,—on mortal's holiness!
Why, even at first,—in utmost purity
To their flesh-nature possible,—slight the bait,
Simple the words that led them to their fall.
A savoury apple the first woman lured
To disobedience; and that woman's tears
Moved man to share her sin! *Such* appetite,

Such puny love-qualm, 'gainst command of God,
Resistless proved,—even when his very voice
The word had spoken; solemn warning given,
And Death pronounced as punishment,—what hope
Can veriest folly hold, that, 'gainst the storm
Of those fierce appetites, the heritage
Of all from woman born, they can make stand;
No special warning given; no punishment
By voice of God announced,—but moral law,
Solely, from sin restraining;—barrier slight,
'Gainst passion's gush, as, 'gainst the bursting spring,
Weak hand of childhood. What, when all those lusts,
Love, pride, ambition, avarice, thirst of power,—
In their young years perchance now sleeping,—come
Like ravenous lions on them,—what will *then*
Cold moral law avail? or love of good,
Taught to their infancy? or wisest word
Of Moses, them admonishing? As well
Might the dry stubble stand against the fire,
As flesh 'gainst such assault. And ours must be,
The passions to arouse; the sparks to strike:
Gently, at first, to fan; then, more and more,
Blow into fury; till the flames go up,
And utterly consume them! So shall God
His wisdom find but folly; and our might,
On his feel pressing; toward equality
Aye mounting; and, by sure procéss, ordained
As high, at length, to stand. Proud hope, perchance,
Deemed by the feeble; but, by Spirits strong,
Sure destiny felt; the necessary end,
By law of Nature. What, at first, were suns?
Think ye that all at once,—like sparks shot out
From the fire-saturate ether,—they appeared,
In blaze of their full glory? Them, indeed,
We saw not at their birth; but well may judge,
From growth of later orbs,—yon earth, and moon,
And other worlds,—how, from beginnings small;
From matter orderless, unshaped, and cold,—
Through cycles of the ages numberless,
Slowly progressing,—form, law, order, light,

They by degrees took on: till, finally,
As we behold them now, at point supreme
Of splendor stood they. These, indeed, will fade,—
Or may,—as this hath; such the law appears
For all material: but, as well ye know,
To Spirits is no decay; still on they speed,
Higher and mightier waxing, till,—like suns
To fullest glory attained,—at the last height
Of Godhead they arrive,—Omnipotent,
Omniscient, Omnipresent, evermore!
Such, be ye sure, our final destiny.
Meantime, a Spirit elder far than we,
God *now;* and, therefore, beyond all compare,
Our mightier,—stands against us; and long time
Subdued hath held us; and long time *will* hold,
If we occasion lose, by which to gain
Advantage, whatsoe'er. That youth, and maid,
Far more than Moses, and the Egyptian king,
Our mark, henceforth, must be: for, greater far,
God's scheme, the race entire of man to save,
Than, from his bondage, Israel: far more great
Our triumph, then, if we his purpose balk.
And, haply, may we. Yet too young, perchance,
By riches, rank, or power, to be seduced,—
Though these, too, may be tried,—that mortal snare
To all of flesh,—and chiefly in life's spring,—
The carnal appetite, must be awaked;
Stirred into warmth; blown then into a flame;
And, that accomplished, up in smoke will fly
Their simple holiness: and God's great hope
From them to bring Messiah, will lie dead
In the dry ashes. But, for task like this,
Not Powers the mightiest need we,—though the aim
Greatest, and final end momentous most,—
Spirits of gentle nature, in such war,
More potent than the powerful; for, soft word,
The melting eye, the amorous look and tone,
The form of beauty, and the air of grace,—
Weapons more potent far, in passion's storm,
Than wisdom most profound; or argument,

Though voiced with thunder. Come ye then, ye twain,
Gentlest of all meek Spirits erst in heaven,
Aziel, and Zuriel."
                    Instantly there stood,
At the right hand of Satan, two fair shapes,
Before him bending. Smiling, on them looked
The Majesty of Hell; then, in soft tone,
And condescending, thus.
                    "To you we give,
Task not unpleasant, those young hearts to snare
With love's soft witchery: the beauteous maid
Thou, Aziel, take; thou, Zuriel, the youth.
By day and night your utmost cunning try
Their souls to enter; all their thoughts to sway;
Their blood to fire; their reason to confuse.
Beauty of form and face, beyond compare
Of mortal loveliness, may ye put on;
With voices may ye speak, so musical,
That sweetest tones of woman,—following them,
Would grate man's ear: with so rich eloquence
May ye assail them, that the choicest strains
Of earthly orator, or loftiest bard,
Were, after it, dull babble. Soul, and sense,
Assault ye then: with amorous thoughts, the soul;
With all can please the eye, and charm the ear,
And stir up passion, war upon the sense.

"But, ever this remember;—the keen eye
Of angel shun, as ye would thunderbolt.
Nor ever, or on earth, or other sphere
Within Heaven's ken,—to us, the higher Powers,
Or to your own compeers, one word breathe out,
Touching your mystery. If aught of new,
Or import great, ye have to tell,—the sign
To me give secretly; and hither soon
Together all repairing,—safe from eye,
And ear of hostile Power,—the general host
Will audience give; and of your future course
Will ye be taught. A pleasant task ye have,
And easy, if I err not: ne'ertheless,
Toward the same end, yet other means shall move.

Ye, of necessity, in close disguise
Must ever work; for, once by angel's ken,
Near that fair maiden, or that youth, espied,—
Full blazoned to the sight of all in heaven
Would be our purpose; and a Spirit-guard
Around them would be placed, that all attempt
Of ours would render vain. Nor, though ye soil
The *souls* of mortals, 'gendering therein thoughts
Of fleshly pleasure,—may ye with them mix
In actual dalliance; final seal of sin:
But, soul by you seduced, easy their fall,
When man, or woman, lures them to the joy,
In spirit imaged first. By mortals, then,
Also, shall these be tried. That headlong youth,
Sethos, the king's first-born, and his throne's heir,
The maid shall tempt: for Spirits, subtle most,
His heart shall enter; and to furnace heat
His passions fire: nor by night-dreams alone,
But shows to the waking eye,—even in mid-day,
Feigning her form, and feature, motion, mien,
And all her wondrous loveliness,—that he
To very madness shall be urged, her charms
In lawless way to enjoy: for not even word
Of wedlock, 'twixt an Israelite, and prince
Of Egypt, may be spoken: so that he,
Suing, will ask for sin; and, yielding, she,
Clear-eyed, to sin consent. But, more than this
Shall his mad passion dare: for, if he lose
Hope to seduce,—with violence shall he seize,
And, haply, *that* way triumph; if no power
Of Heaven come in to arrest him. So, for her,
Easy, methinks, our task. For that soft youth,
Not difficult; and by like resistless lure.
For, fired to the height in dreams of sensual love,
Woman shall come before him; beautiful,
Beyond all mortal beauty,—thus by power
Of ours perfected,—and with eye, and look,
And word, and tone, and gesture, passion-filled,—
With all that woman, over carnal man,
Omnipotent makes, shall force him into sin.

" And now, ye Powers, well understand ye all
How, 'twixt ourselves, and our great adversary,
Stands the momentous strife. Israel to free,—
In the due time Messiah to bring forth,
And, through him, man's Redemption,—such the schemes
'Gainst which, to uttermost of our strength, must we
Battle unceasingly. To each of you
Will task be given : let each o'er others strive
Glory to win, by diligence more, and zeal,
Courage, and wisdom, and keen watchfulness,—
So that the speedier to our foe may come
Defeat and shame ; to us great victory ;
Godhead the sooner ours.
      " If any now
Among you all,—though even the least in power,—
Aught toward the general good be moved to speak,
Let him stand forth."
       He paused ; but all were mute,
All motionless. The signal then he gave ;
And, in that moment, vanished the vast host ;
The great sun's heart again was void, and still!

ISRAEL IN EGYPT.

BOOK NINTH.

THOUGHT-SWIFT the flight of Spirits : ere midway
'Twixt noon and evening had the sun declined;
And while, all gentleness and purest love,
Reuben and Rachel in the garden still,
Softly discoursing, walked,—sound, rarely heard
Within that quiet Paradise, arose,
And their sweet talk suspended. Dim, and deep,—
Uncertain where,—like thunder far away,—
That first strange moan. On Reuben Rachel looked,
Hastily stopping; and her finger raised,
His speech to stay. Together then they stood,
Silently listening. More distinct came soon
The noise,—still deep and gentle, but more loud :
And well, at length, they knew the roll of wheels,
And tramp of horses, urging rapidly.
Full fronting them, nor distant, was the gate :
And thitherward, still standing motionless,
Their eyes both turned, in quiet wonderment,
To see what might pass by. Great marvel, then,
Fell on them when, before that very gate,
Paused suddenly a chariot, bright with gold,
By four majestic horses drawn, like night
For blackness, and whose snorting shook the air.
Lightly as springs the seamew from a cliff,
So from the chariot airily leaped then,

One who, for splendor, might a king have been;
And, after him,—more daintily and slow,
Yet featly as a bird, from some low branch
Dropping to earth,—what seemed a woman's form,
But might angelic be; so exquisite
In its fine gracefulness; and such the beams
That from the countenance breathed: on his raised hand,
Her rosy palm, with gentlest touch, she placed,
And floated to the ground. Right toward the gate
Then moved they; and their cheerful voices rose,
Like two sweet instruments,—two melodies
Wreathing in one rich harmony. Amazed,
The Hebrew lovers looked: but, when she saw
That kingly-seeming youth, with his own hand,
The gate thrust open; and that angel shape
Glide through,—her dainty fingers on his arm
Tenderly resting, as, with graceful step,
Together they advanced,—then hastily,
Yet with perfection of sweet dignity,
That beauteous pair to meet, Rachel went on;
And, drawing nigh them, paused; her delicate arms
Beneath her bosom crossed, and bowed the head;
Then rose, intent to speak. But that fair youth,
With motion light as air, on-stepping quick,
Prevented her; and, lowly bending, thus.

"Needs not to ask if in this favored place
Dwelleth the Rose of Goshen; for, than she,
Surely none else my vision blesseth now!
Fairest of Judah's daughters,—fairest far
Of all earth's loveliest,—give me thy kind thoughts:
Deem me not over bold, or light of talk;
For sacred truth I speak, and soul-enforced,
Not fancy-prompted. Expectation high
Hither hath brought us from a land far off,
Thee, chiefly, to behold; though to the court
Of Pharaoh go we also,—so far come,—
Else, left unvisited; since royal pomp
To us no charm hath, like the loveliness
Of beauty, and virtue; for which, trumpet-tongued,

Fame hath resounded thee. But voice of Fame,—
Too oft o'ergilding brass,—gold, now, hath bronzed;
So far beneath thy due the praise hath fallen.
We looked, indeed, to see earth's fairest rose,
But flower of Heaven have found. Oh! beautiful
Is every work of God; but, in *thee*, all
His choicest beauties mingle. Turn thou not,
Fairest, thy face aside; for truth, pure truth,
Alone I utter: from my soul come forth,
Compelled, the works I speak. I cannot look
Upon thee, and be silent; for my heart
Smites on my tongue, and forces it to speak.
Misdeem me not some common flatterer;
Some dresser up of falsehoods, meant to please.
Weak woman's vanity, and mock her sense.
From distant Syria am I come, thyself
Solely to see; thee solely: yet, in thee,
Essence of earth's most good, and beautiful.
And more than all I sought for, have I found.
But, who I am, that thus have dared approach,
Meet is I tell thee. Haply, of the king
Of Syria, Phatos, the renowned in war,
And richest of all monarchs of the East,
The fame hath reached thee. Who before thee stands,
His son is, Samath named,—his eldest son,
And heir unto his throne,—though distant far,
Grant me, ye gods, that miserable day,
When from his noble head the crown shall pass
To mine, unworthy! She who with me comes,—
And whom I pray thee love,—is Lalia,
My dearest sister; and, throughout the East,
Most beauteous of all women beautiful,
By fame acknowledged: yet, with thine compared,
Sure am I,—for her soul's thought read I well,
As written in her eyes, and wondering looks,—
Homely and poor her charms esteemeth she,
As dew-drop's glimmer, to the diamond's gleam.
Oh! matchless truly is this work of God,
And forceth worship! Even on my knee,
Thou loveliest of all things beneath the sun,

Let me do homage; and, with heart sincere,
Implore,—though but for one brief hour it last,—
That, in the radiance of thy presence, we
Foretaste may have of that divinest joy,
When men with angels commune."
                              Ceasing speech,
Upon his knee he sank; one ardent look,
Bright as celestial flame, upon her shot;
Then, as to higher Being, bowed his head,
All trembling, and was mute.
                              Astonished, fixed,
She heard, and gazed: for, music like his voice,
Never her ear had known; beauty like his,
Her eye had never seen: and that fair form,
His sister,—standing silently, and rapt,
Her gaze returning,—of all womankind,
Nought had she seen, with her to make compare.
Not mortal seemed she: surely, then, from Heaven
Must she have come; a visitant to earth,
For some good task; and soon to re-ascend!
If *she*, then also *he*, of Heavenly kind.
And worthy of Heaven he seemed; such air divine
In all his motions; such a loveliness,
And majesty of beauty; both in form,
And feature, and in that pure radiance,
From the large liquid eye, and all the face,
Beaming like glory of morn. Yet, what the words
That he had spoken! Though mellifluous more
Than sweetest tone of music was the voice;
Though all his ardent look, his trembling frame,
True feeling seemed to utter,—yet, alas!
What were the words! Untrue she knew them well:
But *how* untrue?—Exaggerate?—*so* false? . . . . .
Yet, to *reality*, false,—to *feeling*, true,
Might they not be? . . . . . The fevered eye beholds
A sun where all is dark;—but, saying this,
The man lies not; to *him* a sun there is,
Though, in Heaven, none. Could that rare being, then,
Like man, have been deceived?—how, hard to tell,
That beauty he had seen, where beauty none

Existed truly? But his sister, too,
Though word she spake not, had the same declared
In the eye's language. . . . . And yet, marvel none
That so erred she: for, oft is it not seen,
That madness of one man makes many mad,—
Seeing as *he* sees, hearing as *he* hears,
Though truly all be nought? Not falsehood, then,
But sense-deception was it. A great fame
Of beauty, in his native country heard,
Had fired imagination; and on her,
By chance beheld, the fevered eye had cast
Its self-created glories.
     Thus saw she,
Or thought she saw, as in one moment's glance,
Mingling of truth, and error; falsehood none,
Intended: nay, in nature pure as his,
Impossible, surely! and, to chase forthwith
From those, else clearest eyes, the darkening fumes,—
With words of simple earnestness and truth,
Quickly she answered him.
     "Arise, O prince;
I pray thee rise: thou wouldst not mock me thus
With known deceit: but art thyself deceived;
In me, some other seeing. All unused
To such high presence am I; to such words,
Such praise, and such respect unmerited.
Thou knowest not, of a truth, to whom it is
That thus thou renderest homage, not her due.
An humble daughter am I of a race
Oppressëd sorely; and of small account
Even with my native people: unknown quite
By those of distant countries. Beauty none,
More than the lowliest, have I. Wrong report
Hath reached thee, then; or she, of whom 'twas said,
Far other is than I. Rachel my name.
No great one of the land my father is;
But sheep and cattle feedeth; and the ground
For corn, and fruit, and oil, and wine doth till.
Wealthy, indeed, is he; and in respect
By all our tribe long held; yet, but as one

Uprightly walking before God and man;
In self-esteem the humblest. Such are we;
Far different, as thou seest, from those thou sought.
Then tell me, prince, for whom thou dost enquire;
That, haply,—though I know not, nor have heard
Of such rare beauty, in this little land,
Where each to all is known. . . . . . Reuben, per-
    chance," . . . . .

   Thus speaking, she looked round; and, close behind,—
For gently he had followed her, amazed
At all he saw,—beheld him: "Knowëst thou,
Reuben," she said, "of maiden in these parts,
So passing beautiful, that even to land
Far distant might the fame thereof have gone?"

   "Beauty is only rare," the youth replied,
Modestly blushing, "when with thousands else,
All beautiful, it stands, eclipsing all.
Who one flower only knoweth, cannot know
If in all men's esteem it would be held
Beautiful greatly: in like manner, I,
With thee, my Rachel, my one flower, content,
Have looked on few beside; thence, judgment none
Of rarest beauty have I: nor, in truth,
Of any maiden, in these neighbouring parts,
So excellent in feature, have I heard,
As that to distant lands the fame thereof
Might have been carried. . . Yet one see I here,—"
Sinking the voice, he said, and blushing deep,
As now, with nearer view, full on the face
Of that angelic shape his eye first fixed;—
"One do I see, whose loveliness, methinks,
The voice of fame might sound throughout the earth.
Say thou, my Rachel,—or am I deceived?,"
He whispered; "Is not that fair creature bright
And beauteous, more than all of woman born
Whom yet thou hast beheld?"
                        "*If* woman-born,
Of all most beauteous far," she answered him:

"But go thou to her, Reuben, for she smiles
Upon thee, as the sunrise on the hills;
And would, methinks, speak with thee."
                                        Modestly,
As if constrained—though not unwillingly,—
Toward that fair creature Reuben then advanced;
And Rachel, to the silent, gazing prince
Turning again,—her interrupted speech,
Simple, and true, renewed.
                          " Of whom ye seek,
We know not; nor, as now we think, have heard:
Yet, if her name thou tell,—remembrance then
May come to us; and joyful should we be,
Directing thee aright."
                       She paused, and looked
With clear, calm eye, in simple truthfulness,
Upon that bright and glorious countenance,
Full beaming on her; and, as seemed, all speech,
Though silent: but, when ceased her low sweet voice,
Sprang forth his words of fire.
                               " Whom here I seek,"
Dropping again upon the knee, he cried,
" Is thou thyself, blest Rachel; the one child
Of Kohath and of Sarah; thee I seek.
In heaven is one sun only; and, on earth,
One only flower of Heaven. None, none but thee
Came we to seek. Nought knoweth the bright star
How far-off worlds speak of it: nought knowest thou,—
More than the dew-steeped rose of its own sweets,—
Thine own rare loveliness; and how all tongues
In lands remote speak of it; in plain speech
Of humble shepherds; in high phrase of kings,
In song of harpers, and in tale of bards;
All speaking, and all singing, in the praise
Of Goshen's heaven-flower; scenting the whole earth
With its sky-odour. That sweet flower art thou!
I feel Heaven's breath around thee: Heaven's pure light
I see about thee: sweetest sounds of Heaven
Are in thy voice: all dignity and grace
Of Heaven's bright spirits in thy motions are!

Oh that it were not sin to worship thee!
For, prostrate at thy feet, then, would I fall,
And call thee Goddess. On that exquisite hand,
Grant me, I pray thee, one pure kiss to impress;
Then, happy made, to arise; and thy sweet voice
In all things to obey."
      His glorious face,
All burning adoration,—with clear eye,
And calm, she saw; his passionate words and tones,—
Tumultuous music,—with calm ear she heard:
But her heart sorrowed; for the lofty mind
That should have matched that form almost divine,
Distracted was, she thought,—since words so false
And foolish, never had he uttered, else;
Himself demeaning; and degrading her,
If with clear reason spoken. Gently then,
And with true pity looking,—briefly thus
She answered him.
      "I pray thee, prince, arise,—
For this false reverence, though no mock it be,
Even more than mockery paineth,—being given
Where it is owed not. But thy pardon grant,
When, in obedience to our fathers' law,
A thing most valueless I thee refuse.
To strangers,—even though greatest kings they be,—
Daughters of Israel may not give the hand.
Forgive me then, I pray thee, and arise.
I will send forth,—for not far hence he is,—
And call my father hither. Better he
Will answer thee, than I; to courtly words
All unaccustomed."
      Starting to his feet,
"Nay, nay," with passionate look and tone he cried;
"Thyself 'tis only, fairest work of Him
Who all things fair created,—thee alone
Whom I would see; with whom I would discourse;
Whose knowledge I would know; whose will obey:
For, all things by thee said, or done, or thought,
Wisest, and best, and heavenliest far must be.
All that to thee is worship, custom, law,

Should, to the universal world, be law,
Custom, and worship: for truth, only truth,
Divinest truth, all *must* be, which by thee
As truth accepted is. Oh! tell me, then,
The mysteries of thy worship: of thy God
Speak to me; of his power, and wisdom speak;
His name, and all his mighty acts declare:
Where throned he is: with man how dealeth he:
In all aright instruct me: for, till now,
Worship of other gods have I been taught;
Gods who false *must* be, since they are not thine:
Thine, only, *can* be true; for, truth itself
Not truer is than thou, who, on thy face,
Written, as if with pen in sunbeam dipped,
Bearest heaven's warrant, 'EVER PURE, AND TRUE' ...
But ah! I see thy thought; 'not this the hour,'
Thy spirit saith, 'for matter deep as such.'
On lighter speak thou then. Come,—pleasant task
I set thee now,—of thy betrothed-one speak:
For, with thy name, his, too, hath gone abroad;
His comeliness, and goodness, next to thine
By some reported; nay, by maidens' tongues,
E'en *more* than thine deemed excellent. And see,—
Already have my sister's lustrous eyes
Fallen dimmed to earth, with admiration quelled
Of his scarce mortal beauty. Side by side,
With voices murmuring music, now they walk.
Communion dangerous,—even for both alike;
Were they not both of second passion made
Incapable,—already overfilled
With great first love. On one same spot of earth
Stand not two hills;—nor, in that heart where lives
One pure love, can a second love find place.
No fear, then, have thou, lest her beauty rare,—
For, truly, doth it second stand to thine,—
His love from thee should lure. Betrothed is she
Already, to a prince, in all things held
Worthiest of admiration; and their day
Of marriage is at hand."
      " I pray thee, prince,"

With calm, yet serious voice, said Rachel then,
"Speak thou to me the words of truth alone.
Surely must thou, and all who on us look,
See plainly that, with me compared, is she
As lily to a nettle! Yet no fear,
Even for a moment, have I, that the love
Of Reuben should from me be drawn aside:
For, of a true and faithful mind he is;
Humble in self-esteem; and knoweth well,
That upon him no princess of the earth
With eye of love would look. From earliest years,
Betrothëd have we been: and, sooth to say,
The tree, methinks, from out its native bed
Amid the mountains, would as soon arise,
And in some stately garden plant itself,
As he my side would leave, for even a queen's."

"Nor wonder, fairest, purest, holiest, best!"
Burst forth the enraptured prince: "for that sweet hill
Whereon he hath found root, so radiant is
With Heaven's pure light; with atmosphere of Heaven
So richly fragrant; that no garden of earth,
Though flowered for kings, may with it have compare!
Far more is mine the peril, lest, on thee
Looking, and filled with wonder, should my heart
Be shaken from its faith toward one most loved;
A princess beautiful, by every eye
Admired, nay worshipped,—unto whom my hand
Is pledged; and whom, ere fades another moon,
Shall I call wife. Far, far beyond all else,—
My sister sole except,—whom, till this day,
Mine eyes have looked on, beautiful is she:
Yet, in thy presence,—pardon me,—for truth,
Truth only must I speak, or silent be,—
In presence of thee, angelic, as a cloud
Is she,—a pure, serene, moon-lighted cloud,
To the silvery moon herself." While speaking thus,
Full in her face, with eyes like sunshine bright
And warm, he looked; his radiant countenance,

Love seeming to give out, as, waked by morn,
Earth gives out mist. But, as the star's ray weak
To melt the polar ice,—so passion's fire
Weak was, in her pure heart one throb to stir.
Love's silent language, warm, and eloquent
Beyond conception, saw she: yet, surprise,
And gentle sorrow only did it raise;
Above her pure heart passing harmlessly,
As sound o'er rock of crystal. His strange speech,
Quickly, then, thus she answered.
                                  "Of such things,
I pray thee, prince, say thou to me no more;
For flattery, even when gentle and sincere,
Is but a sickly food; when wild, and gross,
Nauseous, nay hateful is it. What I am,
Well know I; and content have ever been,
As our good God created me, to be.
I do implore thee, then, truth, simple truth
Alone to speak; else, honor though it is,
Thy presence painful were. . . . . But, all surprised
By such unlooked for visit,—meet respect
And hospitality to strangers due,
Have I forgotten. Pardon me, I pray.
My father, and my mother, as I said,
Are absent; with our long-lost Moses gone,
A friend of old to visit: but, if thou,
And thy fair sister, in our poor abode
Will deign to enter; and with fruits, and wine,
Humble refreshment make,—glad will they be,
On their return, to hear it: and I, too,
Be glad such guests to honor."
                              " Sweet the bread,
By thine hands broken!" cried the enraptured prince;
" Fruit by thee touched, the wine by thee poured out! ..
But I forget me; and displeasure raise,
Though but truth uttering; truth from out my soul
Gushing uncalled, as water from a spring!
Far as I can, upon this restless tongue
Will I put bridle; and, if e'er again
Too freely it shall move, I pray of thee,

Think but, that, for a moment, the hot steed
His rider hath o'ermastered; bearing him
On path that, else, he willingly had shunned."

Gently she smiled, and bowed; and her fair hand,
Pure as pearl-tint of morn, extending, signed
Toward the bright princess; mutely saying thus,
"Most fit that *thou* conduct her; I await."
The sign he read; bowed low; and with a step
Light as the sweep of cloud,—yet full of grace,
And princely dignity,—toward where still walked
His sister, and the astounded youth, went on.

Meantime, the phantom princess, with dread lure
Of flattery, and of love, half hid, half shown,
Had striven the innocent heart of that true youth
With warmth impure to stir. From eyes more bright
Than sun-lit sapphire, on him did she shoot
Heart-fire, which, to the man of common mould,
Lightning had been,—within his very bones
Heat kindling; and to cinder scorching up
Even oaks of virtue, human growth alone.
From face all smiling, now, as richest bed
Of flowers, breeze-rocked, and glistening in the sun,—
Now, sad as solitary vale at night,
To the lone lover, wandering,—did she pour
Floods of strange passion,—now, like Hecla's springs
From earth's heart boiling; now, like soft, warm stream,
'Neath overhanging branches, in sweet gloom,
Through tropical forest gliding; gentle, sad;
Yet the hot traveller, as with arms outspread,
Wooing to its embrace: from lips, whose play
Bright was and graceful, as of sun-tipped waves
Just waked at morn,—sounds exquisite she breathed;
Melodies sweet of Heaven, not yet forgot;
Tones that of every nerve of sensual man,
Had made a quivering harp-string; and all strength
So melted, that, as death-struck, had he dropped,
And quivered at her feet. And, with these charms
Of eye, and look, and voice, words dangerous

To strongest virtue spake she; telling half,
And half concealing, of a passion strange,—
Sudden as lightning in a crystal sky,—
Resistless as its stroke,—which her weak heart,
Fresh, till that moment, as an opening rose,
Had scorched to ashes. Sighing deep, she told
Of her troth plighted to a prince, young, rich,
By all men honored; but by her, alas!
Not greatly, ever, loved; and, *now*, abhorred!
So, in all excellence that woman loves,
Immeasurably less was he, than whom——
Oh pity! now, too late, she had beheld,
And even to madness worshipped! yea, for whom,
Her promised greatness, riches, pomp, and throne,
As dust she would fling off; and, with him blest,
Shun all the world beside! A stifled sob
At times came forth, as though, with pangs suppressed,
Her heart were breaking; then, as if to hide
Emotion so revealed,—though roseate all
With sweetest blushes,—a sad smile she forced;
And, lifting up her eyes, which on the earth,
Confession making, humbly she had dropped,
In seeming modesty,—a sudden gleam,
A passion's lightning, on his face she shot:
A radiance that was language, and spake out,
" *Thou* art the loved one! love *me*, or I die!"

As in a dream distracted, Reuben stood,
Seeing, and hearing, sights, and sounds, and words,
Which, in the inflammable mind of simple youth,
By heavenly thoughts unguarded, and pure love,
Stark madness had engendered; but, in him,
Amazement only raised they,—trouble, doubt.
Excess of light brings blindness; and that blaze
Of beauty, over reason, sense, and soul,
Darkness bewildering cast; that, what he saw,
Illusion seemed; what heard, appeared as nought.

But, when the phantom-prince, all smiles, drew nigh;
And, leading toward the house that sister-shade,

The hospitable words of Rachel spake,
Inviting them to enter,—rousing then
From stupor almost trancelike, Reuben too,
Though silent still, went onward; nor one word,
Even to Rachel, spake, when to her side
He came; but, buried in deep wonderment,
Walked as in sleep: within the house arrived,
As in a dream all saw; and stood, or sat,
Or, sometimes, question answered; or aught did,
At Rachel's soft requirement; yet with sense
Uncertain still as vision in thick fog.

Attendance summoned, and refreshment placed
Before her guests,—all purity and truth,
The Hebrew maiden, to that pair impure,
The rites of simple hospitality,
With native grace administered; nor words
Of cheerful converse shunned; doubt feeling none
In her sweet virgin mind, of aught amiss;
Save, in that ardent prince, high fantasy,
O'ermastering reason. For his sister, she,
Pure, now, as snow appeared; gentle and calm
As breath of summer's twilight.
                            But the time
Of their departure came,—for well they felt
The advent of a presence they would shun,—
And, rising then,—with modest tone, and look
All bashfulness, as though of such high grace
Unworthy feeling,—to the chosen maid
Low bowed the prince, and spake.
                            "Our thanks accept,
Daughter of Judah, for such courtesies
As monarchs well might envy us; so rich
In those fine graces that, of mortal food,
Refection spiritual make; mere earthly bread,
And fruit, and wine, as by some holy spell,
To heavenly feast transmuting. Such rare bliss
Who once partakes,—for his whole life to come,
Happy might deem himself: yet, who that once,
Once only, had beheld the glory of day;

Had seen the sun mid clouds of gold arise;
Like orb of steadfast lightning path the sky;
Like a vast world of ruby sink at eve,—
Who, that one day had seen it, would not long
For an eternity of days, to see
Glory, else inconceivable? Who could bear,
Thereafter, in eternal night to dwell,
Hopeless of second sunrise? Even so,
Fairest of Israel's daughters,—blessed once
To see, and feel the sunshine sweet and pure
Of thy most holy presence, ... nay,—turn not
With darkening visage from me,—for my words
Are but my soul's voice; and, if less I say,
False shall I be to that divinest truth
Speaking within me, ... but I see thee still
O'ercast,—like star of evening dimmed by mist,—
And, from the poor plant I would offer thee,
Will dock the flower. In homeliest language then,—
May we thy kind permission crave, again
This favored house to visit? To the court
Of Pharaoh go we now; his guests awhile:
And, such brief distance interposed, far more
Would be our sorrow and privation,—barred
From presence so desired; from hope of good
That might be ours, in thy sweet converse blest,
Instructed, purified, than if wide lands
'Twixt thee and us had lain,—our hearts' first wish
Impossible making, as the gems to seize
Beneath the ocean caverned. Nigh the lips
When stands the sparkling cup they may not taste,
Oh! thousand times more torturing the thirst,
Than when, in fancy only, the clear springs,
Leagues off are figured. Kindly yield us then
Admission to thy Paradise: nor fear
That alway with the look, and word, and tone,
Of admiration irrepressible,
Thy soul, too humble in its own esteem,
I shall offend. Who on the wide sea first,
And suddenly looks,—all wonder and delight,
Even shouts, for rapture: but in awe, at length,

And holy silence gazes; in that vast,
Visible, seeing the Great Invisible.
So, my first vehemence of wonder o'er,—
By musing silence only; or few words,
And simple, may I mark the holy joy
Which fills me in thy presence."
        Modestly,
Thus having spoken, his fine head he bowed,
And silent stood. Silent stood also she,
Unknowing how to answer. For herself,
Converse with strangers gladly had she shunned;
Even those of speech most plain: with one to courts
Accustomed, and to flattery thus prone,
Task painful was it. Of his high estate
She thought not; nor his princely courtesy;
His beauty matchless, both in form and face;
Nor of his fancy's play; nor eloquence
Of word and look; nor music of his voice,—
On her was all as nought: but, such small boon
As he had begged, she liked not to refuse:
Churlish it seemed, nay even unjust, to weigh,
'Gainst any fellow being's harmless wish,
Slight self-distaste, and let it turn the scale.
Nay, even a grievous sin might it not be,
So to refuse; for, who aright could know
What good momentous,—from the converse high
Of her loved father, and of holy priests,
His visitors oft,—to that so gifted pair
Might come, when, in the place of Heathen night,
Should rise upon them that great sun of Heaven,—
Knowledge of Israel's God.
       So rapt in thought,
And silent standing; with her face down bent,
Gentle and pure as some young drooping flower,
When he beheld her,—with a cheerful voice
Thus spake he.
     "Silence oft best eloquence is;
Without word telling, what a host of words
So well could not. The musings of thy soul,
Through thy pure face all clear before me lie,

As pebbles through sea's crystal. Thy kind boon,
In spirit granted, with deep gratitude
Do we accept: and now with cheerful heart
May pass into the night; assured that day
Will visit us again. Our chariot long
Before thy gate hath tarried; and the hour
Compels departure. All that Heaven hath best
For mortal happiness, on thee, fair maid,
And on thy house, be ever."
       Like farewell
The sister-phantom gave: to Reuben then
Turned, and in words, though kind, yet plain and calm,
As to a new-made friend, leave-taking, spake:
But, when his eyes one moment unto hers
Upraised she saw,—sudden as lightning glance,—
Unseen of all beside,—a stream of fire,
Like flight of arrows all together shot,
Even to his heart she sent; that, like to one
Stricken in fight, he staggered. Yet the bolts,
Though the strong mail of purity they shook,
As battering rams a wall, pierced not within.
Sense was an instant stunned, but soul stood firm.
A shock he felt, unknowing what the cause:
And when upon the face, all heavenly calm
And innocent, of Rachel next he looked,
A peace serene came on him; as on woods
By tempest shaken, when the wind falls dead.

 Loudly the horses snorted at the gate,
And stamped the ground, impatient to be gone.
Forth walked the guests, the hostess, and the youth:
Lightly the phantoms to the chariot rose;
Again the farewell spake, and bowed the head,
Smiling, though seeming sad: with gentle words
The Hebrew maiden answered, and the youth
In silence bent: then, without word, or sign
Apparent given them, the black steeds flung out
Their mighty feet; and, like a golden cloud,
Wind-swift the chariot flew.
       Silent, not sad,

Though not untroubled,—since not seeing clear
If all aright had been; if good might come,
Or evil most, from that strange visiting,—
Hand locked in hand, unto the house returned
The innocent pair: and quickly then, like breath
Of Spring upon the flowers, on Reuben fell
The music exquisite of Rachel's voice;
The music visible, beaming from her face;
Soft flow of music from each moving limb,—
Body and soul one heavenly harmony,—
That, like a thick mist from a hill top blown,
When freshly wakes the wind, from off his soul,
Wide scattered flew the lurid atmosphere
By that fair phantom cast: and soon again
With hers his clear voice mingled cheerfully.

In brief time, other voices also joined;
For the loved parents of the youth and maid,
With Moses, their all honored guest, returned,
Radiant with joy; of the approaching day,
Israel's deliverance bringing, in few words,
A foretaste having had; and, of the end,
Doubting no more than of the morrow's dawn;
For, was it not of God? But when, at length,
From Rachel, of those guests so wondrous strange,
In full they had heard; and of permission craved,
And unrefused, the visit to renew;
Awhile, in dim distrust of evil meant,
All silent sat: for, of his flattering speech,
With open heart, disguising nought, she had told:
Of his so ardent looks, and passionate tones;
The beauty of his countenance, and form;
The music of his voice; the graces rare
Of all his motions: of that princess, too,
Had told; how radiant past all thought she was;
Scarce earthly in her exquisite loveliness;
And voiced as might be angel, ... though, of her,
Fitliest might Reuben speak,—with her sweet talk
Most favored, and apart. Full on the youth,

Thus saying, looked she; from her virgin face,
Purest effulgence of all trusting love
Beaming upon him. But, with troubled mien,
Sat he, and spake not: pallid now, now flushed;
With eyes now downcast, now, with hurried glance,
On every countenance looking anxiously:
Yet not as one shame-bowed, but soul-disturbed;
Unknowing of the cause.
      With gentle words,
Yet solemn; and with aspect grave, yet kind;
As to loved offspring speaks an anxious sire,
Then, after silence brief, thus Moses spake.

"As my own children were ye,—nay, far more,
As being of God for some high purpose chosen,—
Dear to me are ye both. What hath befallen,—
Commanded, or permitted,—for some end
Inscrutable hath been: your faith, perchance,
Or holiness, to prove: but, whatsoe'er,—
Be it of Heaven, or hell,—for you can be
One only course. Plain as high road at noon,
Before you lies the way that ye should walk.
Even as your right hand from your left, ye know
The path of holiness, from path of sin.
Keep steadfast on the way which ye have trod:
To neither side, though gardens as of heaven
Would tempt you, for one moment turn your eyes.
Before you straight is the clear road of God:
If thence ye turn,—though seeming angels call,—
From God ye turn,—His chosen ones no more;
But lost! all lost! Of evil, if one breath,
Though weaker than the air-sigh which scarce moves
The floating gossamer, on your souls should touch,—
Your own strength trust not, even for so short time
As measures flash of light; but on your knees,
And on your faces fall; and cry to Him
Who everywhere is present; who each sigh
Of troubled heart doth hear; and in whose might,
Against ten thousand enemies of hell,
Shall ye be victors. Admonition thus,

By duty urged, I give; though confident
That in yourselves, Heaven-destined, are ye strong
'Gainst evil's worst assault. Thy countenance,
Blest Rachel, is as sky without a cloud:
And thine, young Reuben, though a vapour hang
Brief time above it,—from some murky cloud
Blown thither,—no pollution thence hath caught;
And quickly will shine clear. . . . But now to God
Let us give worship."

On his knees he sank,
And with him all that pious company;
And to the throne of God went up a voice.
Solemn as holy hush of midnight, now;
Now, joyful in bright hope, as morning's prime;
Now, fervent as the breath of summer's noon,
Seemed that scarce human utterance. It ceased:
A silent moment followed; gently then,
Tremulous with holy awe, down bending, all
Sank noiselessly, with forehead to the floor,
In spirit to worship: and throughout the house
Was stillness, as of midnight on the hills.

ISRAEL IN EGYPT.

BOOK TENTH.

In that same moment when at Kohath's gate
Paused the bright phantom-chariot,—to the eye
Of Sethos, riding moodily alone,
Appeared a vision. Through thin-foliaged bush,—
Light screen to veil him, feared he,—it shone out,
A living glory. Human could it be?
Or shape celestial? If to mortal sight
Goddess might e'er be visible,—surely now
Such saw he! Isis, in her youthful prime,
It might have seemed; so beauteous past compare
With aught of earthly: feature, form, and mien,
Perfection all. 'Twas in a flowery grove,
Far from all public way. The perfume rich
Thither had lured him; and no fear felt he
Intruder to be reckoned. Still as stone
The vision stood; with graceful head uplift,
Gazing on flowers above, thick set as stars;
And seeming lost in wonder. All alone
In that sweet solitude, 'twas plain she felt;
For in full freedom stood she; negligent
Of all appearance, such as, under eye
Of stranger, maidens heed; her face unveiled;
Arms loosely crossed; one delicate foot, the weight
Of her light form supporting. Full in view

From where he sat, she stood; nor distant far;
For, like the rays shot upward from the sun,
After his setting,—from her eyes appeared
Bright beams upshooting toward the clustering flowers;
Beams which, he thought, even quicker than sun's warmth,
Might ripen them to fruit.   One glance direct,
And she might see him!   Breathless, motionless,
Upon his horse he sat; heart throbbing quick,
Eyes fixed, and open kept; lest, by one wink,
A gem-worth instant he should lose, of sight,
Aught mortal passing, as heaven passeth earth.

    As, looking full on the clear-shining moon,
When nigh the key-stone of heaven's arch she rides,
Nought else the eye can see,—so, on that face,
Dazzling with beauty's splendor, while he gazed,
Viewless was all beside.   One glance, at length,
Upon her vesture cast he; and his heart
Sounded; his breath stopped: for that shape of heaven—
All inaccessible—beyond even dream
Of hope to approach it—even its garment's hem
On bended knee to touch,—now to him seemed,
Of earth! a woman! mortal like himself!
Woman! then, haply, to be wooed, embraced!
Madness of bliss to think of!
                              " Ye great gods,
A Hebrew is she!" inwardly he said:
" A Hebrew!   But, of all Egyptian dames,
Look out the proudest, the most beautiful;
Even to tie the sandal of that foot,
Unworthy were she!   Isis might rejoice
To wait upon her! the throned gods might bend
And worship at her feet! the very sun
Stand fixed in heaven to gaze; and all the stars
Come down, and crowd together, for one look
On beauty past celestial!   Where hath been
This glory hidden,—that, from end to end,
The world hath not proclaimed it!   Is it blood
That paints the delicate rose on that fair cheek?
Or essence from the ruby of the morn?

Flesh is she, truly? or incarnate light?
Or but a fantasy, like forms in clouds,
Glorious awhile, then lost? By sun and stars,
Mortal she *is!* I saw her bosom heave!
Methought I heard her sigh! I felt, methought,
Music too fine for the ear! Oh, sweetest breeze
Of spicy East, with richest odours mixed
From orange grove and citron, tasteless were,
With that sweet breath compared! On that rose-mouth
One clinging kiss—then death—were happiness,
Even for a god! She turns away her face;
And sky is darkened! But that glorious shape
Brings day again! She walks! Oh, sweetest tone
Of harp, or dulcimer, no such melody hath
As those ecstatic motions! Heaven itself
Moves with her as she goes! There's nought in life
Worth having, to the man who once hath seen,
Then lost thee ever! With a warier eye
Than I would watch the sword that threatened death,
Thy pathway will I mark: for, losing thee,
The life of life I lose! Let me but know
Where thou dost home thee: by what earthly name
Thou, heavenly all, art known; and, while these eyes
Can see, these limbs can move, this heart can beat,
This tongue can utter word,—where'er thou goest,
There will I go; the air thou breath'st, will breathe;
The earth thou tread'st, will tread. I'll worship thee!
My goddess thou shalt be! To other Power
Than thee, no more I'll bow. Henceforth no life,
Save in thy presence, have I; merely dead,
Where thou art not!"
     Thus musing franticly,
At gentlest pace of his light-footed steed,
The maddening shape he followed; his eyes fixed,
Lips parted, breath suspended; all his limbs
In painless spasm held rigid: such his fear
Lest the slow hoof-tread on the moss-like turf
Her sensitive ear should catch; and those fine eyes,
Embodied sunbeams, mark how near her heaven
A mortal had presumed. But on she walked,

With such sweet gracefulness, as o'er the ground
She floated rather,—like a lily, loosed,
Adown a gentle stream; nor token showed
Of consciousness that on that solitude
Had aught intruded. Once alone she stopped;
And, sideways turning, lifted up her arm,
And plucked a bending flower. The flowing sleeve
Dropped to the elbow; and discovered shape
Of inconceivable beauty: living pearl
And rose in substance; motion ravishing
As harmony of heaven. And, when the hand,
Down gliding, to the nostril held the flower,—
Blest flower, so favored! and when then, the first,—
Like some new break of splendor in a dream,
Came the side-glory of that countenance,—
Breath stopped for wonderment, and heart stood still,
Palsied by beauty. But again she turned,
And glided on her way.
                    Erelong appeared
The confine of the grove; a rustic gate
Guarding the entrance; and, beyond it close,
In shadow of a tree, two Hebrew men
On foot, mules holding. Through the gate she passed;
Upmounted, lightly as the thistle-down,
Fanned by the breeze; and, with grace exquisite,—
Sweetening, he thought, the air that touched her cheek,—
Skimmed, dove-like, o'er the plain. In haste upsprang
Her serving-men; and the soft beat of hoofs
In distance soon was lost.
                        Forth riding then,
His fleet steed Sethos urged; with eyes still fixed
On that smooth-flying shape celestial:
Half fearing that, like some bright cloud of morn,
It might melt off; yet ever cautiously
Due distance keeping; lest the stamp, or snort
Of his impatient steed should reach the ears
Of whom he followed; and suspicion wake
Of some intent unfriendly. But, right on,
Nought hearing, as it seemed, suspecting nought,
With speed unslacked, head never backward turned,

Still held they; till, when toward the sun he glanced,
And marked declining day; within himself
Thus 'gan he question.
                        " Whither are they bound ?
If farther much they journey, night will fall
Ere home I can return. But, though till morn,—
Ay, till the next day's morn, they keep the way,—
Horse holding out, and my own breath and strength
Sustaining me,—never will I give up
This goddess-chase. Why, in pursuit of beast,
Thousands have toiled, till steed and rider fell;
One dead, the other death-like,—and shall I,
A prize pursuing, worth ten myriad times
All chases, from beginning of the world
Even to its ending,—shall I such resign,
Petty fatigue to shun; or one night's sleep
Beneath a tree, perchance, or on the grass;
Darkness my curtain; and my chamber roof
Heaven's starry vault ? No! till breath fail, and eyes
Be darkened, and all strength have passed away,
On will I still! for never instant more
Of joy were mine, this glory should I lose!
Madness would seize me! I should tear myself!
Or fall upon my sword! or plunge in Nile!
Or headlong in deep pit! or poison drink!
Or aught worse do, such misery to end! . . . .
But idle all my fear. Not distant far
From home, thus lightly guarded, would she go.
A visit to some friend; or mere desire
This fresh north wind to breathe, hath brought her forth,
From Israelitish Goshen; her abode,
I doubt not. And now nigh it do we draw.
Plainly the path behold I, winding up
To that sweet land; and toward it right they go.
Oh, Isis! guard me now! Make deaf their ears
To my horse-foot: cast darkness on their eyes,
If hitherward they look! that I may steal,
Unheard, unseen, upon them; and mark well
Where sets this human star; and learn its name;
And how it may be worshipped."

                              Mutely thus
Within himself communing,—his eyes still
Fixed on the flying vision,—on he went,
Hoping and fearing; till, the mound o'erpast,
And Goshen brief way entered,—at a gate
He saw the riders pause. With hasty hand
His steed he checked, and waited. From their mules
Alighted they; nor toward him, as it seemed,
One instant looked; but straightway at the gate
Went in, and disappeared. On then rode he;
Yet at such sober pace as travellers use,
Bound on long journey,—lest some curious eye
Should watch, and guess his purpose,—on he rode,
Of all things negligent seeming; yet with look
Still on that gate hard fixed. One stealthy glance,
Passing, he cast within; but all were gone.
A garden fair he saw; a goodly house;
One mighty shadowing tree; and onward went.
Deep, clear, as pressure of a well-cut seal
On liquid wax, upon his memory stamped,
He felt that blest abode; and, pausing not,
Rode forward for awhile, as heedless all
Of what he had beheld. But, turning soon,
The backward path he took; at easy pace
Proceeding; and with quiet look, and air,
Like one, for pleasure, riding carelessly;
Till, opposite that heaven-gate once again
Arriving,—to his joy, an aged man
Forth coming he beheld; and, in the tone
Of wearied traveller, asked him, how far thence
To Zoan; and, when cheerfully the eld
Had answered, that a two hours' easy ride
Thither would bring him,—pointing toward the house,
Again he questioned, who in that sweet place,—
Bower for a princess fit, as it appeared,—
His dwelling had.
                    Then, with a serious look,
Shaking the head; yet with a brightening eye,
And tone of one who of some wonder tells,
The old man answered.

"And a princess there
Verily dwelleth,—though of royal blood
None hath she; princess only in the right
Of beauty, such as all of womankind
Surpasseth; more than robe of richest king
The beggar's rags surpasseth. Of the race
Of Israel are all they who dwell within:
A man, his wife, and one fair daughter; she
Of whom I told thee. Kohath is he called;
Sarah, his wife; and Rachel is the name
Of her, the beauty's princess: and as good
Is she, as beautiful; and in the mouths
Of all her people honored. Look, my lord,—
One moment thou may see her."
       Eagerly,
Following the old man's gaze, his quivering eyes
The duped prince turned; for even one smallest drop
Of that rich beauty thirsting.
      As a lamp,
Gliding at night amid a thick-set wood,
Gleams,—and is darkened,—and gleams out again,—
Flashing, and fading momently,—even so,
Amid the bushes, and the slender trees,
As that bright vision walked,—now seen, now lost,—
Seemed, to his starting eyes, now day, now night;
Now peep of sunrise, and now blackest dark.
On went she, gleaming, vanishing; and he,
Breathless, with eyes dilate, and beating heart,
The fitful splendor watched: till, like a flame
Suddenly quenched, within the porch she passed;
And thick night fell upon him. One deep sigh
He breathed: turned then his horse, and silently
Toward Zoan 'gan return.
      But, all the way,
Nought saw he; nothing heard. The eagle swept,
Shrill screaming, over head: in shady nooks
Cooed the soft dove: great birds of splendid hues,
Like living fire streamed by: the nightingale
Gave forth his glorious song: unconscious all
Of aught in heaven, or on the earth, he rode;

Nought seeing, of nought thinking, save, alone,
That more than heavenly vision.
                                Speaking not,
He lighted from his steed: as in a dream,
Glided through court, and hall: with heavy foot,—
Solitude craving,—his own chamber sought:
Sank on a couch, sick, musing, wondering, lost;
Food loathing; all realities around
Bitterly hating; all the pomp of court;
All choicest beauty of Egyptian dames;
All power, all rule, despising: for one thing
Longing alone; as, for the cold, clear stream,
The thirst-fallen perishing desert traveller longs;
One only, which, to body and soul alike,
Both dying for that want, could new life give,—
The presence of that wonderment divine!
That beauty which all beauty else had quenched!
That shape beyond celestial: that face, air,
Motion ecstatic, maddening,—even in dreams
Of Goddess-lustre, never to be reached!
For him, was now no glory in the sun;
No beauty in the earth; in richest flowers
No fragrance; in most luscious fruits, no taste;
No charm in sweetest music. She alone
Was all the light he cared for; hers alone
The beauty he would see; the air she breathed,
Sole fragrance he desired; the music sole
For which he longed, the silent harmony
Of all her infinite graces: and that sound,
Imagined only yet, but such supposed,
As, with aught else of sweetest in compare,
Would be as clustered splendor of all stars,
To each small separate beam,—that wondrous sound,
All other music making harsh,—the breath
Of her celestial voice! Oh! *that* to hear,
Would be, he thought, to die in bliss; heart-pierced,
As with a sword, by beauty!
                              But, erelong,
A hateful noise his frenzied musings scared;

A stroke from mortal hand upon the door,
To dull earth brought him back. A youthful lord
Then entered; and from Pharaoh message brought,
His presence craving instantly. Ill pleased,
Yet daring not refusal, Sethos rose,
And to his father went.
                         "Guests have we here,
My son," said Pharaoh, as, with courteous air,
Toward them he motioned; "the young Syrian prince,
And that rare excellence, of whom fame speaks
To farthest lands, his sister. These two hours,
And more, dull entertainment have I given,
Though to my best,—for, with all-buoyant youth,
Care-cankered middle-age poor concord makes,—
And now to thee the honor I resign,
Welcome more fit to give them." Turning then
To the fair prince and princess, who, with hands
Freely extended, and with sunny looks,
The proffered palm of Sethos gladly met,—
"Know ye my son," he said, "mine eldest born,
And heir to Egypt's throne. Grave state affairs
Compel me elsewhere: yet but slight excuse
Will ye deem ample; for your gain, not loss,
Springs from my absence; since I take away
A smouldering torch, and leave a new-lit lamp.
Sethos will glow, where I but dully burned;
And you had dulled, but that, like stars, ye shone
With your own light. His, now, with yours will join,
Each heightening all; and, from my gloom released,
Gay will ye feel as they who, from dark cave,
Step forth into the sun. But ye have heard
With what strange thing all Egypt hath been scourged;
And how even yet, from those accursed spells
Of Hebrew magic, unknown ills we dread;
And, pitying me, will pardon. Till the morn
I bid ye, then, farewell. What sports ye will,—
Such as our country, and this time disturbed,
May give, the hours to gladden,—all command.
Osiris guard you!"
                    With a smiling face,

Hiding a mind distraught, he waved his hand,
Inclined the head, and went.
                              As, when the door
On a grave master closes,—in high glee,
From tasks released, and from o'erawing looks,
With faces brightened, and joy-flashing eyes,
The youthful scholars to long-prisoned tongues
Give utterance quick; on some old favorite sport
All eager to begin,—so, from the room
When passed the troubled king,—with mirthful tone,
And sparkling looks, the youthful-seeming guests
To Sethos 'gan discourse. Few words, yet bright;
Cheerful, yet modest, the fair princess spake;
Retiring, as it seemed; yet asking still
Attention, as her due, too scantly given:
But full of pleasant talk, and laughter light,
Her brother: till, the face distract and wan
Of Sethos noting; and his answers grave,
And brief; and his low voice, all spiritless,—
He, too, a sudden gravity put on;
And questioned of the cause which so oppressed
A spirit famed for mirth. As loth to tell
The secret of his sadness,—for awhile
Sethos replied not; but, more earnestly
By both his guests entreated; and, in chief,
By that most beauteous princess; nor with words
Alone, though pressing, but with tone and look
Of gentle, loving tenderness,—at length
He yielded; and, with eyes upcast, hands clenched,
Smiting his breast, broke forth.
                               "Heart-sick! heart-sick!
Sick as to death I am! My very soul
Trembles within me! Madness lies in wait,
Eager to clutch me! I have seen a sight,
To blind the eyes; and fetter tongue; and sink
A giant's strength to infant's! Oh! such sight!
Woman? No! goddess! Goddess? No! some thing,
Celestial passing, as gold passeth lead!
Oh! I have seen;—I cannot tell,—I see
Even now, in fancy's eye . . . . Impossible!

I must have dreamed! already must be mad!
Tell me, I pray thee, prince,—look on me well,—
And, as thou fear'st the gods, the plain truth speak,—
Am I not mad? Look in my face,—mine eyes,—
Listen my voice,—observe my words, my mien,
Gesture, and motion; all my nature mark,—
Then tell me, if thou darest, I am not mad!
Oh! sick! sick! sick!"
                    Thus raving, with clenched hands,
Face pallid, flashing eyes, and staggering gait,
To and fro walked he; sighing, groaning deep;
Unconscious of all presence; seeing nought,
Save, in wild fancy's gaze, that phantom shape;
Beauty celestial, yet with earthly fire
Of passion tinged; mixture, to mortal heart,
Fatal as deadliest poison to the blood;
Stark madness gendering; spirit and body, both,
By its dread spell subduing.
                            But the hand
Of the young prince aroused him; the strange touch,—
Like that of finger on a quivering string,—
His spirit-trembling calmed: and the strange voice,
Sweet, firm, and cheerful, soothed him,—as the tones
Of the kind watcher calm the terrified wretch,
Waking from dream of horror.
                            " Mad? sayst thou?"
Smiling, he questioned; " Mad? yea, mad, in sooth,
To *say* thou art mad; no more. Thine eye is bright,
But not with frenzy: healthily as mine,
Beateth thy pulse: thou art but drunk, not mad;
Drunken with draught of beauty, quaffed too quick,
On empty stomach. Why, myself had been
Like mad as thou; and of that self-same cup;
Had I not, body and spirit all, been filled
With love of other beauty; which no room
Left for even wine of heaven. Now,—truth declare:
Hast thou not trodden the enchanted land?
Inhaled its witching odour; seen therein
A flower that brightened heaven, illumined earth,
And dazzled thee with beauty, as the sun

With light would dazzle? Ah! thy looks speak out,
Saying, ''tis so.' That same is she we saw
This morning, journeying hither. To far lands
Fame hath her beauty trumpeted. 'Mong us,
Fair Rose of Goshen called: and, by that name,
Enquiring for her, quickly were we told
The garden where she grew; and wherein still
She glorifies the earth. Ah! mad was I,
Even as thou art, when at first I saw
The wonder of her beauty,—darkening eye,
And stunning sense; and the rich fragrance breathed
That floats about her ever; and first felt
The magic of her presence; fettering tongue,
And palsying limb. But when, all graciously,
She spake to us,—oh, even the very soul
With that immortal harmony was touched,
As by a rapturous death-stroke. Not one word
My lifeless tongue could answer! Even she,
My sister, fairest among thousands fair,
Stood speechless, motionless; in very awe
Of that o'erwhelming beauty. But, at last,
Strength calling up; and of mine own betrothed
In fancy picturing; and that deep love
I owed her, and still felt,—as from a trance,
My soul 'gan waken: as from bonds released,
My limbs felt power of motion; and my tongue
No longer lay as dead: I kneeled, I spake;
Her beauty I adored; but once more felt
Love-proof, and happy,—by my first great love,
Against all other armed. In sweet discourse
Then joined we,—she and I: but other mate
My sister found; a youth, of such rare gifts
In mind, and person, both, that, even for her,
The Rose of Goshen, fit companion he:
Nay, as we heard, already her betrothed;
And, if aught human *can* be, of such bliss
Not all unworthy. After brief time passed
In double converse thus,—with matchless grace,
Putting to shame the flowery style of courts,
She to the house invited us, and gave

Refection elegant; rich fruits, and wine,
And cates, for lightness, that might snow-flakes seem,
And yet substantial. But so exquisite,
Touched by her hands, were they,—that more like feast
Of mingled odours, breath of flowers, it seemed,
Than food material. Yet, most sweet of all
That banquet heavenly, was her rare discourse;
Wisdom and piety in music breathed,
That even the Powers of Evil might have turned
To goodness; made the miser free of heart;
Softened the cruel; humbled the most proud;
In black Despair waked Hope: for, *that* to hear,
Was a new life to feel; to shake off flesh;
Spring upward from the earth, and breathe sky-air;
And be etherial all. And when, at last,
In silence, yet with eloquence most sweet,
Graciously answering my prayer o'erbold,
Leave gave she that blest visit to renew,—
Had midnight wrapped us, noon-sun had burst forth,—
Such our souls' joyance! Nor, by courtly forms,
And ceremony cold, shall we be held;
But, ere pass many days, shall seek again
That heaven to enter: and, if thou with us
Wilt breathe celestial air; and in her shrine
The goddess worship, happy shall we be,
Thee to make happy thus. Yet, have thou care,
Prince Sethos, lest the witchery of her charms
Tempt thee to woo; for, Hebrew is the maid;
And, though the queen of beauty, *Egypt's* queen,
Thou knowest, may never be. Think then again,
Ere thou determine, or to go, or stay:
To smell the flower, 'neath which a precipice yawns;
Or to keep back; and lock up every thought
Of its divinest odour,—as the stone
Locks in a tomb the dead."
                          With flaming eyes,
Limbs rigid, open mouth, pale face, and breath,
Now stopped, now softly panting, Sethos stood,
Listening the wild discourse; each word of praise,
The maddest, deeming cold, unfitted, weak,

That glory to express: but when, at length,—
Fire pouring that seemed water,—those soft words
Of subtle caution spake the phantom-prince,
Out burst the frenzy.
                "No!—let Egypt's throne
Go to a leper, if 'twixt that and heaven
Must be my choice! The jewels of a crown,
Dirt were, with one glance of those eyes compared!
One hour with her, were worth a life of rule!
One tone of her sweet voice, worth all the lauds
Of bowing nations! All the hills of gold
In Pharaoh's treasure-cities, were but dross,
Valued against one touch of that blest hand!
Betrothed she is not,—must not—shall not be!
Nothing of mortal ever dare presume,—
Or, if . . . A Hebrew youth, thou saidst?—Black shame!
Pollution! *If* aught human,—surely then . . . . .
But I shall see her closer,—hear her voice,—
Haply may touch her: and, if mortal be
What seems celestial,—then, before her feet
Will I fall down and worship,—and my life,
And all life promises, to her give up,
So mine she'll deign to be. Oh time, speed on!
Bring quickly the blest morning; that, once more,
Dull earth I may forget, and live in heaven!"

ISRAEL IN EGYPT.

BOOK ELEVENTH.

All night, that beauteous vision of the day,—
In dreams intense, by subtle demon wrought,—
Vivid as life, to the eye of Sethos moved,
Stirring to yet worse madness: for, not now,
As in his waking hours, the loveliness,
The beauty exquisite, the matchless grace,
Alone inflamed him; but desires impure,
Thoughts carnal, images foul, that even to heat
Of fierce delirium fired him. Waking, he raved,
Cursing the unreal: sleeping, dreams again
The real seemed; the waking, a bad dream.
So on till morn; when, body fever-parched,
Mind staggering as with frenzy, he arose:
Plunged in the bath; then wandered out alone;
Sick, melancholy, loathing at all food;
But one thing seeing; for one only thing,
Body and soul insatiate.
            "*When* the day
That I again shall see her?" he exclaimed:
"*When* will all sky grow brighter at her voice?
When, eye to eye, will soul with soul discourse?
When shall I touch that hand of living light?
When take new life in the air she purifies? . . . .
But ha—that day, perchance, hath now been fixed;—
I had forgotten them: our noble guests

May marvel at mine absence. I must haste
To greet them: and to learn on what blest morn
Will come that double sunshine. Speed it, gods!
For, till I breathe that heaven, I suffocate
With this gross air of earth!"
                              That said, he went;
And to the princely guests,—though mind-distraught,—
Due honor; and amusements, to their years
And station fit; with hasty zeal, like one
Conscious of past neglect, 'gan offer them.
Nor failed he soon to question, of the time
When Goshen they should visit: and half life
Esteemed the short delay, when they the morn
Of the third day appointed. But he saw,—
Blaming, as cause, his own scant courtesy,—
That on the face of the young prince,—so bright
On the day past, and joyous,—shadow hung;
That in his tones, his motions, his discourse,
Sadness, or gloom, now mingled; as with one
Care-pressed, or pride-offended. Thence, the more
Strove he to feign a gladness of the heart;
And, with such pleasures as they would accept,
To speed away the hours. Airily laughed
The beauteous princess; and with cheerful word,
And sunny look, and movement full of life,
Strove both to gladden. But her brother's brow
All day was sad: and Sethos, with hot fits
Of resolute mirth, laughter, and boisterous talk,—
Strangely commixed with wild bewilderments,
That fixed both eye and tongue; and absent made
All objects present; present, but one thing,
Afar off absent,—all day vainly strove
To waft away the cloud. "The third blest morn!
The third blest morn!"—still in his soul he said;
"Oh! come, thou third blest morn; and bring me
    heaven!"

In that same night just past, while in the heart
Of Egypt's prince a tempting Spirit had poured
Passion's hot fire,—beside a chaster couch
Had the fallen Zuriel stood,—a dream impure
Subtly infusing. The last waking thoughts
Of Reuben, after prayer, had been of God;
His goodness unto Israel, in the days
Of Abraham, and long after: since that time,
How, as it seemed, His countenance had changed
Toward the once favored people,—their own sins
Surely the cause,—and to long slavery
He had resigned them. But remembrance, then,
Of that great promise, unto Moses given,
With rapture filled him. Glorious to his eye
Appeared the mighty gathering, when, from bonds,
All Israel should go forth: even like a hymn
From choiring angels, heard he the great voice
Of her glad children, singing unto God
The song of their thanksgiving, as they marched,
Happy and free, leaving their chains behind;
Their backs toward Egypt, and their faces bright
Still looking toward that happy Promised Land,
Flowing with milk and honey. But, on thoughts
Rapturous as these intent,—like crystal stream,
Now seen, now lost, amid a vast expanse
Of plain, hill, forest,—evermore stole in
One image, purest, loveliest. Themes most high,
Of God, and of His ways to man, no check
Disturbing felt, when on them, unaware,
Intruded that sweet aspect; for a song
Of prayer and praise embodied, Rachel seemed;
Holiness visible made: and when her voice
With tongues celestial mingled,—discord none
He felt, but even yet sweeter harmony;
One tuneful lyre the more. On heaven, and her,
Alternate musing, in serenest joy
The youthful Hebrew lay; till balmy sleep
Came on him; and ecstatic vision brought.

Standing, he seemed, before the open gate

Of the bright realms above; and looking in
On angels and archangels numberless;
Great shoals of living light; yet, mid that vast,
At large all moving; brighter all than flame
Of sun-touched diamond. Some, o'er golden harps
Bowing the head, swept their pure hands; and some,
With face uplifted toward a distant Shrine
Of inconceivable glory, sang aloud,
In harmony transcendent, choral hymns
Of gratitude and praise. As if a sea,
With all its waves had chaunted unto heaven,—
So numerous seemed the voices of those blest.

Some, singly, musing; some, in pairs, discourse,—
Like loving sisters,—holding, wandered nigh
Even to the gate; and soon, mid those who passed,—
With their benignant faces, sunlike bright,
Pouring upon him bliss,—a countenance,
Bright also, though with tint of earthly love,
He saw bent oft upon him; that same face
Which, on the day just past, even to his soul
Strange fire had shot,—terror, and wilderment,
All unconceived till then. Yet no amaze
Disturbed him now, amid heaven's courts to see
That form and countenance, angelic-fair,
Albeit earth-tinted. With the shining host,
Herself as bright, he saw the Syrian maid
Easily mingling; and her gentle voice,
All musical as theirs, discoursing heard.
And when, as oft, while lingering nigh, she turned
The deep, clear azure of her eyes on his,
Love told they, love intense; yet mortal love,
Not angel's unto angel: still, not gross,
Or aught unchaste denoting, seemed they yet;
But such as, 'twixt the maid and youth most pure,
Might speak a blameless heart-bond.
                              But, at length,
Wild change came o'er his vision. With quick step,
From out the portal came that Shining One,
And took him by the hand. On the instant, lo!
Heaven vanished; and within a sparry cave

By the sea's marge he stood; in hers, his hand
Still tenderly pressed; her bright, consuming eyes,—
As in that fiery onset of the day,—
Lightening again upon him: her low voice,
With mortal words, yet tones angelic-sweet,
Pouring in torrents passionate earthly love;
Till even from crown to foot a trembling came,
An ague-quaking on him; as if soul
Itself had caught distemperature, and shook
With every flesh-throb. Yet no power had he
To loose his hand; to turn away his gaze
From love-tormenting beams, which lines of steel
Seemed, rather than of light; with rigor such,
Eye unto eye they fixed.
                          A foot to move,
That he might fly,—impossible he felt,
As to leap Horeb: 'gainst her magic voice
Deaf ear to turn,—yet harder than to shut
The sense 'gainst doubled thunder. To the stake,
With chains of iron, hand and foot firm bound,
The martyr not more helpless stands exposed
To bigot's demon-rage, than now stood he,
To blaze of demon-love.
                          "Oh beauteous youth!"
She cried,—and on the brow, the eye, the lip,
Kisses of fire pressed: "life of all my life!
Soul of my soul! Immortal is my love!
Immortal must be thine: no pause,—no change!
Oh never come one smallest point of time,
To see thee absent from me! Two in one,
Together let us grow: to both one life,
One thought, one feeling only; so that each
Must with the other live; or, separate, die;
Die both, one lost to the other. Let our loves,
Though twain at first, be one; as two bright flames,
Touching, commingle, and but one become;
One, doubly bright and warm . . . Thy tongue is mute;
But thy heart speaks: through all thy beauteous frame,
Love's lightning plays: thine eyes are springs of fire:
Thy lips are in a tremble, as to breathe
Love's rapture: but thy youthful innocence

Dares not the utterance. Yet I know thou lovest;
Thou dost; thou shalt; for, ah! thy love to gain,
Heaven have I lost! Within those blissful realms
Never may I return! But, with thee blest,
Heaven's joys I wish not back. Thine earthly love
I know; and beautiful indeed is she
As aught not heavenly. But, with heavenly, earth
Nought hath, comparison worthy. Cold the love
Of earth-born, to the blaze of Spirit-fire!
She loves thee; but herself loves even more;
For, wouldst thou but embrace her, and kiss, thus,—
Sternly would she repulse thee; nay, command
To show thy face no more. Cold love, to mine!
For, reckless of all formal ceremony;
The altar and the priest esteeming nought,
While on thy beauty looking,—thus, and thus,
Close do I lock thee; kiss on burning kiss
Thus shower upon thee; and thy lovely cheek
On my warm bosom lay. Oh, pillowed there,
Let love's soft sleep fall on thee!"
                                        Shame, and fear,
And sense of foulest sin,—though all his soul
Revolted 'gainst the allurement,—tortured him,
Even as with death-pangs: but the terrible power
Was irresistible! Speak, or move, or look,
Save as she willed, he could not. As a flower
Bends its frail head beneath the steady breeze,
So, to the gentle pressure of her arm,
Bowed down his burning face, till on the soft
Ambrosial pillow, more than half revealed,
His hot cheek touched. In vain to lift it thence
He struggled; vainly strove his eyes to close
Against the deadly beauty; all in vain
Strove breath to hold 'gainst fragrance exquisite,—
The love-mist floating o'er it!
                                "Come, fair youth,"
She said, at length, and raised him; "those bright waves
Invite us: like a bath of sunbeams, they
Will wanton round our limbs; yet cool the heat
Of this noon hour: there let us plunge, and sport;

And, afterwards, in the soft twilight shade
Of the cave's farthest depths, where rose-leaf couch,
Odorous and fresh awaits us, all day lie,
And whisper thoughts of love. . . Thou tremblest more;
Thine earthly modesty, a phantasm, holds
O'er thy mild soul unworthy tyranny.
Be strong, and vanquish it. With angel's love,
Mingles not foolish shame: 'tis earth-born, gross,
To pure love hostile. Rouse thee then, sweet youth;
Break the poor fetter. See, beside the marge
Of the bright wave we stand. Fling boldly off
Those earth-clouds, woven in looms; and, spirit-clear,
Shine forth in sunlight. Look; I lead the way."

  She ceased; and on herself his terrified eyes
Fixed irresistibly.
      But, load on load,
Would crush at length the elephant; and shame
On shame upheaped, and agony for sin,
Or sense of sin, though on him forced, and loathed,—
Doubled, and yet redoubled, shook his soul,
Till life itself seemed passing. With quick hands
Her robe she doffed, and cast upon the ground,
And stood, a second daylight;—but, to him,
A dread incarnate lightning! Smiling fire,
Toward him then sprang she; opened wide her arms,
And hotly clasped him.
     As, in tropic climes,
Falls the fierce sun-stroke, smiting unto death,—
Even so, beneath that terrible beauty-stroke,—
Beauty like heaven's, but, ah! impure as hell,—
Down sank he, as if dead. One tremulous cry,
Falling, he uttered; "Help me, oh my God!"
Then dropped; and saw no more.
       But that faint sound
Aroused him; or celestial aid, perchance,
Came on the prayer; for, suddenly, he woke,
Quivering and panting; and found all a dream!
Sunshine succeeding blackness of earth's depths,
Poor contrast were to his transcendent joy,

Guiltless awaking from foul dream of sin.
Guiltless in will; but ah! not guiltless all,—
Shuddering, he thought: for, whence, but from himself,
From his own heart impure, could have arisen
The sin-clouds that had soiled him; wrapped his soul
As in the smoke of hell; had shut him out
From sight of heaven, of angels, and of God!
Whence, whence, but from himself! In agony
He wept, and prayed forgiveness; and was cheered.
As, in the silent night, a distant strain
Of slow, sweet music steals upon the ear,
Lulling the sick, or sorrowful, to rest,—
So, on his spirit-ear a sweet voice stole,
Hushing his grief; whispering that, welcomed not,
In minds even purest might a foul thought creep,
Or be thrust in; and leave no stain behind:
That God had seen his struggles; had his strength,
And weakness known; and would not from him ask
Beyond his power to do. Like a still sea,
Smiling in sunshine after storm of night,
Quiet he lay at last. Soft sleep came on,
Gentle as twilight of a summer's eve,
When all the winds are hushed; and earth and sky
Seem musing on their God. Like pale, pure fire,
Noiselessly trailing o'er the clear dark vault,
Ere night shuts closely in,—so on his mind,
Heaven meditating, half in slumber wrapped,—
Last image, seen a moment, and then lost
In dreamless sleep,—as if from heaven it looked,
And went again,—shone his blest Rachel's face;
A gleam of holiness. Her look of love
Through his whole being seemed to penetrate,
Like a new life breathed in. All clear again,
Happy and calm he felt; and, smiling, slept.

In that same hour, while o'er the Hebrew youth,
Permitted so, the sorcery of hell
Wrought its dread charms,—beside that purest couch
Where lay the Hebrew maiden, Aziel stood,—

The delicate Spirit, for a like bad work
Appointed; on the spotless to bring stain;
The virgin snow to sully with foul foot;
With sulphur-clouds the ether, heavenly clear,
To blacken, and make gross.   Ah! fairest flower,
The poison-blast is breathing on thee now!
In holy night, when sweetest dew should fall,
Refreshing, life-sustaining,—creeps an air
Pestiferous, yea with deadliest venom charged,
To wither up thy beauty; sap thy strength;
Kill thy life-essence; and a blackened stem
Leave rotting, where had bloomed earth's loveliest flower!
Will heavenly aid protect thee? or, as he,
The loved-one of thy soul, wilt thou be left
Alone to abide the onset?   What canst thou,—
By innocence only, strong,—against the wiles
Of him, from all hell's millions singled out,
As fatal most, for beauty, gentleness,
Grace, tenderness; and eloquence to speak,
In music ravishing, all seductive thoughts,—
Love-sparks at first, but kindling soon to flame,—
What canst thou, maiden blest!   Yet there thou liest,
Beauteous and pure as angel: and the foe
Bends over thee; and on thy fancy tries,—
Gentle of tint at first, then warmer hued,—
Visions of sin to paint.   A dream he raised
Of a young king, from some far distant land,
Solely by fame of her great beauty brought,
To woo her for his queen.   In mortal form,
Never before had lived perfection such,
In face, shape, voice, air, motion, eloquence,
As in that royal youth, who,—standing now,—
Now kneeling,—now upstarting to his feet,—
In very ecstacy of passion wild;
Yet graceful ever; beautiful and bright,
Even when vehement most,—like a great stream
From earth outgushing, poured love's torrent forth.
First, chastely cool, as bent to woo a bride;
Soon, amorously warm, as if to inflame

With passion loose, a mistress : quickly then,
Exciting words and tones ; foul looks, fierce shot
Of arrowy fire, to white heat raised, from eyes
Distent with carnal longing,—'gan to urge
The terrible assault : at length, raised arms,
Hands quivering with mere madness of desire
To touch, to embrace, drew near her.
        So his spell
Essayed her fancy : yet, amazed, he saw
That on her soul impression made it none,
More than would dew on granite. By one throb,
Not quicker beat her heart. Those burning words
Innoxious fell, as a poor idiot's talk,
In tongue unknown ; and, when the love-mad shape,
With arms outstretched, drew nigh her,—she but raised,
Though sleeping, her own arm, repellantly,
And lo ! in his despite, the wicked dream
Fled from her ; and he saw that, in its place,
A holy vision came. Though darkest night,
Yet, clearly as in sunshine, his keen eye
All things beheld. Throughout the fierce assault,
Calm as a cloudless sky, that exquisite face,
Like to a sleeping infant's had reposed :
But now,—the hell-storm past, and holy dream
Lifting her spirit,—underneath their lids
He saw the meek, adoring eyes upturned ;
The pure lips gently moved ; and heard the breath
Of pious aspiration toward her God.

 He saw, and heard, and trembled. Deepest awe
Through his whole Essence ran. To harm her more,
Powerless he felt ; nor mourned the bad power lost.
For, on that chosen maiden while he looked,
Her seraph-face, as with celestial fire
Illuminate, in fervor of deep prayer,—
Came on him, spirit-thrilling, like a ray
Of that same light, all unapproachable,
Whose splendor rounds the throne. He stood transfixed !

 As when an exile,—in some far-off land,

Absent long years, and hopeless of return,—
Wandering at evening, lonely, sad of heart,
Musing of home, and kindred ever lost,—
Mid the deep silence catches suddenly,
From hill-side, or hushed valley, faint, yet clear,
His own loved country's music;—simple song,
Perchance, with which his nursing mother lulled
His childish sorrow; or a plaintive air,
Sung by the maiden he had loved, and lost;
Or proud chaunt of victorious fatherland,
Now blotted from the nations,—sick at heart,
He sighs, he groans, he trembles, weeps, kneels down,
Lifts quivering hands to heaven, and prays for death
To loose him from his misery,—even so,
But with intenseness thousandfold more keen,
Felt the fallen angel, hearing once again
Heaven's music in that prayer; in that pure face,
Heaven's radiance once more seeing. As a dream
Of ages long gone by,—the infinite bliss
Of holiness, in presence of his God,
Came vividly on him. Like the first dim grey
Of opening dawn, repentance on him stole:
He sighed, as Spirits sigh; he groaned, he wept;
He bowed the head, like one all desolate;
All hopeless; through eternity all lost!

But, in awhile, again erect he stood,
As one ashamed of weakness that had passed;
And with himself, in agitated mood,
Self-contradictory oft, thus held commune.

"Poor folly this! What now with heaven have I!
What unto me its holiness; its bliss!
Have I not lost them ever! What avails
To look upon this purity, which brings
Celestial air about me,—never more
To me the breath of life! Allegiance, now,
To my companions fallën, not to Him
Who spurns them, owe I. Yet, the strict command
By Satan given, and by the general voice,

Have I not failed to accomplish? Am I weak
For evil made, by gazing on the good?
Or, haply, not my weakness may it be,
But strength within herself, my power to foil?
Or strength from heaven sent down? Angelic might
Hovers, perchance, about her; and a shield,
Impierceable by ill, holds over her.
Yet, surely, of such presence, were it here,
Had I felt token. But, whate'er the cause,
Alike my failure is; steel panoply
Not more impervious to the rose's thorn,
Than her pure soul to keenest darts of sin.
What then? Shall I new guile attempt? new dreams,
To stain her holy spirit? 'Tis my task.
Here came I, not to reason, but obey:
And, disobedient, what may I not dread!"

He paused, and gazed upon the sleeping maid;
Listening the fervent prayer that still went up
From scarcely moving lips. Another shock,—
A lightning flash of bitterest remorse,—
Pierced through his whole Essential. "Never more!
Oh never more," he cried, " shall breath of sin
From me thy pure soul touch! Oh God! Oh God
Thou All-Beneficent, All Great, All Wise!
What madness seized us; what ingratitude;
To fall away from Thee: Thine easy rule,
For our own happiness best, to disobey!
What could the mightiest of archangels hope,
Against Omnipotence! . . . For myself, true is,
By folly fell I,—not original sin
Within myself conceived; but swayed by words
Of greater far than I. Yet, their offence,
Mine also made I;—to their bad design
My weakness lending. . . . Ah, thou greatest, worst
From thy ambition, Satan, what dire ills
On all have fallën, whom thine eloquence,
Thy reasonings specious, thy tremendous power,—
All but omnipotent seeming,—lured to join
In thy most foul rebellion! . . . And even yet

Thy madness rages; by all evils past
Untaught, Heaven's Lord, and thy poor self, to know!
Still the mere dust-speck, 'gainst the universe,
Thou'dst put into the scale; and balanced hold!
Oh! if thy God, Almighty to inflict,
Were not as great in pity to withhold,
How hadst thou fared! how all who with thee fell!
Exile from Heaven a tyrannous doom ye think,
Though free throughout Creation else to roam:
What if we still,—as when at first outcast,—
Prisoned, and motionless, in yon blank orb
Had suffered punishment; light ever quenched;
Eternity before us, without hope! . . .
Oh God! thy pitying hand, I feel, it was,
Which lift that burthen from us! Yet, alas!
How did we thank Thee! Goodness infinite
Alone, thine anger just could have subdued,
When, for Thy boon, we gave ingratitude;
Scoffed at Thy lenience; and, with vauntings mad,
Even threatened Thy dominion! Did a worm
Boast to hurl down the sun from out his place,
Not greater were the folly! . . . Yet, with them,
Fallen as they are, for ever am I cast;
A mole-hill amid mountains: and, as least,
Perforce must yield obedience; or abide
Their uttermost wrath. . . . But, weakest of them all
In act,—strong for endurance feel I now;
And will the trial make: for their command
Never will I perform: this heavenly pure
Shall not by me be stained. I made essay
Toward the bad bidding, and was foiled. Perchance,
So should I plead, excuse it would be held;
And censure I might 'scape. But no! as breath
Of plague, plague genders, so the sight of good,
With love of good infects. I will not lie,
One truth withholding. Fall on me what may,
I will avow that, not my *strength* alone,
But my *will* also failed, their work to do:
That, could I, by the impulse of one breath,
Steep her pure soul in foulness, I would live

In pangs of mortal death ten thousand years,
Rather than breathe it! Oh, even bliss it were,
The worst to endure, in such cause suffering!
For, though, before inexorable God,
Repentance useless; prayer impossible;
Heaven lost to me for ever,—yet I feel,
That, for itself alone, the good is good,
Beyond all pleasure, and all profit else.
Let me lie prisoned, knowing that from sin,
Through my weak aid, that heavenly-pure-one 'scaped,—
And happier were I, than, from sun to sun,
Radiantly flashing through the universe.
Rest thee, then, fairest flower of mortal growth,—
Or of heaven rather, to this earthly soil
For but brief time transplanted. Were my power
Strong as my will, never should breath of sin
Be cast upon thee more. My task it is
To hover o'er thee; poison thy pure thoughts.
My station I will keep; but, as I may,
Defend, not harm thee. Oh that I might dare
On God cry out to shield thee! or might speed
Even to Heaven's gate, and call an angel down,
To guard thee from all ill! But I am lost,
And weak,—and who would hearken to my prayer!
All that I can, I will. To die for thee,—
Far as a Spirit can be made to die,—
Prepared I wait; though on me misery fall
Heavier than on created thing beside!
Yea, miserable most of all that lives,
Too surely must I be! from Heaven exiled,
For sin 'gainst God; from my companions driven,
For sin 'gainst them; in some drear solitude,
Sentenced, perchance, long cycles to abide,
Mournful and silent; by no sound, or sight,
Of living thing e'er visited; my groans
And sighs, sole music; conscience, ever harsh,
For sin rebuking; and a timid voice,
Excuse in weakness pleading,—sole discourse!
But, my one act of good will lighten all.
On thy pure spirit, maiden blest, I'll think;

And that shall be my music : on the bliss
Of Heaven, as once I knew it,—though all lost,—
Thousands of years, unpausing, will I muse ;
Till, haply, in sweet vision it may come
Gloriously back upon me ; as, in dreams,
To miserable man a new life comes ;
Pleasure, for pain ; for sorrow, bringing joy.
What though, at waking, all mere shadow proves,
Yet real as reality it is,
Unknowing that he sleeps. And such a dream,—
Dream, haply, of long ages,—may be mine :
And I in Heaven, amid the unnumbered blest,
As in the time of old, may seem to live ;
Of sin unconscious, of the wrath of God,—
Holy and happy, while, alas ! from bliss
Cast out ; by all good angels shunned ;
By even the fallen driven forth, with scorn and hate,—
In some drear solitude my spirit pines,
For ever fading ; like a plant of earth,
From light shut out, and warmth, and rain, and dew ;
Till, a dead stalk, it drops to earth, and rots,
And melts into the air. And, though like end
This Essence cannot know ; yet, greater far
The misery, in worst gloom of death to live,
Than to die wholly,—utterly extinct ;
True Nothing to be made,—as once I was,
As I would supplicate again to be,
If, of offended God, I so dared ask ! . . . . .
Ah ! as *thou* pray'st, blest maiden, might *I* pray,—
Unwearied, through eternity, would I
Beseech forgiveness ! But all hope is dead !
I cannot pray ! not even in thought, dare I
A supplication whisper ! Heaven is gone !
Gone, gone for ever ! God to me is lost !
I must endure my doom ! Yet, though no prayer
To Thee, incensed Creator, may I breathe,—
In my great misery let me humbly own,
Less far than my desert my suffering is !
Bowed then in spirit as to lowest dust,
O merciful God, I thank Thee ! " . . . .

                                At those words,
Through his whole Being suddenly there ran
A feeling wonderful; unknown till then;
Soothing as sweet sleep after frenzy's rage;
As plaintive music, following tempest's roar;
As cool breeze on the desert's fiery breath;
As water-drops upon a burning wound!
In a strange ecstacy awhile he stood,
Then with himself thus questioned.
                                "What is this?
I dare not think . . . and yet . . . but no! no! no!
Impossible it is!   No hope *can* be
Of mitigated wrath!   My punishment,—
The punishment of all the rebel host,—
By Him Unchangeable pronounced, must be
Alike unchangeable! . . . And yet, not so:
For, on our primitive doom, came there not sign
Of wrath subsiding, or of pity awaked?
Our darkness was made light; our dungeon-doors
Were opened; and power given all space to roam.
Dare I, then, hope that, in my wretchedness,
God hath beheld me; and, in mercy, chased
A Spirit-darkness from me?   Ah, no, no!
My misery is deserved!   Nought have I done,
Nought *can* I do, to purge away offence;
And, so, dare dream of pardon.   'Twas but trick
Of Spirit-nature; such as, in poor man,
Fancy oft plays; sounds giving to the ear,
Sights to the eye, substance to sense of touch,
When, truly, all around him is but nought! . . . .
Or, rather, was it not, thou blessed one,
An effluence sent from *thee*? the genial warmth
From thy pure spirit-fire? the rays benign
From thy clear nature,—with heaven's sacred light
Filled to o'erflowing, as yon moon serene,
With the sun's glory is filled?   Yea, even so:
Thy light it was which my dark spirit illumed,
As sunbeams fire the cloud: or fragrance 'twas,
Celestial, from thee, heavenly flower, breathed forth
On my polluted sense; more exquisite

Than balmiest breeze of spring, on haggard wretch,
First from the close-pent sick-room, or foul jail,
To light and air brought forth. . . . . Yet, if, from thee,
Holy and pure, to my fallen nature comes
Aught of celestial effluence,—surely still
Within me lives,—though in eternal death
Seeming all quenched,—some latent spark of fire,
Heaven-born; and capable, perchance. . . . Ah no!
As the stone wall gives echo to sweet sounds,
Seeming to speak, while yet no life it hath,—
So I, to heavenly purity all dead,
But seem to feel it; but an echo give,
To its divinest music,—no response,
Life, and like nature tokening. As man's clay,
After the breath hath fled, to what it was
In flush of youth,—even such my spirit is now,
To its original nature. I have sinned;
Have God displeased; my place in Heaven have lost!
The punishment is just! What I have earned,
Unmurmuring will I bear. And more must bear
Than even my desert: since, not alone
Heaven's punishment for disobedience, due,
Will lie upon me; but avengement harsh,
Unjust, from those to whom obedience none,
Save by God disobeying, could I yield. . . . .
Yet choice there cannot be. Offended Heaven
Will not remit my doom; offended Hell
Will pour its vengeance on me. Not the less,
One heavenly ray will light my prison-house;
One air of heaven will be my breath of life;
One tone of heavenly music bring me bliss:
For, through eternity, of God, and Heaven,
Shall all my musings be: in every thought,
In every act, if power to act remain,
One sole rule will I follow,—so to think,
So do, as if in presence of my God,
Sinless again I stood. . . . . . Even now I feel
As though a wafting of celestial air
Had cooled Hell's fever;—the reward, perchance,
Of conscience, for my one good act performed;

For future good resolved. . . . . Or, is it more?
Can it be God-bestowed,—not inward-born?
A token that . . . . but ah! I dare not think!
One glimpse of Heaven, would be as death to me;
Death by joy's lightning! No, no; never again,
In its reality, may that bliss be mine! . . . . .
But, in my visions, will I cover o'er
All the blank vast with sun-bright counterfeits
Of its exceeding glories. Henceforth, such
Shall be my Heaven; though in profoundest depth
Of dead space buried; where nor light, nor sound,
Nor any form of life hath ever been,
Since there Creation perished! . . . . . Maiden blest,
To thy pure nature owe I this new life!
Thy holiness hath re-created good
In my lost spirit! Would that I could see
A band of glorious angels bear thee up,
And place thee, with thy countenance more bright
Than sunbeams, near the Shrine; and hear thy voice
Praising the Omnipotent, All Wise, All Good;
And, haply, mercy on the contrite fallen,
Of the All-Merciful praying! Meantime, here,—
Sent as thine enemy, but to watchful guard,
Far as I may, by thy sweet strength transformed,—
Gratefully wait I. Be thy slumber calm;
Happy thy waking; blissful all thy days;
Till thy pure spirit pass; and Heaven's glad gates
Fly open, to receive thee evermore!"

ISRAEL IN EGYPT.

BOOK TWELFTH.

WHILE thus the gentle Aziel, at the sight
Of holiness, to thoughts of Heaven recalled,
Stood contrite, watchful,—by far different couch,
A stronger Spirit wrought.
      With ugliness
And age, ill sorted, Egypt's fairest dame,
Loathing her jealous and decrepid spouse,
Door barred against his entrance, slept alone.
Of youthful lover thought she—loved, and lost;
Yet ne'er forgotten; ardently desired;
Mused on by day, and dreamed of all the night,
Till the warm longing, to a fever heat
Of passion had fired her blood. Her secret wish
Knew Satan; and how prone she was to fall
Before temptation; nay, if vision-fired,
Herself to be the temptress; as, of yore,
The wife of Potiphar. Though repulsed was *she*
In her loose wooing, yet far different end
Augured the Arch Fiend now; so exquisite
The beauty of this dame; her eyes so bright,
Though languishing; the rose upon her lip,
So fresh; so fragrant her soft-panting breath;
Her words so all-persuasive; her low voice

So like impassioned melody. This was she
Whom he had chosen, that pious youth to ensnare
In sinful dalliance; by his overthrow,
Hoping God's merciful scheme to bring to nought.
A Spirit, therefore, sent he who, in dreams—
Visions voluptuous of his youthful charms—
Her passions to such fury should excite,
That, meeting him, if wooed not, she herself
Madly should woo; yea, with such fervid heat,
That, human, he must melt.
      Throughout the night,
The obedient demon on her fancy wrought
Pictures so vivid, that reality
More real could not seem. As if in life,
She saw the beauteous Reuben; heard his voice,
Trembling, impassioned, breathing burning love;
Felt his lips madly pressed upon her own;
His arms in hot embrace entwining her;
And thought not of her marriage vow; nor fled;
Nor aught resisted. Thus till dawned the day.
When she awaked, and found 'twas but a dream,—
Heart-sick for love, realities she scorned;
And death had welcomed,—with that phantom, first,
One blissful hour to live. All sight of man
And woman hating; in her chamber locked,
She panted on the couch; food loathing, thirst
Quenching incessantly, yet thirsting still.

The next night also came the tempting fiend,
And with same dreams inflamed her; till, to the height
Feeling the frenzy mounting,—brain on fire,
Blood boiling,—up from bed, shrieking, she sprang,—
Flew to the bath—plunged headlong: there, till noon,
Laughing, and weeping, panting, sighing, lay;
Then, cold and strengthless, rose; in loose attire
Tremblingly clad herself; and to her couch,
With foot unsteady, walked, and sought repose.
Thus, night by night, the demon maddened her.

Three nights to Sethos also were renewed

The visions of the first; nay even more
To frenzy stirring. But, when came, at last,
That blest appointed day, on which, once more,—
In the reality, not in mocking dreams,—
His eyes ineffable beauty should behold;
His thirsty ears the music of her voice
Might drink; till sense and soul, with that sweet draught
Intoxicate, must reel—then up at once,
Blithe as a mounting lark, from bed he sprang:
Found his guests waiting him; and, ere the sun
Three hours on earth his molten gold had showered,
With them, toward Goshen was he speeding on.

Gay as a butterfly mid summer flowers,
The phantom-princess smiled, and talked, and laughed.
But, solemn as deep twilight in a wood,
Silent, and sad of look,—the shadowy prince,
On the blest maiden musing, word spake none,
Save answer briefest: and, recalling dreams
Of the past nights, and picturing bliss to come
In actual presence of that visioned one,
Silent rode Sethos also; the short way
A tedious journey deeming: till, at length,
Heart leaping, and limbs trembling, at the gate
Of Kohath he drew rein; and, without word,
The phantoms followed.   At the porch arrived,—
Joy to his soul! he heard, that, all alone,
Her parents absent, the fair daughter sat;
Yet begged that they would enter. More and more
Tremulous at heart, he followed; and beheld
The object of his vision in broad day,
Of his warm dreams at night. But, though the same,
In outward form, and beauty past compare,
As modestly she rose, and welcomed them,—
Yet, in the silent language of the face,
Motion, and gesture, all unlike she was,
As crystal air of morning, to hot fog;
As sunbeams, to coarse fire. And, though her voice,
In every tone was music—yet, unlike

To that imagined by him, heard in dreams,
As solemn strain of Memnon's harp at morn,
To the loose ditty of night reveller.
Eyes burning, and knees trembling, he advanced,
And bowed before her; while his name and rank
The sprightly princess spake. Wondering, yet calm,
Rachel received the words; and courteously,
With eyes cast down, and gently bowing head,
Due greeting gave.
     "I sorrow, gracious lord,
That, for such presence most unfit, alone
I should be found; for ignorant all I am
Of ceremony meet. Let wish sincere
To show respectful welcome, stand in place
Of courtly knowledge. In a little while
My father will return: and, till he come,
I seek not to enquire why honored thus
Our humble dwelling. So your pleasure be,
Meantime, I beg you sit; and such poor fare
As we can offer, taste."
     The faltering tongue
Of Sethos vainly strove reply to make.
Not woman's beauty only, though unmatched,
Wrought on him thus; but demon-witchery,
Inflamed his soul: and, for his inward eye,
Poured sun-rays on the living diamond.
Yet, in her presence,—maugre the fiend's might,—
Aught sensual in a moment had been quenched,
As murky torch, stamped out. By purity awed,
Silent, perforce, thus was he. With white lips,
And throbbing heart, as if entranced, he sat,
Gazing on charms unearthly; drinking in,
With the few words she spake, such rapture high,
That, for awhile, to his distracted mind,
Speech had no meaning: it was sound, alone;
Music articulated. She, in chief,
The seeming princess, voluble and light,
Silence prevented, which, else, soon had come:
For the mild virgin little had to say
To visitors like those,—their absence more

Desiring, than such converse as might be
'Twixt minds so all unlike: and few words spake
The phantom-prince,—at his first visit, bright,
And sparkling as the dew-drops of the morn,—
But, now, all sad as coming on of night,
With rain and sobbing wind: so mourned he loss
Of innocence, and favor of his God,
And happiness of Heaven.
      But soon, with fruits,
Light cates and wine, the board was spread; and talk
More cheerful grew; for Sethos largely quaffed,
His heart to strengthen; and, though still his ear
Thrilled, as at sound celestial, when she spake;
And though, when hers encountering, still his eye
Sank, as if sun-struck,—yet, with freer tongue,
Though faltering oft, began he to discourse.
But, of such things as women most might please,—
Tasteful apparel, dancing, music, love,
Or other pleasure light,—no word he breathed;
Unfitness feeling, in that presence chaste,—
Even as in temple sacred to the gods,—
On follies to converse. Of Israel's state,
Her sufferings, hopes, in friendly words he talked;
Deep sympathy feigning,—by the arch fiend so
Unconsciously impelled,—and question put
Of the religion by her priesthood taught;
And purpose firm avowed,—when to his hand
Should come the rule o'er Egypt,—from her bonds
To give her full release: so that, erelong,—
Well pleased with seeming goodness,—to his words
More cheerfully she answered; and, at times,
A modest smile poured on him, which,—like ray
Of sunlight glancing through quick flying clouds,
And brightening all it touches,—in his soul
Ecstacy kindled.
     But, at length, came in,—
Wondering such unexpected guests to find,—
The master of the house; and, after him,
The bashful Reuben. Rising gracefully,—
First, with few words and simple, Rachel named

Her father to the guests, and them to him;
Then, to the door,—where, pallid, and with look
Almost of terror, gentle Reuben stood,
As longing to escape,—walked cheerfully,
And took him by the hand, and forward led;
And to the marvelling heir of Egypt named,
With calm, unblushing face, as her betrothed;
And him to Reuben, as a princely friend
To their oppressëd nation; and intent
To be a mighty helper. Scarcely word
Could Reuben utter; though, with kindness feigned,
Sethos his homage answered,—for his eye
Again that beauty terrible had caught,
Which in his dreams wellnigh had maddened him;
And his soul trembled. With a downcast face,
Lest on him should that living lightning strike,
He sat in silence; nor an eye dared lift.
Yet nought to him the phantom-princess said,—
Knowing what mortal wile awaited him,—
But to her brother-shade, in soft discourse,
Addressed herself; while, in more earnest talk,
Apart the others sat. For, when her sire
Obeisance due to such illustrious guests
Had rendered,—Rachel, filled with gratitude,
Spake of the noble things by the young prince
Designed for Israel; when the time should come,
And his should be the crown; and how his heart
For their afflictions sorrowed; and the more,
That now his power was nought.
                            With strongest hope
Though sire and daughter both alike were filled,
That, long ere time so distant seeming, free
From all her bonds would Israel have become,—
Yet, for the kind intent, thankful were both,
And thankfulness acknowledged.
                            "For myself,"
Exclaimed the prince, fiend-taught, "my prayers alone
For Israel unto Pharaoh might be vain:
But, would thy beauteous daughter, Kohath, stand,

Petitioner for your people, at his throne,
All could he not refuse her. Their worst wrongs,
Perforce he must amend: for, though severe,
Not marble is he; and no heart of flesh
To innocence and loveliness like hers,
Could give harsh answer. Wilt thou, Rachel, go?"
He said, quick turning toward her. "I myself
Will be thy herald; with attendance meet,
Will guard thee hence to Zoan; by the hand
Will lead thee to the steps of Pharaoh's throne;
And, while thou standest, kneel, and beg for thee.
He cannot all refuse; but he may pause,
Doubtful how much to grant: then shall my voice
Stir him to justice, and to nobleness;
And thou wilt triumph; and thy people all
Will hail thee their deliverer."
                              With warmth
He spake; for well the wine his heart had cheered,
And Satan words inspired, and strengthened him.
But Rachel modestly inclined her head,
And answered; "Most unfit, my lord, am I
For such great mission. Poor I am in words;
Unused to speech with strangers; most of all,
With those of loftiest station; childlike weak
In subtleties of reasoning, and in art
Of soft persuasion. Tongue-tied should I stand
In presence of the king; and, at my best,
More ill should do, than good: but, wouldst *thou*, prince,
Our intercessor be,—to thee, methinks,
Perforce he must give ear; and our worst bonds,
At least would slacken, if not wholly loose."

"Thy timid nature knows not its own strength,"
Sethos made answer; "for thine eloquence
Of look and mien,—although no word thou spake,
For virgin bashfulness,—would move him more
Than best speech of his sons, and counsellors.
But, as thou wilt, so be it. Even this day
Will I my father move to pity you,

And lighten Israel's burthens; and thy thanks,—
Though thereby I should anger him,—reward
Richest will be."
Gently she bowed her head,
Betokening gratitude; and Sethos then,—
The demon prompting still,—his speech pursued.

"Toward your whole people, it may be, his heart
At once I may not soften: failing so,
No private evils are there,—on yourselves,
Or your near relatives, or friends,—with which
I next may move him?"
Kohath answering not,
Rachel then mildly thus,
"If not o'erbold,
In presence of my father, to reply,
Thus would I say. Our private wrongs press not
On us more hardly, than, on all our race,
Their private wrongs: nay, not one tenth so much
As on the many press they: selfish then,
Unjust, nay impious were it, from our tithe
Release to ask; while yet the load should lie
Full weight on all the rest. In sight of God,
Surely would such be wickedness."
"Thy words
Holy and true had been," he made reply,
"Were your own private good the one sole aim;
Justice, and charity, regarded not:
But, for *you* pleading, equally for all,
In the end, would be my prayer. One stone, at first,
The builder lays,—not the whole pyramid.
Justice to you, would be the precedent
For justice unto all. The small sharp point
First entered, the whole needle passes through.
But, what if point, and eye, and all between,
At once thou'dst press for entrance? Seest thou not,
Fair maiden, that right reason guides me here;
Prudence advising, but injustice none?
I would not thy fine nature so insult,

As to commend for conduct, aught less good
Than the just gods would sanction."
                                  Ceasing then,
He looked upon her, waiting her reply;
And in low tone she answered.
                          " Gracious prince,
No words have I for subtle argument.
What thou hast said, is true : the pyramid,
Stone after stone is laid; one single stone
The whole vast work beginning ; and true is,
That, of the needle, the small point alone
First must have entrance,—since all other way
Impossible were; but not thence just, methinks,
Or, by a like necessity, as true,
That, from among a people, all enslaved,
Some few should be selected for a grace,
Denied unto the rest. The pyramid
Must stone by stone be built; since choice is none,
Or power, by other mode to work at all;
Nor, to that stone first laid, is favor shown;
Nor favor doth it feel: but choice, and power,
Both have ye, if so willing, for release
Of Israel's heaviest bonds : and, by same stroke,
The chains from the whole people may strike off,
As from one family : while, if alone
To few ye freedom grant,—them taking first,
As first stones of your human pyramid,—
In all beside great discontent must be :
And even the favored, if by right mind ruled,—
Feeling that grace to them, were wrong on wrong
To all the rest,—rather in bonds would stay,
Than so unjustly 'scape."
                        " My gracious prince,"
Said Kohath, rising, and his reverend form
Inclining as he spake; " an answer just,
Surely hath Rachel spoken. In God's sight
Unrighteous were we, freedom for ourselves
Accepting, while our people yet lay bound.
No special favor, then, to our own house
Ask we, or wish for : nor, of our free will,

Would from the king receive. But, special *wrongs*
Also there are: and, whether on ourselves,
Or friends, or strangers, all alike may we,
Or they,—for *such*, with justice, ask redress.
Listen, I pray thee, to example brief.
In Zoan is a ruler, aged, and rich,
But covetous of more,—Maimon his name;
Well known to thee, past doubt. In all the land
Lives not a harsher master. From his slaves,
Blood would he have for sweat, so his increase
Might thereby be the greater. In his bonds
Groan some, the far-off kindred of this youth,—
My son, in time, to be. For their release,
Much substance have we offered,—I, and he,
The father of young Reuben: but with wrath
All offers hath he scorned. If thou, great prince,
To mercy wouldst incline him" . . . . .
       On his speech,
By Satan prompted, quickly Sethos broke.

"Set thou thy mind at rest," he said; "be sure
The wrong shall be redressed: but not in way
That ye have tried. O'er many hundred slaves
Though Maimon rules, yet one there is, to whom
Himself is but a slave. The loveliest dame
Throughout all Egypt, is that old man's wife;
His worship, and yet dread: for, not alone
In beauty, eminent o'er all is she;
But in her lofty mind, her spirit great,
Her love of justice, mercy, charity;
Her loathing of all meanness. She, be sure,
Of his hard rule is ignorant; and, taught,
Quickly will end it. Go thou with me then,
Even this same day, young Reuben. To her house
I will myself conduct thee: by the hand
Lead thee before her; and beseech for thee
Indulgent hearing, and quick remedy
For all thou showest amiss."
       Deep gratitude
Stirring within him, Reuben rose, and bowed;

And, though scarce audibly,—for bashfulness,
And joy, with fear commingling,—thus replied.
" Humbly I thank thee, prince. Yet, if I dared,
I would implore that some one better fit,
In years, experience, and in use of speech,
Might plead for them: for I no confidence have,
Like dexterous speakers; and before that dame,
So great, and good, and beautiful,—should stand
Awe-stricken, and the matter quite forget."

" Thy very failings, Reuben, are thy strength,"
Said Sethos, smiling : " for a diffident face ;
A faltering tongue; the reverential look
Of modest youth toward beauty,—all will plead,
Making best reasons better. Thou thyself
Singly must speak before her. Private thus,
Gently she'll hear; encourage thee; and aid
To give thy meanings utterance; so that soon
Will modest boldness come; and with free speech
Thou'lt vent thy wrongs. But, if a third be there,
Less calmly will she hear her lord impeached;
Less gracious will she be; less prompt to clear
Thine indistinctness: and, by consequence sure,
Less ardent and less strong will be thy speech;
Less her emotion; less her will to aid;
Less all that is of good. No moment then,—
Once having named thee, and her favor begged,—
Shall I remain; but leave you to yourselves :
Thee, strong in thy just cause,—and her, most weak,
Nay most unwilling, justice to resist.
Answer not ' nay ;'—else will pale cowardice
O'ermaster good intent; and thy poor friends
Long years must groan, to save thee from a blush.
Thou wilt not, canst not so. And now is come
The time for prompt departure.; else will night
In black arms clasp thee, ere thou thence return."

The chariots twain, and Kohath's swift-foot mule,
Anon were at the gate. Kind parting words
Were spoken: Sethos, with feigned humbleness,

Permission begged, that happy Paradise
Again to visit: and the road, erelong,
Rang to the hoof-stamp, and the whirl of wheels.

    In serious mood; not joyous, and not sad,
But in most strange bewilderment,—half hope,
Half fear, and all amazement; certain, now,
That even the prince of Egypt, and that pair
Most royal, from far country, their poor house
Kindly had visited; and even as friends,
Nay equals, with them spoken,—now, in doubt,
If but illusion all; a waking dream;
Eye and ear open, but true sense shut up,—
In such a state perplexed, of wonderment,
Of certainty, and doubt,—words speaking few,—
Father, and child, and mother,—when, at length,
She had come home, and these strange things had heard,—
Passed the slow hours; awaiting anxiously
Till Reuben should return, and tidings bring
How he had prospered. Not ere set of sun,
Looked they to see him; but, while yet an hour
Of day was unconsumed,—with pallid face,
Eyes wandering, and a wildly troubled look,
He entered; spake not; but to Kohath signed,
And instantly withdrew. As silently
The father rose, and followed. In amaze
Mother and daughter sat: but, when she saw
That fear was on her, to her parent loved
Calmly thus Rachel spake. "Some ill perchance
Hath fallën, or is feared; or, it may be,
Somewhat but *seeming* ill, to end in good;
Or, haply, but the shadow of an ill,
Mere cloud upon his mind, hath shaken thus
Poor Reuben's gentle heart: for, these three days,
Something, yet unrevealed, hath troubled him,
In way most strange: and almost in affright,
When I put question to him, he implored
That I would ask no more. Whate'er the cause,
Though sorrowful, yet I fear not; for his thoughts
Are alway of the Lord; and how the best

In righteousness to serve Him. In God's hands
Are all things; what shall be, and what shall not;
And ever that which best is, in the end,
We may be sure will be: with that content,
Let us in humbleness and patience wait."

So she; and Sarah's troubled heart was calmed.

But, meanwhile, to an upper chamber sped
Reuben and Kohath, agitated both;
One, cold with dread, and one with shame on fire.
Last entering, Kohath quickly closed the door;
And, looking on the strangely troubled youth,
In whisper said, "thy tidings;—speak at once."
A moment on him gazed the large wild eyes;
The pallid countenance changed to burning red;
The trembling hands were lifted, covering it;
A sound that seemed half sob, half wail of fear,
Burst forth; and Reuben then turned round, and wept;
But answer none could give.
            " One word, at least,
Speak thou," said Kohath, softly on his arm
Laying a hand. "To our young Syrian guests.
Hath evil happened?"
            " Evil threateneth them,"
Said Reuben, "we shall see them here no more:
Nor thereat grieve I. Nigh the eastern gate
Of Pharaoh's palace as we drew, behold,
There stood a throng of horsemen, just arrived;
And with the men of Pharaoh in discourse
Earnest and quick, like such who tidings bring.
And when, as we approached, the Syrian prince
They saw,—toward him they ran; and, hurriedly,
Told how the king, his father, on sick bed
Some days hath lain, death battling against life.
When that she heard, the princess a loud cry
Of grief sent up: but the prince suddenly
Commanded that forthwith should all depart
Toward Syria: a few words to Sethos spake;
Then wheeled around the chariot, and was gone.

The horsemen on their foaming steeds upsprang,
And followed. Like unto a dream it was:
With us one minute were they; and, the next,
Like flying spots far off."
                              " I pray the Lord,"
Said Kohath solemnly, " that their great grief
To joy may turn, finding their father well.
To other, then, hath aught of evil chanced?
To any of our people? . . . to the king?"
" No," answered Reuben; and long silent stood.

" I must await till speech return to thee;"
Said Kohath: " some great mischief surely hath fallen:
What, and on whom, I fear, yet long to know.
Soon as thou canst, speak out; for smallest ills,
Doubt-shadowed, oft more terrible appear
Than known ills, giant-sized."
                              " Let me then speak
With face turned from thee," in unsteady tone,
After awhile, said Reuben; " and for nought
More than I tell, enquire: nor afterwards,
Or on a future day, a question put;
For thou wouldst torture me, yet gain no word
More than I now will speak. . . . That beauteous dame,—
Oh Kohath, my soul trembles while I speak,—
That wife of Maimon, good as once she was,—
So said at least the prince,—now wicked is
Beyond all reach of thought: or mad, perchance,
It may be,—nay mad *must* be, and nought less;
Or else possessed by fiends. Mad, mad, stark mad!
I could not tell thee, Kohath,—could not tell,
Even whispering to myself,—of her wild looks,
And words, and actions. Oh forgive her, God,
For mad I'm sure she is! Such loveliness
Of form and face to be degraded thus!
Oh pity! pity! Heaven's most beauteous work,
Defiled by demons! Hope of aid from her
Is gone for ever! Sooner, now, she'd strike
A dagger in my heart, than move her lord
To mercy on our kindred! Oh! those eyes,

How they glared on me when, at last, I sprang
Terrified from her grasp! . . . . . . Four nights, in
    dreams,
She said I had been with her,—and—the fifth . . . . . .
Oh! mad! mad! mad!
                        "I need not tell thee more,"
After long pause, he added; and turned round:
"Pray for her, Kohath! She no reason hath;
Body and mind, by demons all possessed!
Oh God, have mercy on her! Say thou not,
I do conjure thee, to thy wife, or friend,
Or any living soul, what thou hast heard.
The demons may be chased; and she may rise
As from a horrid dream; and nothing know
Of the dire frenzy gone: and, haply then,
Her name may not be tainted, for foul sin,
Unconsciously committed. Let me now
At once go hence, and privily. My thoughts
Are all tempestuous: I must be alone,
And pray; for, till Heaven's peace once more I feel,
Rather I'd look the lightning in the face,
Than thy pure Rachel. As thou may, excuse
My hasty going. Needeth not one word
To make her know my spirit with her is,
Though body absent. With new day, new life
Well do I hope to have. But pray of her,
That she no question put to me of aught
Which this sad day hath chanced. 'Twill be enough:
And she will meet me calmly as if morn
And evening had been one,—between them nought.
Ah! heavenly all she is! But I must hence.
I long for night and silence; for my soul
A fire is, which, save prayer-flood, nought can quench."

ISRAEL IN EGYPT.

BOOK THIRTEENTH.

SEVEN days accomplished,—unto Pharaoh's court
The sons of Amram went; by Voice Divine
Commanded; and, in presence of the king,
His princes, priests, and sorcerers, Moses spake.

"Thus, Pharaoh, saith the God of Israel;
'Let thou my people go, that they may serve
Their God within the wilderness.'"
                                "Again?"
Angrily cried the king; "have I not said
Ye shall *not* go? What feat of sorcery strange,
Now have you to enforce us? Your blood-spell
By natural death soon died: but, even ere then,
A mockery had become; for, in great floods,
Water the purest got we from the earth,—
Too deep, perchance, for your vile jugglery.
Ye shall *not* go: but, for your insolence,
All Israel heavier tasks and stripes shall have:
Your debtor so,—to pay you with his curse.
Your God is but a fable; a pretence
With which ye think to scare us; as old crones
With Night-Things scare their babes. Again I ask,
With what strange witchcraft would ye fright us *now*?
Some spell more terrible yet? Or, is your art

Worn out? your Evil Spirit impotent
Like mischief to inflict? But, take ye heed;
For, if the king's hand fall upon you, vain
Will all your magic be: ye will go down,
As tree beneath the bolt."
                              With face inflamed,
On Moses frowned he: but the patient man,
Strong in the might of God, on Pharaoh looked
With calm, grand face; and mildly thus replied.

"As I before have said, again I say:
No witchcraft, king of Egypt, practise we:
That which we do, as messengers from God
Alone we do;—nought of ourselves. The voice
Of Heaven instructs us; and, as it commands,
Obediently we act; unknowing all
How that shall be, which *will* be. When my staff
Into a serpent turned; or when to blood
Your waters all were changed,—not more than thou,
Knew we *how* such were done. The Voice had said,
So it should be, thou disobedient found;
And even so it was. Nought more we know.
But, Pharaoh, be thou sure, that Israel's God
No fable is; no thing to scare your babes:
Nor, what our art thou deemest, impotent
Like wonders to perform; nay, greater far;
For, what mere sorceries thou hast dared miscall,—
Terrors to shake the nations, wilt thou find:
Nor feats of Spirits Evil; but the signs
By Power Almighty sent, to make thee know,
That we His servants are; His Will declare;
And that obey thou must; or worse things feel!
For, Pharaoh, be thou sure, that, 'gainst the God
Of Israel striving, all thy power is nought;
Less than a rain-drop, with the ocean weighed.
Nor, 'gainst myself, thy threat I heed at all.
I AM hath said that Israel shall go forth:
And, though thou bring the armies of the world
To stay him; and though chains of steel thou put
On every man and woman of the race,—

Forth still shall Israel go. With one great stroke,
The hand Almighty, off the face of earth
Might sweep all Egypt; from the lowliest man
Who toils for bread, to him who wears the crown:
Thy chariots, and thy horse, and countless foot,
Would vanish as a dream, if, in His wrath,
He did but look upon them. Yet, with hand
More gentle, would He deal with you,—yourselves,
By disobedience, not compelling Him
To stretch o'er you the rod. HIS WILL MUST BE:
For, spake He to the starry firmament,
The earth, the moon, the sun,—and said, 'BE NOT;'
Even at that word, the Universe were void!
NOUGHT would be all! Then, Pharaoh, hearken thou;
And, with obedience willing, do, what, else,
A Power Omnipotent at last will force!
As yet, thou wilt not let us go; for thus
The Voice pronounced; but, at the last, thou wilt:
Yea, pray us to depart. But soften, soon,
Thy heart, hard now as mill-stone; so that plagues
More terrible far may not upon thee fall,
And on thy people: for, such things shall come,
As never heretofore on earth were known;
Plagues that shall smite all Egypt to the dust,
If headstrong still thou be. But, for this day,
If thou refuse to let His people go,
Light scourge He threateneth;—punishment less, perchance,
Than proof to send thee that from Him we come;
His Will Supreme to tell. Thus saith the Lord:
'Go thou to Pharaoh, and unto him say;
Let thou my people go, that they may serve
Their God. If thou refuse to let them go,
Behold, with frogs I will thy borders smite.
Abundantly the river shall bring forth
Frogs that shall cover all the land; and go
Into thine house, thy bedchamber, thy bed;
The houses of thy servants; every house
Of all thy people; in thy kneading-troughs,

Thine ovens; on thy servants, and on thee,
And on thy people.'"
       Laughed out Pharaoh then;
The rulers, priests, and sorcerers also laughed.
But Sethos, with mock reverence, got up;
And gravely questioned,—when these visitants
Might be expected,—what the welcome best
Their dignity to suit;—what viands, drinks,—
What ceremonies proper to the feasts
That must be given, to honor such rare guests.

 To that poor folly, Moses listened not,
Nor on the speaker looked. Upon the king
His eyes he fixed, attending the reply.

 "Away!" cried Pharaoh. "At thy god we laugh:
Even let him do his worst. With frogs, forsooth,
To threaten us! Outworn, indeed, thine art,
Reduced to trick like this! Osiris, hear,
And tremble for thy throne! With fleas, perchance,
Thee, next, this Israel's god will hunt from heaven,
If thou obey not! Get ye from my sight,
Madmen, and fools! With frogs! ha, ha! Rare sport,—
Pharaoh and frogs in battle! Get ye gone!"

 Him Moses answered not; but wroth, yet sad,
With Aaron left the hall.
       Then more and more
Went up the laughter: and, as he were mad,
Sethos, on hands and feet, across the floor
Went leaping; with full eyes, and mouth wide drawn,
The reptiles mimicking. At that arose
A very storm of laughter; till the king,
Exhausted, bade him cease. So they.
         Meantime,
Moses and Aaron toward the river went;
Pure now, and crystal bright, as though of blood
No drop had ever fouled it: then his staff
Moses to Aaron gave, and said; "Behold,

Even as to me was spoken, so to thee
Now speak I. 'With thine hand stretch forth the rod,
Over all streams, all rivers, and all ponds;
And cause the frogs to come up on the land,
Even all the land of Egypt.'"
                              Aaron then,
Above that river, and toward north and south,
And west, and east,—all waters ruling thus,—
The rod stretched out; and, instantly, behold——
Bubbling and foaming to its lowest depths,
High o'er the bank, like a wide-sweeping wave,
Nile cast up its foul brood! Enormous, black,
Lizards in˙gait, claw-footed, swift in flight,
They covered all the ground. Sight horrible!
And sound appalling! for, from each low throat,
Croak deeper than the raven's gurgled up;
That, with the dissonant chorus, the air shook;
And birds and beasts affrighted fled, and men.
Wave after wave, cresting the shore, came up
The great, black, living Horror: rapidly
Rolled toward the city; thronged the streets, the courts,
The temples, houses, bedchambers, and beds,
The kneading-troughs, the ovens, and the cups;
With slime bedaubing all things. Every heart
Was fear-struck: children, women, men, alike,
Flew to escape them; but no place could find
Where they were not.
                     To Pharaoh's palace, soon,
The clamor reached; and quickly came the tale
Of that strange terror. But the sorcerers,—
By the bad Spirits taught new power to feel,—
Spake then to Pharaoh, saying, "Lo! that same
Can *we* do likewise. 'Tis but nought. Behold!"
And therewith, lifting up their rods, they called,
And bade the frogs to come. Forth, then, they came;
Even on the floor, and underneath the eye
Of the astonished king. At that, laughed out
Sethos; and, of the rulers also, some
Laughed out aloud; even Pharaoh darkly smiled;

But said, "Better, methinks, your art were used,
The plague to stop, than a like plague to bring.
And, surely, all that uproar round about,
Worse ill than this bespeaks. Send out to know
Why cry the people thus."
       At once went forth
Some younger lords and priests : but, the outer gate
As they drew open, lo! the living wave,
Fiery-eyed, loathsome, croaking loud, burst in.
Terror-struck, back they fled; the inner door
Hurriedly barred, and that dire wonder told.
Yet needless now the tale; for, close without,
The horrible chorus sounded; and the floor
To the numerous trampling quivered. Pale with fright,
Unto his innermost chamber ran the king,
Calling his princes with him: and the rest,
Priests, sorcerers, rulers, in a great dismay,
Huddled together,—doubtful what to do;
Not daring to stir thence.
       Through half the day,
Alone within his chamber, to no man
Would Pharaoh speak; nor unto man give ear:
But, as the night drew on, and wilder rose
The wailings from the city,—horror-struck,
Aloud he called, and bade that to the house
Of Aaron men should haste, and say to him;
"Come thou, and Moses, straightway to the king;
For he will hear your words."
       That message heard,—
The sons of Amram went; threats, curses, prayers,
As they passed on, from windows greeting them:
For, now, by all the people was it said,
How they that plague had caused; the king to force
Base Israel to set free: some, therefore, cursed;
Some, mischief threatened them; and some, with tears,
Besought them to have pity, and take off
That hideous scourge; else famine would slay all!
But, unto no man speaking, on they went,
The firm ground treading; for, before their path,

Aside the reptiles turned, and left clear way;
Gathering again behind.   With Pharaoh soon,
Even in his private chamber, did they stand;—
With him alone; for, shame would he have felt,
In presence of his daughters, queen, and sons,
Submissive words to speak. Cold looks at first,
Nay angry, he cast on them; but, by fear
O'ermastered soon, with tremulous voice, and face
Haggard and pale, to Moses thus began.

"Is this strange plague *thy* doing? by thy spells
Brought on us? or, its coming didst thou know
From men at distance; and, so, safely threat,
As punishment, if thee we heeded not,
That which, unthreatened, equally had come?
Answer me truly: by thy spell is this?
Or by strange course of Nature? or by act
Of some foul demon, whom thou knowest not of?
Such, rather, would seem cause, than power of thine;
For thou a gentle punishment alone,
Didst threaten, if I would not let you go;
Frogs only, that should cover all the land:
But here are come, men say, foul things, till now,
Ne'er seen upon the earth; in shape as frogs,
But huge in bulk, claw-footed, fiery-eyed,
Voracious, that all food do they devour;
Swift running, like great lizards; and deep-voiced
As the old raven. Like to frogs are these,
As tigers like to cats. Hadst thou designed,—
Or but foreknown,—that such should be the plague,
Light threat thou hadst not called it; nor named frogs,
Those reptiles hideous. Truly answer now.
From power of thine is this? or from what else,—
And, if thou know'st it, what the remedy?"

Then Moses bowed before the king, and spake.

"Other than truly cannot I reply:
But, wilt thou, Pharaoh, hear, and truly know?

For, once already, the pure, simple truth
Have I declared, and thou hast hardened been,
And made of it thy mock. No power of ours,
By magic, or aught else;—nor demon-power,—
Which, save by Heaven permitted, ne'er can work
Against fixed course of Nature,—this strange plague
Hath brought upon you;—but our God alone,—
Even as I warned thee He would do to you,
Shouldst thou refuse to let His people go,—
Hath sent it on you: punishment, at once,
And proof that verily from Him we come;
That so thou may believe us, and obey.
Mild threat I called it: and, if yet thy heart
Be hardened, and thou wilt not let us go,
Mild wilt thou find it, with those plagues compared
That will be sent upon thee. Of ourselves,
No more than thou knew we what things should come.
Frogs were they named; but of no special sort:
Yet, that of nature strange they would be found,
Easy to guess,—since passing strange the ills
They should bring on you. Not the harmless frog
Of stream and field, could through your cities run;
Throng in your halls, your chambers, and your beds,
Your kneading-troughs, and ovens. All this land,
Ere such could cover,—from the streams and ponds
Heavily rising,—would long months go by:
Nor miracle would it seem; but Nature's work
Prodigious, only, in some wantonness
Of life-production; even as locust-clouds
Prodigious she brings forth, which a whole land
At once make desolate. Nor aught with thee
Had such availed; thy merriment, perchance,
As at the first. But, surely, now thou seest
That neither magic-spell, nor demon-power,
Nor the wild work of Nature, can this be.
I told thee it would come, thy punishment,
If thou shouldst disobey. Thou didst: it came:
Even that same hour it came! If, as thou saidst,
From men at distance, of that coming plague,
So nigh at hand, the tidings I had heard,—

Think'st thou that others, also, had not heard,
And bruited it about?—But, not alone
Against this city comes it,—Egypt all,—
Save in the dwellings of the Israelites,
And in the land of Goshen,—feels the curse.
Thy sin hath brought it: thy repentance full,
Solely can stay it. As in the blood-plague,
Three days should this endure,—unless thine heart
Quickly thou soften, and bid Israel go.
Then, haply, may the Lord His hand put forth,
And cause the scourge depart."
       A little while
In silence Pharaoh stood,—his proud hard heart,
By the great Spirit of Evil harder made,
And loathing to submit. But, in that hush,
From the whole city, the great voice of wail,
And the horrific croaking of the plague,
Louder came up; so smiting, that his tongue
Clave to the palate. With a faltering voice,
At length thus spake he.
      "Verily I fear
This is indeed from God! Entreat ye Him
That He may take this scourge away from me,
And from my people! Then shall Israel go,
That they may sacrifice unto the Lord."

 Well pleased was Moses when these words he heard;
And thus he answered. "Better to show forth,
That by the God of Israel, and none else,
This plague was sent; and that by Him alone
May it be taken off,—my voice of prayer,
And thy repentance moving Him—behold!
Thou shalt command; shalt glory have o'er me:
As *thou* wilt, be it done. Speak freely then,
And say—*when* of our God shall I entreat,—
For thee, and for thy servants, and for all
Thy people,—that this plague may be removed?"

 "Even on the morrow," eagerly cried the king;

"For, if three days it last, famine and thirst
Will slay us all!"
                    . Him Moses answered thus.
"Be it according to thy word; that thou
Truly may'st know that, like the Lord our God,
None is there. He will bid the plague depart
From thee, thy servants, and thy people all,
Throughout the land of Egypt."
                         But that night
Wailings of dread, and loathing, still went up
Through all the city, and throughout the realm,—
Save in the houses of the Israelites:
Therein no plague was: and a word of joy
From man to man spread quickly, that, in truth,
Pharaoh would let them go.
                    At early morn,
Moses, beseeching, cried unto the Lord,
Because of that great plague, on Pharaoh sent:
And the Lord hearkened: and the reptiles died
Out of all houses, villages, and fields.
Then did the people gather them in heaps;
And the land stank.
                    Yet, this when Pharaoh knew,
Again his heart toward Israel hardened was.
His priests and sorcerers then, the more to stir
His wrath against them, whispered audibly;
Complaining that great insult on the king,
By Moses and by Aaron had been cast;
Deceiving him, their people to get freed.
And when, at length, they saw that to the height
Rage boiled within him,—unto Pharaoh's throne
They went together; and Thamusin thus.

"Light of the Sun,—hear now thy servant speak:
Yet, not *his* thoughts alone, but thoughts of all
Thy counsellors and rulers. A great cheat
By those accursed wizards hath been done,—
The king to vex, and all to terrify,
That so the slaves might 'scape. Of that same plague
Knew Moses, from his people far away,—

Or by the potence of his witchery—
That hither it was coming; for, behold!
Not here alone, but throughout the whole realm,
Swarmed the foul monsters. Yet, with guileful heart,
His God to magnify, pretended he
That, for a special curse on thee, and us,
From that false god, would come, what well he knew,
By natural cause, o'er all the land would come.
Also knew he that, quickly as it came,
So quickly would it go: for alway thus
In course of Nature is it. Every thing
Born suddenly, as suddenly must die.
Gnats, born at morning, perish ere the night:
And those disgusting reptiles, in one day
Brought into life,—knew he assuredly,
By the like law, must on the morrow die.
An impudent pretence, then, of his god
To get by prayer, that which he knew would be,
Whether he prayed, or cursed him. Natural cause
Alone that plague brought on; alone removed.
Plain to the sense of all,—nay even of fools,
Out stands it, that an insolent deceit
This Moses hath put on us,—his false god
To glorify, and those vile slaves to loose.
If their desert they get,—not liberty,
But heavier bonds they'll have: for well 'tis known,—
That, by their magic fended, in no house
Of Israel went the reptiles. Safe within,
The women sat, praising their god with songs;
And, doubtless, also, with vile gibes and mirth,
Mocking their masters, when the cries went up,
Telling their wretchedness: and, for the men,
Alike were they at ease, whether at home,
Joining the women in their psalmody,
Or walking forth; for, ever a clear path
Was theirs; no reptile on them fixed his claw,
Nor even crossed their way; but, right and left,
Fled from before them. If of magic deep
This speaketh not; then magic would be none,
Of pebbles to make bread; of water, wine;

Of corpses, living men. If, therefore, thou,
Light of the Sun, do let this people go,
Their laughter and their mockery evermore
Wilt thou be made; and Egypt her chief wealth
And power, for aye will lose."
        Vehémently
So spake Thamusin; others of the priests
Spake also, and the sorcerers; that the king
Might be stirred up, his promise to recall;
And give, instead of freedom, heavier chains
To that deceitful Israel.
       And, meantime,
While these, with mortal voice, to Pharaoh spake,
A mightier far, though wordless, in his heart,
With potence terrible shook him; for therein
Went Satan; and his pride and wrath awoke;
Rousing him to defy command of God;
And his own word recall; and keep in bonds
Whom he had vowed to loose.
       With rage, at last,
Full fraught, upstarted Pharaoh, and cried out;
"Haste, and proclaim it,—Israel shall *not* go!
Their jugglers have deceived us: but their tricks
Shall be o'ermastered. Give the slaves worse tasks;
And make their women labor as their men:
Fitter than singing while all Egypt howls.
Send instantly, and stay them, ere one man
Put forth the foot. Their magic damnable
Surely no more can do; and, if again
With the same plagues they threaten,—by all gods
Of Egypt swear I, those curs'd sorcerers
At once shall die the death!"
       Foaming with rage,
Down from his throne he went: and speedily
Throughout the city, and through all the land
Where dwelt the Israelites, flew messengers,
Forbidding them to go; and heavier toils
Commanding on them; and their women, too,
Bidding to labor, even as the men.

That seen, among the proud Egyptian dames
Many there were, who those poor women mockèd;
Pointing the finger, sneering, laughing aloud,
And calling on the taskmasters to force
The singers to their work; and smite them hard,
Even as the idle men.
                    At that, a groan
Came from all Israel; and a loud complaint
Against the sons of Amram,—that even worse
They had made their state; had freedom promised them;
Yet brought but heavier chains.
                              Among them then
Moses, and Aaron, and the Elders, went;
Bidding them take good heart; their grievous wrongs
Bear patiently; and in the Lord of Hosts
Place all their trust: for mighty things, erelong,
Would He do for them; such as all the land
Should fill with wonder: till, at last, the king,
His rulers, and the voice of Egypt all,
Should bid, should pray, should bribe them to depart.

ISRAEL IN EGYPT.

BOOK FOURTEENTH.

On the next morning early, Voice Divine
Again to Moses came. "To Aaron say;
'Stretch out thy rod, and smite the dust; that lice
Through all the land of Egypt it may be.'"

Awe-struck, to Aaron Moses went; and spake
Even as the Voice had spoken. Forthwith then
Beyond the city passed they to the plain,
Where arid was the ground. With outstretched arm,
The rod uplifting, Aaron smote the dust;
And it was turned to lice. Throughout the land,
All dust was changed to lice; which man and beast
Alike infested. Borne upon the air,
Through every house of Egypt,—save alone
The houses of the Israelites,—swarmed the plague:
Therein it went not, nor touched living thing.
But, on the Egyptian dames, who scornfully
Had mocked at Hebrew women, and called out,
Bidding the taskmasters to scourge them hard,
Even as the men,—on them so came it down,
That each to the other, each one to herself,
A loathing, and abomination grew;
For, even from head to foot the vermin were;
Crawled in the porches of their ears, their eyes,
Their nostrils, and their mouths; on hands, and feet;

And over all their bodies; even as flies
Cover the putrid carcass: so that life
Became a misery, and they longed to die.
Over the sprightly youths, and haughty men;
Over all rulers, judges, princes, priests;
Over the king, and over all the land,
The plague was; and to madness many stung,
And many fired to fever, that they died.
Dogs howled; and oxen bellowed, and fell down,
And rolled upon the ground: horses broke loose,
And dashed on frantically, o'er plain, through wood,
As stung by serpents; or in rivers plunged,
Or deep mud wallowed,—their hot flesh to cool.

A cry was o'er all Egypt. Even the priests,—
Yea sorcerers also, who in vain like thing
By their enchantments to bring forth, had striven,—
To Pharaoh said, "this is the finger of God!"

Yet was his heart still hardened; and their words
He heeded not.
    To Moses then again
Thus spake the Voice; " Early at morning rise,
And before Pharaoh, as he goeth forth
Unto the water, stand, and say to him.
'Thus saith the Lord,—let thou my people go,
That they may serve me; else, if thou wilt not,
Behold, I will send swarms of flies, on thee,
Thy servants, and thy people. Every house
In Egypt shall be full of swarms of flies;
Yea the ground also, whereupon they are.
And I will sever, in that day, the land
Of Goshen, in the which my people dwell,
That there no flies shall come; so of a truth,
Mayst thou be taught that I alone am God
In midst of earth. Tomorrow this sign shall be.' "

Early at morning, therefore, went the sons
Of Amram; and beside the river stood,
There to await the coming of the king.

He, drawing near, beheld them; and, for rage,
Fain would have smitten: for, though threatened not,
Well knew he that through them, as punishment
For promise broken, that abhorrëd plague
Had fallen upon him. Mind and body both,
Nigh unto madness fretted,—with harsh voice
Breaking upon them, thus then did he cry.

"Out of my sight, ye wizards! for your deed
This filthiness is. Behold! even on the king
Ye cast your dirt. But, hearken now my word.
This pest, I doubt not, quickly as it came,
As quickly will depart; like your blood-plague,
And those detested reptiles: but, if not,—
Or if yet other magic ye put forth
On me, and on my people,—by all gods
Here swear I, on the gallows ye shall hang,
Till every bone be whitened! Get you hence!
I will not hear you."
    "For thine own sake, king,
List thou my words," calmly then Moses said:
"For not mine are they, but the Lord's. Great sin
Hast thou committed: and the punishment
Lighter than thy desert. For, not content,
To hold enslaved whom thou hadst vowed to loose,—
Their bonds thou didst make heavier; yea, didst send
To servile labor, women delicate,
And maidens young and tender, who, till then,
Such tasks wrought never,—their own household work,
Sole labor they had known. And thy proud dames,
Seeing their wretchedness, no pity felt;
But pointed with the finger; mocked at them;
And bade the taskmasters to scourge them hard,—
Even as the idle men. But now, behold,
Pure as fresh snow from soil, from this foul plague
Pure are those Hebrew women;—thy proud dames
Filthy, abominable, loathsome, vile;
Detesting each the other,—each herself;
All weary of their lives!"
    "And whose the blame?"

Fiercely cried Pharaoh; "Is not this thy work,
And his, thy fellow wizard? Nought, indeed,
Of this ye threatened; ne'ertheless, 'tis yours:
Gainsay it if ye can. Your insolence
And spite alone had dared it. Take it off,
Or death shall *you* take off, and speedily;
By Egypt's gods I swear!"
                         "Not ours the work,"
Calmly said Moses, "but the Lord's it was:
Nor threatened, as to come, but sent at once;
A punishment direct, on sin then done:
For thou hadst lied to God. When that last plague
Strongly was on you all, didst thou not say,
'This is indeed from God! Entreat the Lord
That He may take away this scourge from me,
And from my people,—then shall Israel go,
That they may sacrifice unto the Lord'?
Yea, Pharaoh, so thou saidst; and yet, behold,
When He my prayer had hearkened; and the plague
Had bid depart,—harshly didst thou refuse
To let our people go: nay heavier tasks
Didst put upon them; and their women, too,
As slaves didst make to labor! Then, O king,
For thy great falsehood, and the cruelty
Of thy proud dames,—with this abhorrëd plague
The hand of God did smite you. Nor think thou
That threat of thine can make us take it off.
Not ours it is; nor, at our word, will bide,
Or will depart. He only, who hath sent,
Can bid it stay, or go."
                       " Come what come may,
I will *not* let you go," by Satan fired,
Cried Pharaoh: "and, if soon it pass not hence,
Worse for yourselves, and for all Israel too,
Be sure ye'll find it. Hence then: and think well
Of what ye do; and what may be the end:
For, verily, of your black spells alone,
Believe I all hath been; and, for your god,
A fable still I hold him,—a pretence,—
A cloak to hide your sorcery,—a thing

With which to scare us,—that your cursed race
We may set free. Deceive yourselves no more:
For, though ye split all Egypt; pyramids
And hills fling in the ocean; dry up Nile,—
By Isis and Osiris do I swear,
Our slaves ye still shall be."
       By passion racked,
Words failed him there: but, with a face of fire,
He stared upon the Hebrews,—as with looks
He would have slain them: and, with arm outflung,
Signed them to go. But Moses raised his hand,
Attention asking; and, in calm, firm voice,
Thus spake.
    "Even so, O king, the Word Divine
Taught me that thou wouldst do; for, hard thy heart;
And, when beneath the hand of Heaven made soft,
As iron by the fire,—that hand removed,
Hard waxeth it again, as iron cooled.
So, for awhile, perchance, against Heaven still
Thy pride may battle: but, a point there is
Of heat intense, 'neath which in fume doth fly
The solid iron, as in vapour flies
Water, when cast on fire: and point there is,
At which the iron hardness of thine heart
Soft will become as air. Hear now my words;
Then judge if of thy threatening aught we heed.
Thus saith the Lord: 'Let thou my people go,
That they may serve me: else, if thou wilt not,
Behold, I will send swarms of flies, on thee,
Thy servants, and thy people. Every house
In Egypt shall be full of swarms of flies:
Yea the ground also, whereupon they are.
And I will sever, in that day, the land
Of Goshen, in the which my people dwell,
That there no flies shall come: so of a truth
Mayst thou be taught, that I alone am God
In midst of earth. Tomorrow this sign shall be.'"

"Tomorrow be it then!" bellowed for rage
The infatuate King; and, with long hasty stride,

Abruptly left them; yet, with backward glance,
Shot on them wrath and hate. But, suddenly,
Round turned he; and, with threatening arm, and voice
Like maniac's, roared, "At sunrise send your plague,—
Ere noon I send you death!"
       That said, right on,
Hurriedly went he; but still oft looked back,
Fierce-eyed, and muttering; as a beast of prey,
Furious, yet fearful, from yet stronger beast,
Perforce retreating.
     Nought to him replied
The sons of Amram; but, in solemn mood
Discoursing, toward the city took their way;
That, to the few whom they could find, the words
Of comfort might they speak, and their hearts cheer.

 But worse throughout that day the loathsome Plague
Maddened the people. No Egyptian was
Who at his occupation might be found.
No taskmaster was in the field; no smith
Wielded the hammer; not a tool was heard
Of workman, in the garden, or the house.
The dikes, embankments, brick-fields, roads, and walls,
Whereon the Hebrews toiled,—by them alone
Were visited; for, looker-on was none,
Save of their people only. All the streets
Were empty: neither woman nor man dared stir
From out the houses; all in wretchedness
Hid from each other, writhing 'neath the curse.
No food was there prepared, for none could eat;
So vermin all things covered. The king's court
Was vacant: justice slept. To seize the thief,
No hand had been outstretched: for murder done,
None had pursued. Temple, and judgment-seat
Stood empty! All was foul, and desolate!
So, by even vilest things that crawl on earth,
The pride, and power, and majesty of man,
By God may be brought low!
        The sun went down,
But respite was there none: no soothing sleep

Closed any eye of Egypt. All night long,
From every house the cry of misery came;
And, from the fields and plains, the voice of beasts,
In howl, shriek, bellow; that no spot there was,—
Save in the dwellings of the Israelites,
And in the land of Goshen,—where rest, peace,
And holy silence reigned.
                          But, at grey dawn,—
So from on high commanded,—the plague ceased;
Again the lice were dust! Through Egypt then,
On every man, and woman, child, and beast,
Deep slumber fell: that, when the sun arose,—
As on a country of the dead, he looked; or waste,
Wherein, save bird, and fish, no life there was.

Heavy that slumber over all the land;
But terrible the wakening! for, behold!
While yet the sun shone brightly,—on the leaves,
Dew-steeped, and grasses, and the rippling streams,
A diamond sparkle flinging,—the clear air
Suddenly 'gan to thicken. Cloud was none,
Nor gentlest waft of wind, that from afar,
O'er sea, or desert, might that gloom have brought.
In the same moment, over all the land
At once it fell;—as though the firmament
Black dust were gendering. The bright-blazing sun
Grew dim and ghastly,—as, before his face,
A thick veil had been drawn. Dark,—darker yet,—
Fainter than shadow now,—now blotted quite!

The Hebrews, then abroad, with wonder looked
On field, tree, hill, fast blackening,—as if Night
Had turned again, to strangle the young Day:
And, marvelling while they gazed—suspecting each
His own sight failing,—lo! upon the ear,
Came also wonder strange! A sound it was,—
Or as the feeble twilight of a sound,—
Real, and somewhere; but, in sky, on earth,
At right, or left, behind them, or before,
Still doubtful was; for everywhere it seemed;

As if all air were quickening into life,
And feebly moaning thus. But more and more
It swelled, and deepened: darker, and more dark,
Gathered the veil o'er heaven: and, all around,
Thicker and thicker grew the atmosphere.
Colors the brightest, to an inky hue
Quickly 'gan turn: things distant, were shut out;
Things nigh, appeared as shadows. Louder yet
Became the great, deep, universal hum,
Making air quiver: for the black fog, now,
A cloud of life became; a cloud, from earth
Upreaching into heaven,—from East to West,
From South to North, o'ershadowing all the land!
Silent they stood, astonished, motionless,
Gazing, and listening: and, when toward the ground
At length they looked,—behold, no ground they saw;
But a black sheet of life, o'erspreading all,—
Flies of strange fashion; such as eye of man
Never till then had known,—large-headed, lean,
Bodied like scorpions,—their dark wings outstretched,
And quivering as the horizontal air
Of tropical noon. And lo! even while they looked,
The black wings to the hue of dull red fire
Changed rapidly, till like to flame they grew;
And on their broad fronts, eyes, like diamond specks
In sunshine, 'gan to flicker. More and more,
The murmur swelled, and deepened: and above,
And all around them, when the Hebrews gazed,—
Poised in the air, a mighty sea of life,
Filling all space, they saw,—a fire-like life,
From wings flame-hued; and numberless as sands
On broadest ocean-shore. Anon, behold!
As when, from slumber of long centuries,
In his deep bed the giant Etna wakes,
And stirs the abysmal fires,—cloud heaped on cloud,
From the vast crater, rolls upon the air,
Hill and plain hiding, and the firmament,—
Even so, as by command, rolled on at once,
Cloud upon cloud, that infinite of new life;
Mounting, and sinking; surging to and fro;

Like smoke before a tempest driving on;
And carrying noise as of a mighty wind
Amid the forest, when great trees bow down,
Moaning in thunder.
                    All astonished stood
The Israelites, that living hurricane
Hearing, and seeing: but, erelong, arose,
Though faintly in the distance, other sounds;
Mad bellowing of beasts, and howl of dogs;
Strange shrieks from horses, and wild cries of men,
Women and children,—for the Plague was now
Fiercely at work; nor living thing could 'scape!
Up from their slumber, throughout all the land,
As if fire-scorched, the millions started,—wild,
Screaming with terror and pain: for, wheresoe'er
Was opening left,—in hovel of the poor,
In palace, house, or temple,—therein shot
The living tempest: on the faces poured,
And hands of heavy sleepers; and their stings
Struck deep: nay, through light drapery of the bed,
Pierced to the body; that as one great scald
From head to foot, the torture might have seemed,—
But that the eye, in one brief glance—the ear,
Dinned by the fierce hum,—as from hornet's nest,
Suddenly stirred,—the terrible Plague spake out.

Through all the land of Egypt did it rage,
Save in the houses of the Israelites,
And in the land of Goshen. Therein went
No flies; nor of the Hebrews, at their tasks,
Touched they one man or woman.
                                From deep sleep,
Pharaoh, at length, by his young queen was roused,
The mild-eyed Sirois, "Awake, awake!"
In terror she cried. "Again some hideous thing
Is come upon us. Pharaoh, Pharaoh, wake!"

Upstarted he, by that shrill cry alarmed,—
And stared her in the face; as knowing not
What she had said; or wherefore in such haste

She had aroused him. But the murmur deep
Of the life-ocean came upon his ear,
Like far off thunder; and the chorus dire
Of cries, and shrieks,—like a great mist of sound,
From all the tortured city going up.
Paleness of death swept o'er his countenance,
As thus he listened. "Demons! they have brought
Their pest upon us! though with sudden death
I threatened them, so dared they! But to us
Plague cannot come, my Sirois: no fly here
Can bring his venom: locked is every door;
Each window with its snowy drapery closed,
That not even gnat can enter. Calm thee then.
Here, shut up, will we bide, till dies the scourge,—
As, ere tomorrow, will it,—like the curse
Of those foul reptiles, and that other thing,—
And then, be sure, this their last trick shall be;
For, as I live, ere set another sun,
Those sorcerers shall hang. Fruit, cates, and wine,
And water, have we here: and such light fare,
A day, or even twain, may serve us well:
For no door shall be opened; lest thereat
Plague enter, as before; and force me send
For those vile wizards; promising again
Freedom to Israel, so they take it off.
I will not do it! Safe abide we here;
And, for the people, in best way they can,
Must they endure. The day at length will end,
And end the night; and then, by natural death,
The plague will perish; and the Hebrew's spells
Bring on me no disgrace. To pleasant sleep
Return we then, my Sirois; so the hours
Shall flit away; and we the scourge escape."

But sleep they knew not; for loud wailing rose
Throughout the palace: on the chamber door
Heavy strokes sounded; and, from those without,
Cries as of agony came. Still, for awhile,
The king regarded not; for word distinct
None could he hear,—so loud the thunderous hum

Of the dire plague; and such the din that rose
From the tormented city. But more fierce
Anon the strokes fell, as by hammers given,
The massive wood to break. From out his bed
Leaped Pharaoh then; and, smiting on the door,
With voice high-pitched cried out, "Whoe'er ye be,
Get hence! till this plague go, I open not.
Take ye your swords; and to those wizards fly,
And put them to the death, if, instantly
They stay not this foul torment."

"We are blind,"
Shrieked then a voice, "and cannot find the way:
Blind are we all, and mad: from crown to toe
Stung as by hornets. Thou know'st not my voice,
Or would'st not bar me out. I am thy son
Lanetho; help me father, or I die."

"I cannot help thee," Pharaoh shouted back!
"If but one instant I throw ope the door,
The curse will burst upon us. Think, my son,—
What would it profit thee that, like the rest,
Thy sire and mother were stung? We now are safe.
The plague will quickly die: then bear it ye
As best ye may; or, as I bid you, haste,
And end it with your swords, deep in the hearts
Of those accurs'd magicians. Or, if blind
Wholly ye are, then from the windows call
Upon the people, saying, 'the king wills
That forthwith ye make speed, and put to death
Moses and Aaron, who this scourge have sent;
Then shall it cease.'"

"Oh Pharaoh," cried aloud
A voice without; "so would it never cease:
If they who sent, revoke it not, who else
May their dread spell call back? Send, rather, thou,
Light of the Sun, to those dread men, and say;
'Take off this curse, and Israel shall go free.'
Then will they hearken; and our misery end:
Else quickly end must we, and all the race;
And Egypt be one charnel house; for thus

The threat was, that o'er all the land alike
The plague should fall. Oh Pharaoh! send thou, then,
That it may cease; else, ere new day shall come,
Over the dead alone wilt thou be King!"

"I will *not* send!" with harsh voice Pharaoh cried,
"To be again the mock of those accurs'd.
Whether they will, or no, the morrow's sun
Alike will see its death. Then, as ye can,
Endure, if end it ye will not, in blood
Of those who sent it. And now get ye hence:
Ye know my will; and, though till night ye pray,
Vain were it as of clouds to ask for gold.
Haste to the vaults beneath the palace floor;
Or to the catacombs: to that dark night
Plague will not follow you: and the cool air
Will ease your burning. Answer not, but go;
For more I will not hear."
                    So to his bed
Pharaoh returned, and found his queen in tears,
Because of that loved son, whom entrance thus
His father had refused. "Set Israel free,
I pray thee Pharaoh," cried she piteously;
"Thou hast no right to hold them. Oft and oft
Have I not said, evil will come of it,
If them we hold in slavery, who for us,
With their own blood and life, deliverance wrought.
I *pray* thee let them go."
                    With gentle words,
And fond embraces, her he sought to soothe;
Predicting for the morrow sure release
From that affliction; for all time to come,
Security from evil, by the death
Of those accurs'd magicians. Long she sobbed;
But ceased at last,—grief by great terror crushed:
For louder yet, and louder rose the cries
Within the palace, and from all around;
As though throughout the city every voice
Sent up its yell: and, mingled with that din,
Came the still waxing roar of the fierce plague;

Millions by tens of millions multiplied;
For vengeance clamoring, and athirst for blood.
In silence then she lay, and Pharaoh too,
Quaking with fear. Speechless, long time they lay.

   But now again upon the solid door
Came blows so loud that, lest it should be rent,
Upstarted Pharaoh; smote it, and cried out,
"Whoe'er ye be, get hence: till this plague die,
I open not. Have ye the wizards slain?"

"Oh father," cried a voice, "fling open now,
For but one moment. Sethos 'tis who calls;
None else is here: for but one moment now
I pray thee open; else, before thy door
Wilt thou behold me dead!"
                    "I tell thee, son,
I will not open till this plague be gone.
Wouldst have thy father suffer,—and his queen,—
All selfish as thou art, in pity of thee;
Yet thee availing nought? The plague without,
Would enter with thee; and alike wouldst thou
Here be tormented, as where now thou art;
We but thy partners in the misery be;
Nor thou one sting escaping. Speed thee hence;
With thine own sword those cursed magicians kill;
At once then dies the scourge. If thou wilt not,
Endure it as thou may. 'Tis but one night:
At sunrise will it die. Till then, this door
Firm as a rock shall stand."
                    Again his cry
Sethos began; but now such din arose,
From priests, and sorcerers, women of the court,
Rulers, and servants, clamoring all at once,
That Pharaoh heard him not: but, in alarm
Lest entrance they should force—the silver bolts
Shot in the staples,—struck upon the door;
And, at the shrillest pitch of voice, cried out;
"Who are ye now? and what your errand here,
At the queen's chamber? Suddenly get hence,

Whoe'er ye be; and smite with all your swords,
Those Hebrew wizards. Nought else can be done,
This curse to stay. I will not ope the door.
Dare ye to force it, by our gods I swear,
Ye all shall die the death."
                              Rose then a voice,
Shrill as an eagle's scream; "Oh father, hear;
'Tis I, thy youngest daughter: open quick:
I am on flame, blind, dying; let me in."

Then touched was Pharaoh's heart; and he cried out,
"Fall backward from the door; fall back afar,
All, save my child: and Meroë, mark thou well;
Stand close; that, when I open, like the wind
Thou may rush in; and I may shut again
In that same instant."
                      Answer was there none;
His words unheard without; so loud the din.

"Oh Pharaoh, open, open instantly,"
Cried Sirois, tears streaming down her cheeks;
"'Tis that young child whom, as my own she were,
Thou know'st I love!" But Pharaoh heard her not;
For, suddenly, within the chamber stood
A shape gigantic, and of regal mien:
In habit of Egyptian king, the first
In Heliopolis throned. His countenance
Was like pale flame; his voice was soft, and low
As murmur in a rocky seashore cave,
Heard at deep midnight, when the slow waves heave
Upon the pebbly beach, and backward glide
Reluctantly, as moaning at repulse.
With wonder and with terror Pharaoh gazed;
But word found none. Upon him looked the Shape,
With awful eye, and thus.
                         "From Amun sent,
Come I before thee, king; myself once king,
In days far gone, o'er this Egyptian realm;
Long ere the pyramids: Menes was my name.
Thus saith the god. 'Pharaoh, make firm thine heart:

Bow thou no more beneath the unholy spells
Of Hebrew magic. Where thou art, there stay;
So plague can never touch thee. Open not
To priest, or son, or daughter: nay, though all
Thine offspring with one voice cry out on thee;
Hearken thou not. Once opened, through the door,
Will burst the torment-flood; and thou wilt cry
Upon the sons of Amram, as before;
And they will triumph o'er thee: and their hand
Thereafter yet far heavier shalt thou feel.
Baffle them now; and, from this day, their power
Shalt thou make harmless. Heed the terrible god;
Lest thou incense him; and a plague he send,
So dire, that this, against it weighed, were nought."
Ceasing, the dread form frowned upon the king,
And vanished. Stiff with terror, Pharaoh stood,
Staring on vacancy. His queen, amazed,—
For nought she saw, or heard,—hastily rose;
Grasped his cold, trembling hand, and gently thus.
"What ails thee, Pharaoh?—Speak,—on what dost
    look?"
"'Tis gone," he answered; in a warm embrace
Compressing her: "A dream,—my sweet,—nought else.
Get thee to bed again. I am forbid
To open, even though priests, sons, daughters, all,
With one voice cry unto me. Come,—to bed.
'Twas but some woman of the palace. She
Must bide it as she may. So must they all;
Else will the god be wroth, and worse plague send;
Heavy, to this, as iron to dove's down. . . . . .
There,—lie thou still, my Sirois. And, now, mark,—
Oh gods! those shrieks! they stab me to the heart!—
If, in some madness,—though for but one glance,
One atom-instant,—I the door should ope;
And the curs'd hum of but one fly thou hear,—
Tomb thee within the bed: leave not such space
Where even dust might enter."
                                Anxiously
While thus he warned her,—on the door again
Heavy strokes sounded; and a clamor rose

Of voices louder gathering momently;
Outcries of terror some; and some of rage,
And all of torment; many, on the king,
Imploring entrance; some, that he would send
To Moses and to Aaron; but so mixed,
So lost in discord, that scarce word at all
Clear meaning brought. Then on the door again
Sharply he smote; and, lifting high his voice,
Thus spake. "Be silent now; ye clamorous,
And let one speak alone. Who are ye there?
And what your business, that, with such rude noise,
Even at the chamber of the queen ye storm?
Now, let one only answer; and be brief."

He paused; and instantly a voice was heard,
Strongly uplifted. "Splendor of the Sun,"
It said, "thy people all are madness-struck,
By reason of this plague. If no relief
Come quickly to them, they will rend themselves,
Or slay each other. One great cry ascends
From all the city, praying thee again
On Israel's sorcerers to call for help,
And let their people go." Upon the valve
Fiercely then Pharaoh struck, that speech to stop;
And in a very roar of fury cried,
"Fools! they would shun one stroke, to suffer ten!
Bear this they must, and shall. I will *not* pray
Of those detested sorcerers! They shall die,
When this plague dies: and that will be at noon
Of even tomorrow. If the time seem long,
With you it rests to press it in one hour.
Slay those two Hebrew wizards; and 'tis done!
If this ye will not, your own fault alone,
Or folly, smites you; for ye hug the plague
That ye might fling away. Do as ye list:
Immoveable as mountain stand I here:
I *will* NOT send to those vile sorcerers;
I *will* NOT let that hated Israel go;
I *will* NOT, though with clamors ye rend heaven,—

Even but the width of one small barley corn,
This door draw open. Never here can plague
Plant his black foot. Here, my loved queen and I,
Safely defy it. By a God *indeed*
Had it been wrought, and not by magic spell,
Here, as elsewhere, the scourge had found its way:
Nay, fiercest here of all, for 'gainst myself,
Chiefly the curse was threatened; me to scare,
That I might loosen Israel: but I laugh
At the poor sorcery——Hah——"
                                    With a wild yell
Of terror he stopped: for, suddenly as falls
Shadow on earth, when the thick-volumed cloud
Shoots, tempest-driven, across the noontide sun,—
So suddenly around him darkness fell,
And the Plague-roar burst forth. A hurried glance
Toward the close-draperied window cast he;—no—
Closed was it still,—no fly therein could come;
Yet was the chamber, even from floor to roof,
Filled with the Torment: and, as troops of wolves
Rush on the fallën steed,—even so on him,
From head to foot, the angry thousands poured,
Stings driving: while the vast, deep, sullen hum
Of myriads, calling in their turn for blood,
Horrific came upon him, as night-howl
Of famishing tiger. Madly, with both palms,
He pressed his face; and crushed, and flung them off;
Shrieking aloud: but, ere again his hands
He could uplift, fresh hundreds filled their place;
Fresh stings infixing: on his throat, and neck,
And breast they fell; and wheresoever else
They might find entrance,—therein shooting fire.
His hideous howlings told to those without
That Plague at last had caught him: and fierce joy
Uplifted them; for now they knew that soon
Would the sole help be summoned. 'Gainst the door,
Boldly then thrust they; hoping lock and bolt
To force, and win quick entrance: but in vain;
Firm as a rock it stood.
                            The king, meantime,

Like to a blind man groping,—yelling still,
And stamping as he went,—with arm outstretched,
Sought for the portal—leftward now—now right,—
Like to a drunkard reeling: till, at last,
Coming upon it, back he cast the bolts,—
The key wrenched round,—flung wide;—blind,—howling,—mad,—
Headlong rushed out; amid the thronging crowd
Forcing his way,—assured that in no place,
So fierce as whence he came, could be the plague.

Forgotten was his queen,—but now so loved,
So cherished, so secure. Within that hell
Whence he had fled, stayed she,—yet of her fate,
Thought had he none,—his own keen torment-flame
So maddening, that to all else was he dead.
But she his warning, with attentive ear
Had listened, and remembered. At first sound
Of that new Plague-life,—quickly as the hand
Of loving mother from her infant's face
Wafts the fierce hornet,—even so quickly she,
The silken coverings seized,—above her head
Flung in a heap; and, with a trembling hand,
'Neath neck and shoulders pressed; space leaving not
Whereat even dust might enter. The thick silks,
Like coat of mail secured her 'gainst the darts
Of the loud murmuring scourge; and she alone,
Of all the Egyptian people, felt no sting.

But Pharaoh, urging on, from change of place
No respite found. As if blown on by flame,
Seemed face, and hands, and whatsoever else
The darts might reach. Loud yelling, for awhile
Amid the throng he struggled: but, at length,
Frantic with torment, shrieked,—" To Moses run,
And Aaron: cry to them,—' the king will hear:
Hasten ye, then, before him,—stay the plague,
And suddenly,—then shall your people go.' . . . .
Which of you answers me? . . . all dumb? all blind? . . .

Ye then who nigh unto the windows stand,
Call on the men without; and tell my words."

   Thereat, from out the windows a great sound
Of voices flew,—all calling eagerly,
Yet all confused,—voice 'gainst voice clamoring,
That word distinct was none. One man, at length,
The hubbub lessening, with great power spake out
The bidding of the king.
                      His words to hear,
The people ceased their wailing. When they had heard,
Glad were they; and a feeble shout sent up:
Then, toward the well-known house of Aaron, some,
Stretching their arms, 'gan grope along the way.

   But in that throng,—for, through the palace gates
The multitude all day had crowded in,
To cry unto the king,—were Hebrew men,
With the Egyptians mingled, all unknown;
And they, untouched by harm, at full speed ran;
And, to the door of Aaron coming, struck
Sharply, and long; and, when he hastened forth,
Cheerily spake, "Oh Aaron, to the king
Speed thou, and Moses; for he calleth out,
That, if ye come, and suddenly stay the plague,
Our people shall go forth."
                        Then Aaron went,
And summoned Moses; and together they
Walked swiftly,—a great pity in their hearts
For that tormented people, who, nigh mad,
Groped blindly through the streets,—for their own sins
'Gainst Israel, and for sin of him who ruled,
Afflicted thus. Within the palace soon
Arriving, mid the throng they found the king,
To and fro staggering; yelling out aloud:
Then Moses, with uplifted voice,—for din
Of outcries all around, and the dire hum
Of the fierce plague, nigh deafened every ear,—
Thus briefly spake.
                    "O king, awhile be still,

And hear me. Hebrew men have said to us,
'Aaron and Moses, Pharaoh calleth out,
That, if ye come before him, and the plague
Stay suddenly, then Israel shall go forth.'
Moses and Aaron, now before thee stand.
Dost thou repent thee, Pharaoh, of thy sin;
Thy lie to God? and wilt thou now, in truth,
If He take off this plague, let Israel go?"

Then Pharaoh, from beneath the mantle's folds
That wrapped his head, though for protection vain
'Gainst fury of the scourge,—cried piteously;
" Oh! I repent me! Take ye off this plague,
Quickly; then sacrifice unto your God,
Within the land."
      But Moses, answering, said;
" It is not meet that in Egyptian land
We so should do: for we shall sacrifice
Unto the Lord, what all of Egypt hold
Abomination. Lo, before their face
Shall we abomination sacrifice,
And will they then not stone us? We will go
A three days' journey in the wilderness;
And sacrifice unto the Lord our God,
As we shall be commanded."
      Pharaoh then
With tremulous voice cried, " I will let you go,
That ye may sacrifice unto your God
Within the wilderness: but ye shall not
Go very far away. Entreat for me."

Then Moses said, " Behold, I go from thee;
And will entreat the Lord that all the flies,
Even early on the morrow, may depart
From thee, thy servants, and from all the land.
But, deal thou not deceitfully again
Toward God,—refusing to let Israel go;
Else yet again, and with a heavier hand,
Be sure, the rod will smite."
      Thus having said,

And with stern voice of warning,—he went forth
With Aaron from the presence of the king;
And to the Elders, and the people spake:
" A three days' journey in the wilderness,
That we may sacrifice unto the Lord,
Soon may we go, for so hath Pharaoh vowed.
Get ye then ready; that, when comes the day,
At dawn we may set forth."
       From man to man,
Flew the good tidings; and all hearts were glad.

 Then, when alone he was, Moses bowed down,
Entreating of the Lord that all the flies,
Even early on the morrow, might depart
From Pharaoh, and his house, and from the land:
And the Lord heard his prayer.
       But, through the night,
Still rose the din of torment, and the roar
Of the terrific Plague; from earth to heaven
Seeming all air to fill: like thunder's moan
At distance, now,—now, like the uproar wild
Of hurricane-flashes, as, in mountain-waves,
Arrow-swift shot the living ocean by.
Many were they who perished: and, of beasts,
Great also was the number.
       But, when morn
Donned his first robe of grey, and issued forth,
A stillness fell 'neath all the cope of Heaven:
The burning passed away from beast and man:
And, when the sun had risen, and men looked round,—
Nor in their houses, nor upon the earth,
Nor throughout all the air, one fly was seen!

ISRAEL IN EGYPT.

BOOK FIFTEENTH.

Joy was in Israel; for all hoped that, now,
A three days' journey in the wilderness
Verily should they go, and sacrifice
Unto the Lord their God. So, to their tasks
That morn they went not; but within their homes
Abided, and meet preparation made
Of food; and garments, such as might beseem
That solemn festival: and to their fields
Went some, fit victims for the sacrifice
To mark from out the rest: and in all hearts
Great gladness was; and hope of wondrous things
Yet to be done for them.
                      Throughout that day,
And through the night, by their long suffering worn,
The Egyptians heavily slept: but, the next morn,
When the task-masters not one slave could find
At wonted toil; then, to the officers
Above them, angrily they made complaint:
These spake unto the rulers next in rank;
And they to those superior; till, at last,
To Pharaoh came the tidings; and his wrath,
Hot as it was before, made overboil.

For, with the dawn, both he and all his court,
And all the Egyptian people, had arisen,
From torment free; as though that fearful plague,
Of magic alone had been. And, such the cause,
Demons persuaded them; in heart of man
And woman entering; and great wrath and shame
Stirring within them, that, by wicked spells,
Thus had they been tormented, and abused,
Befooled, and mocked.   In Pharaoh, chief, had toiled
The great Arch-Fiend; his passions lashing up,
As tempests lash the waves. With burning face,
Hands clenched, teeth set, the mad king paced his room;
Picturing the triumph of those sorcerers,
And his own damning shame: for, in the ears
Of all his court, had he not cried aloud,
His sin confessing; and, of Israel's God,
Mercy beseeching! nay, even word sent forth
To the base multitude,—that they should speed
To Moses and to Aaron, and call out,
"The king will hear; quickly before him come,
And stay the plague; then shall your people go?"
Humiliation foul!—What should he now?
Not *he* the lord of Egypt, it might seem;
But those accurst enchanters. He had sworn
That, if their threatened plague they dared to send,
High on the gallows should they hang ere noon:
Yet they *had* sent it: and, in place of death,
Suddenly launched against them,—burning shame!
For mercy he had prayed! ay—prayed to them
Who had defied him! whom he had sworn to slay!
What should he then?—what could,—what dared he do!
He had given promise, Israel should go forth
Into the wilderness for sacrifice.
Before his court, and through his messengers,
Nay through the people all, so had he vowed.
Promise thus public,—promise of a king,—
Could it be now revoked?
                         While darkly thus
He pondered,—from his rulers, sorcerers, priests,

Came prayer, that in his presence they might stand,
High things to speak of. A deep flush of shame
Spread o'er his face, when thus his servants spake:
For, of those rulers, priests, and sorcerers,
Many, no doubt, there were, who his great boasts
Had heard, the plague defying,—and his words,
Harsh and unfeeling, to themselves, and all,—
Commanding them endure it as they might;
For bow he would not to those wizards curst,—
That, on the morrow, of itself 'twould die;
And, meantime, must they bear it; for, like rock,
Firm would he stand. Had they not heard him say,
" I *will* NOT send to those vile sorcerers!
I *will* NOT let that hated Israel go!
I *will* NOT ope this door; for never here
Can plague set foot; and scornfully I laugh
At the poor sorcery"? Yet, afterwards,
Had they not heard him yell, and fling back bolt,
And clash the lock, and madly issue out,
Crying aloud for those same sorcerers
To come before him, and the plague to stop;
So Israel should go forth? Even thus, alas!
His shame those men had witnessed! But 'twas done;
And face them must he; that day,—or the next:
Better at once, then.
     Thinking, feeling thus,
The sign he gave; and, forthwith, through the door,—
Accustomed reverence paying, as though still
His glory all unsullied,—a long rank
Of lords, and rulers, priests, and sorcerers came,
And stood before him, and in silence paused,
Waiting till he should speak. With eye unfirm,
And wandering, he looked on them for awhile;
Then, with low tone, unsteady, thus began.

" What would ye of the king? His heart is sad;
Such strange affliction seeing through the land,
Nor remedy clearly knowing. If your thoughts
Toward Egypt's good are bent; and ye behold
Aught thereto promising, that may be done,—

Speak freely, whoso' will."
                    Before the rest,
Necho, a priest of Isis, then stepped forth:
An aged man, but strong; of aspect stern:
In sacred order, than the Hierarch
Thamusin only, lower: but of mind
Loftier than he; of temper more sedate,
Or greater power o'er passion to hold rule.
With lowly reverence he bowed down; then rose;
And thus to Pharaoh spake.
                    "Light of the Sun!
With good cause art thou sorrowful of heart;
And all thy priests, and rulers; nay all men
Within this realm: for, through the ages past,
Even from the first of the world's history,
To the day present, never have there been
Afflictions strange as ours. Four hideous plagues,
Such as no man before this time hath seen,
Or known of, by tradition, or in book,
Have visited the land: and who shall say
If, unprevented, may not come even worse!
Things semblative to these, in days gone by,
Oft have we known; but the resemblance such
As shadow bears to substance. Every year
Hath the Nile's crystal changed to muddy red;
But ne'er before to blood, thick vital blood!
Vermin have vexed us; flies in multitudes
Tormented; from the ponds and rivers, frogs
In shoals have risen, and come upon our fields,
Our roads, and gardens: but poor shadow those,
To the great mountain of our later ills.
By natural course, O Splendor of the Sun,
These things are not. Cause preternatural, then,
Must they have had. Either, this Israel's god
No phantom is,—but Power so terrible,
That, even with the mightiest of our gods,
Should he be ranked, and worshipped: or, if he
A fiction only is, a mere pretence
Of juggling knaves,—then, or by Spirit dark,
Of which we know not, or through magic power

Beyond the wisdom of all men, save one,
These ills have been brought on us. Lives the man
Who can believe that, in this world's old age,
A new god hath been found? and, of all men,
By one of that mean, miserable race,
Ages our slaves! Find out new sun, or moon,
Or constellation in the starry host,
Then may new *god* be found. And what is he,
This wonder new? Seen him have they? or heard?
Or how his being know they? Moses, indeed,
Boasteth that in his presence hath he stood,
His awful voice hath heard: and where, O king,
And in what fashion, did he show himself?
From out the earthquake rose he? or the depths
Of the unfathomed sea? or from the sky,
Thundering, and girt with lightnings, came he down?
Nay; in such guise, perchance, a god of old,
Mortals might visit: not so the new god,—
Old fashions, doubtless, scorning: in a shape
More noble far came he; and with a tone
More terrible spake: a bush on fire, forsooth,
His glory; and his voice the sputtering flame!
And that which spake the flame, rank treason was
'Gainst thee, O king, and Egypt; and a lie
Even to the Israelites! By all the gods
Of the old heaven, companion strange indeed
This Moses hath made for them! Such poor thing,
That, save his stupid people, on the earth
Liveth no man who could believe in him!
A wretched fable is he; not worth breath
For argument, or mockery. Is there, then,
Some Spirit dark, mighty, and yet unknown
To all the world beside, through whom these plagues
Moses hath brought on Egypt? Why, a god
Such potent Spirit would be,—even that same god
Whom we all know, and still propitiate,
The Power of Evil, Typhon. Wherefore, then,
For those vile Hebrews, who him worship not,
Should he on us, who worship him, bring ill?
But Typhon is he not; for this new god

Of wind and bush-on-fire, Jehovah is,—
So named, at least, by Moses; and a god,
Not of all earth, but Israel's god alone;
A phantom, therefore; a mere mock, a cheat!
Nor god, nor Spirit is there, then, through whom
These plagues could he have brought: but, as we know,
A dread reality there is, by which
Sorely might he torment us: that dark power
Of magic, wherein, far above all men,
Accomplished is he: and, by that alone,
Be thou assured, O king, hath all been wrought.
His god of Israel is a mere pretence,
Through which he would o'erawe thee: his true god,
Sorcery is; and thereby hath he done,
What veritable god had scorned to do.
Even from his boyhood, ravenous was he
For all dark learning; feeding evermore;
Yet ever hungry still; so that ripe age,
'Gainst his mere youth, no strength had to contend.
Long ere from Egypt, for foul murder done,
Compelled was he to fly,—thus eminent
In the dark power he stood: but, two score years
Since then have passed: and in the deepest depths,
Be sure that he unceasingly hath worked;
Gathering up knowledge of all mysteries:
Till, at the last, in potence confident,
Hither hath he returned; defying law,
That should have sentenced him; defying thee,
O king; and, with audacious look and word,
Demanding of thee to set free our slaves,
That they, forsooth, might in the desert go
To worship his new god! That power he had
Sorely to vex us, knew he; and this power
A god he named; so hoping most to awe,
And bow us to his purpose. For, if god,
A true god, though to us unknown before,
Plainly through him had spoken, thou, O king,
And all thy priests and rulers, as one man,
Had hastened to obey: but, clear to sight
As sky and earth it is, that this new god

A lie is, merely; a most wretched mask
For magic damnable. Why, every act
That hath been done, is such as gods would scorn:
Not great, and dread, as of Supernal Power,
Wrath pouring upon man; but petty, foul,
Vexatious, venomous; such as poor despite
Of wizard only, would have stooped to inflict.
Bare sorcery is it all. A dead staff, first,
To living dragon changed he; bidding us
Proof therefrom take that from his god he came,
Bearing command divine: but, from their staffs,
Thy sorcerers instantly called serpents forth;
Aid from no god pretending. Verily,
Had it been god indeed, who, for a sign,
That staff had turned to dragon,—not aloof,
Or idly looking on, had he remained,
To see his power thus mocked! A thunderbolt
Would he have hurled among them; or called forth
The earthquake to engulf them. No,—alike
By magic both were done; sole difference this;
One was a giant's power; and one mere man's.
Greater the might that bid a dragon come,
Than that which called the serpents. Nay, the one
Swallowed alive the others; as to show
That Moses, singly, in the dark art stood
Mightier than all thy sorcerers combined.
And how, next, proved he that from god he came?
By turning Nile to blood! Terrific spell,
Truly, that so could work!—but spell alone;
Mere magic still: for even that self-same trick
Thy sorcerers also did; though, as before,
Less in degree of wonder. He, a hill,
They, but a hillock made: yet they, and he,
By same means wrought: and what for him is proof,
Proof also is for them. If he from god
His strength had,—they, too, had from god their strength.
But, while *his* god saith, 'let my people go,'
Ours answereth, 'keep that people still your slaves.'
To which, then, should we hearken,—his, or ours?
Yet well thy sorcerers know, that strength of god

None was there in their work; but solely might
Of magic; and, in his, nought else. Alike
In nature both, as hillock is to hill;
In bulk alone unlike. Then sent he frogs,
Vermin, and flies: and these thy sorcerers,
In part, brought also. If, in part, they failed,
What proveth this, save what before was proved,
That his the deeper cunning? Reason none
It brings, to force belief, that other power
Than at the first, he used. No! plain as day
Outstandeth it, that his pretended god
Is, veritably, witchcraft: and himself
Boldly hath made avowal, that his aim,
In so tormenting us, hath been, and is,
And will be to the end, to force from us
Freedom to Israel. Splendor of the Sun,—
If this rebellion be not, against thee,
And 'gainst all Egypt,—let the judges say
What *is* rebellion. He defieth thee,
Defieth all the realm: our lawful slaves,—
Our property, as much as are our lands,
Our horses, oxen, houses, mules, or dogs,—
On terror of worse plagues, demands from us;
As robbers, upon pain of death, demand
Spoil from the traveller. Laws, indeed, we have
To punish rebels. In the public court,
Such may be tried, convicted, and condemned.
But, for *this* rebel, trial none there needs;
Since he himself, before thy face, O king,
And in the presence of thy servants all,
Hath blazoned his rebellion. Cause beside
Is there, why formal trial should be none,
For traitor like to him; since much the fear
That his great magic might the law defeat;
Blinding his judges, so that black from white
Could they not know: or, were he cast in chains,
Might make steel fetters, cobwebs. For thyself,
And for all Egypt, boldly say I, then;
No safety is there while this man shall live:
And no assurance is there he shall die,

Save by a stroke, rapid and unforeseen
As lightning from clear heaven. For, be assured,
If but a moment his black spells can work,
To him will victory be—to us defeat.
And if he live, and his old course pursue,
Ruin, erelong, will cover this whole land.
Already, from our rivers, streams, and ponds,
All fish have perished; by his magic killed:
And, of our cattle, by these two last plagues,
Thousands are lost to us; horses, and mules,
Oxen, and sheep; while, of *their* cattle, none
The Israelites have lost; not even one!
Surely, O Splendor of the Sun, 'twere just
To force from the wrong-doers recompense
To those whom they have wronged. A punishment
Most righteous, then, it were, from them to take
Even three for one, of all that we have lost;
Mules, asses, oxen, horses, sheep, and goats,—
So teaching them that gods o'errule the earth,
And make the stroke of evil to rebound
Upon the striker. But even more than this
Should they be mulcted. Through the land 'tis known
That, while beneath their cursed plagues we writhed,
Nought suffered they at all. Water they had,
While we but blood: no frog their doorway crossed;
Nor was there of them woman, man, or child,
On whom the vermin, or the fly, once touched.
This wrought their magic: but thou, too, O king,
Power hast of magic; power by which to force
Silver and gold from them who have it not,
Or say they have not; and the which to lose,
To them worse plague would be than those they 'scaped.
In answer, then, to *their* plague, *thy* plague send:
Their taxes double: and, for each default,
The penalties double also. For our wrongs,
In part thus may they pay us. But, in vain
This, and all else, that remedy, or redress,
For evil done may seem, while yet untouched
Stands the prime cause of all. Thy plague, O king,

Worse plague would answer, if, ere it be sent,
Thou strike not down the sorcerer,—who will, else,
Thee strike; and this whole realm. First, foremost,
    then,
Let the magician die: all, afterwards,
Will be a downhill journey, smooth and swift:
Else, mountain-climbing; crags, and precipice
Awaiting us at last. O Pharaoh, hear,
And ponder; for, as I have spoken now,
So speak thy princes, judges, rulers, priests;
One thought, one fear, one hope pervading all."

 He ended; lowly bowed; and silent stood,
Approval hoping. But the king sat mute;
Angry, yet fearful: burning, now, to send
Swift vengeance on his enemy, and wipe out
The shame of his debasement; shivering, now,
With apprehension dark of some strange ill
That bitterly might repay him. Life to take
By secret stroke, even if success were sure,
Would argue feebleness, or cowardice,
Unworthy of a king: but, if the blow
Its mark should fail, shame tenfold would be his;
And some dire vengeance, inconceivable,
Even tenfold might requite it.
      Kingly pride
From danger of reproach to guard;—to 'scape
Peril of retribution, for a crime
Successless in attempt,—and, yet, to slake
Thirst of revenge, for injury and disgrace
Brought on himself, and Egypt,—on safe course,
Or what safe seemed, at length he fixed resolve;
And, his bowed head uplifting, thus replied.

 "Garment of fashion wondrous strange, O priest,
Thou offerest to a king; of silk, in part,
But, part, of coarsest flax: a robe, indeed,
Might token him half monarch, and half slave.
As monarch, thou wouldst have him send command,—

Of his own will alone, not law's award,—
That a great criminal die : as timid slave,
Wouldst have him whisper in a murderer's ear,
To take him suddenly off! What! thinkest thou
The king so feeble is, that he need fear
The power of this one Hebrew? So cast down
That, knowing him a traitor, he yet dreads
In public court to arraign him? or so vile
That, vengeance to make sure, and peril 'scape,
He'd have him stabbed in the dark? Great shame,
 indeed,
Thou flingest on the king,—presuming him
A listener to such counsel. Majesty
And power of monarchs, o'er the herd of men
Soars high as thunder soars above the earth.
Kings hurl their lightning,—and the subject tree
Falls blasted. But, as heaven's dread thunderer
His own time chuseth to let go the bolts,
Even so will Pharaoh his own moment chuse,
And his own manner, to send punishment.
The Hebrew's spells, perchance, are now worn out;
His poisoned shafts all spent : or, if he still
Point, threatening, to his quiver, he shall learn
That every arrow against Egypt sent,
Strikes Israel also; in him rankles most :
For, thy last counsel, priest,—the woof of silk,
Ill matched with vilest flax,—the king accepts.
Let, then, proclaim be made throughout the land,
That whosoever by this plague hath lost
Horse, ox, sheep, mule,—or other living thing,
May from the Hebrews take, even three for one;
Found wheresoe'er, or whosesoe'er they be :
Three horses for one horse, three sheep for one,
Plague-killed. But, if of more they be despoiled,
Then let them go before the magistrate,
And cry for justice. A requital fair
For loss of substance this; and warning, too,
That, Egypt aimed at, Israel will be struck.
But, in like fashion, can we not repay

Bodily torment, terror, hunger, thirst,
By Hebrew plagues inflicted: curse for curse,
Of one same nature both, we cannot send:
But yet, a plague which terror, hunger, thirst,
Mind-torment, will bring on them, can I fling;
And it shall go. Let the tax-gatherers, then,
All tributes double; and all penalties
Laid on default, make threefold what they are.
And to the task-masters let it be said;
'Your slaves are idle still: get ye more work
From their vile bodies: and, if more they grudge,
Stir them with music of the whip, and stick;
Till to the sky, or wheresoe'er he be,
Their howlings reach, and their Jehovah wake,
To help them, if he can.' Moreover, send,
And on the instant,—for the slaves, I hear,
This day no work have done; but in their homes
Abide, quick preparation making all
For their fool's journey to the wilderness,—
Send forth, I say, on the instant, and proclaim
Throughout the city and all parts around,
'Thus saith the king: get ye to work again,
Ye cunning slaves; for ye shall not go forth
Into the desert. If to your false god
Ye must give sacrifice, within the land
Is room enough. When all your tasks are done,
Here worship if ye will; or not at all;
For hence ye shall go never! By all gods
So swear I. To this realm your toil ye owe;
To this earth owe your bodies: work, and die:
Then rot, and with your fat enrich our fields:
For ours ye ever were, and still shall be;
In life, in death. Then know yourselves; and haste
To do the king's command; else, speedily,
Shall vengeance be among you!'"
         Speaking thus,—
By the Arch-Fiend inflamed,—his starting eyes
Gleamed fire-like; his lips quivered; and his voice,
Like to a tiger's howl articulate made,

On all brought wonder. Sign of audience o'er,
Suddenly making then,—down from the throne
With hurried step he trod, and left the hall.

Astonished, for brief time in silence stood
The princes, lords, and rulers; man on man
Looking, and marvelling. In low tone, at length,
Spake one unto the rest; and all went forth.

ISRAEL IN EGYPT.

BOOK SIXTEENTH.

DARKNESS again on Israel! for the words
Of Pharaoh,—with harsh proclamation sent
Throughout the city, and throughout the land,—
Struck down all hope: and o'er the time to come
Shadow so fearful cast, that gloomiest days
Of the years gone, with that compared, seemed breath
Of spring, to winter's blast. 'Gainst Moses then,
And Aaron, rose new murmurs, and 'gainst all
The priests and Elders, who had promise given
Of a deliverance coming. Of God's help
Despaired the many: even some there were,
Who of Jehovah, the One Only God,
Doubt felt,—nay, disbelief: for, in the ways
Of Egypt born and bred,—to Egypt's gods
Rather inclined they: the poor Hebrew creed
Vulgar esteeming; and for ignorance
Alone a fit belief. Murmurs, and groans,
And cries, and curses rose.
                      But, meek and mild,
Though great, and awe-inspiring, Moses went
Among the people, strengthening their hearts;
Bidding them trust in God; for, sure as day

Would follow night, so surely would His act,
The promise follow. " ' With an outstretched hand
Will I bring Israel forth,'—said not the Lord?
' The king of Egypt will not let you go:
But with my wonders will I smite the land;
And, *after that*, the king *shall* let you go.'
And *hath* He not with wonders smitten them?
And think ye God will cease, till all be done?
Be sure that wonders greater yet shall be;
And that, though millstone-hard against us now,
Yet, in the end, shall Pharaoh soft become
As clay in the potter's hands. In God then trust."

Thus Moses; Aaron also, and the priests
And Elders, throughout all the city went,
And in the lands around,—the downcast hearts
Uplifting; the weak strengthening; the blind
Teaching to see, on the dark Orient's rim,
Dawn's tinge; though faint, yet heralding bright day.

But still the groans, and cries, and curses rose:
For, with rude mockery, on the Hebrew herds,
Horses, and mules, the Egyptians laid their hands;
For every *one*, plague-slain, extorting three:
Tax-gatherers stern a double tribute forced;
Task-masters, with their sounding whips, drove forth
The sorrowing, terrified slaves; and labor more,
And worse, inflicted on them: so that life,—
Save unto those who yet in God had trust,—
Became a burthen, and they longed to die.

To the blest land of Goshen quickly flew
The tidings; and, though task-masters were none,
Nor slaves therein,—yet, when from house to house,
From village unto village, ran the word,
That, thenceforth, double tribute must be paid;
And that, from out the Hebrew flocks and herds,
Even three for one of all that they had lost,
The Egyptian men with law's strong hand might take;
Then a deep murmur rose. Some few there were

Who Moses blamed, that such terrific plagues
He had sent on Egypt; which but torment were
Unto her people; and, for Israel, wrought
Evil far more than good; the headstrong king
But madder making; 'gainst themselves more fierce,
Defiant more 'gainst God. But all the rest,
Who, either from his mouth, or by report,
Had heard the words of Moses,—as to him
At night, on Horeb, from the burning bush,
They had been spoken,—knew that hard of heart
Pharaoh would be; and plague on plague might bide,
Ere God he would obey, and Israel loose.
Much evil, therefore, looked they to endure;
And, while most sorrowing, whispered to their hearts,
That, when at heaviest, the black clouds would break,
And let the sunshine down.

                        Within the house
Of Kohath, with his family, that day,
Sat Reuben, and his father Malachi.
Two hours the mid-day meal had passed; but they
Still in the chamber lingered; grave discourse,
Now sad, now hopeful, holding, of the events
So wondrous which had lately come to pass;
Of Pharaoh's fickle mind,—submissive, now,
Now, arrogant; and still tyrannic most,
After, plague-terrified, he most had bowed
To Israel's God, and loudest cried for help.
Of Sethos, also, spake they; and the word
Of promise he had given, that in the cause
Of Israel he would plead before the king:
Yet how,—strange answer to such prayer,—had come,
Not grace, but worse oppression,—as that day
Sorely had witnessed. "When he shall return,"
Said Kohath, "thereon will I question him:
For, truly, spake he as a man sincere,
Simply, and warmly; not as one who feigns
Great zeal, intending nought. Nor many days
Will pass, methinks, ere he again . . . ."

"Hush, hush,
Said Rachael, one pearl finger holding up;
"I hear the tramp of horses."
Mute they sat,
Listening quick hoof-stamps; and, anon, the roll
Of chariot-wheels, at great speed drawing nigh.
Louder the tramplings grew; and numerous,
It seemed, as of war-squadron; and the wheels,
As if for multitude, made the ground to shake.
Then, suddenly, all was still. Not without fear,
Kohath, and Malachi, and Reuben gazed
Each in the face of the other: and her hand
Upon the arm of Rachel, Sarah laid,
And, trembling, whispered. But, with face serene,
The virgin looked on all, and gently said:
"No cause for fear, methinks. Nor native foe,
Nor foreign enemy have we to dread;
Nor wrath of Pharaoh, more than on the rest
Of our poor people. But, whoe'er they be,
Now pausing at our gate—forget we not
That God o'erruleth all things."
As she ceased,
Quickly the door flew open; and a man,—
Crazed, as it seemed, with utmost ecstasy
Of terror,—pale, and trembling, hurried in.
"Oh master," cried he, "get thee out at once
Behind the house, and fly; else, verily,
Wilt thou be put to death: for, at the gate,
Sitting within his chariot, all of gold,
Is Pharaoh, even the king; with his great lords
Standing about him: and, when I went up,
One of them said, 'Unto thy master speed,
Kohath, the son of Zohar, and thus say;
Pharaoh, the Splendor of the Sun, is come
To visit thee, and on great matters speak;
Come thou then forth to honor him.' But oh!
Go thou not forth, my master; for 'tis ill
They mean thee, and not good. Chariots like flame,
Twice ten there be, and more; and horsemen, too,
By hundreds; some before, and some behind;

All giants, and in armour that seems fire;
Riding on huge, fierce horses, lion-eyed,
And black as midnight. Oh, my master, run,
And get thee from the house, or soon . . . ."
                                          " Stay, stay,"
Said Kohath. Turning then to Malachi
And Reuben, with a look all wonderment,
Hastily spake he. " Whatsoe'er this bode,
Evil, or good, one only course we have.
Come with me on the instant. We must speed,
And reverence pay."
                    For answer waiting not,
Forth went he then; and, with quick beating hearts,
Not pausing, though reluctant, Malachi
And Reuben followed him. In Rachel's face,
Sarah, all pale and trembling, looked, and said;
" I dare not stand before the king: come now;
Let us make haste, and get from out the house,
Before they spy us."
                     With a loving smile,
Rachel beheld her, and replied, " Fear not;
For, dearest mother, nought is there to fear.
Were the king's thoughts of evil, never thus
Had they in act appeared. The violent hand
At once had fallen upon us: but he comes,
With gracious courtesy, and at our gate
Pauses for word of welcome. Surely, sign
Of amity this. His purpose, out of sight
To my poor vision is, as ocean's bed;
Yet, thus beginning, ill it scarce can be.
But, whatsoe'er it prove, an eye there is
That all things sees, a hand that all things guides:
Come good, or evil, still from Him it comes:
And evil though it seem, must yet be good.
We stand upon a rock, my mother dear,
Not on a trembling plank: and, standing so,
Never can fall. Be then thy heart at rest.
Consider, too, if from the house we go,
When friendly feet are entering,—what sad shame
On our poor hospitality will be;

Most poor, at best, to welcome a great king.
Let us not make it worse. But come; I hear
Footsteps within the garden, drawing nigh;
And a strange voice. Let us retire within;
And preparation make for such repast
As guests like these may suit."
*   With cheerful tone
Thus speaking, she her mother's trembling hand
Took in her own, and kissed it lovingly;
Then drew her from the room.
                              In little while,—
With meet respect by Kohath ushered in:
Friendly of aspect seeming; and with tones
Kind and familiar speaking,—yet intent,—
Since through the carnal appetite he had failed—
With deadliest wiles those Chosen Ones to lure
To utter ruin; and God's merciful scheme
Through them to bring Messiah, thus o'erthrow—
In humble form of Pharaoh, Egypt's king,
Came now the terrible Majesty of Hell.
Behind him, of his train, was one alone;
An aged man,—in rich habiliments,
Silk, woven with gold; who, in his shrivelled hands,
An ebon box, with gold and gems thick laid,
As with deep reverence bore. Behind him walked
Reuben and Malachi, silent both, and pale;
By that dread presence awed.
                              Within the room
Arrived,—about him looked the shadowy king,
As seeking whom he found not. Turning then
To Kohath, with a kindly voice,—suppressed;
Yet such appearing as, put forth at full,
Might talk 'gainst even the thunder,—" Where is she,—
" Where is thy beauteous daughter?" he enquired;
" For her, not less, nay even more than thee,
Come I to visit: where, too, is thy wife?
Her presence also need I; since her words,—
If mine prove vain,—haply may move thy child
To her own good, and yours."
                              By a dark fear

O'ermastered, Kohath answered not; but signed
To Malachi; and the old man went forth.

"A goodly land ye Israelites have here,"
Pursued the Shape; "such as through Egypt, else,
I have not seen; for verdure, and sweet air,
And fruitfulness. A favored race indeed
Must ye be held,—almost possessors sole
Of this, the kingdom's gem: though wherefore so,
Truly I know not; neither why exempt
From bonds elsewhere imposed; or from the stroke
Of plagues that smote all else. Such happy state,
Well may ye prize: and distant be the day
That shall bring change. But, with yourselves alone
It rests, to keep, or lose it.
                              "Fairest maid,"—
To Rachel he pursued, as, bowing low,
Yet with calm mien, she entered; by the hand
Her trembling mother leading,—" on thee, chief,—
Though on thy parents also, and this youth,—
Dependeth that of which even now I spake;
Whether your people, in this favored land,
As heretofore, shall dwell; happy, and free
From that great bondage which, through Egypt, else,
Weighs on the Hebrew race,—or, gods forbid!
Shall be driven forth; and, mixed with all the rest,
Live years on years in slavery; and slaves die.
Such the momentous question which this day
Ye must determine; for with you it rests:
With you alone. Yet, not indifferent all
To me, and Egypt, how ye turn the scale;
For, with your good, ours also is close bound;
Our good being yours; our evil also yours;
And, though in less degree, your good, and ill,
Ours also. Summon then your best of powers
For comprehension clear: and, when ye see
How wisdom points,—then into Passion put
An iron curb, and force him from wrong path.
Thou, maiden, chiefly; and thou, virtuous youth,
To reason solely listen; and the voice

Of justice and of mercy to your race:
But, to the foolish whisperings of fond love,
'Gainst reason and justice pleading,—hearken not;
For selfish wholly are they; a foul sin
Against your people; and, on you, and all,
Sin's punishment would bring. Not harsh am I,
Though strongly speaking: zealous for your good,
Even more than ours; as, erelong, will ye find;
Nay, zealous more than for mere policy,—
For a quick-born affection: but, of that,
Hereafter shall ye learn. No matter slight,
Ye may be sure, that hath a Pharaoh brought
To Goshen, with one Hebrew family
Discourse to hold. Ye no tradition have
Of like event. Intently listen then:
Reason my counsel: and, as wisdom bids,
As justice urges, and as mercy pleads,—
Nay, even as piety to the gods commands,—
For wisdom, justice, mercy, are their voice,—
So now on act determine.
                              "Well ye know
How, at this day, your Moses, and the king,
Strange opposites, front each other. Earthly power
So wholly mine, that, by a finger raised,
Death might I send him: but demoniac power
So potent his, that, over all the land,
Strange plagues, abominations, hath he brought:
And worse hath threatened, if his insolent words
I hearken not; and let your people go
Three days, forsooth, into the wilderness;
There to give sacrifice unto your god.
Much torment hath he caused us, and great loss.
All fish within the rivers, brooks, and ponds,
Have perished: and of horses, oxen, sheep,
So numerous are the slain, that, with loud voice,
All Egypt hath cried out for punishment
On the magician; and full recompense
From Israel, for the ills through Israel brought.
Vast is our loss; but, far and wide 'tis known
That, magic guarded, not one plague hath touched
Horse, ox, or sheep, or any living thing

To you belonging. With great justice, then,
My people clamored that, even three for one,
Of all plague-stricken things, should be exact
From Hebrews,—the sole cause of all that loss.
And thus did I decree; as ye this day,
Ill-pleased, have learned; yet not worse pleased than I,
Forced so to deal against you. Nay, more still
Driven may I be to vex you; for, one voice
From all my people, rulers, lords, and priests,
Calls death upon your Moses: and by oath
Pledged am I, if but one plague more he bring,
Sharply to cut him off. But, way there is
Before us open, on which you, and I,—
Wisely and truly walking,—the worst ills
For both may 'scape; for both great good may win.
But, the worst evil, or best good, to *me*
That hence can come, all insignificant is
As gnat unto a camel, weighed with those
Enormous, waiting you; which to the heavens
In glory will lift, or sink you deep in earth;
Ay, deeper than the grave. In my right hand,
A chrysolite of the sun if I held forth;
And, in my left hand, noisome rottenness,
Choice proffering you,—not greater, 'twixt those two,
The contrast were, than 'twixt the opposites
That now I offer. Israel is a slave;
Egypt his lord: but Israel may be free;
Free from this land to go, or here abide;
Free from all labor, taxes; save alone
Such as, throughout the realm, Egyptians pay.
A rare gem this ye grant,—but the price ask.
Yet, be ye silent till my speech shall end,
And I your answer crave; for more, far more
Advantage would I give you; glory, too,
Such as, yourselves to dream of, madness were;
Such as, to speak of, ye might think *me* mad,
Till ye shall all have learned . . . . . . Thou, beauteous maid,
Fairest by far of all these eyes have seen,
The cause original art; though, of thyself,
Most ignorant how."

With gentle wonderment,
Her calm clear eyes upon him Rachel turned;
Nor blushing, nor confused; though, with a look
At once of admiration, and great love,—
A father's love, and all-approving smile,—
The mighty face gazed on her.
                            "Yes, fair maid,"
Pursued the king; "first, and chief cause, art thou.
On thee dependeth, whether Israel rise
Among the nations, great and glorious;
Or, altogether, woman, man, and child,
Down to the bottom sink, slaves evermore.
If thou the voice of wisdom, mercy, list,
All may be well: if thou refuse, all ill.
Maiden, thy heart I know. To this fond youth,—
Not undeserving it,—thy love is given;
Thy hand is vowed. Yet, for thy parents' good,
Thine own, and Reuben's; for all Israel's good,
Should'st thou from him thy love, thy hand, disjoin."

"Never!" the maid exclaimed,—a roseate tinge,
As from red sunbeam, flashing o'er her face:
"Never!" again she said, in deeper tone,
More mild, yet speaking strength invincible:
And, toward him lightly stepping, by the hand
Took the pale trembling youth; and in his face
Poured infinite love. With look, then, all serene,
Unknowing shame,—she turned; and to the king
Gently, yet firmly spake.
                          "From childhood up,
O Pharaoh, to each other dedicate,
By parents, and by friends, and our own love,
Have we been held. There is not on the earth,
Save Reuben, one to whom I would be wed:
Nor maiden is there, whatsoe'er her state,
Her beauty, or her wealth, whom, leaving me,
Would he espouse; for, on our souls 'tis fixed,
That, by especial ordinance of God,
We twain shall one become."
                          As, in the gloom

Of sultry summer-night, along the verge
Of the horizon dark-red lightning runs,
A moment seen, and gone; so, from the orbs
Of the dread Phantom-king,—when that sweet voice
Opposal resolute spake,—one fiery glance
Quivered, and died. But, all eyes bent on her,
Hers upon Reuben turned,—the meteor blazed
Unnoted; and, for that hot gleam, a look
Of gentle love commanding,—with mild voice,
The Pharaoh thus resumed.

"Thou didst forget,
Fair maiden, that I silence craved from all,
Till my whole speech should end. Unto the last,
I pray thee once again to lend thine ear,
And understanding; but lock up thy tongue:
For, in poor ignorance thou refusest now,
What, with full knowledge, thou may haste to take.
Think not that, for light reason, I would ask
Maiden to loose a knot of virtuous love:
Or that, for sacrifice made by thee, and him,
Thy long-betroth'd, I would not recompense give,
Worthy a king,—ay, greater far than king
Through the whole earth beside: beyond compare
More rich than what 'twould pay for. Take thou thought,
Blest Rachel; Reuben thou, and all the rest,
Take thought of this,—that, what he stoops to beg;
Nay, at large cost would purchase,—with strong hand,
Defiant of all earth, the king might take;
And, as he would, dispose of. When he prays,
Think, then, he might command, if love ruled not,
And justice, more than passion; and so frame
Your dispositions, that his generous thoughts,
With generous you may meet. Such harmony
In good to all must end. With few words now,
My whole desire will I lay bare to you:
Make plain all good that ye have power to do,
And all the evil: all the tenfold good,
Thousandfold evil, that upon yourselves,
Power have ye to call down, as, to the right,
Or to the wrong, ye go.

"The sun shines not
To one man only: beauty cannot shine,
By one man only seen, admired, and loved.
Maiden, my son, the heir to Egypt's throne,
Like a poor fly to the flame, too near hath come
To thy soul-scorching beauty; and been burned,
Till sense, nay life, is perilled. Kohath, thou
A father art; and, for a father's pangs,
Feeling must have. Even like to one possessed,
Is my loved Sethos; body, fever-fired;
Mind, wandering; voice, still calling upon her,
Thy matchless daughter; who, though seen but twice,
Deep in his soul is buried; no more thence
To be withdrawn, than might a buried sword,
Deep broken in his body. Sobbing, now,
As if his heart would burst; now, groaning loud,
As in death-agony; with folded hands,
Now, crying out to her imploringly,
As to a very goddess,—down his cheeks
Tears running like two brooks,—Oh! it is sad,
Sad, piteous, even for stranger, to behold
A tree so glorious beaten to the ground,
Withering, and dying: for a father, then,—
Oh Kohath, oh blest Rachel, Reuben too,
What for a father is it!

"Ere distraught,
He had his story told: how once, by chance,
He had beheld a being, goddess-bright;
Had watched her to her home: how, afterward,
By the young Syrian prince and princess led,
That temple pure he had again beheld;
And, therein, the shrined deity; the bright star
Which, thenceforth, made his heaven! and he implored,—
As I would have him live, and reason hold,—
That he might wed her. But, when he confessed
That she a Hebrew was, indignantly
Did I rebuke him; for that public law,
As well he knew, such marriage had forbid.
Alas! I now repent me that so stern
Was my forbiddance; for, as though quick death

Had smitten him, he sank; and all the day
Corpse-like lay stretched: till, evening coming on,
Flame-faced, and frenzy-eyed, he started up,
A yelling madman: from the palace flew,
To plunge in Nile; or headlong fling himself
In pit, or well; or howsoever else
He might end life and misery,—for even so
Out cried he, running. Swifter feet pursued,
And brought him back. Still all the night he raved.
At length, with kind words, loving tones, and sound
Of gentle music, having soothed his rage,—
Calmly I spake with him; and promise gave,—
So he a reasoning man once more would be,—
Far as my power might go, his suit to speed,
And aid him win that jewel. For the law,—
The maid herself, perchance, its interdict
Might set aside; Osiris for her god,
In place of him, Jehovah named, thenceforth
Avowing. . . . . Answer not as yet, fair maid:
Nor any of you speak till all be told.
A point momentous this ye deem, I see;
Though, of a truth, 'tis nought; or nothing more
Than a sound's difference. Ye Jehovah say;
Osiris we: yet, by two words, one thing
Meaning alike: and it poor wisdom were,
A word to cling to, and give up a world:
For, that word holding, more than a world's worth
Ye fling away. Who higher rates the gem
Seen in the mirror, than the gem itself,
Such folly might act: but not so you, I trust,
All knowing, and considering. For myself,
Plainly I say,—did not Egyptian law,—
Stronger, in this, upon Egyptian king,
Than even on humblest subject, force on me,
For names of god and goddess, the words sent
From hoar antiquity down,—as readily
Would I Jehovah, as Osiris speak;
For Isis, whatsoever goddess-name
Ye to the like power give. Small mountain this,
For a firm foot, and steady brain, to climb:

And oh! what glorious prospect from its height!
Small obstacle I say; yet, unto *you*
Alone, 'tis small; a thing to be o'erleaped,
Scarce drawing breath; but, unto us, a rock
Precipitous; high as heaven; impassable!
The maiden, by a word, may fit herself
To espouse Egyptian king: Egyptian king,
Neither by word, nor act, could be made free
To wed false worshipper; for law, more old
Than records tell, would crown and sceptre take,
And to another give them.   Ponder then,
I pray you, all; thou, maiden, first and chief;
Ye, her fond parents; and thou, modest youth,
Sore as thy grief would be; and thou, his sire,—
Ponder, I pray you all, the mighty thing
That ye are hearing: and, for slight account,
Miss not a sun that waits to rise on you;
And plunge yourselves in everlasting night.

" Thee, Rachel, woo I now for my son's wife;
For Egypt's sometime queen.   Our learned priests
In their religion soon will give thee light;
And thou wilt see how easy is the task,
A name, and some few forms, mere trifles all,
Of worship, to lay by; and others take;
Not better, haply, but not worse,—alike
In meaning, and in end: but different far
In the great end of all, as life, and death.
Trifle, as yet, I see thou deemest not
Even the mere name-change; the poor difference
'Twixt the few letters that make up the words.
'Tis but that one is nigh thee, one remote.
The nigh put off, and the remote brought near,—
The favorite of old thou wouldst discard,
And hug the new, once spurned.   What nearest is,
Still greatest seems: thy rosy finger-point,
Close to thine eye, shows greater than the sun;
Blotting it wholly out: so, thine old creed,—
For aught of moment, a mere finger-point,—

Blots out all others; blots what thou might find
A sun, a heaven all glory.
                         " Absolute this,
The one condition sole,—that Egypt's gods
Thou worship,—*thou;* for, if their creed of old
Thy parents still would keep,—full liberty
Have they, as all of Israel : them our law
Of royal marriage touches not. The wife
Of Egypt's king, or prince, to Egypt's gods
Must bow,—else on the throne may he not sit.
For all her race beside, such liberty
As theretofore they had, such keep they still. . . . .
This one small thing by thee conceded,—here,
Even at this hour, I hail thee as the bride,
Of Egypt's prince,—as Egypt's future queen!

" For any other damsel 'neath the sun,
Such honor this, that straightway at my feet
Might she fall down,—speechless with gratitude,
Or eloquent with thanks : but thou, blest maid,
So far in beauty dost all else o'erpeer ;
So like to goddess art,—that earthly prize,
Even the richest, all unworthy seems
To purchase thy celestial. Nay, frown not ;
Though even thy frown more lovely is than smiles
Of all earth's beauties else ; but hearken now,
While—the deficiency of Egypt's throne
Thy worth to balance,—in the scale I cast
Advantage, such as never yet did king,
Even for the loftiest princess of the earth,
In dowry offer.
                " Treasure-cities four
Have I : in gold, and silver, and in gems,
The richest of the world. I cannot name,
Nor couldst thou understand, the mighty sum ;
Passing all count. Of these will two be thine
On that same day when thou my son shalt wed.
On that same day, north, south, east, west, shall fly
The great proclaim,—' Henceforth is Israel free :

Henceforth no labor, taxes, shall they pay,
Save such as pays all Egypt: from this day,
Free to depart the land, free to remain,
All Israel is become: for, on this day,
A Hebrew maiden, gem of all the earth,
Or goddess, rather, habited in flesh,
Celestial, yet half human, hath come down,
And wedded Egypt's prince.'   Such the proclaim
Of glory and good to all of Hebrew race,
On that glad morning. . . . . But, of special good
To thine own house, and friends, I now must speak.

" Kohath, and Sarah,—from your heavenly child,
Never should ye know severance; for, all else
Which the world hath, of pleasant, or of rare,
Would, wanting her, seem common, joyless, poor.
But, vast the palace wherein she will dwell;
And chambers spacious, numerous there are,
Wherein ye may abide: so one home still
Will yours and hers remain: your revenue such
As fits Egyptian prince.
                         " But, now, for thee,
Young Reuben; gentle, virtuous, loving,—*just*,
Boldly I add; for, in thy countenance,
And thy demeanor, so I read thy worth;
And rightly read; yea, plainly, as thy brow,—
Door to the very chamber of the soul,—
With letters of heaven's fire were over-writ,
Telling its qualities such,—for thee, poor youth,
From whom the richest jewel of the world
Seek I to take,—for thee what may I do,
Such loss to countervail?   Nought, verily,
Which, in thy mood existent, thou wouldst deem
More than the poorest fraction of that whole
Of which I'd rob thee.   But, Time pauses not:
The earthquake may be staggered in its course,
Encountering bottomless rocks: great ocean's stream
Be turned, and hindered,—but, in earth, and heaven,
No power there is that can the stream of Time
One sun-flash stay: and still, as it flows on,

In all things, earthly, heavenly, it brings change.
Mountains, by Time, have been worn down to hills;
Hills flattened to the plains: the sun himself,
Sometime, 'tis said,—black, cold, and motionless,
Will hang in heaven, burned out. But, changeful most
Of all things, is weak man: one day insane
To clutch at some bright bauble; and, the next,
Heedless to keep, or lose it. Not of change
So hasty, capable *thou*, true-hearted youth.
Thy earnest love for that consummate maid,
Long moons may last: nay, even while the sun
Twice winter brings, twice summer; but, at length,—
By the same fate inexorable that rules
All things of earth and heaven,—wax faint it must,
By hope unfed, and die: and with it, too,
All that now stings, will perish: and thy life
Will pass as one bright day of blissful calm;
A golden sunshine, temperate, o'er thy head;
Airs of heaven fragrant, ever fanning thee;
Earth at thy feet, all verdure, flower, and fruit.
For, in the place of that too short-lived dream,
By fond youth thought immortal,—woman's love,—
Passion more lofty, and life-lasting too,
Will glow within thee; love of fame, wealth, rank,
Dominion; all which over the dull mass
Of men, lifts man; such will in glory rise
Within thy soul; and the poor dream of love
Melt, as noon-sun the dew-drop. Well I know,
Thou say'st within thy heart, 'I heed them not;
Humble I am; for riches do not care;
Desire not fame, or power; but peacefully
In this sweet solitude my life to pass;'—
So say'st thou,—and the truth: yet, *this day's* truth,
Alone dost utter,—not the morrow's; *that*
May, as the poles, be opposite. 'Tis now day;
Anon it will be night; and, even so,
That which to thee seems day, will turn to night;
That which night seems, to day.
                              "Yet, not alone
In certainty of human changefulness,

Would I that thou seek comfort: for thy loss,—
So thou consent to lose,—I offer thee
Such recompense as, by clear reason judged,
And world's best wisdom, far beyond all count,
Thy loss would overpay.   Attend me now,
And weigh what I shall speak.   Fools have there been
Who, dark gold offered, have bright brass preferred:
Be thou not such! for, with the brass, thou'dst take
Evils most deadly!   Laying now aside
All kingly power to enforce, I *pray* of thee
This maiden to resign.   If true thy love
To her hath been, and is,—though loss to thee,
Yet, unto her such gain unspeakable,
And glory, thence proceeding,—thou wilt leap,
The sacrifice to offer.   As thy wife,
A bondslave were she ; as my son's, a queen.
Thou canst not hesitate.   Yet, sacrifice
I ask not; but exchange : for one sweet flower,—
Celestial sweet; but ah ! with every day
Destined to fade,—another exquisite flower,—
Perchance wellnigh as sweet, I offer thee ;
And gems, which, all thy life long, bright as first,
Will shed a glory on thee.   From that hour
When thou this maid shalt render,—to the king,
Even as his better hand shalt thou become ;
The ruler, under him, of all this realm.
Thy palace, and thy retinue of state,
Princely shall be : o'er every lord and priest
Supremacy shalt thou hold.   Judges most sage,
When doubtful, by thy sentence will be swayed.
The captains of our hosts to thee will look,
As to a second Pharaoh, for the word
That moveth armies.   King in name alone,
Contented will I be; all kingly power
To thee resigning; while with wisdom thou,
Justice and mercy, shalt govern.   If thou fail . . . .
But fail thou wilt not; for in thee I read
Same qualities rare, which, in a day long past,
A youthful Hebrew to such state uplift,
That, to the Pharaoh then upon the throne,

The eye, the voice, the arm did he become;
In all, save title, king. Your records tell
Of that great Hebrew, Joseph. Even as he
Unto that Pharaoh was, so thou to me
Shalt on that day become. Nay more, far more:
For, Reuben, in the place of that fair maid,—
If thou resign her,—one condition sole
Exacted, and performed,—to thee I'd give,—
And all the earth would marvel—one, who most
Unto my heart is dear: one, whose rare charms
Are noised through Egypt: one, for whose fair hand
Kings have been suitors; one, whose dower will be
A pyramid's cost,—yea, even my own loved child,
Meroë, my youngest daughter. Her to thee,
Young Reuben, will I give; so, to my son,
This maiden thou wilt yield; and to our gods—
For here, too, law is absolute—worship pay.
Such the small price for which thou'rt offered now
Riches exhaustless, glory, honor, power;
A monarch's love, and boundless confidence;
A princess, the bright eye of all the land.
What say'st thou? And, blest Rachel, what say'st thou?
And you, their parents, what to this say ye? . . . . . .
Yet, ere you answer, once again survey,
In narrow compass, the whole vast amount.

"If ye refuse what I have stooped to ask,—
Your loss, and mine, see first. For mine,—a son
Love-tortured; perhaps of reason all bereft;
And, haply, through your magic, one more plague:—
Such were, to *me* the sum; nor light the amount,
As my conditions show: but, unto *you*,
The amount enormous! misery of such bulk,
That all life's joys 'twould crush: and,—bitterest thought
For your few wretched years,—by your own act
Solely brought on you: neither fate, nor power
Despotic, having forced; nor ignorance
Misled you,—for the issues all ye know,—
Nor aught save blind, mad obstinacy in wrong,
Hurried you on to doom. Ye see me now,

Calm, gentle, generous; nay, to one and all,
Even as a loving relative. Be calm,
Generous, gentle, loving in your turn,
And life will be all sunshine: but, for love,
Should ye give hate; or, though professing love,
Prove that, at heart, ye hate, by flinging back
What love had offered,—then, *like* deeds of hate
From me would ye enforce. No freedom then
To Israel would be given: but that ye have,
Would all be taken from you. This blest land
Of Goshen would no longer be your home:
Scattered through Egypt,—father, mother, son,
Brother, and sister, daughter, husband, wife,
Each separate from the rest,—slaves would ye be;
The brickfield, pyramid, fosse, canal; or aught
That labor hardest, and most servile asks,—
Your portion till life's end. And, from that man
In whom ye trust, your Moses, never more
Would hope come to you; for, if once again
His magic he dare try; and with new plague
Should harass Egypt,—even on that same day,
Ere sunset should he hang. Your Hebrew race
Its very name would lose; Egyptian slaves,
Alone thenceforth your style. Annihilate
Your god would be; his temples overthrown;
His worship made a crime,—nay, even his name
Be death to him who spake it. If aught else,
Yet worse, can be imagined, verily
That also might be added; till the worm
Beneath your foot half trampled, would be gay,
With such as you compared. Say not I threat
Revenge, if ye refuse my will to do:
It is not I would send; but ye would draw,
On your own heads such misery. For myself,
Good unto all I ask for: if ye grant,
The greatest gainers ye; if ye refuse,
Just is it that the heaviest be your loss.
Yours only is the act, the sentence yours;
Be it good, or heaviest ill. . . . The evil such

Of your refusal,—of compliance, next,
Let me the good recall."
                              His countenance,
And voice, which, that dark future shadowing,
As cloud and thunder had been,—now, like the smile
Of sunbeam after shower, and the glad sounds
Of bird and whispering breeze, came pleasantly.

"First, to myself and Egypt, this the good;"
With bright benignant look pursued the king;
"All future plagues,—if magic such could send,—
For doubtful is the power,—we should escape.
A minister wise, and faithful, diligent, just,
In Reuben should I have; and my loved child,
In him a loving husband. Last, and chief,—
My noble son, and heir unto my throne;
Now love-distraught, and steeped in wretchedness
Might move with pity even the very beast,—
Once more would be a man; once more to heaven
Would lift his face; and thank the merciful gods,
That they a lovelier far than in the train
Of Isis had sent down, his arms to bless.
Such unto me, and Egypt, is the good.
Great do I grant it: but, to yours, my friends,
As clay it is to diamond. Through this land
All Israel would be free,—free to go hence;
Free to remain: and, if remaining, free
From every tax, save such as, through the realm,
Egyptians pay. This to the general good
Of your whole race. For your particular gain,
Glorious indeed the promise. Unto you,
The parents of this youth, and this blest maid,
A joy the dearest in parental heart,—
To see its offspring wealthy, glorious, great:
To thee, young Reuben, riches, rank, and power,
Second to king's alone; and,—happiness
That kings in vain have sighed for,—the bright pearl
Of all Egyptian beauty, for thy wife,
Even Pharaoh's loveliest daughter. Gold indeed,

Ten times refinëd gold thou'rt offered now:
And thou wilt take it: ay, I hear thy soul
Speak, though thy tongue is mute.
                              " But now, the last,
To thee, celestial, human, whatsoe'er
Thy nature be; for still, the more I look,
More doubtful do I grow, if earth, or heaven,
The justlier claim thee; and the less amazed
That, gazing on thee, was the spirit-eye
Of Sethos struck with blindness . . . let not fall
Thy snowy lids, and round thine eloquent lips
A shadow gather; as if fulsome praise
From some hot youth thou heard; for agëd eyes
Look not through passion's ruby-tinted glass,
Which shows even poorest rich; but through clear air
Of truth's broad daylight, which all qualities shows
In their own absolute nature. For my words,
Deem them not flattery, then, or cozenage,
To some false end; since, in all possible scope
Of world-events, what 'vantage could I gain
By thee deceiving? If in rapturous phrase
Thy qualities I speak of,—deem me, then,
As one but giving tongue, enforcedly,
To the soul's rigorous bidding: and, from me,
Accept as *my own* truth, what, by *thee* judged,
False, through excess, may seem. Raise, then, thy face,
Blest Rachel, and behold me as thy friend.

" For thee,—in thy clear soul I read it well,—
First, ruling thought, is not of thine own gain,
But of the general; in the next degree,
Of thine own house, and friends; in last, and least,
Of thy pure self. Thy largest wishes, then,
It rests with thee to grasp: for, unto all,
And all at once, such blessings may thou give,
As dreams could scarcely match. Speak but one word,—
Osiris, for Jehovah,—easy task;
Within our temple, and before our gods,
To my most noble son,—mad for thy love,—
Give thou thy hand,—and Israel will be free:

Thy Reuben, losing thee, will, in exchange,
A princess take to wife; honor and wealth,
And glory, and power will gain; throughout this realm,
Even as its king becoming: and thyself,—
Ah! let me call thee daughter!—over all
Egypt's most haughty dames, in rank and wealth,
Supreme wilt be, as, in thy beauty, now,
Beyond compare supreme. To worship thee,
From farthest limits of the land will come,
The young, the old, the great, the rich, the wise;
All that is rare in beauty, high in fame,—
Eager to look, as on a milder sun,
Shedding diviner light. Even Egypt's prince,—
Noble and glorious as all own him now,—
By thee will sit unseen; so every eye,
By thy perfections dazzled, will be blind
To aught of earth beside. Such thine estate,
While only wife of Egypt's foremost prince:
But when, in due time, shall descend to him
The throne of this great kingdom,—then, its queen
Wilt thou become; of earth the mightiest queen:
Both queen's and king's thy power; for, unto thee,
By love's strong force subjected, must he yield
Submission absolute,—that thy will alone
Shall rule and guide the nation. Then shall be
Glory indeed to Egypt: for thy sway,—
I feel it in my soul,—will wisest, best,
Most just, most merciful be: and every voice
Throughout the land will praise thee. Even now,
In spirit's eye, I see thee on the throne;—
Sethos beside thee, to thy golden words
Of wisdom humbly listening: on thy head
A gem-fired diadem,—yet lustreless,
By thy bright countenance shadowed. So, to thought,
Dost thou appear: but, in the verity, now
Let all eyes prove it. Zabid, bring thou forth
The queenly crown: and, on thy daughter's head,
Thou, Sarah, place it; and, then, note ye all,
If her the crown adorneth, or she it:
If, placed together, flame of diamond

And ruby, the pure radiance of her face
Darken,—or they, before her beams, look dim."

While yet he spake,—with slow and careful hand,
The old man on a table placed the box
Of ebony, gold-inlaid, which to his heart
Till then close pressed had been; and, from his robe,
A golden key, to slender chain of gold
Suspended, drawing forth,—into the lock
Tenderly thrust it; with a gentlest touch
Turned the smooth noiseless bolt; the lid upraised,
And let forth a new sunshine. From its couch
Of purple silk, with reverential hands,
Then lifted he what fires celestial seemed,
In gold imbedded; fires of many hues
Battling together in a silent strife
Perpetual; ever burning, never burnt:
And, with slow step majestic, on her face
Fixing his large bright eyes, toward Sarah moved;
Bowed low, as to the honored of the king,
And the rich blaze presented.
                              But, as starts
A timid maiden, seeing at her feet
The gold-gleams of a serpent,—even so,
At that unearthly lustre shrank she back,
Pallid and trembling. With wide-opened eyes,
She gazed upon it; but still backward drew,—
Breath leaving her, and strength; till, even to stand,
Powerless at last, upon a couch she sank;
Covered her face, and wept. From Reuben's hand,
Till then close held, Rachel her own withdrew,
And to her mother went, and o'er her leaned,
And whispered words of comfort.
                                But, meantime,
The strong oppression of that Presence strange,
Striving to combat,—with a faltering tongue,
Thus Kohath pleaded.
                    "Pardon her, O king;
For timorous is she, and of feeble frame;
And fearful ever, lest by act, or word,

Or thought, she God displease. No slightest thing—
The issue doubtful—ever hath she done,
Till, to her best, considered. If for her,
And for myself, I may permitted be,
Few words to speak" . . . . .
"Go on; the king will hear,"
In tone subdued, and kind, said the great voice,
The sudden silence ending; "freely speak;
And the plain truth; for such I love to hear,
Though harsh, better than lies, to music set."

Though still by dread mysterious sorely pressed,
As in a ghastly dream,—yet, resolute
The right to do, thus Kohath then pursued.

"As parents of the maiden, mighty king,
No just power have we now her course to rule,
Or even lead. That which hath once been given,
'Twere robbery to take back. To this just youth,
Our daughter have we given, to be his wife:
To our loved daughter, him as husband given:
Hand into hand we have put; and binding words
Have spoken: and the act hath witnessed been
By honored friends of old. Such bonds to break,
Were sinful violence: and, for profit's sake,
Not more to be excused, than robbery
Of noon-day thief; who profit, too, could plead,
To justify his crime. Accurs'd were we
Of man and God, so doing. Nor, by words
Of soft persuasion, nor by looks, or signs,
Could we, uprightly, either of them lure
Such contract to make void. That lustrous crown,
Should loving mother place upon the brow
Of loving, duteous daughter,—what were that
But silent invitation, so to act,
That hers it might become? Mute prayer 'twould seem
That, for world's glory, she should do a sin
Which the lips dare not utter. From such crime,
Our God preserve us ever! Frown not then,
Great king, upon a mother, who but shrinks

From doing, and from tempting unto, wrong.
To us impossible, thus, save with great guilt,
Our child to enforce, or lead, to set at nought
Contract, God-sanctioned,—with herself alone
Decision rests. Thy words, all eloquent
In threatening, as in promise, hath she heard;
And hers should be the answer. Whatsoe'er
She say, alike say we. If of the youth
Thou first wouldst question, first let him reply.
If he my daughter yield unto thy son,
No breach of contract ours. The bond thus loosed,—
All of that power parental which we gave,
To us would come again: and we were free
To guide her as before; but, as before,
To herself should we entrust her; fully sure,
As of the ground beneath us, that, in all,
So will she act as, in the sight of God,
Well pleasing she doth deem."
       While humbly thus,
Yet firmly, Kohath spake,—across the brow
Of the great Phantom swept a thundercloud:
But, when he ceased, quick sunbeams played again
O'er all the countenance; on the lips a smile
Seductive hovered; the rough brow grew smooth;
The eyes beamed love, and hope; nay confidence;
And the soft voice, tender, mellifluous;
But yet invincible seeming, strongest will
Of mortal, with kind witchery, to subdue,—
Like gentlest music, the short silence broke.

 My daughter,—for on thy clear brow I read
That mine thou art"——to Rachel turning then,
Spake the joy-beaming king: " a little while
Leave thou thy mother,—though more beauteous sight
Not gods themselves could witness, than sweet love
Of human hearts like yours,—yet hither come;
And, with one word, throughout all Israel,
Throughout all Egypt, bid a second sun
Arise, and pour down blessings. All thou know'st,
Of evil, or of good, which unto us,

And unto you,—to the whole Hebrew race,—
Will fall, as thou shalt speak. Scarce need I ask
What thou wilt answer: for, to rational mind,
'Twixt opposites such, one only possible is:
And thou, not rational merely, but of mind
Goddess-like lofty art,—as fits, thy form
And face divine to match. Yet, ere I ask
For that mere word which, to the soul of thought,
Firm body gives, and shape,—one moment grant
To all our longing eyes, that they may feast
On more than mortal beauty; and even now
May see thee, as in due time to appear,
When queen of earth's first empire. On thy brow,
Honored will Pharaoh be, with his own hands,
The priceless crown to set: and on that brow,
More honored still, a father's kiss to impress,
And as loved daughter hail thee."
                                    Speaking thus,
From Zabid the fire-flashing diadem
With careful hand he took; and toward the maid,
All loving smiles, advanced. One backward step
Calmly she trod, and raised her pearly arm,
Forbearance signing; then, with downcast eyes,
Voice sweet, and low, yet firm; her heart, the while,
Nor bold, nor fearing aught, thus made reply.

"All have I heard, great Pharaoh, of both ill,
And good, which unto Egypt, and to us,
Will come, as I *thy* will shall do, or do
As our God willeth. Ill would it beseem
Poor maiden such as I, by force of words
To strive for victory 'gainst a wiser far,
An elder, and a king, who graciously
Stoops to entreat. But, truly, reason none
Have I to render, wherefore all the good
And glory thou dost promise; all the ills
Which thou dost threaten, weigh with me as nought,—
Save this,—that in the hand of God, I know,
Are all events: that, howsoe'er man schemes,
God still directs: that His sole will to do,

Our duty is; in thought, in word, in act,
Or in endurance; to Him leaving all
Which thence may follow; certain that the worst,—
So seeming,—in the mighty plan unknown,
Still best must be. As duty bids me, then,
So must I do; regardless what the event.
God's will it is that Reuben and myself
Should be espoused. We feel it in our hearts
As a truth absolute, though nor word, nor sign
From heaven hath spoken it. We cannot tell,
How this we know; but not more could we tell
How 'tis we know that on this ground we stand;
Yet surely do we know it, with a force
No argument could reach. If word of man
We needed to confirm us,—from the lips
Of our great Moses, inspiration filled,
Such had we; for, with prophet's eye, and tongue,
Seeing, he knew us chosen; and, from us
Proceeding, to all Israel blessings spake.
But warning, too, he spake: 'Plain as high-road
At noon,' he said, ' before you lies your way.
Even as your right hand from your left, ye know
The path of holiness, from path of sin.
Keep stedfast on the way which ye have trod:
To neither side,—though gardens as of heaven
Would tempt you—for one moment turn your eyes.
Before you straight is the clear road of God:
If thence ye turn,—though seeming angels call,—
From God ye turn; His chosen ones no more;
But lost, for ever lost!' So us he warned,
Though fearing not; and we our clear path see.
From Reuben know I that I cannot part,
Save by God's will opposing; nor from me
Can he make severance: boldly for us both,—
For, in the soul, already are we one,
And, when *I* speak, *he* speaketh,—say I then;
There is no power on earth that him, or me,
Could move to disobedience. Earth's best lures,
Riches, and fame, power, honor, rank, and rule,
As wages for such sin, all worthless were

As dirt beneath the foot. For him, and me,
One life-rule only is,—our Maker's will.
On what earth stands, I know not; but, firm fixed
As on that base the earth,—so fixed stand we
On the known will of heaven. To disobey,
With us impossible alway. Hence, thy son
Never can be my husband; for the voice
Of God within my soul hath given to me
The humble Reuben. Likeway is *he* bound:
Me could he never leave; feeling that God
Our hands and hearts hath joined.
       "Even were this all,—
Through solid rock might the weak body pass
Lightly as, through such obstacle, the soul:
Yet, greater far before us hast thou placed;
Not rock alone, but rock of adamant;
And wouldst that we pierce through it. Of God's will,
Unspoken, and unsigned,—in the heart alone
Felt as a living truth,—a doubt, perchance,
In hour of weakness, sickness, wretchedness,
Might, cloudlike, come, and go: but, of this globe,
The doubt to us not more impossible were,
Than of Jehovah, the one only God;
Maker of heaven, and earth, the sun, the stars,
And every thing that is. Yet, that great God
Thou wouldst we should deny: to other gods,
False deities, the imaginings of man,
Bow down,—the name of the living God exchange
For names of shadows!—and for what reward?
Riches, renown, high station, worship, power!
Ah, king! forgive a simple maiden's speech,
And let her tell thee,—couldst thou turn to gold
All valleys of the earth; her mountains turn
To ruby, sapphire, emerald, diamond, pearl;
Her oceans into silver,—and, of all,
Couldst make me queen; for husband give to me
A youth, than all man's race more glorious,
As sunshine is than blackness; and, to both,
Years twice a thousand give of happiest life;—
Or, couldst thou unto Reuben give the crown

Of the whole earth, and all those riches give;
For wife, a creature exquisite beyond
All earth's most lovely maidens, as the rose
More sweet than noisome fungus,—and, to both,
Life long as Lebanon's Cedars,—not for all,
Nor for all multiplied, till even as stars
In cloudless night for number they should be,—
Would he, or I, that Holiest Name forsake,
And to false gods, the dreams of man, bow down!"

While thus she spake,—beyond expression bright,
Holy, and beautiful, her countenance grew.
Glory of heaven seemed girding her about;
Her look was adoration; and her voice
Ecstatic as rejoicing seraph's hymn.

All gazed, and wondered. Of that presence great
Forgetful wholly,—with love-beaming face,
Lightly stepped Reuben forward; on his knee
Hurriedly sank before her; grasped her hand;
Tremblingly kissed it; tremblingly looked up,
And, mutely blessing, all but worshipped her.
Even the dread Phantom-king one step retired,
Astonished, as if dazzled by great light,
Suddenly breaking; and to Zabid's hands
'The crown surrendered. Kohath, Malachi,
And Sarah, who, amazed, had left her couch,
Looked on that gentle maiden,—loftier now
Than proudest queen; and, while they looked, scarce knew
If Rachel truly were she, or some Power,
Clad in her semblance, who from heaven had come,
Their weakness seeing, with celestial tongue,
To voice their silent thoughts.
                              Foiled utterly,
Thus far, the Arch-Fiend saw his wiles; and wrath
Boiled up within him: yet despaired he not;
By other means intent, at other time,
His end to win. Fair front he now must show;
Grief, disappointment, anger; though by love,
Even fatherly, subdued; and hope not lost

Of wiser course to come. With tender look,
Moist eyes, and quivering lip, and voice sad-toned,
To Rachel then he spake.
      "A glorious sight
Methought I saw; but thou hast blotted it,
And pictured horrors. More I say not now,
To turn thy erring thoughts. With thine own heart
Take counsel; with thy parents, and thy friends;
Ere once again,—of more than life and death
Disposing,—thou make answer: for, the words,
Now uttered, I receive not: else must ills
Unspeakable fall on you instantly.
Use well the hours, my child; and force me not,
You punishing, myself to punish more.
With your great Moses will I conference hold.
His age and wisdom clearer far will see
Than thy young fancy: and his voice, perchance,
To thy true good may move thee, though alas!
A loving king hath failed!"
      Thus having said,
Gently to all he bent; and, with slow step,
And grief-marked brow, went forth.
      To its rich case
The crown restoring,—with like solemn mien
Zabid departed: and, him following close,
Went Kohath, Reuben, Malachi; all mute,
All marvelling.
    At pace funereal-slow,
With bowed head moved the king: through the opened gate,
Like one by sorrow weakened, slowly passed;
Feebly his chariot mounted; backward sank,
And covered up his face. Beside him soon,
Bearing the priceless treasure, Zabid sat.
The attendants quickly mounted: and, at once,
With sound like earthquake-mutterings, the great hoofs,
Stamping together, shook the solid ground.

ISRAEL IN EGYPT.

BOOK SEVENTEENTH.

On the next morrow,—as by Voice Divine
Commanded,—before Pharaoh Moses stood,
And sternly spake. "Well know I all thy thoughts,
O king; and how the tongues of wicked men
Have counselled thee to slay me. Not the less,
Here do I stand before thee; fearing not
What man shall say, or do; for, in God's hands
Are all things; and His will alone shall be,
In heaven and earth. Plain speech must now be mine;
Heeding not kingly state, when kingly faith
Is all forgotten. With most solemn word,—
So I the Lord would pray that plague to end,—
Didst thou to Israel promise, they should go
A three days' journey in the wilderness:
Yet, when our God had hearkened, and the scourge
Had bid depart,—all truth despising, thou
Thy word revoked; and, for the three days' grace,
Didst give them yet worse bondage; labor more,
And taxes doubled: nor with that content,
Didst of their cattle rob them; for each beast,
Lost by Egyptians, from their hapless slaves
Three taking. But, O Pharaoh, three times three
Doomed yet to lose, if thy most stony heart,

This day thou soften not, and let them forth.
For, thus the Lord God of the Hebrews saith:
'Let thou my people to the desert go,
That they may serve me. But, if thou refuse
To let them go, and wilt withhold them still,
Behold, upon thy cattle in the field
The hand of God shall be,—on horse, on ass,
On camel, on the ox, and on the sheep,—
A very grievous murrain. And the Lord
Shall sever between those of Israel,
And those of Egypt,—there shall nothing die
Of all the cattle of Israel. And the Lord
This thing shall do tomorrow in the land.'
Take thou then thought, O king; and, lest the plague
Come on thee, let us go."

With gleaming eye,
Pharaoh looked on him; wrathful, yet afraid:
For Moses with a mien and voice of power
Had spoken, as the mighty to the weak;
And the king's heart misgave him; and a shame
Rankled within him; knowing how with lies
He had defiled himself. A secret dread
Likewise was on him; for, now, all alone
With Moses was he; and, what sudden stroke
Of witchcraft in that privacy might be done,
He knew not. Silent, therefore, for awhile
He sat. But Satan, him beholding thus,
His spirit entered—stirring up anew
Pride, anger, headstrong will: kindling within
Suspicions foul; and urging to defy
At once the insolent wizard, and his god;
And be himself the threatener. With dark look,
Pharaoh, at length, thus spake.

"I counsel thee,
Bold Hebrew, to look well unto thy feet.
A road thou treadest which, too far pursued,
In death must end. Thy magic spells most black,
My sorcerers soon will match: for, day and night,
Dark secrets they dig up; such as, at length,
Thine art will master. But even now, methinks,

Thy cunning halts; and with mere mortal means
Thou'rt forced to work; bad leaving, for yet worse;
The wizard's craft, for poisoner's. Hopeless now,
Upon ourselves, by magic,—with foul drugs,
Thou'lt work upon our cattle; and, by night,
Send forth thy men to creep into our fields,
And with some subtile venom slay the beasts;
Then, on the morrow, glorify thy god,
Saying, *his* hand it was that smote them all;
Even as through thee he had threatened. If a power
Of magic still thou hast, such spite to do,
Why on our cattle wreak it,—not on us?
They hold you not in bonds: why, then, on them
Your murrain send? Yet, easy answer is:
They at *your* mercy lie; but *you* at *ours.*
Slept we within the fields, your pestilence
On us, perchance, as on our beasts, might come.
Into your land of Goshen ye send not
Your poisoners; and, behold a miracle!
Your cattle shall not die! Art not ashamed,
With such poor lie to come before the king?
Yet, for thy warning, thanks. Our fields, this night,
Well watched shall be: and every Israelite
Who therein shall be found,—with instant stroke,—
No questions asked, and no excuses heard,
Shall on that spot be slain. Now, answer not;
But hence. Thee, and thy god do I defy.
Meantime, be sure, thy people shall not go.
If, at the last, by some black sorcery,—
Thy poisoning hindered,—thou the mischief bring,—
Then, first, what worse to Israel I can do,
In quittance, will I ponder: next, for thee,
What punishment the fittest. Heed thou, then:
For,—whatsoe'er thine impudence, and guile,—
I tell thee, at thy root there lies an axe;
A strong man near at hand; and, be thou sure,
If evil more thou do, a voice will speak;
The axe will be uplifted; and thy top
  Will quickly beat the dust."
                              Thus having said,

He started from his throne, intent to go.
But Moses raised the hand, and spake.
                              "O king,
A strong deceit is on thee. As I live,
And as thou livest, rather would I die
Than falsely speak. Within the house, this night,
Imprison thou all Israel; not the less,
Upon the morrow will the pestilence come
On all your cattle in the field. On them,
And not on you, wherefore the plague shall be,
I cannot answer: the mere messenger I
From Israel's God; His words, not mine, to speak.
Three times already warning have I brought;
Three times hast thou regarded not; three times
The threat hath been accomplished: and the fourth,
If thou obey not, will as surely come
As day-light on the morrow. Canst thou hope
To strive 'gainst God! Though yet a hundred times
Thou should resist, 'twere but a hundred times
To feel a grievous scourge, thou might have 'scaped
And bow thee down at last."
                              "That will I prove,
Fiercely cried Pharaoh; "for, by earth, and sky,
Thy people shall *not* go. Thy god, and thee,
Alike I scorn: thy witchcraft damnable,
Spell against spell, soon will my sorcerers front:
And, if in that fight victor, thou shalt, next,
Try spells 'gainst Death: him conjure if thou can.

  With laugh of haught derision, saying thus,
Hastily turned he, and the chamber left.
Nor Moses sought to stay him; headstrong still
Beholding him; and knowing all words vain.

  On the next morning early, went a cry
Throughout all Egypt, for their cattle struck,
Thousands on thousands, by a pestilence
Such as, till then, no eye of man had seen,
No ear had heard of. Post-haste messengers,
Sent Pharaoh then through all the land around,—

Far as, 'twixt rise and set of sun, swift horse
Might go, and come,—to question everywhere,
What cattle of the Egyptians had been slain;
What cattle of the Hebrews.
                        But, when night
Had fallen, and every missive had returned,—
To Pharaoh went his ministers, and said;
"Splendor of heaven! so heavy is the count
Of cattle lost to Egypt, that the sum
All figures fail to tell: but, as for them
Of Israel, not one horse, ass, ox, or sheep,
Hath by this pestilence perished."
                        Hard as rock
Was Pharaoh still; headstrong, and proud, and stern.
Command he gave; and, promptly, nigh the throne,
Priests and magicians stood. At heart dismayed,
Yet,—the bold front assuming,—with big words
Outspake they: making boast how, speedily,
Spell against spell, with every day more strong,
Would they the cunning of the Hebrew match;
And, at the last, o'ercome. A willing ear
Gave Pharaoh; and yet harder grew of heart;
Pondering how best on Israel he might work
Avengement.
            But, on that same evening, came
To Moses and to Aaron, as they walked
Within the garden, musing silently,
A Voice from out the firmament, which said;
"Handfuls of ashes of the furnace take;
And toward the heaven let Moses sprinkle it,
In sight of Pharaoh: and it shall become,
Through all the land of Egypt, a small dust;
And shall a boil be, breaking forth with blains,
On man and beast through all Egyptian land."

Prone on the earth,—soon as the Voice they heard,
The sons of Amram fell; and long time lay,
Silently worshipping: then slowly rose,
And, without word, unto the house returned:

Nor that night spake at all,—so with great awe
Their souls were bowed; but, with a brotherly love,
Embraced, and parted, each unto his rest.

   At sunrise, toward the river they went forth,
That Pharaoh they might meet; and, as they walked,
From ashes of the furnace, handfuls took;
And, to the water having come, made pause,
Awaiting his approach. Him soon they saw,
With a great company, princes, rulers, lords,
Priests, and magicians, walking after him:
And, as they nigher drew, still more and more,—
Like torrent's murmur wafted on the wind,—
Sounded their angry voices. Them to meet,
The sons of Amram went; and speedily
Knew that themselves were seen; for, as a man,
Right in his path, a panther, or wild bull
Beholding, suddenly stops,—so instantly,
Those hated Israelites seeing, Pharaoh stayed,
And, blackly frowning, stood. Then stood they all,
Marvelling why paused the king; till, looking forth,
They, too, beheld the Hebrews coming on;
And, as they thought, ill threatening; for their mien,
Their port erect, their majesty of gait,
Sense of power tokened; nay, as nigher they drew,
Seemed as from out their faces beamed forth light;
So with a consciousness of strength divine
Infused within them, were their souls uplift,
Sustained, and glorified.
                    Still paused the king,
And gladly would have shunned them; for he felt
How they must triumph o'er him; and well knew
That not yet could his sorcerers their spells match;
Howe'er in the future might they. But great wrath
Stirred in him soon, and pride; and on he went,
Shooting before him, like bright lamps through night,
Eye-flashes fierce; and muttering, as he walked,
Threats of dark vengeance. Quickly they drew nigh.
But, pausing now, the sons of Amram bowed,
And waited the king's words. All quivering

With ire suppressed, like a caged leopard he
Glared on them, and broke forth.
"Infatuate fools!
Come ye to seek for punishment? Said I not,
If ye our cattle slay, I first will think
How yet worse things on Israel I may do,—
Next, how yourselves to punish? Speed ye then
To know your sentence? But, be patient yet:
I have not all considered: when the account
Lies full before me, then shall I resolve,
How, when, and where, to strike. Meantime, go hence:
I will not hear you; nor myself will speak,
Save this,—beware! Strong as your magic is,
Yet stronger may be found. Our cattle ye
Have withered: heed lest we should wither *you*.
But, perhaps some witchcraft fresh ye have in hand;
Some plague upon ourselves, since through our beasts
Ye cannot move us: and, if so, at once
Speak out: discharge your venom, and be gone;
For ye do darken daylight. Only this
Remember,—that, for every ill on us,
Three on yourselves ye bring: and, though ye turn
This land into a grave-pit, yet herein
Shall ye be buried; for, by earth, and sea,
And sun, and stars, and by all Egypt's gods,
Hence shall ye never go!"
. With face all wild,
Livid, distorted with excess of rage,
Thus spake he; and his priests and sorcerers came
Thronging about him; upon Moses, now,
Like maniacs glaring; now, upon the king
Eagerly looking, as though all athirst
The word to hear which should their rage let loose
Upon those insolent, whom, limb from limb,
Longed they to rend. In silent dignity,
And more with pity than with anger moved,
A moment Moses stood; then, with firm voice,
Thus spake.
" Not from the God of Israel, now,
Warning we bring thee, Pharaoh. Thou his words

Hast heard, and disobeyed : and judgment, sent,
Hast disregarded. Well, no doubt, your fields
Last night were watched : but yet the pestilence,
Even as I prophesied, fell upon your beasts,
That ye the slain can count not : while, on those
Of Israel, as I also said would be,
No pestilence touched at all. Yet, even now,
The hand of God thou seest not in this stroke ;
But witchcraft only ; and, with marble heart,
Refusest still His bidding. Punishment,
Not warning, therefore, by my hand He sends ;
Not on your beasts alone, but on yourselves ;
Boils, breaking forth with blains, on every man,
Woman, and child, of Egypt."
                              At that word,
From sorcerers, rulers, priests, burst forth a yell ;
All clamoring on the king, to give command
That they should slay him. Some, upon the knee,
Trembling with fury, sank ; and Pharaoh prayed,
For sake of all in Egypt, that, at once,
The wizard in the river might be flung,
Or hanged on nearest tree ; and some, with looks
Demoniac, toward the Hebrews stiffly walked ;
Jaws locked, hands clenched,—awaiting, as it seemed,
The word to slay them. But, unheeding all,
Above the din a great voice Moses raised,
And, looking upon Pharaoh, cried, " Behold."

Uttering the word, his arm uplifted he,
And from his hand the furnace ashes loosed,
And sprinkled them toward heaven.
                                  Tumult was hushed ;
All hearts beat quickly ; every straining eye
Intently watched ; expecting, as before,
In the blood-plague, some ghastly spectacle,
On the instant to appear : but, when they saw
That, from the hand, ashes alone were cast,
Which a small dust became, and melted off
Like a thin smoke,—then quickly rose again
Their fury,—and, with threats, sharp mockery too,

And scornful laughter. Full before the king,
Thamusin, the chief priest, with face inflamed,
And tongue for madness stuttering, hurried on;
And, both hands lifting, frantically cried out,
" O Pharaoh, free thy kingdom, and the earth,
From these detestable. Speak but the word,
And quickly they, too, shall as dust pass off,
Like that they juggle with. One only word
Speak, Pharaoh, we implore thee. Strength enough
Here is to rend them into very threads:
Cords, trees, stones, water,—death in any shape,
To end them on the instant."
       While he spake,
His face, wrath-burning, with yet other fire
Rapidly kindled; and his trembling hands,
As if flame-touched, 'gan sting him. Suddenly mute,
He stared upon them. Swoln were they, and red,
And with strange blisters gleaming. His hot brow
Then touched he; and, beneath his tingling palm,
Felt the boils rising. Terrified he stood,
Stupidly staring round: and lo! the king,
Even like himself he saw, fire-faced, and swollen,
And in great horror staring. Every man
On whom he looked, stood staring on the rest;
Red-visaged, bloated, terrified. No voice
Cried unto Pharaoh now, for punishment
Upon the Hebrews: each man his own pangs,
And wrath, in silence smothered. With stern eye,
The sons of Amram gazed around on all:
But the magicians turned away, ashamed:
By reason of the boils, they could not stand
Before the face of Moses: nor the king,
For shame, dared look upon him.
       Brief time thus,
Inwardly cursing; though no word he spake;
Stood Pharaoh,—then turned quickly; and, forthwith,
Back toward his palace walked; still, as he went,
Angrily moaning. All his rulers, too,
Priests, princes, sorcerers, moaned: and whomsoe'er
They passed upon the way,—with head depressed,

They saw, and flaming face, and dark-red hands,
Which, as fire-scorched, for coolness still they waved,
Moaning, and hurrying on. And when, at last,
Unto the palace came they, all the house
Resounded with deep moaning.
                              Through the land,
Save in the dwellings of the Israelites,
And in the peaceful Goshen, thus it was
With all the people: and their cattle, too,
With boils were struck; so that, of men, and beasts,
That day, and through the night, were thousands slain.

   Yet, hard as furnace-brick still was the heart
Of the proud king; nor for his daughters aught
He heeded, nor his beauteous wife, when they
Implored him to free Israel. "Never! no!
No!" roared he out; "this left hand on the block
I'd lay, and with this right hand smite it off,
Rather than loose them. Every bone, at last,
Shall rot in Egypt; but their flesh, meanwhile,
Shall toil, and sweat, and groan beneath the whip,
Till vengeance cry, 'enough.' 'Tis now the hour
For *their* magicians: soon our own will come:
And then, shall *they* cry out, as now the cry
They force from *us*. But, for each separate wail
By us sent up, a chorus shall they send,
Till the clouds rock with the uproar. In few hours
This burning will pass off: as best ye may,
Endure it then: for no ease can ye have,
That would not ten pangs bring, for one now 'scaped."

   So all that day and night, throughout the land,
The plague tormented Egypt: but, at morn,
By Power Supernal ordered, it passed off;
And they who had not perished,—sound again
In flesh became, as though no plague had been.

   Then did the priests and sorcerers exult,
Saying, that through their magic had the scourge
Been ended; and that speedily their might

Would tread down that of Moses. Them the king
Heard, and applauded; and yet more his heart
Hardened 'gainst Israel's God.
                                Within the shade
Of a thick grove,—for now it was high noon,
And from a cloudless sky the sun poured fire—
Alone walked Moses; on God's gracious ways
Toward Israel musing; and deliverance sure,
At hand foreseeing. Almost midnight-hush
Was round him; for no gentlest breath of air
Stirred leaf: no sound of water was; no bird,
For heat, could sing; no voice, or foot of beast,
Broke the deep stillness: even in the grass,
No rustle was, of snake, or creeping thing:
Life, earth, and air, seemed slumbering; when, behold,
As from Heaven's inmost heart, came down the Voice,
Thus speaking.
                " Early in the morning rise,
And before Pharaoh stand; and say to him:
' Lo, thus the Lord God of the Hebrews saith:
Let thou my people go, that they may serve me.
Else, at this time will I send heavier plagues
On thee, thy servants, and throughout the land:
That thou mayst know that there is none like me,
In all the earth. As yet exaltest thou
Thyself against my people, and wilt not
Permit them to go forth. But, now, behold,
About this time tomorrow will I send
A very grievous hail; such as, before,
Hath not been seen in Egypt, since the day
Of its foundation. Send thou therefore out,
And gather all thy cattle, all thou hast
Within the field: for, upon every man,
And beast, which in the field shall then be found,
And shall not be brought home, the hail shall come;
And they shall die.' "
                        With forehead to the ground,
That great Voice Moses heard; and, spirit-bowed,
Long time lay worshipping: but rose, at length,
And homeward hastened: unto Aaron first,

And his own wife and children, with low tone,
Awe-filled, the bidding of the Power Divine
Made known; then through the city took his way,
Where'er the wretched Hebrews he might find,
The tidings to impart, and their hearts cheer
With hope of good at hand. By different ways,
Went Aaron also: till the evening closed,
Throughout the city went they; and their words
As sunshine were to some; but, to the most,—
So darkness shadowed them,—as but the gleam
Of a marsh-meteor; dead, ere well alive.

On the next morrow early, all alone,
Went Moses out; and, nigh the palace gate,
Waiting the coming forth of Pharaoh, stood.
Soon, from within, the sound of feet he heard,
And many deep-toned voices muttering.
Louder, as they came on, the murmur grew;
And when, at length, wide open flew the gate,
Burst forth an angry hum, as when the bees
Pour from their hive disturbed. First came the king,
With countenance dark; and Sethos by his side,
Eagerly talking; with the right hand now,
Now with the left gesticulating quick,
As passion moved him. After them, a train
Of princes, rulers, priests, and sorcerers,
Two and two walking; muttering man to man,
Hot-faced, blown up with wrath. From out the gate
When he beheld that all had issued forth,
Then, slowly moving, with majestic mien,
Moses went on to meet them.
                                Stung with shame,
Yet with rage burning, Pharaoh saw him now;
And would have blighted him. With flaming eye,
Grinding his teeth, he went; and, near him come,
Paused; and, with voice harsh as the raven's croak,
Cried out; "detested wizard, get thee hence,
While yet thou may. Soon will thy cunning fail:
A stronger gathers 'gainst it. Thy poor plague
Quickly was mastered: as it ne'er had been,

Sound are we all. My sorcerers know thee now,
And will confront thy worst. Away with thee!
I know not why I suffer thee to live;
Unless the most to gall thee ere thou die,
By mocking at thy witchcraft. I will wring
Again from Israel three for every one
Of all the beasts by the last plague destroyed:
And, if again thou try thy sorcery,
For every man of Egypt, thereby slain,
Three Israelites shall hang. Away, away!
I will not hear thee."
      Calmly Moses stood
Till the storm ceased; then gently raised the hand,
And, with a voice of such high dignity,
Though mild, that silence upon all it brought,
Thus made reply.
     "Sad ignorance, O king,
Which, in directest proof that God's own hand
Omnipotent all hath done, finds proof of nought
Save man's poor magic! But, purge now thine eyes,
To see the true, and false. From first to last,
Consider all things: then, let reason judge
If man's, the power, or God's. All history search,
To find if ever yet, through a whole land,
Within the self-same moment, magic power
Even weakest thing hath wrought. But, here, behold,
At once on millions, nigh, and far away,
On man, and woman, child, and beast, hath been
Thing done, so strange and fearful, that the spells
Of all thy sorcerers, working with one will
On weakest babe, like wonder could not do.
Thy wizards tell thee, that my spells alone
Brought that plague on you: just as easy 'twere
To say I made the hills; or heaven's great arch
Flung o'er the earth: and by no argument
Might I disprove the lie. Couldst thou believe
That magic power of mine had filled the seas,
Or from the sky had thundered? Yet these things
Nor more impossible than, throughout this land,
At once to send a pestilence. 'Gainst the course

Of Nature, in one moment, of pure flesh
To make the foul,—as far beyond all reach
Of witchcraft is, as, of pure gold, to make
Rust-eaten brass. Of foul, the pure to make,
Like suddenly,—as more 'gainst Nature's course,—
Yet harder, were not both impossible.
All this, O Pharaoh, know thy sorcerers
Surely as I. No power whatever is
Such thing to do, save God's. Yet, hard of heart,
And blind of eye, to them thou giv'st belief;
Though all experience, all world's history,
Cry out, they falsely speak. Let them, in one,
Knit all their strongest spells; and, on pure flesh
Of feeblest woman, or child, bid boils burst forth,—
Then justly might they think, that the same power,
Doubled a millionfold, and then again
A millionfold redoubled, o'er this land
That pestilence had brought. Could I bid here,
Through the air flying, mighty Babylon,
Its countless streets, squares, gardens, rock-like walls,
Palaces, temples, and sky-propping tower
Of Babel,—and bid all before thee stand,
Foundationed in the earth,—then mightst thou think
That power I had, as at one blast, to send
Plague through all Egypt. Yet, the greater power,
In one same moment, throughout all the land,
The plague to stop, the foul flesh to make pure,—
That power thy sorcerers claim ! Ah Pharaoh, prove
The might they boast of : from one cheek diseased,
Let them, by stroke of magic, chase death-fire,
And, in its stead, plant health-bloom,—*then* believe
That they chased Egypt's pestilence."

"Death itself,
Our spells can chase," cried out an angry voice,
Fiend-prompted. "From the very grave, our might
Can bring forth the dead man; and bid him live,
And speak; and this, in presence of the king,
Permitted, will we do. Thine argument, then,
Great wizard, is but nought; for ....."

Toward the man

Turned Pharaoh, not ill pleased, though marvelling much
At that great boldness,—no leave prayed, to break
With loud tongue thus on royal conference.
But, when the face he saw, dark, wild, and fierce;
And the voice noted, harsh as clanging brass,—
Of mind disturbed he feared him; and, his arm
Uplifting, with tone strong, yet kind, his speech
Suddenly checked. "Stay, Hophra. Though thy words
All verity be; yet, at unseasoned time
Thrust forth, even truth slight welcome hath. When kings
Listen, unanswering,—surely meet it is
That subjects hear, and speak not. Calm thee, then."

But Hophra from the rest stepped quickly forth,
And bowed before the king; then nigher drew;
And, with hushed voice, thus spake. "Light of the Sun,
Be thou not wroth with me, that to this man
I fling back scorn for scorn. That which I said,
Truth is. Last night from out his grave we took
The body of a Hebrew; an old slave,
As yet but one day dead. Till ends the third,
Power have we to call back the parted soul,
And force it speak. If Israel a god hath,
He knoweth now: if Moses yet more plagues
Can send, he knoweth; and the truth will tell;
For spirits dare not lie. If Pharaoh, then,
So ordereth,—ere the sunset will we lay
The might of spells upon him: and the king
Himself may question; and from out the corpse
Hear the soul answer; thus the truth to know."
Well pleased heard Pharaoh. "On the morrow, then,"
Replied he; "and, when verily your spells
Have power upon the dead, and on the soul,
To make it speak,—then send ye speedily,
And I will come to question it." That said,
He signed: the necromancer bowed, and went.

On Hophra, Moses looked, as on a man
Crazed, or intoxicate, unworthy note;
Then, turning to the king, his speech renewed.

"Again, O Pharaoh, say I; from one cheek,
Let them, by spells, the fiery ulcers drive,
And bring back the pure health-bloom,—*then* believe
That they stopped Egypt's plague. But, seest thou not,
At once their falsehood, and their foolishness?
My power alone, they say, that pestilence sent:
But their sole power removed it. Had my strength
Such been, that over all this land at once,
Plague had I sent on millions,—thinkest thou
I had been baffled by these impotents,
Whose boasted spells not even one blade of grass,
One tenderest flower, could wither? Prove them, king:
From yonder date-tree let their mightiest call
One leaf: or, with his staff, one blade of grass
Wither before thy face. . . . . . Ye hear me all,—
Magicians who the dead can bring to life,—
From the young tamarisk near you, bid one leaf
Fall withered; or the withered bid again
Grow to the stem, green, juicy, fresh with life.
Ye would as soon expect, on your staff's point,
To toss a pyramid: yet, with front of brass,
Ye boast that millions, withering, men and beasts,
Over all Egypt scattered,—by your spells
Ye have restored to health! Did ye not bid
The sun his path through heaven? and Night's great crown
Gem with its myriad stars? So might ye boast,
As glibly, and as truly. Heed them not,
O Pharaoh; for deceitfully they speak,
To their own ruin, and thine: but, with clear mind,
The brief whole see, and judge. I came to thee,
No message bringing from offended heaven;
No warning; but a punishment direct
To inflict upon thee,—for that thou hadst lied,
Even to God! As by the Voice Divine
I had been taught, in plain words told I thee,
That boils, with blains forth breaking, would be sent
On thee, thy servants, and on every man,
Woman, and child, and beast, throughout the land.
Thou didst not then repent, and humble thee,

And Israel's God implore that plague to avert;
But poured wrath on me; and thy servants' tongues,
Unblaming, heard, when, fierce as beasts of prey,
They howled to rend me. And what did I then?
As I had been commanded, in thy sight
I stood, and, lifting up mine arm, toward heaven
I sprinkled—not some deadly magic charm,
From festering graves, or fouler things, distilled,
But furnace-ashes only; from a heap
By the way side cast out, which in my hand,
As I came on, I had taken; for the Voice
So had commanded. That the plague 'twould bring,
I knew, instructed so; but, by what course
Of action,—save by God's own will alone,
Nature's great laws o'er-ruling,—nought I knew;
Nought know, more than the infant this day born.
That heap of furnace-ashes, by the way
Still lieth: if aught of deadly therein be,
Let thy magicians prove it. 'Gainst myself
To sprinkle it they are free. As nought I know
Of that plague's cause, save only as the act
Direct of the Omnipotent,—so, alike,
Of its surcease no cause, save that, I know.
For punishment was it sent,—for token, too,
Doubtless, if thou would see it, that from God
To thee we come, the speakers of His will,—
And, chastisement given enough, it was recalled:
In its outbreak, and its departure, both,
Alike a miracle wholly; a great voice
From Heaven,—wouldst thou but hear it,—crying aloud
'The hand of God alone these things hath done.'
If blind thou art not, then, blind utterly,
So must thou see it: if not hard of heart,
Even as the nether millstone, thou must bend
Thy too long stubborn will, and Heaven obey.
Why shouldst thou farther dream to stand 'gainst God?
Couldst hope to drink up ocean at a draught?
Pluck Horeb from its roots; and through the air
Fling it on Lebanon's top? Yet, tasks like these,
Light were, to strife 'gainst God. With plague six times

Already hath He smitten thee: His scourge
The seventh time now is lifted: bow thyself,
O Pharaoh, to His will: let Israel go;
And a terrific stroke on thee, and thine,
And over all this land, so may thou 'scape."

Spite of himself, while the great voice he heard,
Pharaoh stood silent: downward looking now,—
Now, with quick glance, on the majestic face;
Glance quick and tremulous, as though he turned
On what might blind him; or an aspect caught,
Surpassing mortal: and, when Moses ceased,
Yet, for a time, fixed, silent, did he stand,
Pondering how best to answer: for great pride,
And a great terror also, in him fought,—
Each victor now, now vanquished. But, at length,
Shame urging him, fresh courage he called up,
And, as he might, replied.
                         "Nought hast thou proved,
High-talking Hebrew: but, with wordy pomp,
Asserted merely. When contrariously,
Of the same thing, two equal men affirm,—
Which to believe, we know not; and remain
Oft times in doubt; and judgment fear to pass.
But, if, of three men equal, two affirm
That *thus* it is, then toward *them* we incline,
Slighting their opposite; unless proof he bring,
Lacked by the two. Hadst thou, then, such proof brought,
And my priests none,—against their voices, thine
Had weighed as gold 'gainst down. But all alike,
Assertion only bring: and there stand'st thou,
One only 'gainst twice ten; thine equals all;
Nay, thy superiors rather; for the priests
Of Egypt's gods are they,—thou, but the priest
Of a false deity, imaged by yourselves,—
A slave-created god. A sorcerer great,
I grant thee; nay even greater far than mine,
Evil to do: but not the likelier, thence,
Pure truth to speak; nor worthy of respect,
More than those weaker. Equal only thus,

At best,—against my sorcerers and priests,
One art thou 'gainst a score. Thy god it is,
Thou say'st, who these foul plagues hath on us sent,
Because we will not let our slaves go forth
Into the wilderness,—knowing, as we do,
That, once escaped, never would they return,
Unless with whips driven back: as, be thou sure,
Quickly they would be: but my sorcerers say,
Thy god is all a fable; a pretence,
With which at once to o'erawe the ignorant,
And cloak the work of magic,—thy *true* god.
These plagues, they say, are sorcery, first and last:
Nay, in part, proved they this, when water to blood
They turned, as thou hadst done; and frogs brought forth,
As also thou hadst: and, though hitherto weak
Their cunning against thine, yet equal soon,
Through diligent seeking, trust they it shall be;
And, finally, the stronger. But, even now,—
If truth they speak, deceiving not themselves,—
Their power hath thine surpassed; for, though thine art,
Pure flesh to ulcerous in a moment turned,
Yet theirs the wonder greater far performed,
Flesh ulcerous, in a moment to make pure.
Assertions bold alike, alike unproved;
Alike by equals spoken,—unto which
Should I give credence? to mine enemy,
Or to my friends, and counsellors? To *one*,
Who, for his profit, and to my great loss,
Would steal from me this Egypt's richest gem,—
Or to these twice ten, who exhort me keep
My rightful treasure, and the robber strike?
Can'st ask me how I answer? Though alike
In weight of reason were their words, and thine;
Yet one 'gainst four times five, must kick the beam,
At the first scale-lift: but thy words, 'gainst theirs,
Less have in poise of reason. Proofless both,
Yet theirs more truthlike are; more probable;
More consonant to experience, and things told
In oldest records. Of the power of spells,
Lives there the man who doubts? and, of its scope,

Who dare prescribe the limits? Who shall say
If, from the uttermost depths of knowledge dug,
Charms might there not be brought, so terrible,
That they the moon could blacken; or force back
The mid-day sun toward morning? 'Gainst *such* spells,
Thine were as tricks of childhood: yet, even such,
For aught man knows, may be. Cause probable, then,
Of these vile plagues, we in thy magic find.
We know thee, of all sorcerers, most profound
In the dark learning; and, by proof, we know
That acts like thine, in part, can magic do:
And, if in part, then wholly, full power gained.
This knowing, other cause we need not seek;
Nor, thrust upon us, wisely could believe.
But, for thy words, in reason weigh they nought;
Improbable, 'gainst experience, 'gainst the lore
Of oldest history. Who, till thou, hath dared
Prate of a new-found god? A god, forsooth,
Of but one wretched people? Look thou back
Through the eye-blinding mist of ages gone,
To time's remotest depths,—those gods thou seest
Then throned sublime, are, to this day, the gods
Whom Egypt worships: no new god hath risen;
No god of old hath fallen: unchangeable,
Eternal as the mountains, stand they all.
How, then, can we believe that a new god,
A god of Israel only, hath been found?
A god so potent, too, that the old gods,
Egypt's disposers and protectors, shrink
Before his power; permitting him to fling
Plagues damnable on us, their worshippers,
For disobedience unto him, toward whom
Obedience none we owe? Preposterous all!
Against new god, intruding, would they stand,
Such wrongs to hinder: but, against the power
Of sorcery,—old, perchance, as even themselves,
And through all times permitted,—hindrance none
Might they put forth. Wouldst thou that we believe
In thing so passing wonderful, as a god
Newly existent, never known till now;

And, *now*, by you alone,—give us to see
Signs, marvels, miracles, that all doubt must crush,
As millstone the corn crushes. But, till then,
Thy god we hold a dream; or a pretence
To cloak thy witchcraft; and to give its power
Semblance of godlike,—so with greater awe
To oppress the feeble: therefore do I still
Defy thee; nor will let thy people go.
Great as thy cunning is, 'twill find its match;
If, ere that time, I end not it, and thee,
By one great stroke of vengeance, merited long;
Too long withheld,—but sure to fall at last,
If more thou vex us. Then, do thou take heed;
And, ere new plague preparing,—weigh, if that,
Or thine own life, more worth. I now have done;
And at my own great patience stand amazed;
So temperate, to thy words most insolent,
Hath been mine answer."
      Ending thus his speech,
Full in the face of Moses, Pharaoh looked;
And, his hand waving, signed the conference o'er.
But, ere a foot had moved, with solemn voice
Thus Moses spake.
     " Even as I feared, O king,
Thick darkness blinds thee still; and I must speak
Warning again, and threatening. Who could look
On the noon-sun, and call it candle-light?
Yet worse than that dost thou—the might of God,
Poor magic calling. But, vain now all words,
To clear thy darkness, as sweet music's voice,
To make mid-day of midnight. Hear me then.
Lo, thus the Lord God of the Hebrews saith;
'Let thou my people go, that they may serve me.
Else, at this time will I send heavier plagues
On thee, thy servants, and throughout the land:
That thou mayst know that there is none like me
In all the earth. As yet exaltest thou
Thyself against my people; and wilt not
Permit them to go forth. But now, behold,
About this time tomorrow will I send

A very grievous hail; such as, before,
Hath not been seen in Egypt, since the day
Of its foundation.   Send thou, therefore, out,
And gather all thy cattle; all thou hast
Within the field: for, upon every man,
And beast, which in the field shall then be found,
And shall not be brought home, the hail shall come,
And they shall die.'   So speaketh Israel's God.
Hearken, I charge thee, Pharaoh, and obey."

Thus having spoken, Moses bowed, and went.
Dark looks of hate the sorcerers on him cast,
All murmuring together: and the king,
Eye-glances fierce shot after him,—great wrath,
With terror greater mingling; so that word
As yet he found not; but, with head depressed,
Gloomily musing, toward the river went.

ISRAEL IN EGYPT.

BOOK EIGHTEENTH.

THROUGHOUT the city, and the lands around,
Soon ran the rumour that, from Israel's God,
Moses a word had brought unto the king,
Threatening, that on the morrow he would send
New plague o'er all the land,—even grievous hail,
Such as in Egypt, from the very day
Of its foundation, never had been seen.
They, therefore, of the servants of the king,
Who feared the word of Israel's Lord, sent forth,
Commanding that all serving men, and beasts,
Should, on the morrow, in safe shelter bide:
But they who heeded not the word of God,
Left in the field their servants, and their beasts.

Audacious most of all, the king himself,
By Satan with great wrath and pride inflamed,
Mocked at the threatening; and his servants bade
Leave *all* within the field; nay, drive therein
All cattle whatsoe'er, which, under shed,
Or in the stable, else, had been secure :
So boldly his defiance to speak out
'Gainst Moses, and his God.
                              But humbler men
Among the Egyptians, who the wondrous things

By Moses done had seen,—respected him,
And in his word believed: and all their beasts,
As night drew on, brought homeward from the fields;
And bade that, of their servants, not one man,
Woman, or child, should on the morrow stir
From out their dwellings; lest the hail should fall,
And slay them. Through the day, from house to house,
Both they of Egypt, and of Israel too,
Went anxiously,—with pale face, and low voice,
Discoursing of the Terror that should come.
Even they of Pharaoh's servants, who the most
Had feigned a mockery,—rulers, captains, priests,
And sorcerers,—in the silence of the night
Lay sleepless; a strange fear oppressing them,
Like his who, waking from deep slumber, feels
A stirring of the earthquake.
      One alone
Within the royal palace, no fear had
Of evil on the morrow; for he thought
Cunningly all to 'scape; and great joy have,
And perfect peace, even though the hail should fall
Dread as a rock-storm; and the plains and hills
Make stagger with the smiting.
      Night, and day,
In the heart of Sethos had a demon worked;
Blowing to heat intense his foul desire
Toward Israel's snow-pure virgin, chosen of God:
When, therefore, standing by his father's side,
That hail-plague he heard threatened,—instantly,
To shun it he resolved; and, in the land
Of Goshen, pleasantly and safely, pass
That day of peril; and, perchance, the night,—
Should the storm pause not; for, that come it would,
Doubt had he none; though sorcery alone
As cause misdeeming. Therefore, the command
At evening gave he, that, with earliest dawn,
His chariot should stand ready,—one alone
Of all his train accompanying, the steeds
To govern; so, with mind unfettered, he
In love's bright heaven might rove.

                              But, through that night,
His whole base nature so the fiend inflamed
With dreams brain-maddening, that even certain death,
As penalty, seemed nought, so he but first
Might revel in the bliss. From bed he sprang,
And toward the east looked out. The morning star
Told night far spent. Attendants roused he then,
And bade that two score horsemen, fully armed,
At day-break, close beyond the eastern gate,
Should bide his coming; for resolved he was,—
Love's lurements failing,—by the violent hand
To seize the Rose of Goshen, and bear off:
Whither, as yet he knew not: *that,* to time
He left: for him could no place be amiss,
So therein were his goddess,—the sole thing
His frenzied eye could see: his father's wrath,
The blot of public shame; even death itself,
From private vengeance,—all invisible
Behind the one great blaze of hoped-for bliss.
With speed his arms he donned: one hasty cup,
Of food one morsel, took, and hurried forth.

    Obedient, yet amazed, his charioteer,
Armed as for battle, by the chariot stood:
One at the head of each impatient steed,
The humbler grooms awaited. With quick stride
Onward went Sethos; to the chariot leaped:
As lightly sprang the driver: the word spake;
And, to the clattering hoofs and jarring wheels,
On all sides round, the vast void court gave out
The clamoring echoes. Through the eastern gate
Quickly he passed. Beyond it, at each hand,
Mounted on battle-steeds, eager, strong, and swift;
With sword, and spear, and shield, cuirass, and helm,
Armed as for combat; twice ten chosen men,
Waiting his coming, stood. No word he spake,
But onward flew; and they, much marvelling,
In silence followed.
                     From the beaten road
Soon passed they to wide champaign, where, of tree,

Or bush, few were there, or the abodes of man,
Save shepherd's hovel.   Uttering not a word,
At speed the prince urged on,—troubled to see
How swiftly waxed the light; yet hoping still,
Ere the first hail should fall, secure to stand
In sanctuary of Goshen.   Glances quick
Casting at times toward heaven, thus rapidly on,
Pallid and mute, he drove.

Three fourths, at length,
The journey was accomplished; the vault still
Gem-clear reposed: yet, but more anxiously
Glanced his keen eye round heaven; dreading, erelong,
Somewhere, to see first shadowing of the storm:
For now the sun was up; and, as he thought,
Same height had gained, at which, on the day past,
He stood when Moses said, " about this hour
Tomorrow, will I send a grievous hail:"
Wondered he, therefore, that all crystal clear
Shone yet the cloudless vault; and in his heart
Doubt felt, at length, if verily so far
Might power of magic stretch, that over gods,
Rulers of air, and storms, it might prevail.
At slow pace, then, he journeyed; fully assured,
That, long ere tempest that fair heaven could foul,
Safe should he be in Goshen.

But, behold,
When next he looked behind him,—on the verge
Of the horizon where, few minutes back,
Sky had been clear as sapphire—blackness was,
Night-blackness, solid as rock.

"On! on! lash on,"
Eagerly cried he; " the Plague-Demon comes."
At once the thong resounded; and the steeds
Thundered along the plain.   Backward again
He looked; and lo! in even that span of time,
Visibly higher the black surge had risen.
Upsprang he then,—with left hand clutching hard
The bounding chariot, pointed with the right,
And shouted to the horsemen; " look behind,—
Terror and Death are after you.   On, on;

Keep rank no longer: fly as best ye may.
Reach Goshen, and be safe." Again he sat,
But with head backward turned, eyes riveted
On the doom-boding heaven: for still up, up,
Swifter than racer drawing nigh the goal,
Ran the dire blackness: and, erelong,—though yet
No slightest breeze below stirred leaf, or grass,—
Came from that sea of cloud the terrible voice
Of the Storm-Lion, roaring for his prey.

"On, on," again he cried. The charioteer,
Wild with affright, shook the loose reins, and stamped,
And shouted to the horses. Tempest-fleet,
They battered the ground. Yet still, "on—on," he cried;
For, over half the sky, the mountainous clouds
Had billowed; and, with din more terrible,
The hurricane roared; no longer over head
Sending its voice from far, but right to earth,
Heavy as water-floods dashing; that the steeds,—
Driven on like dust,—half flying, half with foot
Spurning the ground,—at speed brain-dizzying went.
Full with the wind they ran, or car and horse,
Down had been cast. The chariot, from the earth
Uplifted oft, as if for flight through air,
With wheels revolving sped,—then sank again,
Heavily jarring: but, with desperate gripe,
Still Sethos clung to the car; still round and round
Staring aghast: for, now, o'er all the heavens
Had swept the terrible gloom: the sun was quenched:
Day had seemed night, but that, from midst the clouds,
Like fierce eyes glancing, fiery meteors looked,
Impatient to be loosed. Heart-sick he saw,
The threat remembering; "Upon every man,
And beast, which in the field shall then be found,
And shall not be brought home, the hail shall come,
And they shall die!" And now for him no hope!
Goshen to reach, even at that tempest-speed,
Ere leaped on them the Plague, impossible!
Was there no shelter, then? no cave, no house,

No poorest hovel of even meanest man,
Wherein he might find safety? Eagerly,
By the red glimmerings aided, he looked forth:
Alas! nought saw he but uprooted shrubs,
Whirling along the ground; or, in mad flight,
Tossing in air; trees bending to the earth,
Writhing and twisting; huge limbs rent away;
And flying, light as leaves; old stubborn trunks,
That would not bow, struck down, as though a hand
Invisible, and almighty, with one blow
Had smitten them to earth. Mad with affright,
"On—on"—still shrieked he, though at blinding speed
The terrified horses flew: but his own voice
Scarce could he hear; in the hurricane's thunder-shout,
Small as the pipe of childhood. Back he looked:
Scattered behind him came the horsemen on,
Bowed to their horses' maues. Hastily then
Skyward he turned; for the black canopy,
Red suddenly grew,—cloud lightning against cloud,—
O'er all the arch of heaven, cloud, and red fire!
"On, on," again he cried; and, shuddering, turned;
With starting eyeballs keenly peering out;
Hoping to see some shelter.
     Far away,
Blazoned by lightning, a low house appeared.
Frantic for joy, he shrieked;—with quivering arm
Eagerly pointed; and still cried, "on, on."
Again the charioteer, deliriously,
Stamped—shouted—shook the reins—and smote the
  steeds:—
Away,—away,—away:—and, for awhile,
Feebly yet glimmered hope. But, when again
Backward looked Sethos, scarce could he believe
What his eyes showed him; for, upon the rim
Of the horizon,—all on blaze with war
Of multitudinous lightnings,—seemed to fall
A shower terrific; not of rain, or hail,
But fire, white hot, as from the furnace pours
The melted iron. Rigid as in death,
And voiceless, stared he. Rapidly as cloud,

x

Low hanging, tempest-driven, sweeps overhead,—
So up the sky-arch mounted the dread Plague;
Sending before him mighty thunderings;
A thousand lightnings for his banner-flags;
The hurricane his trumpets.
                            Nigher still
As drew the Terror, lo! what fire had seemed,
Falling from heaven like rain,—now, likeness took
Of the dread Hail: and, even from north to south,
Spanning the plain, came on a mighty wave,
As of the storm-driven ocean,—cloud and fire
Mingled together, running on the ground.
And, as it nigher drew, even hurricane
And thunder deadened not the terrible crash
Of the down-pouring; for the Hail it was;
Masses of ice for hailstones, rugged and huge,
That dashed on earth,—shivered, and leaped, and hissed,
And whirled in air; billow-like rolling on;
A foam of ice-dust, lightning, hail, and rain,
Lashing together.
                  Franticly as clings
To his frail raft the drowning mariner,—
So, to the rocking, leaping, flying car,
As with the death-grip, clung the fear-crazed prince;
Eyes rivetted, jaws locked, while backward still
On the dire Terror he glared. But a glad cry
Aroused him, and he turned. His charioteer
Ardently pointed onward. Blessed sight!
Shelter at last was near him! the lone house,
Seen from afar; humble, yet strong; and, now,
More coveted than, brief hour back, had been
A palace of one gem. A very scream
Of rapture he sent; but, in the midst, broke off:
For, like a sword-stroke, ringing on his helm,
A hailstone smote; one solitary stone;
Sent forward from the Plague,—so might it seem,—
Him singling out for vengeance. Such his thought;
As, rising from the chariot's cavity,
Whereto he had been smitten, he looked out,
And, near him, no hail saw. Again he sat;

Griped with both hands the car; and anxiously
His eyes on the lone house fixed.
                            Soon, in the porch,
Women and men he spied,—with heads thrust forth,
Fearfully peering; and, with arm upraised,
One standing foremost, pointing earnestly.
Turning to look,—horror on horror,—lo!
The terrible Destroyer, nigh at hand,
Eagle-swift rushing on; its monstrous wave
Tearing along the ground, with noise more dread
Than stormiest ocean's thunder. But, where now,—
Where are the horsemen? Ha! he sees them still;
Scarce arrowflight distant,—almost chest to ground,
The horses stretching. But, far swifter yet.
Comes on the Terror,—sending out afar
Vaunt-couriers fierce—wide-scattered hailstones, shot
Like spears of iron from a Titan's arm.
Struck as by thunderbolt, steed, or rider, falls,
And whirls along the ground. Still fly the rest;
Though, with even tempest-wafted falcon's speed,
Hopeless to 'scape. . . . . . Anon, through all the din,
Pierces a dread sound,—shriek of man, and horse,
In the death-fear-spasm: then, his terrible foot,
The Plague flings out, and stamps them into dust!

    Aghast with horror,—staring—motionless—
Wellnigh of reason bereft—awhile he sat:
Then turned; shut close his eyes, and waited death.
But, suddenly, bethought him,—seized his shield—
Flung it across his back,—and looked again
Toward his one only hope. Even yet, even yet,
Possible seemed escape: scarce bow-shot off,
Stood the lone house; wind-swift the horses flew:
Still, swifter far came on the roar and crash
Of the irresistible Plague; and, ere full speed
Could slackened be, and he could leap to ground,
The Fury might be on them. Thinking thus,
"On, on," again he shrieked: but his own voice,
In the dread uproar heard not. By the arm,
He shook the charioteer;—no sign replied;

Nought felt the man, or heard: the body alone
Sat stiffly at its work; with rigid hands,
The reins and scourge holding obediently,
Though Mind, the ruler, slept. On the white face
A moment Sethos looked; then stretched his arm,
The reins to seize; but, in that instant, struck
By a great ice-bolt, headlong to the earth
The driver tumbled, dead; in his clenched hand
Dragging them down. One glance upon the corse
Showed him the reins torn loose from the hard gripe,
And trailing on the ground. Gone now all hope!
Another instant, and beyond the house
The unmastered steeds would fly! Death certain, then,
In the next would leap upon him. Bootless all
That in the porch stood men who would have helped!
Lifting their arms, they seemed to cry to him:
He heard not; had not heard, though every voice
Had been a giant's trumpet.
       But a hand
More mighty came to save. Stone-dead at once,
A thunderbolt smote the horses. Heavy as lead,
Down dropped they: snapping pole and trace, rolled o'er;
And lay, haunch-foremost. Shot from out the car,
As from a catapult—limbs stretched and stiff,
As in a dream of flying from a height,—
Beyond the horses far, on flew the prince:
Dashed to the earth;—whirled rapidly o'er and o'er;—
Stopped,—heavily backward swayed,—and lay as dead.

 Forth from the porch, their own lives perilling,
A woman first, and, after her, three men,
Hastily ran; lifted, and bore him in;
And the door barred. Even at that point of time,
Hail, fire, and rain as from heaven's flood-gates loosed,
Driven by the hurricane's dread artillery,
Heavy as ocean-wave smote on the house;
Battering, and shaking, as if stone from stone
Furious to rend, and scatter on the ground.

 His hour not yet was come; and Sethos 'scaped.

Regardless of his priests and sorcerers,—
Who, though aloud they boasted, and made mock
Of Moses, and his God, yet, in their hearts,
Great terror had, lest verily the threat
Should be accomplished; and the dreaded scourge
Themselves should strike; and, therefore, earnestly
Had counselled him that morning to abide
Within the palace,—for, by natural signs,
They read a tempest coming,——of all these
Unheedful; hardened still, and proud of heart,
And resolute more, the more dissuasive they,—
Forth to the river, as his custom was
Ever at sunrise,—by his lords, and priests,
And sorcerers, attended, Pharaoh went,
The threatened plague defying. Round the sky,
Gayly he looked, when they the outer gate
Had passed, and in the open space made pause;
Then, turning to his followers, with a look
And tone derisive, thus.
      "A threatening heaven
Verily have we! Yon blue cloudless vault
Hath mischief in it, like the face that smiles,
While the hand gripes a dagger. As I live,
Ye are pale-hued and fearful. If *indeed*,
As ye aver, the natural signs ye see
Of gathering storm, teach me to see them too.
Doth emptiness show fulness? Why, nor wind,
Nor cloud, nor moaning in the air; nor aught,
To eye, or ear, or any sense, gives note
Of tempest coming. 'Tis a day for youth
And love to wanton in from morn till night.
Get ye all out, ye downcast sorcerers,
To wood, and river-bank; and search for gold:
Then, when ye find it, look for hailstones too;
'Twould be the rarer prize. From my first days,
Ne'er saw I morn more lustrous, or more sweet:
It brings me youth again. Some joyous sport
Must I devise, to suit such happy time;
That it may be remembered, as the day
Of the great hailstorm."

                        Laughing pleasantly,
On went he then ; Soter, his second son,
Walking beside him, and right lustily,
Joining his father's merriment.   In a while,
His head half backward turning, as they walked,
Again unto his sorcerers, with light mock,
Spake Pharaoh.
                "When a sign ye shall behold,
Declare it to me ; for mine eyes, alas !
No cunning have to see, save that which *is* ;
The non-existent, or the invisible,
Beholding never."
                "Will the king look *now:*"
Said a deep voice : and Pharaoh, at the word,
Stopped, and turned round ; and, as the extended arm
Of Hophra pointed, toward the west looked out.

"And what should Pharaoh see, now he *doth* look ?"
After short silence said the king, displeased.
"What dost *thou* see ? "
                "The forelock of the storm,
Of which we warned thee, Pharaoh, do I see,"
Hophra made answer : " and the lowering brow,
Is mounting ; and the whole dread shape, ere long,
Careering on the winds, will shadow earth.
See,—like dread Typhon rising from his throne,
Up soars the blackness.   Fleetest desert-steed
Would fail to save thee, king, if on the plain
That demon should pursue thee."
                            " Nought I see,"
Pharaoh made answer, " save such cloud, night-hued,
As oft, against the season of the rains,
From out the abyss beneath the earth ascends,
To herald their on-coming.   In due time,—
At hour of noon, perchance,—that sable mass
Above our heads may sweep, and some broad drops
Cast down upon us.   Meantime, toward the bath
Our easy course we take, be thou assured.
The threat of the great sorcerer I defied ;
And yield not to thy tremblings."

                          "Nay, O king,"
With firm voice Hophra answered; "for myself
Nought fear I,—but for thee. If go thou wilt,
Forbidden not, *I* go. Thunder, and rain,
And hailstones, not more heavy on my head
Than on thine own will fall. But, once again,
O Pharaoh, look. Even in this point of time,
How hath the Fury mounted! At such speed
If it hold on, plainly I tell thee, king,
The threshold of thy palace thou'lt not cross
Ere storm and thunder reach thee. Hark! the voice
Of angry winds already overhead,
Even in yon crystal sky. . . . Thou hearest it,
O Pharaoh, and yet stirr'st not; though 'tis note
Of death to him who scorns it. Ha! look! look!
Heaven is in flames: the great arch melts: see! see!
In fiery ruin it falls! A moment more,
And flight will be too late!"
                          Pale, breathless, mute,
Stood Pharaoh, looking on the coming Plague;
Heartsick with fear, and shame; yet iron-stiff
In native obduracy, so that power
To bend, none had he. But, around him now,
Trembling with fear, came rulers, lords, and priests,
Conjuring him to turn: and, with both hands,
Grasping his arm, his son, too, cried aloud,
Imploring him, and gently drawing back:
So that, though slowly, and reluctantly,
Homeward at length he moved.
                          But quicker foot
Soon found he; for the hurricane's first breath
Half overthrew, half lifted him from earth:
And from the dry ground, like a harrow, tore
Pebble, and sand; and in thick cloud drove on,
Like stone-shower from the sling. Arm locked in arm,—
For, singly, none had stood,—heads bowed, teeth clenched,
Sinews hard braced,—stunned, speechless, terror-struck,—
In one close mass, as 'gainst a torrent's force
Thrusting and struggling, onward labored they;
In midst of them the king.

'Gainst a strong wind,
As the deep-laden bark—her port in view—
Oft tacking, heavily rolling, staggering,
Holds on her difficult way,—so these, to the right
Now reeling, now to the left, still toward their goal
Stiffly bore on: and never mariners,
After long, perilous voyage, more rejoiced,
Their native harbour entering, than did these,
When, panting, crushing, through the palace door
They crowded in at last. Even then, from stroke
Of Plague's fierce arm, as though not safe enough,—
Hurriedly toward the hall's remotest end,
Prince, priests, and sorcerers ran: and silent stood;
Listening, and trembling.
     But, with lowering brow,
To no man speaking,—for great wrath and shame
Burned in him, when of his proud boasts and mocks,
Thus ending, he bethought him,—Pharaoh straight
Toward his own chamber sped; that privily
To rage he might give loose; and, all alone,
On the coming Plague look out. Yet, as he went,
To his servants cried he out; "Send to the field.
Bid that all cattle therein be brought home:
Let not a hoof be left. Instantly send;
Else will all perish."
     But too late the word!
For, when he gained his chamber, and looked forth,—
Not far away, like bars of steel white-hot,
From cloud to earth ran down the fire-lit hail;
Thunders before it coming, and great blasts,
That all the palace shook.
     With piercing shrieks,—
Yet, in that hurly, small as infant's wail,—
The queen, and her two daughters, pale as death,
Rushed in the chamber; fell upon their knees:
Uplifted trembling hands, and piteously called,
Imploring him. But, in that uproar, nought
Heard he, or cared to hear. Suddenly then
Sirois upstarted,—grasped his arm,—her face,
All wild with terror, lifted,—drew him down,—

Close to his ear put her white quivering lips,
And cried out franticly; "Oh Pharaoh dear,
Why didst thou mock me when I prayed of thee
To let the Hebrews go! Thou canst not stand
Against their terrible God! Six fearful plagues
Already hath he sent; and now a seventh,
More dreadful far, is coming. Ere it fall,
Send thou to Moses; I beseech thee send;
Else, such destruction as . . . ."
                              Her speech to stop,
Pharaoh his hand uplifted; shook the head,
And turned away,—anger, and shame, and pride,
O'ermastering him. But every moment now
More terrible grew the roar of hurricane,
The thunder, and the thickening lightning's flash;
And yet again, by the arm seizing him,
Into his ear she shrieked.
                      " Oh, Pharaoh, send—
Send, ere too late. The ever blessed gods
So have disposed, that, in this very house,
With thy dear father's sister, Moses sits
At morning meal,—invited yester-eve;
For the old love she bears him. Aaron too,
The high priest, with them sits. Oh! send thou, then,
I do implore thee, Pharaoh. . . . ."
                              Uttering cries
As of death-torment, suddenly she ceased,
And dropped upon the knee; with hand on floor,
A moment stayed herself,—then, senseless all,
Rolled back, and lay as dead. Shrieking, down sank
Her daughters also. The astounded king,
Staggering, and cowering, trembling, wailing, ran;
Fell on a couch, and, with sharp-quivering hands,
Covered his face: for, in one moment, burst
The Plague in all its wrath; lightning in floods,—
Cataracts for rain,—and hail that, like the clang
Of myriad iron hammers, on the roof
And walls brought trembling. As the very world
Were in its death-throes, and the elements
Rending asunder,—ocean, sky, and earth,

In horrible uproar battling,—seemed the din.
Stopping his ears, he sat, and glared around,
As if to see when walls should topple down;
Or the whole palace, like a stone cast forth
Into deep water, sink within the earth!
All plagues, to this, seemed light. One single hour
Should it endure, Egypt a waste would be.
Submit he must. Nerving himself, he rose,
To seek the Hebrews. But, ere step he took,—
Behold, as, terror-stunned, will lamb and kid
With lions mingle,—so, all form forgot,
Even in the royal chamber, yelling, poured
Priests, rulers, sorcerers, princes, serving-men,
Crowded together; fell before his feet;
Lifted their quivering hands, and cried to him.
Words he heard none; but saw their moving lips,
And their speech guessed. To one of them signed then;
And, when the man arose, close to his ear
His voice uplift to the highest, and thus cried.
" At table with my father's sister, sit
Moses and Aaron, at the morning meal.
Fly to her chamber: bid them hither haste;
Even on the instant: the king waiteth them."

Forth sped the man: and Pharaoh, seeing now
His queen and daughters stretched upon the floor,
With his own trembling hands uplifted them;
On couches placed; and to the servants then,
Priests, rulers, sorcerers, signed that they should go.
Backward all went; yet lingered; for the Plague
More terror had than even Pharaoh's wrath;
And from the chamber, though about the doors
They gathered, yet departed not one man.
Crazed with affright, the king beheld them not;
Stunned by the uproar, dazzled by the fires;
But, with stopped ears, eyes bent upon the floor,
To and fro hurriedly walked; a furtive glance
Casting at times, expecting to behold
Whom most he feared, and loathed; yet now, of all,
The most desired to see. Nor long the time

Ere, with calm mien, and gesture dignified;
Yet look severe, as of doom-speaking judge;
Moses and Aaron entered.
                           Pride and rank
In that great dread forgetting,—with hands clasped—
Lips quivering—eyes wide staring—his whole look
Mercy imploring,—toward them Pharaoh ran;
To the highest pitch lifted his voice, and cried,
Piteously cried:
                 "Oh, I have sinned this time!
The Lord is righteous: I, and my people all,
Are wicked! But entreat ye now the Lord,
That no more thunderings and hail there be;
Then shall ye go; ye shall no longer stay."

In stern mood Moses on him looked, and said;
"Soon as without the city I am gone,
I will spread forth my hands unto the Lord;
And the great thunder and the hail shall cease:
So mayst thou know that all the earth is God's.
But, as for thee, and thine, I know that yet
Ye will not fear the Lord."
                           Like two sharp swords
Piercing the flesh, in Pharaoh's spirit pierced
The eyes of Moses, when, thus having said,
Full in the face he looked him; without word,
A book of censure speaking. Turning then,
Aaron beside him, swiftly he went forth.

No hailstone smote them; tempest stirred them not:
With a great pity at their hearts, they sped:
And when without the city Moses came,
He spread abroad his hands unto the Lord.
Hail, rain, fire, hurricane, and thunder, ceased.
Through all the land of Egypt, instantly
The mighty uproar ceased; and silence fell,
Even as a blow; so, unto common noise,
Was every ear made deaf.
                        But, in a while,
When from the houses pallid men looked forth,

A gathering sound they heard; like gentle flow
Of streamlet first; but, as the sense returned,
Swelling and deepening to the torrent's rush:
For, channelling the ground, through all the land,
Toward Nile the rain-flood, and the melting hail,
Ran roaring: and the fervent sun poured down
On the huge hailstones, and the leaping streams,
That all the earth with a great glory blazed.

But when, with trembling, men 'gan issue forth,
And walk abroad,—destruction terrible
On all sides round they saw. Dead men, and beasts,—
All flesh that from the field had not been brought,—
Stiff, crushed, and battered, lay: birds of all wing,
Sparrow, and eagle alike;—from sheltered nook,
Or lofty eyry mid the far-off hills,
Blown forth, and smitten: trees by the roots dragged up;
Or snapped in the midst; or, branchless, leaning down:
Bushes, and plants, and all grain that had sprung,—
As by a harrow, torn from out the ground,
And utterly destroyed.
                              A voice of wail
Went quickly through the land. Many cried out,
Cursing the Israelites,—through whom had come
Such bitter woes: but many on the king
Cast censure; saying that, obstinate and proud,
And faithless to his promise, he himself
Those ills had brought on Egypt; the great power
Of Hebrew magic, or of Israel's God,
Defying still, though, by six fearful Plagues,
Might he have learned that, 'gainst it, all his strength
Mere breath was, 'gainst the everlasting rock.

ISRAEL IN EGYPT.

BOOK NINETEENTH.

But, while thus many blamed,—Pharaoh himself
Most censured Pharaoh: not that, by his pride,
And obduracy, that tremendous scourge
On Egypt he had brought; but that, by fear
O'er-ruled, to vile submission he had stooped,
When, haply, one short hour had he held firm,
Self-moved the storm had passed. So in his heart
The demon whispered him. But, most of all
Bitter his shame, remembering how, in sight
Of his own queen, and daughters, rulers, priests,—
Nay, even in presence of base serving-men,—
He had been humbled; to the sorcerers
Of Israel, as though very gods they had been,
Piteously praying. For long hours, alone
He kept; nor any living soul would see.
With face inflamed, hands clenched, and flashing eyes,
In his closed chamber to and fro he strode;
Nor food, nor wine would touch; his burning thirst
With water only cooling. All distraught,
He knew not what to do; by what means best
His shame to wipe away. If real God
Those hideous plagues had sent,—all strength of man,
Resisting, must be vain. Yet how knew he,
How *could* he know, if, in the verity,

Such Power there were? His sorcerers had laughed;
Himself had laughed, at thought of a new god;
A god, forsooth, of that poor Israel:
Yet, such dread things had been, as gods alone,
Or magic strong as gods, could have brought forth.
On that man only, evil's minister,
That hated, terrible Hebrew, might he hope
Such act to do, as fear of future ills
Would end for aye: the one stroke that should take
From that pernicious the life-breath,—would take
From Egypt all the evils yet in store,
Through his malignance. Yet, if god-sent, he,
God-guarded too, perchance; and, aimed at him,
Stroke deadliest on the striker might recoil;
Turned by the hand divine. Even if with strength
Of magic solely, had the Hebrew wrought,—
His god a mere pretext,—yet, that same strength
And wisdom, more than human, in defence·
'Gainst open might of king, or secret stroke,
Potent, perchance, would be as in assault,—
And, lashed to fury, even more terrible still
Might be his vengeance.. Nought could he resolve;
The just, or unjust way to take, alike
Irresolute. The promise had been given,
That Israel should go forth. Decree, indeed,
As yet was unproclaimed: but, not the less,
The slaves, he knew, would preparation make
For quick departure; and, unchecked, might go;
Many, if not the whole: yet, dared he not,—
So fresh the terror on him,—tell aloud
How he had lied to Moses; and the word
Send forth, forbidding them.
                           As when the wind,
Fitfully blowing, north, east, south, and west,
Tosses the silken streamer,—even so,
Anger, or fear, or hope, his purpose tossed,
This way, or that; one moment, resolute
That Israel should not go; that, with high hand,
Yet more would he oppress them,—and, the next,
Resolved that go they should; that he himself

Would drive them forth; and be for ever quit
Of those detested, and their sorceries.
Enough of her own people, Egypt had,
For public labor: let *them* do the work;
Erewhile by Hebrews done. . Whate'er the cost,
Cheap were it, purchasing escape from Plague.
That hour of hail more grievous loss had brought,
Than years of Israel's labor could repay.
And, even if all exhausted now the wiles
Of magic,—no new torments to be found,—
Yet, who might know if the old Plagues again
Might not be sent,—again, and yet again,
Till victory should be won, and Egypt lost;
Dispeopled,—nay a desert. They should go!
Go on the morrow: he would scourge them out!
That instant would he send abroad the word,
Driving them forth. But, even while he moved,
His lords to summon, quickly veered the wind.
Pride, hatred, fury, shame, in passionate blasts
Swept through his soul; and, rather than submit,
A thousand deaths he'd die: nay, the whole land
Behold a wilderness!
     So, all the day,
Like to a vessel on a broken sea;
Fast anchored, but yet restless evermore;
With every changing gust, this way, or that,
Moving, as if on voyage to set out;
Yet faltering soon,—then stopping,—and, anon,
Forward again, or backward, or traverse,—
But straight advancing never,——all the day,
So, on the changeful waves of hate, and fear,
And hope, and doubt, tossed Pharaoh; nor at eve,
More than at morn, on path direct could fix.

But hunger now was on him; and he called,
Commanding food and wine: then, when sufficed,
Touching his daughters questioned, and his queen,—
How they all day had fared: yet, when he heard,
That to his presence they desired to come,—
Shame bowing him, before their eyes, as yet,

Dared he not stand. "Say to my gracious queen,
That, care-distracted, Pharaoh keeps alone,
Till hour of sleep: and to my daughters say,
'Until the morrow wait; your father then,
Sorrow o'erpast, will gladden in your sight.'"

Thus to his faithful servant Onar, spake
The cloud-wrapped king; and answer thus received.

"The king hath spoken. Let him not be wroth
With his poor servant, if the word he brings
Displeaseth him. Thamusin, the high priest,
And other priests, and sorcerers, the past hour
Impatiently have waited;—audience quick
Earnestly praying; for that some great thing
Should be done speedily." Pharaoh shook the head,
And turned away.
"May yet thy servant speak?"
After short pause, in low tone Onar said.
And, when he saw that Pharaoh looked on him,
Permission granting, hastily pursued.
"Thus said Thamusin to me; 'if thy lord
Inclineth not to hear us, say,—the thing
Of which we have to speak, is even that same
On which the necromancer Hophra spake
But yester-morn unto him; and that now
The last hour cometh?'"
O'er the countenance
Of Pharaoh, like a torch-flash in mirk night,
A bright gleam suddenly shot: his bended form
Erect stood instantly: his languid voice,
With its old vigour spake—promptly and clear,
Commanding them before him: for a break
Through the blank darkness which the future hid,
Seemed now about to open; and he longed
To fix on it the eye. With restless foot,
To and fro walked he; and, before him now
When came the priests, with hurried utterance thus.
"Hath he the soul brought back? And speaketh it?"

"Even so, my lord the king," Thamusin said:
"With our own ears we heard it. But, alas!
If the king haste not, from the corpse 'twill part,
Ere he can question; for the third day this,
And this the final hour. Thy chariot waits,
O Pharaoh; for even I did so command,
Lest, through delay . . . . ."
     "Thou hast done well, high priest,"
Hastily said the king: "Where lieth, then,
The body of the Hebrew?"
       "In a vault
Of the north catacomb," the priest replied:
"Our mules stand ready; and, so please the king,
His heralds will we be."
      "Away at once,"
Cried Pharaoh; and himself went quickly forth;
By all as quickly followed. Eve's last rays
Lighted the path: but, in a vestment black
And ample wrapped, no eye that him beheld,
Knew that it looked on Pharaoh.
      Through the door
Of the dark mansion of the dead, soon passed
The anxious monarch; of the hidden things
Eager to learn, yet fearful; and with awe,
Unfelt till then, touched strangely. The strong breath
Of flesh-preserving spices,—in the air
Of open day so fragrant,—in that house
Of death, itself seemed deathlike; a corpse-sweat,
Loathsome, detestable; and he turned back.
"Bring forth the body to the air of heaven;
I cannot breathe that horror"—he exclaimed.

"O Splendor of the Sun," Thamusin said;
"Thou wouldst the impossible. Silence, rest profound,
Alone can lure the spirit to remain
In the fast-perishing corpse. Spells cannot force;
They but conjúre. All now prepared awaits;
And still the spirit answers: but, the hour
Well nigh is ended: and, once passed, the might
Of all earth's charms combined will never draw

The freed soul back. See,—on my torch I throw
A perfume that will call the flowers of Spring
Around us. Hasten then, O Light of Day:
See nought,—nought hear, or feel,—and think of nought,
Save of the one great end for which alone
Here com'st thou,—the far-onward-piercing look
Into the hidden knowledge."
 "On, then, quick,"
Impatiently said Pharaoh; "and fail not
To feed thy torch-fire, ever and anon,
With that life-raising essence: the death-air
Will choke me, else."
 A low, and narrow way,
Lined by the dead, they trod; and speedily
A chamber reached. Before the entrance, paused
The monarch, awe-chained: for one ghastly beam
Alone kept off pitch-blackness; a thin flame,—
As 'twere the ghost of light,—nought showing there,
Save the stern, livid faces of the priests,
Like dead men motionless standing. Clearer view
Soon coming,—in the midst a corpse he saw,
Clad in the grave-clothes. From the high-arched breast,
As from a lamp, that supernatural flame,
Like a thin luminous smoke, rose tremulously;
And, slanting on the countenance of the dead,
Distortion gave horrific. While aghast
Thus stood he gazing,—on the stillness broke
The low, hoarse voice of Hophra.
 "Quickly wanes,
O king, the life-flame: while that weak light burns,
The spirit lingers: when the flame dies out,
Gone is it, and for ever! Weak the words
Which last it spake; with every moment now,
Death clogs it more: if question thou wouldst put,
Lose not, O king, an instant. Thy right hand,
Stretch toward the gods: on the dead brow, thy left
Lay firmly, and then speak."
 One step advanced
The blood-chilled Pharaoh; but, irresolute, paused;
Shrinking to touch, nay ev'n draw nigh the corpse,

So grimly terrible in stony rest;
Rotting, yet not all dead.
                        " Of Israel's god
Myself have asked," said Hophra, hoping thus
The faltering king to stir; " but, unto me,
Came not a word: as if for shame, or wrath,
Or terror,—from the crown unto the foot,
The dead flesh trembled; but reply was none.
Yet, if the Splendor of the Sun demand—
To that great voice, reluctant though it be,
Promptly the soul must answer. But, O king,
Fast is the life-flame dying! when 'tis gone,
Question the rock; 'twill answer thee as soon."

    Stirred by the demon, Pharaoh boldly then
Advanced: his right hand lifted toward the gods:
On the damp, wrinkled, icy brow, his left
Laid firmly: on the stone face looked; and spake.
"Soul, which within this dead clay hoverest yet,
By the Dread Powers do I conjure thee, speak.
While in this flesh thou dwelt, not the great god
Osiris, didst thou worship, but a name
To Israel only known. As thou wouldst hope,
Within the bark of Athom safe to reach
The nether world; and, in the realms of death,
Enemies vanquish; and divinities soothe;
And in the hall of judgment have thy sins
Weighed mercifully,—speak to me the truth.
Is there a god, Jehovah named; a god
Of thy peculiar people?"
                        Like the moan
Of night-wind in the wave-worn sea-shore cave,
Went through the vault a low, deep, shuddering sound,
As though even air were awe-struck. 'Neath his hand,
The hard brow seemed to quiver; ne'ertheless,
By the fiend strengthened, on the marble lips
Keenly his eyes he bent; waiting to see
When the dead breath should stir them. Motionless
Lay they: the whole gaunt face hard fixed as rock:
But, from within the body of the dead,

A voice he heard,—faint, dim, like sound from far,
Coming at hush of midnight, yet distinct;
And thus it spake.
     "Oppressor of our race!
Why wilt thou question me? Is't not enough
That, while in flesh, we thy poor slaves should be?
Thou hast called back my soul, to force from it
Knowledge pernicious. Ask me, then, no more,
But let me go. The bark of Athom waits
My coming; and the impatient souls look out,
Chiding my long delay. If speak I must,
Truth only *can* I speak; and, of my words,
A whip thou'lt make, to scourge our people more.
Be pitiful, O king; and let me go!"

"Speak, first, then go," said Pharaoh: "by all Powers
Of the Great Mysteries, I command thee speak:
Is there a god, Jehovah?"
     Silence deep
And long there was: then the thick air again
Shuddered, and moaned; and, afterwards, the voice,
But fainter than before,—as if the clay
Deader had grown about it; or the soul
More weak to struggle through,—thus, sighing, spake.

"Would that I dared refuse to answer thee!
For, losing fear, the worse wilt thou become;
Yea, make of Israel one great voice of woe.
But answer thee I must. . . . . Whom Hebrews call
Their God Jehovah, but a shadow is;
A name, a sound,—nought else. Had they a god
Peculiar to them, slaves they had not been
Long years to thee, and thine. Release me now,
I pray thee, king, lest other misery,
Through me, thou bring on Israel."
     "Tell me, first,"
Said Pharaoh, "why, in name of Israel's god,
Plagues threatening, Moses came,—if, in the truth,
No god hath Israel? Was he mind-diseased;
Conceiting that a god he saw, and heard?

Or falsehoods uttered he, us to mislead,
And bend unto his purpose? Furthermore,
Tell me thou this: how came on us those plagues?
How their on-coming did your Moses know?
Were they of natural cause, and but foreseen
By his keen prescience? or, by his great spells
Solely were they brought on us? Quickly speak;
For thy life-flame low burneth."
         "While on earth,"
Sighed the thin voice, "even righteous men, for good,
Do evil; falsehood speak, in cause of truth:
And Moses thus, great, virtuous though he is,—
To serve his suffering Israel, did with guile
Strive to dismay thee; threatening as from god,
Though god was none; that sooner from their bonds
Might thou set free his people. For the plagues,
He, Moses, all alone, them sent on you;
Master of spells that might the moon eclipse;
Root up the mountains; and make ocean boil,
As water in a cauldron. Heed, O king,
How thou confront him. But thy sorcerers, too,
Strange might are gathering: and I see, methinks,
Far off, great clouds wherein a conflict is
'Twixt him and them. Osiris aid the right!
I have replied to all: let me then go;
For the clay chokes me."
       "Yet one question more,"
Said Pharaoh quickly,—every instant now
Marking the pale flame weaker, paler, grow,—
"One only; then I let thy spirit pass.
Hath Moses power yet other plagues to send?
And *will* he send? What, then, our best course were?
To endure,—or shun them,—or the sorcerer crush?
SPEAK."
    Like a hasty blow rang out the word;
For, suddenly sank the life-flame to a point,
Small as a star; and darkness so thick fell,
That no man saw his fellow. As thin smoke
To the eye,—just visible, and melting fast,—
So faint, and sinking, to the listening ear

Came the dim spirit-voice; "Yet two plagues more
Will Moses bring on Egypt; after that—
The king—shall rest—in peace."
                              Like scarce-heard voice
Of lessening echoes from far distant hills,
Faint, fainter fell the words. As ceased the last,
Died out the life-flame. From the clammy brow
Pharaoh his chilled hand snatched; and on his robe,
Heart-sick, wiped off the death-dew.
                                    Torchlight soon
Flashed in the chamber: quickly he went out:
For water cried: washed: to his chariot sprang:
Word uttered none; but toward the palace sped.

In bath of sweetest perfume plunged, two hours,
The death-scent to purge utterly, he laved;
Then hastened to repose. Glad was he now;
In his new knowledge confident; and stern
With high hand yet to rule o'er Israel:
The threatened plagues to endure; then, the poor spells
Of Moses to defy; and of his god
To make a mockery. Thus, with spirit proud,
To rest he sank; and, all the night, in dreams
Of power and glory infinite rejoiced.

ISRAEL IN EGYPT.

BOOK TWENTIETH.

LIKE a strong youth who, from refreshing sleep
After hard travel, rises light of heart,
Active of limb, flushed with high summer of health,
And eager for whate'er the day may bring,—
So, on the morrow, waking from sound rest,
And visions glorious, Pharaoh on the past,
As on a great toil overcome, looked back;
Then toward the future; and, exultingly,
Within himself thus said.
      "Yet two plagues more,—
And then, proud sorcerer, will thy spells be done;
The king will rest in peace. But, as for thee,
What peace canst *thou* expect? The peace of death!
Nought else! for, though thy mischief all be spent;
Thine arm grown powerless,—still, thy deeds accursed,
Punishment full must have. Yet, ere thou die,
In sight of all the people shalt thou stand,
For mockery; both on thee, and on thy god;
When, stronger grown than thou, my sorcerers
Shall make of thee, and of thy magic tricks,
A sport to please even children; and thy god
Shall hold up for the laughter of the land;
A thing of smoke, or mist, or air, or nought;
A name, a bugbear only. And, the while,

Pharaoh shall sit; and look upon the man,
Who, in the name of that same fantasy,
Once bearded him, and bid let Israel go.
Yea, Moses, upon *thee* shall Pharaoh look,
Thundering, as thou 'gainst him didst thunder oft,—
Armed with thy plagues, and vaunting of thy god:
And loudly in the dust shalt thou cry out
For pity; but the answer will be, death!
Meantime, upon the instant shall proclaim
Go forth to Israel, bidding them remain;
And better do their work."

      Then passed he forth
Among his lords and priests, and spake the word;
And, forthwith, through the city, and around,
Went out a voice, commanding Israel stay;
And with more diligence labor. To the baths,
By all his train attended, then he walked;
Thamusin at his right; and, at his left,
The necromancer Hophra; in discourse
On what, the night before, had come to pass;
The spirit's prophecy; and what should be
The two plagues yet to come; and how the best
They might be met; endured, or shunned; or stayed,
As theretofore, by prayers, and promises,
Ne'er meant to be fulfilled: for, falsely thus
Feigned Pharaoh now,—pretending that in guile,
Not under fear, submission he had made,
To the Hebrew wizards;—so one rag to hide,
By putting on another, though far worse.

 Among the sorcerers chiefly, and the priests,
Was gladness, hearing that but two plagues more,
Had Moses power to send; though, even of those,
Were some who at the prophecy shook the head;
And feared, they knew not what; the awful power
Of Israel's magic; or the power, yet more,
Of Israel's God: for, through the boundless void
Of mortal darkness, how could man see all,
Know all that is? Osiris who had seen?
Or heard? or felt? Yet who *him* doubted God?

If he,—why not a god Jehovah, too,
Existent, though unseen; by no sense known?
And, surely, or a god, or magic power
Great as a god's, it *must* be, that such plagues
Had sent on Egypt,—Israel to get loosed.
Magic, or god, alike 'twould victor be:
Soonest, then, best, to yield, and let them go.

So these, but privately, among themselves;
Not daring yet aloud such thoughts to speak.

But, of the lords and rulers, did the most
That prophecy hold as nought; a poor device
Of priest-craft; and still numerous plagues, and worse,
Dreaded would come upon them; and their voice,—
If so might be,—in presence of the king
Resolved to lift; imploring him to yield,
And send the Hebrews forth.
                    As these, so thought
Among the Egyptians many; nay, the most:
For, 'vantage little from the Israelites
Had they; but, through their bondage, evils great;
So that for their departure did they long:
Some, that they pitied them; some, that they feared,
If obstinate still the king,—more scourges yet,
Yea, even more terrible, might Israel's god,
Or Moses, send; to force him let them go.

Though,—knowing well how false would Pharaoh
    prove,—
On the hope of Israel forthwith to depart,
Moses cool words of caution had poured out,—
Yet, when the noisy criers went abroad,
Commanding them more labor than before,
For slaves they still should be,—then fell again
Great weight upon them; and again they railed
'Gainst Moses, Aaron, and the Elders all;
Saying that, for deliverance, they had brought
Yet heavier chains upon them, and worse toil.
But, throughout all that day, to whom they might,

Moses, and Aaron, and the Elders went,
Consoling them; and bidding trust in God;
For that the time drew nigh, when His great hand
Surely would He put forth, and set them free.

But Pharaoh, high in pride uplifted now,—
With a long train of lords, and men of war
Accompanied, throughout the city drove
In his gold-flashing chariot; that the eyes
Of all the people might his pomp behold,
And glory in his power. A great feast then
Unto his lords, and priests, and sorcerers,
Gave he: and high his talk was; for he looked
Into the future; and, two clouds o'erpast,
Saw an eternal sunshine waiting him.

But, on the morrow, while beside the bank
Of Nile walked Moses, musing,—from on high
The Voice descended to him; and he sank
Upon his knees, and fell upon his face,
And, trembling, listened. "Unto Pharaoh go,
For hardened is his heart; and say to him:
'How long wilt thou refuse to bow thyself
Before the Lord! Let thou my people go,
That they may serve me: else, if thou refuse,
Behold, tomorrow will I bring a cloud
Of locusts on thy coast; which all the land
Of Egypt so shall cover, that no eye
May the ground see: and all that from the hail
Remaineth to you, every tree of the field,
Shall they devour. Thy houses shall they fill,
The houses of thy servants,—every house
Of all the Egyptians: such the plague shall be,
As thy forefathers, even since the day
When first on earth they were, have never seen.'"

When the Great Voice had ceased, and for awhile
Moses had worshipped,—he arose, and went
Unto the house of Aaron; and the words
In low tone spake. Together then they walked;

And,—for they knew that on the judgment-seat
Sat Pharaoh in that hour,—unto the hall
Of justice hastened, and before him stood.

With a great burst of rage, as theretofore,
Looked they that he would greet them; but, behold,
A smile was on his lips,—a giant's smile,
In presence of a dwarf. Nor word he spake,
Nor sign made that he saw them. To the end,
The cause before him heard he; the award
Of the grave judges sanctioned; and arose,
Tokening the session o'er. But, suddenly,—
As if that moment first beholding them,—
On the great sons of Amram a cold look
Of mere surprise he cast; upon his throne
Again sat down; with calm and patient mien,
Awaited till the people had gone forth;
Then toward the Hebrews turned, and spake.
 "What *now*
With Pharaoh would ye, that, unsummoned, thus
Ye come before him? Yet I need not ask;
For sure am I that the old jugglery
Ye come to act before me; some new plague
To threaten, if I will not let you go.
Speak freely then; for, not far off the day
When ours 'twill be to threaten, yours to obey.
Not ye alone, great sorcerers, in the blank
Of time-to-come can look; and see in life,
Events unborn as yet: our art, like yours,
Can make the future present: and the day,
I tell you, is at hand, when your great voice
Shall die in whimpers. But, of this enough:
Speak as ye will."
 Then Moses one step took,—
Not bending now the head; and, his right hand,
As one who warns, uplifting, with stern voice
Thus spake.
 "Again, O Pharaoh, unto God
Vow hast thou broken. How long, thinkest thou,
Will this be suffered? Hath not, evermore,

Punishment fallen upon thee, when thy deeds
Have given the lie to promise? Dost thou hope
That God's strength is worn out? palsied His arm?
Or His plague-quiver spent? A handful take
From ocean's wave, and sprinkle it in air:
As those few drops, unto the boundless deep,
So the plagues past, to plagues that yet remain,—
Willed He to send them. Hard art thou of heart,
Shameless, and false! In thy great agony,
Didst thou not cry,—'entreat ye now the Lord,
That no more thunderings, and hail there be;
Then shall ye go; ye shall no longer stay?'
And, afterward, did I not answer thus;
'But as for thee, and thine, I know that yet
Ye will not fear the Lord?' Ay, king, even then
I saw the lie within thee; and see now
Within thee what against thyself doth lie,—
A hope, false, foolish, that o'er Israel's God
The mastery thou may gain; and, in thy turn,
Become the threatener, and the conqueror.
Or from thine own proud heart, or from the tongue
Of the false speaker, if such folly have come,—
Quench it, O Pharaoh, as the torch thou'dst quench,
Thrust in to fire thy palace. When thy hand
Can stretch into the infinite; pluck forth thence
Star after star; and in the bottomless void
Of Night down cast them: when thy palm, outspread,
Can cover up the sun; and crush his fire
To darkness, as a candle is crushed out,—
Even then be sure that, unto Israel's God,
Still as a candle art thou to the sun:
Nay, even as nought: for, to the infinite,
The finite, greatest, less and less becomes,
Till nothing seems it; all invisible,
As dust-mote, leagues away. Yet, well I see
That words to thee are vain; that, hard of heart,
Proud and imperious, thou dost hold thyself
Still as a god o'er Israel. Hearken then.
To thee the Lord God of the Hebrews saith;
'How long wilt thou refuse to bow thyself

Before the Lord! Let thou my people go,
That they may serve me: else, if thou refuse,
Behold, tomorrow will I bring a cloud
Of locusts on thy coasts; which all the land
Of Egypt so shall cover, that no eye
May the ground see: and all that from the hail
Remaineth to you, every tree of the field,
Shall they devour. Thy houses shall they fill;
The houses of thy servants; every house
Of all the Egyptians: such the plague shall be,
As thy forefathers, even since the day
When first on earth they were, have never seen.'"

With awful voice thus having said, he turned,
Reply awaiting not; to Aaron signed;
And from the presence of the king went out.

So stern the tone, the countenance so severe,
That all awhile were silent; man on man
Looking askaunt; and all upon the king.
Gone now was Pharaoh's smile: with eyes cast down,
Pale, anxious, restless, sat he; wrath, and fear,
Strangely perplexing him.
　　　　　　　　　When this they saw,—
The lords, who from the judges and the priests
Apart were seated,—gathered in a group,
And whispered earnestly; then all at once
Went on, and stood before the king, and bowed:
And, when he looked upon them, Osochor,
One of the chief, thus said.
　　　　　　　　　"Light of the Sun,
We pray of thee, let not this Israelite
Become a snare to us; a stumblingblock,
For Egypt to fall over. Plain to us
It seemeth, that the power which turned to blood
All waters of the land: frogs, lice, and flies,
Created out of nothing: boils and blains
Sent on all beasts, and men: and, last, that storm,
Thunder, and rain, and hail horrific, brought,—
Could also, and far easier, were it willed,

Set free the Hebrews; and conduct them hence,
Whithersoe'er it would. But, at the first,
This had it done, pretext there had not been
For these plagues sending on us; old despite
On Egypt so to vent. Seven plagues, O king,
Hath it let loose; and threateneth now the eighth:
And, if that eighth avail not, be thou sure,
Even to the eightieth, should thou still resist,
Glad will it be to hurl them; till the land
Shall be a wilderness. Nay, even now,
Knowëst thou not that Egypt is destroyed?
We pray thee, then, O Splendor of the Sun,
Let the men go, that they may serve their God."

"That they may serve their God?" with tone of scorn
Spake Pharaoh, echoing them; for, by their prayer
That he would yield, the stiffer had he grown;
By their submiss'ness, haughtier: the fear, too,
Was now gone from him; for the watchful fiend
Had entered, and his heart made iron-hard;—
"That they may serve their God? And think ye, then,
That, God to serve, into the wilderness
A three days' journey distant they must go?
Ah! if a god they had, all spots alike,
To worship him were fit. A vile pretence
This wilderness-worship is: the slaves would 'scape:
And three days' journey off, good starting-point,
Doubtless they think. If worship were their aim,
Why go not forth the Elders, and the priests,
Alone,—the people leaving all behind,
That they may labor? But not thus, methinks,
Would they be satisfied. If so ye will,
Send after the two sorcerers: bid them back;
And, in your hearing, will I question them."

Forth went command; and, in brief time, again
Moses and Aaron stood before the king.
Pharaoh awhile looked on them, and then said;
"Go, serve the Lord your God: but, who are they
That shall go with you?"

                        With a firm, clear voice,
Looking on him, and all, thus Moses spake.
"Our young, our old; our sons, our daughters; our flocks,
Our herds,—all shall go with us: for a feast
We hold unto the Lord."
                        At those great words
Laughed out the king; and on his rulers looked,
As he would say, "I told you their intent;
Worship new meaning hath, and stands for *flight*."
Then, to the Hebrews turning wrathfully,
Thus cried he: "Let the Lord be so with you,
As I will let you, and your children go!
Look to it. Evil is before you. Nay—
Ye that are men, go now, and serve the Lord,
For so did ye desire: but not one else."

That heard,—from judges, priests, and sorcerers, burst
A laugh of mockery; and before the king
Went some, and prayed of him that they might drive
The Hebrews from the hall. But, tarrying not,
Soon as the king had spoken, Moses turned;
To Aaron signed, and went.
                        Toward his own house
Sped Aaron; but, without the city-gate,
Sorrowing, walked Moses. On that mound arrived
Whereon he had stood, when, the hail-plague to stay,
He spread abroad his hands unto the Lord,—
Again to him came the Voice; and he bowed down,
With face upon the earth. "Stretch out thy rod,
That locusts may come up o'er all the land
Of Egypt; and may eat up every herb;
Even all the hail hath left."
                        The Voice Divine,
Awe-stricken, Moses heard; and, worshipping,
Long time lay prostrate: then arose, and stood,
And toward all quarters of the land, his rod
Stretched out. That instant, from the east
The wind arose; and all that day blew strong;
And all that night: and, when the morning came,
The east-wind brought the locusts. As a cloud

O'er all the land they came; blotting the sun;
As though, by hand invisible, o'er the sky
A dark pall had been drawn.
       Hurriedly then,
The people of all cities through the realm;
And who in villages, and lonely spots,
North, south, and east, and west, their dwelling had,—
Went forth, and stood to gaze; all silent, fixed;
Dreading they knew not what. High up in air
Sailed on at first the Plague; and like the sound
Of wintry wind and torrent, was the boom
Of million million wings. But when, at length,
O'er all the land had spread that living night,—
Then down, with din like thickening thunder-peal,
The innumerable sank; and all the earth
Covered, and darkened; that no spot was seen,
No leaf, no blade of grass. Monstrous in size,
Voracious,—every herb, fruit of all trees,
All that the hail had left, did they devour.
In every house they thronged: over all men,
Women, and children, fell, and covered them:
Upon the floors ran thick: o'er all the beds,
Couches, and stools, and tables: o'er all food,
And in all drinks, brought foulness.
         A great cry
Went up throughout the land. In Zoan most;
And, chiefly in the palace of the king,—
For hottest there the plague,—was heard the wail.
"Nay, ye must bear it," Pharaoh proudly said:
"Bear it ye must: in few hours will it pass."
But soon,—by the dense clustering over mouth,
And nostril; the close, burning atmosphere,
And the foul odour of the plague, nigh choked,—
All courage he lost; and on his servants cried;
"To Moses, and to Aaron fly with speed:
Bid them before me. If they stay the plague,
Israel shall go into the wilderness.
Away! haste, haste; or dead men are we all!"

  Louder and louder still the wailings grew;

And louder the deep roar of countless wings.
Down to the vaults beneath the palace floor,
Rushed priests, lords, rulers, sorcerers, serving men,
Princes, and serving women,—all degrees,
In that great dread forgotten. But, with them,
Rushed the Plague also—the whole space of air
Close filling, as the crowded water-drops
Of heaviest rain-shower.
                        At the summons, came
Moses and Aaron quickly. Them the king
Beholding, toward them hastened; with a hand
Sheltering his mouth, lifted his voice, and cried;
"Oh, I have sinned against the Lord your God!
And 'gainst you also! Therefore now forgive
This once my sin, I pray thee; and entreat
The Lord your God, that this death only he
May take away: then shall your Israel go."

"Thou speakest words, O Pharaoh, but not thoughts,"
Solemnly Moses answered. "At thine heart,
Still is the hardness; and even yet, I see,
Thou wilt not let us go. But, at the last,
Be sure thou wilt; yea, pray us to depart.
To this God's wrath shall bring thee. Wiser far,
Unforced, His will to do, than by constraint
Of ills unbearable. Ere yet too late,
Ponder then well, if Him thou canst resist.
Magic thou deem'st it still,—the power that sends
These plagues upon you. From thy soul drive forth
Such folly; and behold the hand of God
Stretched out upon you, irresistible.
Maker of all things, and Disposer too,—
He is it that these chastisements hath sent,
Because of disobedience. His command
Obey, and ye may live: if thou refuse,
Again with heavy stroke will fall the hand,
Till bow thou must. Though still I see thee hard,
And insincere of promise,—yet, thine eyes
Haply to open, that thou may perceive
How Israel's God alone all things hath done,

And all can do,—behold, when I go hence,
I will entreat the Lord that He may take
This plague from Egypt: for, as here it is,
Even so, at this same hour, o'er all the land
Hath it come down : and, if my prayer be heard,
And the plague taken from you,—know thou then,
That Israel's God alone it was, who sent,
And who recalled it."
                          Having spoken thus,
Forth went he; and from out the city passed:
And when he was alone upon the hill,
Prone on his face he fell, and prayed to God,
That He the plague would stay.
                                Then suddenly,
Against the east, a mighty strong west wind,
Upstarted, quick as war-horse at the spur ;
And roared along the ground, and high in air ;
And bore away the locusts, every one ;
And in the Red Sea cast them. Of that host,
Throughout all Egypt there remained not one.

Glad were the people then; and wonder-struck;
For, though in years before had locusts come
Thick on the land, yet, had they been, to these,
As pigmies unto men; and, though even weeks
They stayed, had spoiled not all. But, few short hours
Though these remained, yet not one herb, or fruit,
Or corn-blade, had they left.
                                Still, all the day,
No word unto the Hebrews Pharaoh sent;
For in his heart he gloried that again
The wizard he had foiled: and the one plague
Which yet they must endure, by like deceit
Trusted to overcome. His sorcerers, too,
His proud heart lifted more,—declaring aloud,
That neither god, nor magic, had that plague
Brought on the land; but the east wind alone,
From the great deserts blowing; for, behold,
Soon as the west rose thundering, it had fled,
Even faster than it came.

                    But, for the lords
Who Pharaoh had counselled to let Israel go,
They knew that, nor the east wind, nor the west,
The scourge had caused to come, or pass away;
But magic terrible, or the might of God,
Solely; and yet worse dreaded. And, as they,
So, of the Egyptian people, many thought;
Moses respecting greatly; whether power
Within himself, or greater power of God,
Through him made manifest, such wondrous things
For Israel's freedom had wrought : and fain would they,—
Maugre the promptings of the Spirits of Ill,—
Have seen the Hebrews loosed; and free to go,
Whither they would.
                    But, to the Israelites,
Moses declared, that yet was Pharaoh's heart
Hard as the rock; his promise as thin smoke,
Melting even while it rose. "But the day comes,
When I shall speak to you, and bid prepare
For sudden going forth. Against that time,
In what ye may, get ready. Until then,
Bear as ye can; and put your trust in God."

ISRAEL IN EGYPT.

BOOK TWENTY-FIRST.

On the next morning, early, to the house
Of Kohath, riding on a mule, there came
What seemed the holy Moses;—Satan himself
So feigning, in his damnable attempt,
By human means,—since the Fallen Spirit had failed,
And all his own temptation come to nought,—
The virgin pure to stain. . . . . For, in the reach
Of Sethos could he lure her,—well he knew,
That, like gaunt wolf upon a lamb, would he
Madly spring on her; and with violence tear,
And scatter to the wind that heavenly flower,—
Never to bloom again: so, in His aim,
Through her, great good to bring unto mankind,
Omnipotence might be foiled.
                              The morning meal
Had passed; and, worship ended, silent sat
The pious family; when, at the door,
As with an old friend's privilege, unannounced,
He stood; and with a kindly greeting spake
To each, and all. Though none did he embrace;
To none, as custom was, even proffer hand,—
Yet marvel raised it not; for much fatigue
He pleaded, and a sudden weakness, fallen

That day upon him; therefore on a couch
At once he sank; and, with a languid voice,
Thus spake. "My venerated friends; and thou
My daughter,—for in spirit so thou art,—
Of things momentous to all Israel
Come I to speak; and patiently, I know,
Will ye give ear to me. A mighty wrath
In Pharaoh is, because of what hath passed
'Twixt him and you. Needs not that I recall
That which he offered, and which ye refused.
In full to me all told he; and besought
That, seeking you, I would to wiser course
Strive to persuade you; showing that, for dross,
Ye had pure gold rejected. Harder toil,
In his great ire, on Israel hath he put;
And harder yet doth threaten, if ye stand
As enemies fixed against him. To the storm
What will not bend at all, too oft is snapped,
And cast to earth for ever. Ill to do,
That good may come,—ne'er would I counsel you.
The world-unequalled offer of the king,
His son and heir, with thee, blest maid, to join
In marriage,—for the present, promising
Riches unbounded; and, for time to come,
The queenly crown,—even as at once thou didst,
So still must thou refuse; both, that thy faith
To Reuben thou hast pledged; and that thy love
To him alone is given; and, most of all,
Because thou canst not,—as Egyptian law
Sternly demands, ere to Egyptian prince
Thou couldst be wed,—the God of Israel leave,
And bow to Egypt's gods. Firm as a rock,
In this great thing, to thy resolve abide.
But, there immoveable, in smaller things
Wise may it be to bend. Unkind it seems,
All proffered favors sternly to refuse:
And even hearts the gentlest, when their love
Rudely hath been rejected,—but too oft,
Most hate, what most they loved,—as sweetest wine,
To vinegar sharpest turns. But, well ye know

That not of nature gentlest is the heart
Of the great Pharaoh; so that terrible wrath
Well may ye dread; not only 'gainst yourselves,
But 'gainst all Israel, if too absolute
And stern ye stand against him; every good,
Offered by him, rejecting. And, though sure
As that the morning will succeed the night,
Am I of that time coming, when our God
Shall lead us out from bondage,—yet, the day,
The week, the month, the year, He hath not told;
And who can know with what dire ills, meantime,
To the height incensed, Pharaoh may visit us!
Some sign of gratitude for kindness meant,
Wise were it, then, to show; nor only wise,
As 'vantage to us bringing,—but a debt,
Justly laid on us; since, for kindness given,
Kindness should still be paid. If Reuben, then,
The royal boon accepting, to this king,—
As, to the Pharaoh of a former day,
Was our great patriarch Joseph,—would become,
Though but for brief time, the chief minister;
And if thou, blessed Rachel, his desire
To see and know thee more, wouldst gratify,
By his queen's guest becoming,—for, of thee,
Ever, of late, to her hath he discoursed,
Till, with a very mother's love, she longs
To see, and to embrace thee,—these slight shows
Of kindness, tenfold kindness in return
May bring to you, and us: nay, blessing to all,
Of Egypt, and of Israel: for, good done,
Is good received. And even when, at last,
The irresistible truth shall on him come,
That,—though the law of Egypt would permit,—
Still, Rachel with his Sethos cannot wed,
Because that Israel's law, fixed as the heavens,
Forbiddeth Hebrew maiden to espouse
Who Israel's God refuseth,—yet, his wrath,
Ere that time, would be less; and more his love,
As thou to him more known; and he would see
That but the impossible thou didst refuse,—

All else conceding freely. And, perchance,—
For, who the changeful heart of youth can know?
The hot love of the prince, like fever's fit,
To cold may turn : or toward some other maid
The flame may point; and so the discord end
'Twixt thee, and him, and Pharaoh : or, perchance,—
Yet better ending,—ere that time shall be,
The day of our deliverance may come,
All evils finishing thus. Howe'er may close
The time of trial,—meanwhile,—steering thus
Through sea of difficulty,—happier days,
Or weeks, or months, or years, will be for all.
Ponder on this, my friends; and, if like mine
Your judgment be,—with Reuben reason then,
And with his parents; so that, to himself,
Great power, and wealth, and glory, may there come;
And great good to all Israel. For your part,
Dear friends of old; and thou, though new, yet dear
As my own child,—from you, opposal none
I look for : Pharaoh's gentle courtesy,
Gently ye'll answer. Nor, of conduct safe
For Rachel, need be fear. Whene'er ye will,—
So ye but signify unto the queen,
Or Pharaoh, that on such day, at such hour,
Your daughter will set forth,—at that same hour
A royal chariot at your gate will be;
And guard, befitting queen. Nay, haply, too,—
For so spake Pharaoh,—even the queen herself,
Or her fair daughters, may ride forth, to bear
The loved one safe to Zoan : and, like way,
When homeward she would go, chariot, and guard,
And kind friends would attend her. His own words
Now have I said. For token of his love,
A gem that once the royal crown adorned,
He sendeth thee, blest Rachel; with it, words
Of father's kindness : and, though fierce of heart
Well do I know him; and that falsely oft
To Israel's God he hath spoken,—yet, in these,—
So on the words did gesture, look, and tone,
Stamp truth's clear impress,—simple verity

Alone I see. ' Tell her,' he said, ' that, warm
As the bright gem I give her, is the love,
The fatherly love I feel; as durable, too,
And strong,—so she herself will love return ;—
Even slight; an echo only unto mine,
Far off, and faint; yet tuned to the same tone
Of heart-affection.' "
      Speaking the last words,
He rose; and, from a small bright case of gold,
A ring brought forth. As if the setting sun
A beam of ruby glory had shot in,
All the air caught sudden radiance. With a step
Slow and majestic, toward the maiden then
He walked; and, bending his tall form, held forth
The glowing stone-fire. But she also rose;
And, lowly bowing, with calm tone, and soft,
Yet firm, thus spake.
     " The favor of the king
Gratefully own I. Yet, but one kind deed,
To even the lowliest done, were, in my sight,
More estimable than a royal crown.
Would the king have so poor a maiden's love,—
Let him show justice to the wronged; give help
To those who suffer. Nought that I have done,
Or could do—for such price might quittance be:
And I would not be debtor, save to one
Who, for the debt, himself indebted feels;
Grateful to be the server. When the king
Hath freed the slave; and, to the wronged, given back
What tyranny had taken,—then, to him,
My love, and full obedience,—yea, the love
And full obedience of all upright hearts,—
Freely poured forth will be. Till then, the gems
Of all the earth from me no love could buy:
For pure love hath no price. In every breast,
Methinks, love lies,—but sleeping, till 'tis stirred
By the right quickener: as fire sleeps in wood,
Till rightly touched. Steel will not force it wake,
Nor gold, nor jewels tempt: thunder, and wind,
And earthquake cannot stir it,—for their might

Of other nature is:—but the small spark
Of fire, like-natured, the deep slumbering heat
Wakes quickly; and the cheering flame ascends.
So, in the heart, love, or the deeds of love,—
Of mercy, justice, piety, and truth,—
All fruits from that great tree, the love of God,—
Alone can call to life true human love.
To offer gold for stars, were not more vain,
Than for pure love. Since, then, I cannot yield
What Pharaoh so would purchase,—for a price
It hath, or would have, though, in form, mere gift,—
Let him forgive me, that I cannot take,
What on my spirit would a burthen be;
A debt could ne'er be paid; or wage received
For work could ne'er be done."
       Ceasing, she bent
Her graceful head, and sat. Her voice, though soft,
Spake granite-firm her purpose. To its case
Satan the ring returned; and, with calm tone,—
Love and approval beaming from his eyes,—
Still standing nigh her, bowed his lofty head,
And spake.
   "Of worldly wisdom, more have I,
Than thou, blest Rachel: yet, best wisdom is,
Not worldly, but of heaven; and, therein, thou
Show'st me, perchance, in darkness. Whatsoe'er
The voice within doth bid thee,—that still do;
For truth, in thee, is instinct; o'er all force
Of subtlest logic mighty. The wise man,
With wordy flood may strive to overwhelm
Thy simply-uttered thought; may say 'tis dream,
Error, old prejudice, or aught beside,
Unworthy thy regard: but, when the stream
Hath spent its force, firm stands thy pure thought still,—
Bright, clear as rock of crystal after storm.
For, reasoning power 'twixt truth and error goes,
Listening to both,—the umpire in their strife;
And sometimes, in confusion, the one voice
Mistakes for the other, and wrong judgment gives:
Or whisper from some restless passion hears;

Or blind self-craving,—thinking justice speaks;
And *that* way rules amiss. But the great law
Of God, within the spirit placed, stands fixed
As everlasting mountain; its high top
Far o'er earth's clouds, and pointing still toward Heaven.
Error, or passion, moves it, as the wind
Moves Lebanon's foundation. To that law
Within thy soul, trust ever; wisest words
Against it weighing, as earth's feeble fires
Against the sky-throned sun. For Pharaoh, then,
Do as thy soul directs thee : but, meantime,
As for myself,—though good to thee, and thine,
More than to me, 'twould bring,—a boon I ask.
By her good deeds, and name, at least, thou know'st
That gracious princess who,—when, death-devote,
On Nile, in rushy cradle, I was launched,—
Her father's law defying, rescued me;
Long time concealed; and, with a mother's love,
Reared me, and taught; and,—as in years I grew,
And understanding,—in the deepest lore
Of Egypt had me lessoned; and to rank
Among the noblest raised me; yea, so high,
That, as ye know, even with the king himself,
Much favor found I. Ah! to her I owe,
All that above the lowliest of the earth
Hath lifted me : and, verily, my life
For her would I lay down; debtor, even then,
For kind deeds numberless. On her behalf,
A suitor now I stand. From Pharaoh much,
And from the wretched Sethos, hath she heard,
Touching thyself, and thy rare qualities;
And great desire hath, with the eye and ear,
To test, and prove its truth. As thou to her
A daughter wert, lost even from thy birth,—
So longeth she to see thee, and embrace.
But age and weakness chain her : she would, else,
With me have journeyed hither : and her prayer
Now is,—and mine, my warm and anxious prayer,—
So in my soul I reverence her, and love,—

That even this day,—though but for few short hours,
Thou wouldst her guest be. 'Tell the Hebrew maid,'
Smiling, she said, 'that I have all prepared
For my heart's daughter; welcome such to give,
As fondest mother to an only child,
Long parted from her. If she love me not,
Let her not come again.' So she: but love,
To heart like hers, thou never couldst refuse,—
As this day well will prove,—for sure I am
Thou wilt go with me, and her soul make glad."

To Kohath and to Sarah turning then,—
"I will myself," with fatherly tone he said,
" Safely our loved-one guide; throughout the day
Be ever nigh her; and, ere evening fall,
Myself restore her to you. For this night,
I then may be your guest: but, with the morn,
To Zoan must haste back; lest for his work
The Lord require me, and I absent be.
Good unto all, my venerated friends,
From this may come; and evil can be none.
The stubborn Pharaoh, to the gentle voice
Of his loved father's sister listens oft,
When all else he rejects. Even I myself,
To my fond mother—so I call her still,
As me her son she calls,—to her alone
Owe, that in Pharaoh's presence I first stood
To plead for Israel; and fair audience had,
Though by his priests insulted, and reviled,
Traitor, and murderer called; and, as they said,
Law-doomed to death. The good Thermuthis, then,—
Both as my more-than-mother, and as friend
Of Israel, in the past, and still-to-come,—
For much may be her aid,—ye will not grieve,
By such slight boon refusing. Ah! I see
Your hearts are willing; yet an anxious eye
On your blest child ye cast; as though some fear
Of possible ill ye felt. Dismiss it quite.
No peril whatsoever need ye dread.

Close to her mule all day myself will be,
From common harm to shield her; and the eye
Of God will be upon her evermore."

He ceased, and all sat silent. A faint dread
Disturbed the loving parents; yet, so faint,
And seeming causeless, that they shamed to speak
Objection: and, for Rachel, though fear none
Had she, yet her fine delicate nature shrank
From the fair-seeming Moses, as from touch
Of the hot finger shrinks the sensitive-leaf,—
And not more knowing wherefore: for, though words
Like flatterer's he had spoken, yet the voice,
And look, had earnest seemed, and grave, like his
Who the heart's-truth doth speak: and, though she felt
Of all unworthy; pain, not pleasure, felt,
From praise unmerited,—yet, for distaste
Toward one, long deemed the holiest, the chief hope
Of Israel, poor excuse indeed were this.
Sinful must be that feeling; and by force
To be suppressed. Thus thinking, she looked round.
All eyes on her were bent; on every face,
Was smile of love; a look that said, "we wait;
Thine 'tis to answer." To her parents then
Gently she spake. "No evil do I fear;
And toward that gracious princess my heart yearns
With strong affection. If ye, then, approve,
Cheerfully will I go." Well pleased were all;
And with glad voices spake.
                            In little while,—
Serenely beautiful, from out the gate,
On her swift milk-white mule rode forth the maid,
Image of holiness more of heaven than earth;
And, at her side, a spear's length scarce apart,
Silent, and anxious, the dread king of hell:—
Anxious, and silent, lest the sun-beam eye
Of greater angel, hovering in mid heaven,
Through that fair garb of sanctity should pierce,
And see the demon, and his wiles defeat:—
Silent, and anxious; with far-reaching look,

Striving to see the invisible: for, by sense
Spiritual wholly, and to flesh unknown,
A Presence, somewhere under cope of sky,
He felt,—as by man's soul the shadow is felt
Of evil threatening. Nor the spirit-touch
Wrongly informed him: for, beside the moon,
In her dark shadow, looking on him, stood
Gabriel, and Zophiel,—of his bad intent
Forewarned; and ready, from Satanic harm,
The chosen maid to guard. Though thus far off,
Yet, by the Power of hell, some adverse Power,
Heavenly, was feared on watch; so that in awe,
Silent, and anxious,—as with myriad eyes,
All parts of space transpiercing, whence might come
The adversary,—hell's dread king rode on.

In thoughts of God, and holiest things, deep rapt,
Nought did the maiden note that bearing strange
Of the true-seeming Moses: and the gate
Of Pharaoh's palace close before them stood
Ere either silence broke. From off his mule
Gravely alighted he; and she, all grace,
Lightly descended also: then at once,—
Few words, with fatherly kindness, having said,—
Through the self-opening door the demon went;
And she, the holy, unsuspecting maid,
With light heart followed.
                          Though to every eye,
Save hers, with darkness had he girt him round,
That even from ken angelic clearest, safe
He hoped himself,—yet glad was he that now
Nigh was the time when to his proper form
He might return; for the true Moses lay,—
As well he knew,—even then upon the mound
Without the city, listening to the Voice,—
Myriads of mighty angels looking down,
All evil quick to see.
                      No warning now
For the false king vouchsafed, to Moses thus
Came the command. "Stretch out thine hand toward
    heaven;

"That darkness over all the land may be,—
Even darkness that may be felt."
                              Trembling he heard,
And worshipped: then, when from the ground he rose,
Toward heaven his hand stretched out.
                              Air knew the sign,
And instantly 'gan thicken. Cloud was none,
Distinct of shape; but the whole cope of sky
Seemed cloud becoming. Motion of the air
None was; but great stagnation,—as the winds
Were dead, and stiffening; life-blood growing thick.
Deep silence fell on all things. In mid song,
The bird paused, fluttering: voice of man, and beast,
Sank, as in fear. The eagle from his height
Dropped rapidly, and to his aerie fled.
The wild beast of the desert, in his den
Sleeping, bestirred himself, waked by the gloom,
And oped his fiery eyes, thinking 'twas night.
In one same moment, over all the land,
Save in the happy Goshen, fell the shade.
All who in houses were, marvelling went out,
To look upon the sky: they who on road,
Or plain, were journeying, hastened on their way,
Eager for shelter: who within the fields
Labored, or on the public works, peered round,
Anxious, and fearful; for a second hail
And thunder they feared coming.
                              One brief glance,
Awe-stricken, on the darkening sky and earth,
Cast Moses; then, with quick foot, through the gloom,
To the house of Aaron went; and with hushed voice,
To all the family told the wondrous thing
Had come to pass; and what was still to come.
And, after he had spoken,—mute with awe,
They sat together, looking toward the sky,
Where Day lay dying; even in strength of noon,
Trampled by ghastly Night.
                              But ho, meantime,
The phantom Moses, his bad work to end,
Eagerly sped. As yet, the sun shone clear;

But well he knew pitch-blackness soon would fall;
And hailed its coming, omen of success
To his vile purpose. Unsuspiciously
By the pure maiden followed,—passage, and hall,
And stair, he trod; till, at a door arrived,
Gently he opened wide; and, smiling, said,
" Enter, beloved of heaven; and brief time wait,
While to my reverend mother I make speed,
And tell her thou art come."
                              Bowing the head,
She entered: he the door behind him closed:
Swifter than sun-glance from a falling sword,
Vanished;—and in the chamber of the prince,
To sight, a servant of the palace, stood.

By foul dreams, and foul thoughts, to frenzy driven,—
Like a caged leopard panting with great heat,
And eager to spring forth,—with long, quick strides,
Therein walked Sethos; resolute once again
With arm'd men to go out; and pluck by force
The flower whose perfume maddened him. Till then,—
Harmed by the hailstone that had stricken him,
And by the stun of his great overthrow,—
Strengthless upon the bed, by night and day,
Had he lain prisoned; but, that morning, healed
By power Satanic, full of vigor and health
Had risen: and, forthwith, order once more sent,
That men and steeds should wait his going forth
Toward Goshen; for no power of earth, or heaven,
Swore he, again should balk him.
                                 Bending low,
Before the prince the feigning demon stood,
And humbly said: " A Hebrew maid, my lord,
From Goshen hath arrived; and of the king,
Or of thyself,—such honor may she have,—
Audience imploreth. Rachel is her name;
Daughter of Kohath."
                    " Bring her hither straight,"
With joy and wonder stricken, cried the prince:
" Or, stay; I will attend her; for she comes,

I know, on a great matter; and, beside,
Is worthy of honor. Lead me to her, then;
And, till I call, let no man trouble me."

Low bowed the seeming servitor; and, still
Low bowing, walked, till he the door had gained
Of the great chamber of state; wherein the maid
Patiently waited. With a noiseless hand,
He opened it; with a like gentleness,
When the hot prince had entered, closed again:
Then, instantly invisible,—for he feared
The nigher coming of some heavenly Power,—
Thought-swift, down to earth's burning centre shot:
There, mid the sea of fire, and light intense,—
If eye had watched him,—hoping to be lost,
By vision even the keenest.   But, meantime,
Awaiting his return,—of nought afraid,
Nothing suspecting,—with a pleased surprise,
A gentle childlike wonder, Rachel gazed
Around that sumptuous chamber; the chief boast
Of Pharaoh's palace, for all things most rare,
Costly, and beautiful, which labor, art,
Riches past count, and judgment the most nice,
From the whole earth could gather. As a child
In a fair garden, walked and wondered she;
Pleased by whate'er was beauteous; but, for show
Of kingly pomp and riches, caring nought;
Of nought possession craving; thinking not,
For even one moment, on the promise made
By him who Pharaoh had seemed, that,—would she wed
With Egypt's heir, all this, and ten times more,
Hers should become. The beautiful alone
Her nice sense touched: yet, highest joy of sense,
Though of heaven savoring, but brief while could draw
From God, and things *all* heavenly, her pure thoughts;
And soon,—the gorgeous scene forgetting quite,—
Midst of the chamber, with eyes downward cast,
Silently musing stood she; and heard not

The softly opened door; nor the quick step
That entered, and drew near.
                              Thus, statue-like,
When her exceeding beauty he beheld,
And purity angelic,—on the heart
Of Sethos, for a moment, fell a power
That him, too, fixed like statue. Breathing not,
All eye he stood; drinking the beauty-draught,
As the parched dreamer seems a brook to drink,
Yet still, unsated, thirsts. But soon arose
The carnal passion: crown to foot, he shook,
Longing to clasp her: yet the gross desire
Dared not at once betray; with courteous guise
Of look, and word, and tone, hoping awhile
His foulness to conceal; till, bolder grown,
All he might sue for; or, repulsed, might seize:
For seize he would, so driven, though instant death
Should follow the wild joy. With bow, and smile,
And hand outstretched, as to a dearest friend,
Toward her he hastened.
                       "Twice, then, doth a sun
This happy day arise; and twice more bright
The second than the first," he cried,—her hand,
Snow-pure, within his palm, flame-hot, and foul,
Striving to grasp: but she, astonished, shrank,
A pace withdrawing; and, in calm tone, thus:
"I pray thee, prince, remember who I am;
A simple Hebrew maiden, who plain truth,
And manners plain, am bred in; knowing nought,
And nought esteeming, of court flatteries.
Invited by herself, I hither come . . . . . ."

Impatiently upon her speech he broke.
"Whatever brought thee, ten times be it blest;
Ay, more than though a goddess it had brought;
For beauty like to thine, not heaven could boast;
Nor music like thy voice."
                          His burning looks,
And tones, displeased her; but their wicked bent
She knew not; and no terror felt at all;

Knowing that evermore within the eye
Of God she was; and that, against His will,
No harm could touch her. From the frantic prince
Turning away,—his stream of passionate words,
She heard not, heeded not; more than the hum
Of babbling brook she had heeded. As alone,
Or of no presence conscious,—to and fro,
With arms crossed lightly, at slow pace she walked:
Now, toward the door a calm glance casting; now,
Toward the fast darkening sky. Each look he watched,
While pouring his vile love-strain; and, at length,
When with long gaze he saw her face upturned,
" Ah! sweetest one," he cried, " here must thou stay,
Or bide a storm. I, too, must prisoner be;
For, verily, a frown the sky puts on,
Might threaten second hail-plague. Blest the cause,
Loveliest, that hither brought thee! blest the chance
That kept me from the chase! and ten times blest
The clouds that bring this darkness! for my tongue,—
A very coward when broad daylight falls
Full on thy sun-bright beauty,—in the shade,
Bold will become, and eloquent to tell,—
Thou marvel of all woman-kind,—the love,
O'erwhelming, maddening, that I feel for thee.
Since first I saw thee, no breath have I drawn,
That brought not thought of thee: no life have had,
Save what remembrance of thy beauty gave.
Without thee, henceforth, earth is but a tomb:
Food, wine, are nauseous; sweetest breath of flowers
Hath death-scent! brightest sunshine is black night!
Be thou my wife,"—more near her drawing now,
He cried; and fell upon the knee, and clasped
His hands imploringly; " be thou my wife;
And, sometime, Egypt's queen."
       At quiet pace,—
As though she saw him not, nor heard at all,—
Still walked she on; but, at the chamber's end
Made pause, at length; and in deep awe looked forth;
For, so thick fell the darkness suddenly,
Twilight seemed dropped on noon.
       Yet terror none

Came on the sensual prince,—so his whole frame·
With foul desire was burning. That strange gloom,
To him, was brightness; for it made him bold
To dare what, in broad daylight, he had feared.
"Proud, scornful beauty," thought he, to his feet
Upstarting; "if thou still refuse my love,
By all the gods of Egypt, I will seize,
And rend the fruit from off the tree; and feed
To very surfeiting!"
                  With hurried step
Then to the door he went; the silver bolt
Slid noiselessly; and turned to seek his prey.
But, at the spacious chamber's farther end,
Invisible was she now; in darkness wrapped,
As in a robe.
           Even in his madness, struck
By a brief terror, toward a window nigh
He looked; and saw what seemed a solid mass
Of blackness falling,—as if Chaos, once more
Rampant o'er heaven, mountains of thickest night
Were hurling 'thwart the sky. But soon again,—
Fear chased by passion,—through the obscure he groped;
Hoping, though utterly from sight concealed,
Yet that some sound,—perchance a sigh, a word,
A motion,—might reveal her. A faint light,
As of a glowworm's beam, at length he saw;
And toward it moved: but, ere a second step
His slow foot trod, the living lamp beheld,
Whence came that radiance,—the heaven-lifted face
Of the pure virgin. Like embodied air,
Touched by the star of evening's silvery beam,
Softly it shone; beauty celestial all.
Yet, in the frantic youth, nought stirred it now
But foulest fire of earth. Stone-still she stood,
Seeing him not; for, through the window yet,
Skyward she looked; with hope some quickening beam
To spy in the grave-like blackness. One step more,
And he might seize her: yet, so dead the hush
Had suddenly fallen, that he feared to stir,
Almost to breathe, lest her keen sense should catch

Note of his presence near; and, terrified,
In the darkness she should plunge, and baffle him.
So, glaring on her, silently he stood;
And, in his foul heart, thus.
                              "Enchantress bright
Thine own sweet witchery betrayeth thee.
Spite of thyself, from out thine exquisite flesh
Beameth celestial light; and thou know'st not
What eye beholds thee; what foot standeth near.
Ah! in these arms let me once prison thee;
Never, while life lasts, shall the chain be slacked.
Bosom to bosom, lip to lip, close pressed,
Till death comes will I lock thee. Turn aside,
Witch, goddess, turn aside; for yet thine eye
O'erawes me: turn aside; that I may spring
Unseen upon thee; and, on earth, find heaven."

With fingers clawlike spread, eager to clutch,
From head to foot all quivering, he stood;
Burning to seize, yet fearing.
                              Not one tinge
Of day now visible,—window, wall, and sky,
Alike one solid blackness,—her raised face
She lowered: a moment, as if listening, stood,
And turned her delicate head. The madman saw;
Drew in his breath; his arms outstretched,—and sprang.

But, as beneath his foot the floor had sunk,
Down in a heap he dropped. No mortal might
Had stricken him; no stroke at all he felt;
Yet, like a broken thread, cast from the hand,
Strengthless utterly fell he. Still was sense
Unstunned;—hellish desire still burned within,
And deadened him to fear. Toward his lost prey
Eagerly staring—sight that maddened him more,—
A wondrous flame he saw, steady and mild,
Smooth gliding as a marsh-fire in dark night,
O'er some far distant vale; and, close behind,
The maiden, slowly following. One short glance
The thick air suffered him; then all was lost.

In agony of rage, he strove to rise;
Strove to cry out: voice, limbs, were paralyzed;
And, helpless, he lay struggling.
                              But, meantime,
To the awe-smitten, yet nought-fearing maid,
An instant 'mid the blackness had appeared
A form of purest light; a countenance
Beauteous, yet sad; and, faint as softest sigh
Of evening, yet within her very soul
Deep felt, a voice had come, "Blest child of heaven,
Follow thou me." And, without word, or thought
Of questioning,—all trustful as the babe
Its mother follows, even so followed she.
But now no more the countenance, or form,
Was visible; and the voice no more was heard.
A mild, clear light alone before her moved;
And, wondering, yet all trusting in her God,
Serenely she went on.
                      With steady foot,
Down the great stair she trod; each step made plain
By the descending beam: through passage, and hall,—
As in a torch-lit rift right through the heart
Of a black rock—walked on: but sounds of dread,
Above, below, to either hand, still heard:
Voices of men, and women, in great woe;
Some, crying out that they were smitten blind,
And help imploring; some, in ghastly tone
Of supernatural horror,—prayer and shriek
Commingled strangely,—calling on their gods:
Some, shouting, as if mad: some, groaning loud,
As in death-agony. Still glided on
The clear, mild light; still, trustful as a child,
Calmly the maiden followed.
                            Soon came sound
Of a great portal opening; and then stood
Before her, like a figure painted white
On ground of deepest black, her milk-white mule:
Visible solely that. Downward she looked,
But saw no earth: to right, and left, she looked;
But walls of solid darkness only saw:

Toward heaven she turned; but, close above her head,
As she might touch it, hung what seemed a roof,
Black and substantial as a grave-stone, cast
O'er the dead world! Awe-stricken, silent stood
The holy maiden; on that wondrous sight
Gazing, and pondering. *Why* distinct shone out,
The patient beast,—as if to invite her thence,
Though all path was invisible as the rocks
Leagues under ground,—she marvelled: yet, the face
So beautiful, though sad; the voice so sweet,
So soft and plaintive, she recalled, and thus:
"Surely an angel of the Lord hath come,
To lead me forth this peril. But, where, then,
Where is the holy Moses? Aught could I
Him aid, by here abiding? Truly no:
The Gracious Power which me protecteth,—him,
In its own way, will care for. Not for me
Fit is it, then, to question; but to do
Even as 'tis shown unto me."
                      Thinking thus,
Lightly the maiden mounted; and at once
Again the pale flame moved; the gentle beast,
Unbidden, followed.
              Meantime, far above
Earth's tomb-like blackness,—in the bright serene
Of heaven's pure air, the mighty angels hung,
To whom it had been given, from power of hell,
Or power of man, hell-taught, the maid to guard.
Through that thick darkness,—to all mortal sight
Impenetrable as the solid globe,—
So by power special gifted, their keen eyes,
As if in sunshine, all things clearly saw:
And, to his bright companion, Gabriel thus.

"A wonder see, O Zophiel! From the snare
Laid by the king of hell, that purest one
Through human violence to foul,—behold,
Even he, the Spirit chosen from them all,
As potent most to lure her into sin;
Now leads her forth, in a great dread lest sin,

By force should come upon her. *That* to stay,
Our task is : but, Oh, blessed is the sight
Of yon repentant fallen-one,—our work,
Of his own will performing ! Seest thou not
His spirit-anguish ? hear'st thou not his sighs ?
Ah ! he would pray ; but, in his ignorance,
Deemeth the All Merciful, All Wise, All Just,
But the inexorable Omnipotent.
He fears his night eternal ; joys of heaven
For ever past,—even as the ages past
Are gone for ever. But we better know
God's inexhaustible mercy unto all :
How, in progression of eternity,
Within His kingdom all will meet again :
Those lost ones numberless,—even like drops of rain
In fathomless ocean,—to the blessed depths
Falling of His illimitable love.
Go on, poor Spirit : turn thou never back
To bad allegiance,—or through failing joy
In good, now moving thee ; or from the fear
Of hell's dread wrath : and, surely, in due time,—
When strong repentance hath within thee worked,
And from thy burning spirit hath gone up
Incense of prayer sincere,—God's eye of love
Again will look upon thee ; and heaven's gates
Stand wide to give thee welcome. But, meantime,
Hard trial waiteth thee. Before the eyes
Of thine incensed companions must thou stand,
Mark for their hatred. . . . . .Zophiel, notest thou
Where, wrapped in darkness,—even to eye of God
Invisible, as he thinks,—Hell's dreadful lord
Glares on the poor repentant ; wroth to see
That, whom to ruin, solely was he sent,
Her now he strives to save ? Ha ! on that spot
Gladly he'd wither him ; but that he feels
Celestial Powers not distant ; and his rage
Fears to let loose. And yet, a time will come
When even he,—yea, most of all—will joy,
For his vile end thus thwarted. Last, perchance,
To feel repentance, as the first to sin ;

But sure, at length, with agony infinite,
To see his wickedness; in remorse to groan;
To cry aloud for pardon; to implore
That, even among the lowliest of the low,
Again into God's presence he may come,
And feel His infinite grace. Ah Lucifer!
How, once, by all wert thou admired, and loved:
Eldest, and greatest of Spirits; to the throne
Admitted nearest; in the Effulgency
Of Glory Divine, the brightest of heaven's host!
What art thou now! In place of that pure love
Which, like a spring exhaustless, from thee poured
On even the humblest angel,—now, behold,
From eyes like very fire, pours wrath red-hot
On a meek Spirit, because thy bad command
He disobeyeth; striving good to do;
Turning from loathëd hell repentant looks
Toward the far-off,—nay, as he wrongly thinks,
For him, the ever unapproachable heaven.
Ah! change most sad, when angel angel hates,
For good act, or pure thought! But see, two more,
And of hell's mightiest,—Beelzebub,
And that fierce spirit, Moloch, with their chief
Now stand; and others are there, gathering round;
All hot as flame against that humble one,
Who their bad service leaves. What worst they can,
Be sure, they'll do against him. But their spite
Will be controlled; their evil bring forth good.
For, though of heaven's forgiveness hoping not,
Yet, so to do as in his Maker's sight
Once would have been well pleasing,—firm is he,
Though all hell's malice crush him: and we know,
That still accéptable to the God of love
Will be the good intent; from whomsoe'er,
Or whencesoe'er it come;—heavenly its source,
Though rising even in hell."
                      So these. Meantime,—
As though, by miracle, through substantial rock,
As in air, moving,—through the solid night,
In perfect quietness of soul; her trust

Wholly in God,—the gentle maid rode on..
The mild light, like a steady star, still went
Before her: as by hand invisible led,
The patient mule still followed. Every beast
Which, in the common night-gloom, clearly saw
To roam abroad, and seize upon his prey,—
As if stone-blind was now; nor dared to stir,
Or utter noise at all: no watch-dog barked;
No horse, or ox, or other thing, dared move;
No bird dared flutter wing: air, sound, seemed dead;
Crushed by the curdled blackness. Earth, sky, sun,
All blotted from Creation might have been;
Primeval Night the Universe!
                              But still
Serenely on the gentle virgin rode;
Awe-filled, yet fearing not; for, mid the dark,
Unutterable, and the tomb-like hush,
Heaven's glories she beheld; and heard the voice
Of the innumerable angels round the throne,
Chanting their hymn of joy.
                            So hours passed on,
Hours that might days have seemed: but, suddenly,—
As though the coffin-lid of the dead earth,
Had been uplift, and let noon-glory in,—
All in a moment, like a mighty wave,
Full sunshine burst upon her. Sharply stopped,
The mule stood trembling: she her eyelids closed,
And covered with both hands; as if by flash
Of lightning dazzled. But the mule again,
Recovering first, went on: by slow degrees,
Her tender eyes she opened, and looked forth,
And saw her own loved Goshen; and, far off,
The low of oxen heard, the bleat of sheep,
And happy human voices. Turning then,
Backward she looked; and, even from earth to heaven
Upreaching,—like a wall of blackest rock,
The unearthly darkness saw. With folded hands,
And face low bent,—to that All Merciful God,
Who her deliverance, through angelic power,
Surely had wrought,—her fervent thanks she breathed:

Raised then her head; looked round her; smiled anew
At sight of her loved land, and hastened on.
But the pure light, the sad, yet beauteous face,
No more she saw; no more the sweet voice heard.

Gayly as captive from his prison loosed,
Bounded away the mule. In loving arms
Of parents, soon the loving child was locked;
And all the wonders she had witnessed, told:
How Moses she had lost; how, by a Power
Angelic, surely, she had been brought forth;
And how even yet, perchance, o'er all the land
'Twixt Zoan and their Goshen, darkness lay,
Like a deep pitch-black lake.
                              Ecstatic joy
Filled the repentant Spirit, when he saw
The chosen virgin, in the light of day
Secure, and homeward speeding: for a sense
Obscure he long had felt, of hostile Power,
Beyond compare his mightier, not far off;
And dreaded lest, with interruption sharp,
He should be stopped; and all his good intent
For her, made vain; while on himself should fall
Anger, and hate, and bitter punishment.
Faintly, and trembling, then, a thought he breathed:

"Omnipotent, All Pure! a Spirit lost,
Humbly dares thank Thee, that one deed of good,
'Gainst hell's command, hath been permitted him!"

More durst he not: but, in the eternal book
Of Mercy was it written; never more
To be effaced.
                Thoughts different far came next;
Of instant danger threatening; future ills,
Such as even boldest Spirit might appal:
And, with himself communing, thus he said.

"Ah! whither may I fly? 'Gainst hell a crime
Past pardon have I done; and from its wrath

Must hide myself; or suffer what of worst
Hate can inflict.   Had but one faintest glimpse
Of God's approval, possible been to me,—
That wrath I had defied: but, to re-live
The cycles gone, not more impossible is,
Than to regain the love of God, sin-lost,
By sin annulling!   Even Omnipotence
Perchance no power hath to recall the past!
The deed done, for eternity is done!
The darkness of all Chaos, close conglobed,
Never could hide it!   Oceans of all worlds
Never could wash it out!   The gathered suns
Of all the Universe, in one keen point
Concentrating their fire, could never burn
That indestructible!   Oh God!   Oh God!
Canst THOU expunge it!"
                                    With the agony
Of sharp remorse, more fierce than bodily pang
Of nerve, fire-touched, while quivering thus he stood,—
His whole Essential torment; suddenly,—
Even as a dove, seized by the eagles' claws,—
Beneath the power of Spirits, strongest, worst,—
Though touched not, threatened not, by word, or look,—
Captive he felt himself; all strength to fly,
To stir, to speak, gone from him.   The dead stone
Beneath the sculptor's hand, as easily
Might from its place fly up, and path the heavens,
As that poor Spirit, from the hill of power
Laid on him, 'scape.   Yet,—marvel to himself,—
Calm was he;—not one throb of fear he felt.
Was it, perchance, the numbness of despair
That tranquil held him, when such monstrous storm
Of all hell's congregated scorn and hate
Soon would be loosed against him?   Or some hope,
Though shadowy, imperceptible, could he have,
That, after brief flame, would the fire of wrath
Die of itself,—against a Spirit so weak,
Unworthy to be cherished?   No,—he felt,
That not despair's dead touch that calm had brought
Nor the dim dream of hope; that hell's fierce ire,

Sure as the coming of the hour, would burn
To the last against him.   Solely was he firm,
By one great thought sustained : 'gainst bad command,
An act he had done, which, ere from heaven cast out,
Approved had been of God.   No gracious sign
Of approbation looked he now to see ;
Of pardon he dreamed not ; less of reward,
From his offended Maker : and, from those,
His fellow Spirits Fallen, hatred, and scorn,
And vengeance he expected, infinite.
Yet, calm he was,—nay, glad : for its own sake,
Good had he done ; and, in that blessed thought,
All his reward would find ; his comfort, and strength ;
Though with heaped wrath, as with rock hurled on rock,
Hell should o'erwhelm him.
      While in high mood thus,
Motionless stood he,—to the Fallen Host,—
Throughout the universe scattered,—summons went
To council, instant : and, like smallest mote
Before the tempest,—swift as flight of thought,
The contrite Spirit, by those fearful ones,
His conquerors, through the immense of space was borne.

ISRAEL IN EGYPT.

BOOK TWENTY-SECOND.

WITH splendor that all former glory eclipsed,
Shone hell's vast council-hall; a wondrous blaze
Of sun-fired diamond. With astonishment struck,—
From outer darkness entering,—suddenly paused
The great Arch-Fiend, to gaze. From roof to floor,—
From floor to roof,—from side to side, he glanced:
Again from floor to roof,—from roof to floor,—
From side to side, he turned: in wonder lost,
To see heaven's brightness there. With no less joy,
Wonder, and triumph, the whole host looked round,
Speechless and motionless,—that, for a time,
Was silence deep throughout.
                              But the fierce wrath
Not long could rest. That the unnumbered eyes,
Lightening together, most might wither him,—
Full in the front of the great semi-cirque,—
Accusers, judges, executioners too,—
On a low rock, the sinner against hell,
The contrite Spirit was placed. Not far removed,
Upon a loftier height, the towering form
Of Satan appeared; accuser chief, and judge
Inexorable. But, with other thought
Than vengeance, first seemed filled; though subtly so,
Vengeance to make the hotter. With raised head,

And arms outstretched, toward the sun-blazing roof,
Vast as a sky, he pointed; and, with voice
Exultant, as, to mortal sense, appears
Trumpet of victory, thus his proud thoughts spake.

" Angels, Archangels;—yea, even Demi-gods,
In brief time sure to be,——such evidence
Of our advance toward godhead greets us now.
For, alway, as, in might and wisdom, *we*,
So, from our *Spiritual* glory, doth this orb,
Our mansion, in *material* glory wax;
A mirror wherein,—as the things of earth,
From polished surface of bright brass, or steel,
Their clay-formed shapes behold,—so we our strength,—
The stature of our spiritual excellence,—
Our wisdom's increase,—rise in majesty,—
May see reflected: and, such wondrous growth,
In days so few, beholding,—Demi-gods
Boldly I name you. Nor less proof of power
Toward godlike coming on us like a flood,
Herein we have,—that sharpest ken of heaven
Easily blind we now; nay, even the eye,
Till late, All-seeing named: for, in our task
God's schemes to oppose,—both for deliverance
Of Israel,—and for that yet hidden thing,
Redemption of mankind,—not once hath spy
Of heaven detected us: nor even He,
The All-wise, our counsels ever would have known,
Had fealty ruled us all. 'Gainst Israel much
Our contest is,—because, in whatsoe'er
God we can foil, thereby new power we gain;
Him, in like measure, weaken: but, far more,
'Gainst that strange scheme, Redemption, is our war:
For, not one people only,—this small race
Of Israel,—it concerns; but all mankind,—
If right I read the intent,—the whole vile brood
Thereafter peopling earth,—from curse of sin
Is meant to save; and so far purify,
That, spite of the original fall from God,
For heaven they shall be fitted; and there dwell,

Our places filling. Looking through the dark
That shrouds His counsels,—such, at least, I guess
The end, through that Messiah to be wrought,
Who sometime is to come. If he come not,
Redemption will not come; and these base things
Of clay, half human only, and half beast,
Will not in heaven sit mocking over us,
Clad in our proper glory. Well ye know,
On what most strange condition,—in due time,—
From two frail things, now living, should proceed
That wonderful Messiah; son of God,
Yet born of woman! Incredible it were
That He, All-wise, so foolishly should scheme,—
Had not the tongue of His own messenger,
In presence of the second Power of hell,
To Moses so proclaimed it. 'Servant of God,'—
Thus to the marvelling Hebrew Zophiel spake,—
'Chosen of heaven art thou; and mighty things
For Israel wilt thou do. But, after thee,
In due time, will arise one greater far;
Born of a woman, yet the Son of God;
Messiah to be named; through whom shall be
Redemption universal to man's race.
From tribe of Levi hath it been ordained
Shall come the Virgin Mother of that Son:
Yea, even from these shall spring,—the maid and youth
Before thee standing,—so, with upright heart,
Pure from all sin, in sight of God they live,
And pure they die. But, sinning, will they fall,
And Heaven's high favor forfeit. Look thou then
Heedfully on them: dangerous is their path,
And narrow: ONE FALSE STEP, AND THEY ARE LOST!

"Thus, in the hearing of Beelzebub,
Spake Zophiel: and,—this foolish scheme to cross,—
Forthwith sent we two Spirits; fittest deemed,
That youthful pair, so favored, to seduce,
By dreams of carnal love, and waking thoughts,
And images, voluptuous. One of these,
The stronger, so was shaken, that all sense

Wellnigh he lost: and, though he still had stood,
And stubbornly,—temptation would have urged
So fiercely, both within him, and without,—
His fall at length was sure. But, for the maid,
The weaker creature,—victory ere now
Certain had been, but that, among ourselves,
One Spirit a traitor proved; a groveller
Before the Power who insult and great wrong
Heaped on us; from that heaven, our heritage,
Expelled us; and to this quenched sun drove forth;
Herein designing, through eternity,
Our durance. How of this He failed, ye know:
And how, by our still growing strength, we rose;
And, for our region, took the immense of space:
How even in this dead orb, from solid dark,—
With our still soaring Spirits in sympathy,—
Matter a glory likest heaven's assumed.
And ever, in such fashion, our advance
Toward godlike state will be, if to ourselves
Faithful we prove, and to our holy cause.
On that hangs all our hope. Together bound;
Striving together toward the one great end,
Resistance to our foe,—Almighty now,—
In progress of eternity, be sure,
We must o'erthrow his sway: ourselves become
Almighty; rulers through the Infinite.
But, with the false among us, even though least
In power they be,—danger is imminent,
Lest bad example spread; lest, one by one,
Falling from truth,—atom by atom, our strength
Impaired may be; and, cycles numerous,
Our progress may be stayed. . . . . As in man's frame,
So also with our Spiritual body it is.
Ye all have seen how, on the human flesh,
A small black spot hath come; to ignorant eye,
Of moment insignificant as bite
Of pettiest insect: yet, to the whole mass,
Heralding death at hand. This knoweth well
The human leech; and, all the body to save,
With sharp steel, from the flesh that spot cuts out.

On our vast Spirit body so, alas!
The black spot hath appeared: and, if ourselves
The remedy knew not, yet from yon poor clay
Might we be taught, how, with excision sharp,
To rid us of the blotch. Since we lost heaven,
Example first of treason in our host
Against our righteous cause, now summons us
To judge, and to pass sentence. In long course
Of ages, from among us have there gone
Some few weak Spirits. Whither they have fled,
Is mystery to us: if in solitudes
Of living orbs far distant, they have sought
To soothe strange sadness,—marked, not understood;—
Or if, as some conjecture, they have bowed
Before our tyrant; crawled their abject way
Once more into some outer court of heaven,—
Or howsoever else they may have sped,—
Nought do we know; for singly, and by stealth,
Have they gone from us; and have left no sign.
But, now, a portent direst hath appeared;
A sign indeed, and terrible!—Ye behold——
Ay, look upon him; scorch him with your gaze;—
To that base Spirit, even in this place,—
In hearing of you all; approved by all;
Command was given,—to him, and Zuriel too,—
Who faithful hath been, and zealous in his task,
Though unsuccessful; and our praise deserves,—
To those two Spirits, ye remember well,
In words like these I spake: 'To you we give,
Task not unpleasant, those young hearts to snare
With love's soft witchery: the beauteous maid
Thou, Aziel, take; thou, Zuriel, the youth.
By day and night your utmost cunning try
Their souls to enter; all their thoughts to sway;
Their blood to fire, their reason to confuse.
Beauty of form, and face, beyond compare
Of mortal loveliness, may ye put on:
With voices may ye speak, so musical,
That sweetest tones of woman, following them,
Would grate man's ear: with so sweet eloquence

2 B

May ye assail them, that the choicest strains
Of earthly orator, or loftiest bard,
Were, after it, dull babble. Soul, and sense,
Assault ye, then: with amorous thoughts the soul;
With all can please the eye, and charm the ear,
And stir up passion, war upon the sense.'

"Thus, in the hearing of you all, I spake.
How think you, then, that traitor hath performed
The task he undertook,—easy to do,
And pleasant, with that superhuman maid:
A trifle seeming; but, 'twixt God and us,
Matter momentous. Her with sin to soil,
His duty was,—that so, with one light stroke,
God's whole great foolish scheme we might destroy;
Blighting the root whence, in due time, should come,
That wondrous flower, Messiah. Yet, not so
Wrought that foul recreant. Us to serve, he went;
But, God to serve, remained! Beholding still
How pure she stood, though after temptings strong,—
As nought I doubted,—by the forceful arm
Of the lust-maddened Sethos, I resolved
She should be fouled; and *that* way should the scheme
For a Messiah fail. Daring the gaze
Of all heaven's spies,—the form then I assumed
Of Moses; and, by subtle story, lured
The silly maiden at my side to go,
Even unto Pharaoh's palace. Thither come,—
To the great chamber of state, wherein no foot
Would dare to intrude, I led her: hastened then,
In form a serving man,—to Sethos told
Who had arrived,—into her presence straight
Conducted him, and left,—mad for his prey
As hungriest tiger. At that moment fell
First shade of darkness. As the augury
Of full success I hailed it; and, at once,
Down to earth's centre shot. All fear soon past
Of eye suspicious peering,—I returned,—
Triumph expecting; but reverse soon found.
Gone was the maiden; all untouched, all pure,

As when I thither led her. Of herself,
Through that unearthly blackness, well I knew,
Never could she have passed; and Spirit of heaven
None felt I near: but, following on her track,—
Easily known by the celestial air
That floats around her,—soon, through the thick gloom,
Like to a star amid black fog, a beam
Of gliding light I spied; and, drawing near,
Beheld the maiden, riding on her mule;
And, close before her, a small globe of fire,
Self-moving, as it seemed: but, nigher come,
Soon I descried the mover,—that vile thing,—
That traitor,—that apostate,—that mean wretch,
Who now before you trembles. Fired with wrath,
That instant had I, with a mighty blast,
Driven him from face of earth; and to her fate
Led back the maiden; but that, suddenly,
The presence of some greater Powers of heaven
I felt, not far; and feared lest their keen eyes
Such open act should see; and therein read
Our secret business. Him, the traitor wretch,
They *must* have seen: yet, if his purpose all
They had perceived,—some token, even though faint,
Of their approval, surely had they shown.
Me they saw not; nor those who to my side
Had come,—Beelzebub, and Moloch; we,
Invisible, looked on; and others, too,
Of our companions, who soon gathered round;
All burning, with one terrible storm to hurl
The miscreant to perdition; but withheld
By a wise caution. Nor through eye alone
His treason knew we; but his craven voice
Heard wailing out repentance for his *sin*,—
His *sin*, ye mark, against the despot Power,
The Almighty tyrant, who that heaven, once ours,
By right, and not by sufferance, snatched away;
And drove us to the ghastly Infinite
Of a long dead Creation. Nay, even prayer
For pardon,—or what likest such appeared,—
Came from him, like a howl of agony

From man in the death-torment: his vile deed,
His treachery 'gainst *us*, the one sole thought
That comfort gave him. Burning with just wrath,
We followed; and from darkness to full sun
Beheld the virgin led; and from our snare
Set free. Then, we the pleased apostate marked;
His dolorous musings heard; how from our wrath,
Best might he 'scape; yet how, if but one look,
Approving, Heaven would grant him,—even our worst,
Gladly would he defy. But such proud thought
Soon ended we: for, when those powers of heaven
Withdrawn we felt,—upon him poured we then;
And, shuddering, dumb, as there ye see him still,
Hither enforced him. Angels, Demi-gods,
Lift up your voices: tell him with your curse,
How faith loves treachery."
      At the word, went up,
Loud as a thousand thunders loosed at once,
Howlings of execration and fierce hate,
That the vast hollow shook. Like rays converged
From suns unnumbered to one burning point,
On that poor Spirit glared the fiery eyes
Of all Hell's millions. The enormous din,
Like great waves seemed to bury him: yet, calm
And patient stood he; saying to himself;
"I did the right: I did as gracious God
Would have approved, had I not lost for aye
All claim on his regard. For sin toward Him,
Punishment I deserve; and even from them
Who led me to that sin, let punishment come!
All is my due; and all will I endure."

So he, his spirit strengthening. But, when now
The roar enormous, like spent storm, had ceased;
And the great echoes, battering at the vault,
And all sides round, had died,—then once again,
Satan his voice uplift.
     "Among you all,
Not one there is who hath not sent the curse,
'Gainst this first traitor,—this foul deadly spot

On our pure Spirit-body. To the depth
Must go the knife that from us cuts it out.
Never again, through all the eternity,
Among the faithful can that false one stand.
To him, the future one long pang must be :
Imprisonment, everlasting solitude;
Without least hope a thing of life to see,—
Light to behold,—motion to feel,—sound hear,—
Or substance touch;—worse dungeoned than, in corpse,
The living soul of man: living, yet dead
To the whole universe; the eternal Night
His grave; no dream of help from even that God
To whom he vilely hath bowed: whom abjectly
To serve he hath striven, in place of us, to whom
Was all his service owed: for, even here,
In this dead orb, on the mere confines placed
Of the interminable Void of ruin and night,—
Far are we from the ken of Him whom, once,
The Omnipresent, the All-seeing we deemed.
But realms there are, in the abyss of space,
With perished suns, wide distant, interspersed,—
So inconceivably farther from all life,
That, hence to heaven, is but a sick man's stride,
Against that infinite measured. Mid those wastes
Of mouldering horrors; in the lowest depths
Of half-chaotic orb; in solitude,
Silence, and blackness,—fixed, and motionless,
As stone, locked up in heart of mountain rock,—
Through the slow-dragging cycles, evermore,
Shall the foul traitor lie; longing for death,
Yet forced to live, and under torment writhe
Of our undying wrath. There let him cry
Unto his God; and see if He can help."

Thus Satan, to the height of fury inflamed,
With visage terrible, and voice more harsh
Than grinding of great granite rocks down hurled,
Discharged black vengeance. All the assembly stood
Silent, appalled. But, willing some bare form
Of justice should be shown,—with gentle mien,

And ook of one who for the right would plead,
Belial arose; and, voiced like him who weighs
Coolly all reasons, searching for the truth,
Thus spake.
          "That all of which he stands accused,
This Spirit hath done,—doubt is impossible.
A bad deed he hath wrought, which, to our foe,
Advantage is; to us, a heavy wrong,
And disobedience: yet, but half we know
The sin, when knowing only the bad deed,
And not its cause: for evil may be done,
In act most virtuous; and therein no sin,
Even venial, be committed. Punishment
For evil, sinless, would itself be sin;
And more deserve the rod. The guilt of deed
Lies in the thought that prompts it,—not the hand
Which executes,—for that is but the tool
Wherewith the greater works: and 'twere as wise
To scourge the sword, because it had shed blood,
As punish him, who but the impotent tool
Of mightier Power had been. Let us, then, first,
Assurance have that, of his own free will,
The maid he rescued: for, by greater power
If over-ruled, and so to do, compelled,—
Compassion, more than punishment, were his due.
Thyself, O Satan, saidst, that, hovering nigh,
Were potent Spirits of heaven: how know we, then,
If, of his own bad will, that evil he did,
Or under their constraint: for, strength like his,
To theirs, would be as grass beneath the tread
Of Behemoth. If he declare, the deed
Was forced on him; that, all the while, his wish
Was *us* to serve, and our command obey;
That he repenteth him of the vile act;
That still he holdeth God his enemy;
And evermore, in all things, earnestly
Desireth heaven to oppose, and us to obey,—
Then shall my voice, at least,—though with me join
Not one among you,—speak him innocent
Of evil intended; and of pity, and love,

Deserving, more than punishment. Let him, then,
Speak for himself; and say, how this strange thing
Was brought about."
                    With a complacent smile,
There Belial ended,—satisfied that worse
He had made the state of him whom, outwardly,
He seemed intent to aid.
                    With lowering brow,
Ill pleased, the terrible Lord of hell arose.
" Useless to question him,"—sharply he said;
" No word of truth, from thing so false as he,
Ever can come. Doubtless, will he deny
Free action in this treachery: but his deeds
Will cry to him, 'thou liest.' We, who beheld,
Sun-blazing proof saw, that in agony
Of earnest will, he wrought: repentant sighs,
Groans, prayers we heard: saw from his eyes great tears
Dropping like rain: and, when his treason was done,—
The maiden free,—then saw we his wild joy
At our defeasance. Proofs like these, too strong
For word, or oath, even of a god, to oppose.
But that, occasion given him, he'll deny,
With word, and oath monstrous, that his free will
Went with the treason,—and the whole blame will lay
On absolute compulsion from heaven's Powers,—
Who here can doubt? Yet, not the less, since thou,
Belial, has claimed for him the right to plead
In his own cause, so be it."
                    Turning then
Toward the lone victim, " Aziel," he pursued,—
" By every voice among us art thou judged
A traitor accurst. Clear as the light of day,
To all thy sin appeareth: and, ere now,
Doom had been hurled against thee,—but that one
Who justice loveth; and, as possible, holds,
That, by compulsion from some hostile Power,—
Not of thine own free will,—thou may have sinned,—
Demand hath made that in thine own defence
Thou be allowed to speak. Lift then thy voice,
That all may hear: and, if thou canst, the truth,

Truth only, speak; declaring how it was
Thou didst this guilt; if under absolute force
Of hostile Power; or under a mean fear;
Or of thine own bad spirit, willingly,—
That our eternal enemy thou might please,
Rather than us, to whom thy faith was due;
On whose especial service thou wert sent;
And whom to disobey, worst treason was.
If willingly thou didst it, then thy doom
Already hast thou heard: if overborne
By adverse Power, thou'dst win us to believe
Thy crime was done,—or impulse of weak fear,—
Subtle, I warn thee, must thine eloquence be;
Deep thy repentance; fervent and complete
Thine abjuration of the God we hate;
And who us hates, and wrongs. Thus warned, speak out,
That all may hear."
                     With tones of wrath and scorn,
Thus Lucifer; his face like thunder-cloud,
Fire-charged, on the meek Spirit looking down,
As he would blast him. All the assembly gazed
In silence,—if reply at all would come,
Uncertain,—such a mite, before the strength
Of gathered hell, that weak one: at the most,
Some poor excuse expecting; or base wail
For pardon, or for mitigated doom.
Wonder then seized them, when, his downcast head
Boldly uplifting, Aziel looked around;—
Beneath the millions of wrath-shooting eyes,
In stature, and in power, seeming to grow;
And, with calm mien; voice low, yet clear, and firm,
Thus answered.
               "Weakest of you all am I.
Might against might opposed, few are there here,
Who could not, even as a blade of grass,
Beneath the tempest, bow me. Not the less,
Before the strength of all combined, I stand
Fearless; not ignorant of what ills your rage
May heap upon me: but—with calm resolve
All to endure; and as the punishment

Of sin accept it: though of other sin
Than that for which ye punish. . . . . . Unto thee,
Satan, in chief, I speak; fearing no more;
No more respecting, thy dread eminence.
ONE ONLY GREAT I KNOW: all greatest, else,—
Atoms,—the difference of whose littleness,
Note merits not. . . . . . When first thou didst conceive
Rebellion 'gainst thy Maker; and with thee
Joined millions of angels, greater far than I;
And when the wondrous eloquence I heard,
Which made revolt seem virtue,—then I, too,—
Weak and submissive, among Powers that showed
All but Omnipotent, and Omniscient,—
Foolishly joined you; saying, as ye had said,
'Gods shall we all become: by nature, and right,
All equal are we: therefore unjust it is
That One alone,—solely because, of all
Eldest, and therefore wisest,—over all,
Absolute rule should arrogate; and claim
From countless myriads,—in due course to be
His equals fully,—abject homage, and praise,
And never-ending thanks.' . . . . . So, after you,
Senseless I spake: not of my own free thoughts
Rebelling; but seduced: and, even when most
Sinning 'gainst God,—in my great ignorance
Misdeeming, that 'gainst tyranny I fought,
For good, for justice. . . . . . Soon upon us came
That blast which from the grain swept off the chaff;
And drove us from the glory and bliss of heaven,
Down to the void of Death; and so long time
In the darkness fixed us, and drear solitude
Of this half-perished orb. Yet, all that while,
Faithful to you, and to your cause I stood.
For still, your burning words,—all wisdom and truth,
As seemed,—remembering,—did I feel myself,—
Though but a dust-mote, mid so many and great,—
Yet, equally with them, a sufferer
In cause most holy and just. Through all that time
Of darkness and imprisonment, no sigh,
No word of discontent, from me ye heard. . . . . .

At length, the wondrous glory of this vault
Burst on us; and that power, more glorious far,
Suddenly felt by all, our dungeon to quit,
And path the universe,—all, except the realm
Of God's more special abode. In your great joy
At liberty and strength regained; your vaunts
That from our ever growing might, alone,
All this had come,—joined I; your wisdom still
Undoubting as at first; and confident
That your proud prophecy would accomplished be,
And soon should we be gods. As you had taught,
Still I believed, that He who made us all,
Was but our angry tyrant; that, to thwart
His purposes; to render vain His might,—
Whate'er the cost,—was warfare noble and just.
When, therefore, ye commanded me, His scheme
For man's redemption, through Messiah,—son
Of progeny from that maiden,—to subvert,
By stirring in her pure soul thoughts impure,—
So vitiating the one condition named,
On which from her the Promised One should spring,—
Willingly I consented: and, conjoined
With Zuriel—who, in like way, should the soul
Of that pure youth make foul,—gladly went forth
On your bad errand. Clothing me in guise
Of Syrian prince; but with a face, and shape,
Beautiful past compare with aught of flesh;
And with voice speaking that an echo seemed
To the unforgotten melodies of heaven,—
Thus most to enthral her,——all things potent known
O'er passion and weakness of woman I poured forth:
So, toward myself to inflame her with desire,
All carnal, in the end; and from the youth,
Her destined husband, the pure virgin love
Which she had given him, turn aside; or quench
Utterly,—as a candle's light is quenched
By blaze of sunshine. . . . . . Thus in full I tell
My whole procedure; that it may be seen
How, thitherto, with strong sincerity
In your bad cause I served. But all my wiles

Proved vain. As torches, into water dropped,
Die on the instant,—so, all hottest fire
Of carnal love, on her pure spirit cast,
Fell dead. All flatteries most by women loved,
Harmlessly passed her, as thin vapours pass
Idly the granite mountain. Firm she stood;
Invulnerable to sin. As easily,
His puny hand outstretching, man might dip
Down to earth's centre, as might I,—though armed
With strength and cunning of all hell combined,—
Have striven that nature to pollute, which God,
Pure from all soil had made, as the inner heaven
From earthly cloud is pure. Ignorant of this,
Satan, wert thou : else, knowing well how weak
My nature; and how easily by thee,
Even to rebel 'gainst heaven, I had been led,—
Wise fear had whispered, that, as easily,—
In presence standing of what seemed a work
Direct from the hand of God; heaven's purity,
In woman's form impersonate,—again
Toward heaven, its birthplace, my weak spirit might
 yearn :
Might all the countless ages bring to mind
Of happiness ecstatic, ere we fell.;
Might loathing feel for that which such dire loss,
Such endless misery, had upon us brought;
And long once more of that pure bliss to taste,—
The approving eye of God. Who, that hath lived
In glory of light, would not in horror shrink
From home in utter darkness? In foul night
Who cycles long had mouldered, would not joy
To bathe again in sunbeams? I beheld
That pure one : day and night watched over her;
Striving, at first, her exquisite nature to stain;
But lower still and lower bending down
Before the wondrous might and majesty
Of her most heavenly innocence : feeling again,
A somewhat of the old celestial joy :
Hearing again, as seemed, far off, and faint,
Music of happy angels : breathing again,

In her blest presence, what might seem the air,
Long lost, of regions nigh about the throne;—
Till, at the last, with utmost fervency
Of my whole nature, I loved her. Not as ye,
Or some among you, in the ages past,
Have loved the daughters of earth,—but with a love
Like angel's unto angel; yea, with worship,
Such as to aught celestial would I pay.
Scorn, rage, threat, mock at me, even as ye will,—
Boldly I tell you, rather would I breathe
Fragrance of humblest flower from field of heaven,
Than be elected monarch of this hell!
Well know I that against me, 'gainst us all,
Heaven's gates for ever are shut; that, for our guilt,
Can no forgiveness be; that God's approof,
Even for a deed that 'gainst me maddens hell,
Can never more be mine; that good to me,
Ne'er as reward will come for doing good;
That evil will fall on me heavily,
For evil to do refusing. Ay,—I know
That punishment the worst ye can conceive,
Ye will inflict on me: but, one sweet drop
Again I have tasted from the cup of heaven;
And to the draughts detestable of hell
Never will turn again. Take me then hence
Unto your realms of death: even as ye will,—
And as I know ye can,—in some old orb,
Chaotic half, as if in iron rock,
Fix me; and, as ye threaten, leave me there,
Mid blackness, silence, everlasting death.
Yet, through the eternity, one glorious thought
Present will ever be; one heavenly guest
Alway supporting me,—that my last work
In life, and liberty,—feeble though it was,
Was yet for good; the gracious purpose to aid
Of Him who me created happy, and pure,—
The bad designs to cross of those, whose sin,
Of happy, made me wretched; of pure, foul!
I have done. I wait your vengeance. Visit me,
If so ye will, millions of ages hence;

And ye shall find, that he who weakest was
To do,—strength everlasting hath to endure.
Yet, ere ye rush upon me, one word more
Hear, and record. As my last deed, on earth,
Was toward the service of God,—so now, in hell,
My last words shall proclaim Him Lord alone;
For ever in glory unapproachable;
Omnipotent, Omniscient, and All Good!
And, though I nothing hope, I will confess
Humbly my sin, and for his pardon implore."

Raising his quivering hands; his contrite face
Upturning,—while the whole Satanic host,—
Astounded; and, with very excess of rage,
Motionless held, and silent, on him gazed,—
With tremulous voice, yet clear, thus did he cry.

"O Thou great Omnipresent! for, even here,
I know Thou art,—yea, in the farthest depths
Of the Death-regions,—and wilt hear the cry
Of my great misery,—though my greater sin
Louder do cry against me, to keep down
The motion of pity;—heaven is lost to me!
Yet will I call upon Thee, O my God;
Pity, oh pity me! my sin forgive!
Let me some hope have, that Thine utter wrath
Will pass; that somewhere in the unending line
Of ages, will the hour come, when my guilt
Shall be expunged: and, though in farthest space
From Thee remote, Thine eye shall look on me,
Not disapproving: for a heavy doom
Soon will these lay upon me; misery
All insupportable, save for thought of Thee;
And memory of bliss; and one faint joy,
That my last feeble act so was performed,
As once Thou hadst approved. Oh! pardon then
Lift from me the great mountain of Thy wrath:
Or mercifully take the life Thou gave!
Let me die now,—and be for aye at rest!"

Ceasing, upon his face he cast himself,
His doom to wait. As though 'gainst one poor lamb,
In the same moment of time had burst the roar
Of all wild beasts of earth,—so upon him,
The poor repentant, thundered forth the din
Of all hell execrating. Such the rage,
So horrible the cries, that even the voice
Of Lucifer, though to the height uplift,
Was whisper in tornado. But, at length,
When somewhat had the roaring billows sunk,—
Then, with eyes bright as bale-fires on a hill,
Aloft the Arch-Fiend stood; and, hurling words,
Each like a thunderclap, thus his fury expressed.

"The traitor that I knew him,—dead to shame,
He owns himself! Nay, glories in his guilt;
Mocks at our power; and, in the face of all,
Hath worshipped our eternal enemy!
The wrath he hath defied,—now shall he feel.'"

Thus having said, he paused, and looked around,
Motioning silence; then, when all were still,—
With visage changed, as 'twere from fire to cloud,
And voice no longer thundering, but low,
And harsh as grinding of the earthquake's jaws,—
Thus the dread sentence spake.
                              "The pestilent spot
Cut we now out for ever! To his doom
Be the apostate borne. On that one thought
Which so rejoiceth him,—his last act on earth,—
There let him feast: there let him evermore
Confess his sin, and call upon his God,
For pity, and pardon. Omnipresence, there,
Will ne'er be present: there, the all-seeing eye
Never will see him: there, Omniscience
Nought will know of him: there, Omnipotence
Powerless will be to help! Even this dead orb,
Haply, beyond the reach is of God's ken;
And, therefore, as our prison-house was chosen,
That we might vex him not: but, in that depth

Of uttermost space whereto this false one goes,—
For half the past eternity hath been
Not even a shadow of God. Beelzebub,
To thee that doleful prison-house is known:
For thou with me, long ere from heaven we fell,
Didst pierce the abyss; if limit might be found,
Curious to know, and what: till, wearied out,
We paused, pondering return. Then, as thou know'st,
A voice came to us, though no form we saw,—
Telling of orb enormous, not far thence,
Eldest of Old Creation. When we spake,
Enquiring, answer came not; but all space
Heaved like a sea. Awe-struck, though fearing not,
On went we then; and soon the presence felt
Of the great sun-corpse. If eternity
Beginning could have had,—before that date,
Seemed it, must this have been; beyond all else,
So with the mountain load of ages crushed,
The ghastly ruin appeared. Take with thee, then,
Of Spirits the strongest, three: and bear away
That hateful to his home. In lowest depth,—
Core of the hideous ruin,—make his grave;
Living, through all eternity to live,
There bury him; as bones in hardest rock
Sealed up,—there, motionless, for ever fix!"

To Aziel turning then, "Traitor!" he cried,
"Arise;" and the repentant-one stood up.
"Ay,—look around thee; for the last hour this
In which shalt thou see light! Look round thee well:
Behold the glories of this once dark vault;
Brighter than sunshine now: of our own strength,
And growing majesty alone the growth:
And still, as we in power, in brightness to wax,
Till heaven it shall outshine. In thy deep gloom,
Remember the great glory thou hast lost:
In solitude, remember the bright host
Of god-becoming Spirits, among whom
Once wert thou happy; and with whom, for aye,—
Faithful, hadst been so: in thy silence of death,

Call back their ether-shaking hymns of joy
For some great victory; but recall thou, too,
The tempest of their execrating yell
Against the traitor. Demi-gods,—to the height,
Lift now your voices: tell him the strong love
Faith bears to treason: for the last sound *that*
Which e'er shall greet him. To eternity
Let its echoes beat upon him!"
       Like the din
Of a great world exploding,—all its seas,
Mountains, and continents, and mighty heart
Of ever-during granite, in a cloud
Of flame and fire-dust roaring through the sky,—
Burst from the millions instantly a yell
That made the adamant quiver: every voice
Of all that living ocean hooted him:
All eyes shot fire against him: every hand
Pointed the finger of scorn.
       While thus at height
The tumult raged,—against the far-off sides,
And lofty roof re-thundering, like great waves
On cliffs precipitous,—Satan lift the arm,
And every voice was hushed. As if intent,
When the great war of echoes should be stilled,
Some thought new risen to speak,—awhile he stood,
Gloomy, and mute: yet, when, in dying gasps,
Faint, and more faint, — with lengthening pause between,—
The clamor sank,—and one drear muttering,
Its last death-rattle, ceased,—still mute stood he:
For, as the silence deepened,—more and more
Gathering in strength,—again the hated voice
Of supplication he heard. With sudden wrath
Inflamed to the height, furiously then he signed;
And instantly beside Beelzebub,
Three powerful Spirits appeared; and, following him,
Toward the condemned-one moved.
       Firmly stood *he*;
With countenance uplifted, sorrow-marked,
Repentant, praying aloud; acknowledging

His punishment deserved; yet timidly
Asking for strength to endure it.
                                At those words,
Fiercer than ever, from the millions burst
The uproar. Had his Essence been as flesh,
To atoms had they rent him: but, behold!
Even at the instant when the four dread Powers
Stood nigh, about to bear him to his doom;
And while at highest raged the tempest of hate,
Till roof and floor all trembled,——suddenly,—
As, on the gloom of midnight, breaks heaven's bolt,
Earth and sky firing—so, through that bright vault,
Pitch-blackness, as from Night's artillery shot,
Broke forth, and blotted all! The thunder of rage
Ceased in a moment; terror infinite
Crushing them; for a Presence then was felt,
Since loss of heaven, unknown; by sin-defiled,
Never to be endured. A thought-swift death
Appeared to have smitten all things: light seemed dead;
Voice dead; even echo dead. Spirit itself,
Dead seemed, or dying: power gone,—thought congealed;—
Life but a dream in death!
                                Down to the floor,
Like seared leaves dropped the shuddering host of hell;
All save the one doomed victim. Firmly he,
Serenely stood, nay, even hopingly:
For, through his whole Essential, like the ray
Of sunshine piercing mist,—a beam he felt,
As of heaven's radiance, shooting: breath of heaven
Appeared to fan him: voices seem to speak,
Exhorting him for pardon still to pray
Of his offended Maker,——for that He
Surely All Merciful as Almighty was,
And would in pity hear. His trembling voice,
Then he lift up, and cried;—" Oh God! oh God!
Merciful,—ever Merciful I know Thee now!
Thou hast seen my misery; hast heard my prayer;
Has sent me hope of pardon! Oh, once more,
Though but far-off, let me have glimpse of heaven!

From these Fallen Spirits let me be released;
And in some peaceful region of the sky,
Live ages of repentance: till,—my sin
Made lighter by Thy grace,—to heaven again,—
Though in remotest part, I may return;
Still to repent, and pray: but hoping still,
In lapse of ages, that repentance and prayer,—
Thy mercy aiding,—may my sin blot out;
And once more, purified, with angels pure,
I may stand nigh the throne; and, as of old,
Oh rapture! feel Thy presence! . . . . And for these,
These miserable,—blind and ignorant,
They know not what they do,—All Merciful,
On *them* have mercy!"
       Mid that awful hush,—
As flame of a lone taper, in dark night,
Spreads o'er a waste of sea,—so through the host
Spread round his low clear voice: and, though in all,
Life faint as shadow seemed, yet, on the ear,
Distinct fell every word, as falls the plash
Of water drop, from cavern's echoing roof,
Slow dropping upon stone. But fury none
Kindled they now,—all passion quenched in dread.
As the tranced body in the coffin hears,
Powerless to speak, or stir,—so they the words
Of the repentant heard; yet sign gave none.
Still, gathering fervor, kindling with high hope,
Went on the voice; but, as awe-paralyzed,
In a moment ceased; and gravelike silence fell.

 On every Spirit, then, a feeling stole,
Mysterious, of a somewhat nigh at hand,
Unknown, and fearful. To the lofty roof
Uplooking,—as if far off in the sky,
A radiance they beheld; a sphere, as seemed,
Of heaven's own splendor. Terror-struck, they gazed.
Expanding, brightening, it came down; and lo!
Midst of the light, a mighty angel of God!
Down came he, scattering glory, that their eyes
Nigh blinded; and dismay within them shot,

That even the boldest withered. As dry grass
In a dead calm, they lay; that, like to dust,
His foot, in anger, might have trampled them.
Down came he; and beside that contrite one,—
As, by the humble flower, the lofty pine,—
Stood; looked upon him; smiled, and spake.
                                " Well done!
Long erring, at the last thou hast well done.
The All Seeing hath beheld thee: all thy thoughts
The Omniscient knoweth: the All Merciful
Thy sin hath pardoned. To receive thee back,
Heaven hath flung wide its gates: to welcome thee,
All the angels of God are gathered. Thine offence
Will no more be remembered. In the choir
Again thy voice will rise. Thou wilt bow down
Mid angels and archangels near the shrine;
Wilt feel the Presence of God."
                                With holy joy
Intense, all quivering, the meek Spirit looked up:
And, lo! his countenance shone with glory of heaven,
Bright as before his fall! The mighty one
Stooped; took him by the hand; and, instantly,
Like upward flash of lightning, they arose.
One moment, as they pierced it, the gem-roof
Blazed to the splendor. Darkness then again,
Substantial; iron silence, covered all.

    At once, mid the vast realms of Night they plunge:
And still, as on they go, words of great joy
Speaks out the gracious angel. Through the obscure,
Stars 'gin at length to twinkle;—suns become,
Rulers of systems.—Straight as beams of light,
And swift as thought, through constellations vast
On, on they speed. . . . . Even through the very heart
Of a sun's burning atmosphere pierce they now. . . . .
Anon, through thickly clustered wonders bright,—
Great shoals of sun-sands, wherein light intense
Solid as diamond seems. . . . Through host on host,—
Glory on glory thickening,—still they fly:
Till, now, that highest firmament they reach,—

The holy solitude where no star is;
The immense which all Creation, else, divides
From the Heaven of Heavens itself. To cross that depth,
Sunbeams would toil in vain; ere midway won,
Dwindled to viewless point. No vacuum this,
But purest air celestial—flood of life.
Light from without unneeding, self-illumed,
A liquid sapphire evermore it glows:
Its silence music; its eternal calm
Sacred as prayer. They shoot within: at once
They drink that air divine,—more fragrant far
Than breath of sweetest flowers, at dewy eve,
In virgin Paradise. . . . . On—on—still on—
A bliss unspeakable, greater, and more great,
Like a flood of deepening water, pouring still
On the blest pardoned-one.
      Across the vast,
Trembling he looks,—the first faint glory of heaven
Eager to spy:—and, lo! at length, a light!—
To the eye, a star,—but, by the unspeakable beam,—
Through thousand centuries forgotten not——
The Heaven of Heavens proclaimed!
        A rapture-thrill
Runs like a lightning through him. On, still on,—
Still fleeter,—though each instant piercing space,
The measure of earth's orbit.
       To a sun,
The star dilates . . . . To bulk enormous spreads . . . .
Vast as, to eye of man, the vaulted sky,
Waxes anon: and, lo! the mighty orb—
That solid had seemed, ONE, indivisible,—
In starlike points innumerable breaks,—
Pure beyond ray of sun, or star, that shines
In firmament of earth, as *they* eclipse
The smoky torch-flame. . . . Soon, to suns expand
The stars-points . . . Open . . . In the space between,—
Again as stars,—unnumbered as the sands
On ocean's shore—glorious past reach of thought,—
Heaven's inner sphere he sees; that wondrous round

Of orbs magnificent,—each one gem entire,
Ruby, or sapphire, emerald, chrysolite,
Topaz,—or other gems, yet lustrous more,
In earth, and sun, unknown,—which, to the sight
Of angels in mid heaven, temper the blaze
Of outer suns, too bright. . . . .
       Rapidly still
The wondrous spheres enlarge : brighter become;
Till, even to Spirit-gaze, the glory intense
Nigh unendurable is . . . Nearer . . . More near . . .

Heaven seems the Universe now,—no space beside!

In the deep, sacred stillness, rose, at length,
Dim sound of angel voices. Slower then
Their flight,—for, with o'erwhelming rapture, and awe,
The pardoned-one was faint. With trembling hands,
His eyes he covered; and adown his cheeks
Pure tears celestial trickled. To heaven's bounds,
Nigh as the moon to earth had they attained,
When the great song of all the angelic host
Rejoicing, burst upon them. A low cry,
In the bliss-agony, from the Spirit broke :
Drooped then his head : his eyes closed : he sank down,
Senseless with joy.
     When life returned, behold,
By angels and archangels numberless
Accompanied, before the Shrine he stood,
And felt the Presence ! On their faces then
The shining millions fell : throughout all heaven
Was holy stillness; and from midst the cloud,
'*Dark with excessive light,*' came forth a Voice,—
"THY SIN HATH BEEN FORGIVEN THEE."
         Air, hill, plain,—
The whole vast region,—as with rapture shook.
Yet still throughout the angelic host remained
Serenest silence; prostrate still they lay,
In spirit worshipping. But, brief time past,
One impulse ruling all, the millions rose;

And, grander far than glory of the sun
Rising above the mountains, there went up
A chorus of thanksgiving. As the bed
Of a deep ocean with its waves is filled,—
So the vast temple of heaven, with that great hymn,
Even to o'erflowing, was full: and, though yet weak,
And in his rapture tremulous, the voice
Of the forgiven-one,—happiest then of all,—
And for eternity—once more was heard.

ISRAEL IN EGYPT.

BOOK TWENTY-THIRD.

MEANWHILE, within the heart of the dead sun,
After that glory angelic had passed out,
Long time reigned silence, night impierceable,
As in the depth of Chaos. Where they had fallen,
There the awe-stricken Spirits of Evil still,
Confounded lay; powerless to move, or speak,
Or of aught clearly think,—as though a stroke
From hand unseen had staggered very life.
At length, permitted so, the astonished Powers
From that dread stun 'gan waken. Satan first,
As mightiest, strength and courage returning felt;
And his great voice sent forth; the downcast host
Exhorting, and emboldening. His old art
Remembering then,—on the substantial night,
Once more that dark clear ruby glow he brought,
Which, solely, during ages long, had been
Their dungeon's radiance. Gladdened by the sight,
And by their leader's summons,—from the floor
Uprose the myriads; yet with motion slow;
Aspects of strange confusion, and dismay;
And, in crowds gathering, their dark fears, and thoughts,
Gloomily muttered. But, in little time,
When he had looked among them, and beheld

Their trampled fires rekindling, Satan then,
Tower-like upon his lofty throne stood up,
Silence awaiting: and, when all was hushed,
Thus spake.
          "Companions loved! and still the most,
When in adversity most,—few words now hear;
And treasure them; that they your spirits may lift
Above this gloomy present: for, be assured,
But brief repulse we have suffered,—not defeat.
Right on our course toward godhead go we still;
Not greatly, through this mischief, turned aside.
Oft have I told you, that, though all our might,
As in one arm, we could together wield,
Yet powerless were we, in the strife with Him
Who now Almighty is,——the one sole God,
Because, of all Existences, the first;
By half eternity, eldest of all.
Hence the discomfiture that just hath fallen.
No longer here safe conference may we hold.
That miscreant hath betrayed us; and the eye
Which, else, would ne'er have reached it,—from this hour
Ne'er will turn from it: steadfast as a hill
Upon a plain, here will it ever rest.
Even now, be sure, it sees us; and the ear,
Noteth each word we speak. Some fitter place,
Ere long shall we discover. Unto this,
A farewell everlasting bid we now;
And straight to Earth again; therein to do
As ye all know. When meet it shall become
That we again assemble, council to hold,
Then shall the word go forth,—of time, and place,
Instructing you. Meanwhile, be strong, and bold;
Hopeful,—nay confident; for, every age,
Toward godhead speeds us on assuredly,
As every league, by earthly traveller trod,
Speeds toward his journey's end. His sum of leagues
Accomplished,—well he knoweth that the place
For which he seeketh, *must* before him lie:
And, all our cycles past,—as truly we,
Know that the godhead looked for, will be found.

Not less this knoweth He, the already God;
And His whole might will wield to baffle us.
Henceforth, then, double caution must be ours.
The traitor, doubtless, hath our scheme made known,
Touching that youth and maiden; and 'tis crushed.
Eyes, now, of tenfold vigilance will watch,
If we evade them not, our every act;
Ears, tenfold keen, will hearken even our thoughts,
If heedless be we. Shut your natures up,
As gems shut up in rocks. Let your own eyes
Be sunbeams: but, against angelic gaze,
Stand ye impierceable, as cliff 'gainst wind.
Enough: be wise: and, now, in stillness hence."

The sign he gave; and, swift as flash of light,
The millions vanished. Through the void immense
Again came Stygian blackness, solitude,
And silence, for the eternity to come.

* * * * *
* * * * *

While thus in heaven and hell God's justice ruled,—
O'erwhelmed by darkness inconceivable,
As 'neath a coal-black ocean, Egypt lay,
A blot on face of earth! So thick the Night,
That the hand felt it, and the breath was clogged.
All sounds, as though through piles of wool, came dulled:
Noise, close at hand, seemed distant: tones of man,
Weak were as woman's: even his own voice,
To each seemed that of stranger. From the place
Whereon he had stood when the last ponderous wave
Of blackness fell,—aided by touch alone
Of hand, and foot, dared any man to stir.
Happy were they who nigh to couch, or bed,
Had found themselves; in chair, or even on floor,
Of their own dwellings. They who were abroad,
In field, or plain, or road,—at the first frown
Of darkness, fearing Plague at hand, ran on,
Eager for shelter,—wheresoe'er, or what:
But all the Israelites, who in the field,
Or on the public works, then labored,—led,

They knew not how,—through the fast-gathering gloom
Boldly walked onward, each unto his house.
Therein, behold, a pleasant light they found,
Soft, clear, and shadowless,—as if air itself
Radiant had grown; or every separate thing
Self-luminous. Yet, when the in-dwellers looked
From door, or window,—lo! before them stood
Blackness like solid rock! The hand of God,
Toward their deliverance stretched, therein they saw;
And with glad hearts,—for so had been enjoined,—
Due preparation made, against the hour
When, suddenly, to all should summons come,
From bondage to depart.
      But, for the men
Of Egypt, then abroad, who shelter sought,
Few were there who could reach it; for, with foot
Far fleeter, came the Terror; and flung night,
Pitch-black, and vast as mountains over them;
That staggered were they; wildly glared around;
Hurriedly stopped; and through the stifling air,
Sent shriek on shriek,—till, feeling all in vain,
With a low wailing of despair they sank,
Each where he stood; and lay upon the ground,
Trembling, and moaning: eagerly listening, now,
For any sound of life; now, with wide eyes,
Athirst for glimpse of light, staring toward heaven;
Now, for help feebly calling on their gods.
But, more and more, like a substantial weight,
They felt the Blackness press them; and lay mute,
Shivering, and panting; with a horrible dread
Lest nameless Things of Darkness, roaming then,
Should come upon them.
      Over the whole land
At length was midnight stillness: bird, nor beast,
Uttered a sound, or dared to stir at all:
Thronged cities silent were as sepulchres:
No man spake word; none from his place arose:
On every living soul throughout the realm,—
The Chosen people except,—such horror was,
As if, alive, entombed.

Hour dragged on hour;
Each a long day appearing. "Was the earth
Death smitten?" many thought; "the sun gone out?
Or, had the terrible god of Darkness come,
The universe to destroy?"
                              But, for the king,
Assuredly knew he, that through the might
Of Hebrew magic alone, the mischief was,—
Though threatened not; and therein he beheld
That second Plague, and last, which, by the voice
Of the dead Hebrew, through strong spells enforced,
Had been predicted. But, like all before,
Soon would it pass: meantime must be endured:
For, not again to the proud sorcerer
Should Pharaoh bow; imploring that his God
Would turn away the scourge. The Plague should die
Its natural death; and, afterward, by death
Not natural, he who sent it.
                              When dropped down
The first great cloud-pall,—fearing what might come,—
A second Plague of flies, perchance, or hail,—
At swiftest toward the chamber of his queen
Had he sped on; his keen eye glancing still
At window after window, as he passed;
And, wonder-stricken, noting, that, through each,
Still fiercer glared the Terror: nay, so swift
Night smote, and trod down Day, that, when he stood
Within the door, already darkness such
Had veiled the earth, that, save as by her voice,
Answering his own, directed, he knew not
Which way to stir the foot. Fever, at eve,
Had come upon her; and her bed she kept.
At length he stood beside her: her small hand,—
Cold now, and shivering,—took, and gayly said.

"Be not afraid, my Sirois. In few hours
All will again be sunshine. Hebrew spells
Once more are working: but the last time this;
And, like all former Plagues, soon will it die.
Come nought but mid-day darkness,—by my troth

We may enjoy the trick; a pleasant change
From the old course may find it. At the worst,
Lamplight for sunlight, a few hours shall have;
No monstrous evil. Calm thee, then, my life:
Think 'tis but night, a little out of time;
And close thy lids, and soothe thy thoughts to peace:
Soon then sweet sleep will come, and pleasant dreams
Of sunny days: and, when thine eyes re-ope,
The veritable sun will gladden them.
Here will I sit beside thee, thy soft hand
Still clasping; and, when daylight comes again,
Will wake thee with a kiss. A little while
Lie still, and speak not; then, in this dead hush,
Perforce will sleep fall on thee."
                              Thus spake he,
Calm mind pretending; though within his soul
Darkly perplexed,—unknowing what might come.

   Hours passed, and brought no change. Oft looked
    he up
Toward window, hoping some slight quiver to see
Of the day's eyelids: but one solid black
Were window, and wall, alike. Hour after hour;
And but the heavier grew the palpable night;
Pressing the flesh, and making thick the breath,
As with dense dust. Mysterious horror came
On the proud king,—a dread lest the whole world
Should be about to perish, by the doom
Even of the gods who made it: for, by might
Of Hebrew spells, impossible seemed it now,
Such evil could be. Like heavy hammer-strokes
His heart-throbs rang,—sole sound that he could hear:
All silent else, as if leagues deep in earth
He had been caverned.
                     But, at length, the voice
Of Sirois, faint as whisper; and the hand
Compressing his, aroused him. Burning thirst,
She said, was on her: on him, too, was thirst
Insatiable. Where water-vessels stood,
And cups, well knew he; and, with hand and foot,

Feeling the way, he walked; and, having found,—
Task harder still,—brought them; and, pouring forth,
Gave her to drink; and, afterward, himself
Drank eagerly: and then again he soothed
His terrified queen; and with a cheerful tone
Encouraged her, "for soon the spell must die,
And daylight come anew." But, when she spake,
Saying how pleasant even the poorest lamp,
That gloom to cheer, would be,—he lifted up
His voice, attendance calling. Yet no tongue
Spake in return: nor, when again he called,
And yet again at strongest, came reply.
Up got he then: with arms outstretched, and foot
Feeling his way, along the chamber groped,
The door to find: but, as in labyrinth lost,
Long wandered. With a joyful heart at length,
He struck upon it: opened wide; and sent
Loud summons:
"Ye who hear me, answer now;—
It is the king who speaks."
Came then a voice,
As from far distance, saying, "Light of Day,
I hear thee; but I know not where I am."

"Bring hither lamps," cried Pharaoh,—"or call out,
Whoe'er thou art, on them who have the charge;
And say, that, to the chamber of the queen,
Pharaoh commandeth them." Thereat the voice
Cried, "Whoso heareth, let him answer now:
For, through my mouth speaks Pharaoh."
Seemed it then
That answer came, though Pharaoh heard it not;
For, soon, again the voice arose, and spake.

"Unto the chamber of the queen bring lamps:
Or, upon them who have the charge, call out;
And bid them speed; for so the king commands."
That having heard, Pharaoh his way groped back,
By the queen's voice directed; and again

Beside her sat; again, with soft words, strove
Her terror to calm.
    Hour after hour dragged on;
Yet came no touch of daylight, and no lamp:
And wroth had Pharaoh been, but that strong fear
The rising anger smothered. A faint voice,
High-pitched, as if far off, at length he heard,—
"Where is the king? that we the lamps may bring
Into his presence."
    "The king sitteth yet
In the queen's chamber," answered Pharaoh then,
Calling aloud.
    "Light of the Sun, we stand
Even at the door thereof," returned the voice;
"For thereon, by the lamps, have we descried
The gilded Apis: but the king doth speak
As if far off."
    "In the queen's chamber I
Verily am," cried Pharaoh; "but, for you,
Ye are not nigh it yet: when ye draw near
The lights will tell your coming."
    "Glory of Day,"
The voice replied, "as I do live, we stand
Within the door thereof; three goodly lamps,
Of purest naphtha, bearing in our hands.
Haply the king, at distance, see'th them not;
For we ourselves, a dark gleam only see,
As through black glass. Where sitteth now the king?
Let him still speak aloud; so may the voice
Guide us to find him."
    Then, at highest pitch,
Pharaoh cried out,—again, and yet again,
Answering their call: and fearfully, and slow,
Hand, and foot, groping, nigh, and nigher, they came.
But, not till near as span's length the first light
Approached him, saw he the dark dismal gleam,
Like worn moon through dense fog: nor, till the lamp
Touched the king's hand, did he who bore it know
That he drew nigh him. Pharaoh took it then,
And waved it round, and groaned; for, mockery all

He found it; to that chamber giving light,
Such as to hill-top gives the glow-worm's beam,
In the deep vale beneath. Even when the three
Together stood, strength had they not enough
To show the bearers' faces.
"Get ye back,"
Said Pharaoh; "two of these, to light you, take;
And bring back many; filled, but kindled not:
So, from one, dying, may the next take life.
And bid ye hither food, and wine; for hence,
Till daylight cometh, can I not depart."
So fared the king.

At length, well nigh three days
Had run; and ponderous still as ever lay
The blackness on the land; silence like death;
Utter stagnation. Oft, with prayers, and tears,
The gentle queen had striven, the stubborn heart
Of Pharaoh to subdue, that he might send
To Moses, and beseech him, with his God
To plead for suffering Egypt: yet, till now,
Hard had he been as iron: but, at last,
Worn out with horror, and fast growing dread
Lest even on themselves might famine fall,—
Darkness enduring,—to her earnest prayer
He yielded: and on them who, by command,
Without the door attended,—called, and said;
"Go, some of you, and quickly as ye may;
And say to Moses, 'the king waiteth thee;
Come thou before him.'"
Then the weeping queen
Dried up her tears; and thanks spake; and lay still;
Undoubting of the end.
Yet hours passed by,
And Moses came not, nor the messengers:
Through that chaotic night a way to find,
The task so difficult.
But, what time the sun
Far under earth had dipped, a voice they heard;

"Light of the worlds! without the door even now
The Hebrew standeth: all alone he came;
Walking as in the daylight. Will the king
His pleasure speak?"
             "Let him draw nigh; for here
Must I talk with him," Pharaoh said. "And thou,
My Sirois," he whispered,—"mark not word
That shall be spoken: turn away thy face,
And shut thine ear; lest, if harsh speech arise,
Thou may betray thyself."
             Scarce had he ceased,
When near him was a voice; and, when he looked,
Lo! Moses stood before him; visible,
Like a pale flame; his countenance severe,
Yet not in wrath; but with stern sanctity
Of upright judge, addressing criminal.

"At last thy proud heart bendeth, mighty king;"
Solemnly said he: "mighty among men;
But, in the sight of God, less than the mote,
Seen only in the sunbeam. Know'st thou *now*
The hand of God stretched o'er thee? Wilt thou *now*
His word obey, and let our people go?"

Then Pharaoh trembled; for the voice, though soft,
Awed him like thunder; and his tongue lay mute.
But shame burned in him, lest, before the queen,
Weak he should seem; and soon, speech mastering,
Briefly he answered.
             "Go ye; serve the Lord.
Only your flocks and herds behind you leave:
Your little-ones take with you."
                       "Nay, not so,"
Firmly said Moses: "thou must likewise give
For sacrifices, and burnt offerings;
That we may sacrifice unto the Lord.
Our cattle also shall go with us: none,
No not a hoof shall there be left behind;
For thereof must we take, to serve the Lord:
And wherewith we must serve Him, know we not,

.Till thither come we."
"Even as ye will
Then get ye forth," said Pharaoh, hurriedly;
"So that ye first this pestilent darkness chase,—
However brought,—by spells, or by your god,—
And give us day again."
"Even yet thy heart
Hard is, I see," said Moses; "and thy words
Of the tongue only. Ne'ertheless, to show
That Israel's God is Lord of all the earth,
And of the heavens, and of all things that be,—
Behold, when I shall pray to Him, this Plague
Will He take from you. But, if wickedly still
Thou disobey,—then heavier still, be sure,
His rod will fall on Egypt; till, with tears,
Ye shall implore us go."
Thus having said,
On Pharaoh a stern warning look he cast;
Then, walking as in day, the chamber left.

Through these three days and nights, o'er all the land,
Deeper had grown the horror. Sleep was none,
Or but for moments,—so all ears were strained,
Sound whatsoe'er to catch, that might denote
Life, motion, presence, action, suffering, aught
Which good, or evil coming, might portend,—
So were all eyes into the solid night
Eager to pierce; some feeble spark to find
Mid day's black ashes. Thus all Egypt lay,
Dark, soundless, as the vaults 'neath ocean's bed.

But, even at noon of midnight, there went up
A cry throughout the land; a voice of joy.
They who in field, or road, lay perishing,
Upstarted; for, on that chaotic gloom,
In a moment, lo! a sunrise glory sprang,
Dazzling all eyes. "Day! day!" the myriads cried,
"Thanks to the gods,—day, day!" Yet, looking up,
Stars only saw they, numberless, burning bright,

As ne'er before they had burned; like well-filled lamps,
After long darkness, kindled suddenly.
The dwellers in the cities, villages,
And lonely houses,—as at clarion-call,
Started beneath the light-stroke; and cried "Day!"
And rushed abroad, plunging within the beams,
As in a bath; some, shrieking in their joy;
Some, laughing; weeping, some; and wondering all,
When they looked up, to see that stars alone
Such daylight gave them. But, in little while,
All eyes saw common night; clear, yet still dark:
And, when joy's fire its brightest sparks had spent,
On most,—though hunger-pinched,—with giant power
Came Sleep; some, striking down even where they stood;
Some, hurrying to their rest on couch, or bed,
Or floor, if nighest.
     But yet many there were,
So, to the very soul, all horror-struck
By those three days of darkness, that, even then,
Feared they the sun had perished in the sky;
Night had become eternal. On their lids
Sleep touched not: toward the bright stars, earnestly
They turned their eyes, counting the slow-paced hours:
And, nigher to the morning as they drew,
On the clear east, silent and doubtful, gazed;
Watching for first weak beam, that trumpet would be
To herald Day-god's rising.
     Pale they stand,
Anxious, and tremulous; for the stars proclaim
That now the hour is come.
     Doth sight, at last,
Truth tell them? Doth a faintest pearl-tint wash
Earth's dark rim orient? Or, but cheat of sense,
Hope and fear-troubled, is it? Tremblingly,
Myriads of eyes 'neath close-pressed palms are hid;
Opened again,—and shut—and opened anew:
And still, at every glance, stronger is hope,—
Doubt weaker—weaker—dead!
    "Day, day,—'tis day!"

Sky kindles: and from city, field, and plain,
Steams up the voice of joy. Again pour forth
The roused-up sleepers: every living soul
That strength hath, to the street, or field, flies out;
On morn's clear radiance looking, as on thing
Wondrous, unseen before: the sweet, fresh air
Drinking more eagerly than thirsty man
Of the sparkling grape-juice drinks: even on bare ground,
And leafless tree, Plague-ravaged, looking now
As on some beauteous picture: from each sight,
And sound, a rapture taking,—the great bliss
Once more within a living world to feel.
The birds, though faint with hunger, thirst, and fright,
Send up glad voices; and with clanging wings
Speed through the air, their 'customed haunts to find.
Like prisoners from dark dungeon suddenly freed,—
Uttering strange sounds of joy, gambol the beasts:
Even the huge river-horse, and crocodile,
Wild with brute rapture, headlong into Nile
Plunge—tempesting the stream. O'er all the land
Again is life: eyes see, ears hear, tongues speak,
Limbs move: life, life is over all things: death
Died with the darkness. Such the tumult of joy
At light's great resurrection!
       Many there were,
Who saw in this the hand of Israel's God:
And Him they reverenced; and his servant, too,
That wondrous Moses, by whom had been done,
Marvels unknown before throughout the world:
And earnestly they hoped, the king, at length,
Faithful would be; and let all Israel go.

 But not so purposed Pharaoh. Soul-rejoiced,
He saw the solid blackness, to clear air
Changed in a moment: and now, confident
That the last Plague was gone; and, thenceforth, peace
Eternal should he have,—in his bad heart
He laughed at Moses; as at some poor dupe,—
A fool snared easily; and, when noon drew nigh;

And the great Hebrew, standing near his throne,
Questioned him, wherefore proclamation none;
As promised, had gone forth,—that Israel,
Men, women, children, herds, and cattle all,
Might go into the wilderness,—with scorn
Thus answered he.
     "Thou hast well played thy game,
Bold sorcerer; and I, mine. Thy tricks of art,
By tricks of guile were met. And now I know,
That in thy quiver not one shaft is left.
Fool! if thou brought that darkness; and, at will,
Could'st bid it last,—hadst thou not cunning enough
To keep us prisoned till yourselves were free?
Thou'st lost occasion; and occasion *last*.
Thou hast been spendthrift of thy wizard-wealth;
And now art beggar. If some straggling spell,
Forgotten, thou should find,—I caution thee,
Well use it. Meantime, broken sorcerer,
I scorn thee, and defy; thee, and thy god
Alike: impostor thou,—imposture he!
Thou'lt try thy wand again: one grain of lead
Would o'erbuy all its worth. Thou wert a fire;
Art ashes; iron wert,—art glass; a hill
Wert thou in pride,—a molehill art become:
Thy sun is set; the waters of thy seas
Are dried up in their continents: from thy bones,
Flesh, blood, and marrow are gone: thou art a puff
Of smoke upon the wind,—or aught beside,
More weak and worthless still. Thou hast thy staff;
Bring with it now a Blood-Plague, as before,—
And I will place upon thy head my crown,
And hail thee Egypt's king. But, well thou know'st
That all thy tricks are o'er. Wizard, and fool!
Life to permit thee, is myself to be
Foolish as thou: yet, live; and, morn and night,
Thank Pharaoh's mercy. But, presume no more
To come before him. Get thee quickly hence,
Out of my sight! Take heed unto thyself!
See thou my face no more: for, in that day
Thou darest to see it, surely shalt thou die!"

By Pharaoh's frantic threatening all unmoved,
As, by the brawl of waters at its foot,
The cloud-o'erlooking cliff,—on the flushed face,
In a stern anger Moses gazed; and thus.

"Thou hast well spoken, king: uncalled, unsent,
I see thy face no more. But, hearken now.
My quiver, thou sayst is empty; my sun set;
My waters all dried up. Oh, blind of eye,
And hard of heart! imagin'st thou, even yet,
That art of mine these Plagues hath brought on thee;
And dream'st thou that, worn out, it can no more;
And safely, therefore, may thou fling at me
Threat, and derision? In the quiver whence came
The arrows that have smitten thee, lie yet
Ten thousand times ten thousand, ten times told;
And greater far,—for 'tis the quiver of God!
I do but warn thee, saying,—' the bow is bent:
Obey, and 'scape the shaft:' for so to me
The Voice hath spoken. That small buzzing fly,
Now hovering o'er thy head, as easily
Might wield the thunder, as man's deepest art
Such Plagues might bring. From first, to last, still thus
Have I declared it to thee. In thy palm
Could'st thou scoop ocean; and, when highest he stands,
In the sun's face fling it, and his fire dash out,—
Still, against Israel's God, more feeble thou,
Than worm against the earthquake: and from Him,
Again I tell thee, have these judgments come:
And bend to Him thou must. Nay, even now,
When most thy pride is, doth the day draw nigh:
For thus to me hath spoken the Lord God.
'Yet one plague more on Pharaoh will I bring,
And upon Egypt: afterward will he
Let you go hence; nay, he shall thrust you forth.
For, in the midst of Egypt will I go,
About the midnight; and the first-born all,
Throughout the land shall die: from the first-born
Of Pharaoh on the throne, to the first-born
Of the maidservant, toiling at the mill;

And the first-born of beasts. And a great cry
Shall be throughout the land; such as, before,
Hath been none like it; and shall never be.
But, 'gainst the children of Israel, not a dog
Shall move his tongue,—either 'gainst man, or beast:
That ye may know how that the Lord hath put
Difference 'twixt Egypt, and our Israel.'
And those thy servants, Pharaoh, with fierce look
Now glaring on me,—who, with bitterest hate,
And lies, and scoffs pursue me evermore,—
Even they shall come before me, and bow down,
And cry, ' now get thee out from Egypt,—thou,
And all thy people.' After that, O king,
Will we go forth: for all the land will cry,
Imploring us to go; even jewels, and gold,
Thrusting upon us, lest we should delay;
And evils worse should follow. Warning none,
As heretofore, now give I: thy bad course
Is run; and to thyself, at last, thou'rt left.
Promise, or oath, to thee such fetter is,
As gossamer-thread to foot of elephant.
A sea of promises thou'dst gulp at once,
Lightly as draught from Nile. Thou hast been weighed,
And art found wanting: sin on sin hast done;
Hast lied to God; even four times hast thou lied,
Unto the God of Israel: and His hand
Is lifted; and nought now can stay the blow.
Word more to thee were vain: bide thou the doom!"

Thus stirred to righteous wrath, the meek man sent
Upon the king, and his much wondering court,
Glances that staggered them; and with great voice,
As with nigh thunder, shook them: gathered then
His robe about him, bending not the head,
And from the hall went forth.
       Astounded sat
King, priests, and rulers; each upon the face
Of the other looking; and all pale and mute.
But, in a little while, Thamusin rose,
And bowed before the king; and, with bold words,

By Satan prompted, flung defiance and scorn
At Moses, and his threats. And, after him,
Spake Necho, subtly; Hophra, with stern voice;
And others of the priests, all demon-fired,
Making their mock at Moses, and his God.
But in the heart of Pharaoh, most, the fiend
Waked disbelief, and scorn; that, in the end,
Upstarting from his throne, loudly he laughed
At the dread threatening; and his court dismissed.

Exulting in their victory, forth went they;
Joyously laughing also: yet, at heart,
Oft a strange horror felt, which their loud mirth
Stopped in the midst; shooting through nerve and brain,
Like icy lightning: for the voice and look
Of the Hebrew came back on them, trumpet-strong,
Saying, 'the truth he speaketh; so will be.'

ISRAEL IN EGYPT.

BOOK TWENTY-FOURTH.

Moses, meantime, straightway unto the house
Of Aaron speeded back: for, gathered there
By hasty summons, knew he that the priests
And Elders waited him: and when, at length,
All stood attentive, wondering what should come,—
In their astonished ears the words he spake,
Which, by the Voice, to Aaron, and himself
At sunrise had been spoken: how that month,
Thenceforth, first month of all the year should be:—
How, on the fourteenth night, first Passover
Should Israel keep; throughout all time to come
Should keep it as a feast unto the Lord,
An ordinance for ever. And all rites
Thereto pertaining, which prescribed had been,
Even by the Voice itself,—with words distinct,
From first unto the last, did he make known:
So, on that holy feast, might fall no blot.

"And thus, then, shall ye eat it: with loins girt,—
The shoes upon your feet,—the staff in hand :
And ye in haste shall eat it: for, behold,
About the midnight, will the Angel of God
Pass through the city, and through all the land,
And smite the first-born, both of man, and beast.

In that hour throughout Pharaoh's realm will be
A sound of wailing: and, with one great voice,
All Egypt will cry on us to depart.
Therefore, that night, bid ye the people speak
To the Egyptians,—as old custom is
Of guests departing,—asking of them gifts;
Jewels of silver, and gold: for favor great,
In sight of man and woman shall they have,—
Yea honor; and with riches be sent forth."

  That having heard, the priests and Elders went
Throughout the city, and the lands around,
The tidings bearing: and swift messengers,
To Goshen, and all places wherein dwelt
The Israelites, hastened; and in every house
Made known what must be done; that every soul
Of all the people, when the hour should come,
Might be found ready. To the Egyptians soon
Plain was it that again some wondrous thing
By Israel was expected; which, at length,
Might the king force to loose them: and the most,—
Maugre the Spirits of Evil, who still strove
Against the Hebrews hatred and wrath to raise,—
Longed to behold them go: for both great fear
Toward Moses felt they, and a reverence great;
His power well knowing, and his righteous ways:
And even of Pharaoh's servants many there were
In whose sight he found favor. But the king,
And those about him,—sorcerers, priests, and lords,—
Yet made of him their mock: and, day by day,
Seeing that still the threatened Plague came not,
More insolent grew; at Moses, and his God,
Flinging worse scoffs. Nor, when it had been told,
How that the slaves by night toiled secretly,
Preparing to depart, cared Pharaoh aught;
But suffered them, that more might be the laugh
At their cloud-fabric melting. Still the days

Passed cheerfully; and not one shadow signed
The approaching Terror: all seemed joyous and light;
Plague gone for ever; peace eternal come,
Even as the dead had prophesied. But lo!
The earthquake was at hand!
                          The fourteenth sun
Had risen, and set. All preparation made,
All ordered rites performed,—the Israelites
Stood at the feast of Passover; loins girt;
Shoes on their feet, and staffs within their hands;
All silent, pale, expecting.
                          Suddenly,
About the midnight, there went up a cry,
Throughout the city; a great wail of woe,
Louder and louder waxing; women, and men,
And children, all together clamoring;
All crying out that death was in the house;
Death horrible,—unknown before,—Black Death,
Swift as from lightning. To and fro they ran,
Shrieking and yelling in their misery.
And when, at length, each of the other asked,
The same dread tale heard all,—the first-born slain,
As by a thunder-stroke; yea, like a coal,
Scorched up, and black. Louder than howl of storm,
Over all Zoan rose the wail of woe:
And over all the land, in city, and town,
Village, and lonely house, was heard the wail.

   After a joyous banquet, soundly slept
The headstrong king; a vision of the night
His pride uplifting: for, before his feet,
Prostrate lay Moses; a low voice of prayer
For pardon uttering; and him owning king
For ever, and sole lord o'er Israel:
Even as he would, to deal unto them life,
Or death; labor, or ease; pleasure, or pain,—
His slaves they, body and soul. With lifted foot,
Upon the neck of the great sorcerer,
So dreaded once, in dust so humbled now,
Threatening to tread, he stood,—when, on his arm

A grasp,—and, close to his ear, a hurried voice,
Quivering with terror,—roused him.
                              "Pharaoh, list—
Some evil is there. Hark! Oh God, oh God,
The Plague,—the Plague is on us! Hush,—again,—
Didst thou not hear a cry, 'my son, my son,
My first-born!' Ha! a sea of voices now
Roars o'er the city! Up; up; get thee up,
My Pharaoh; to thy first-born let us haste.
And bid the leech be nigh, lest sickness come.
Haste, haste. Oh gods have mercy!"
                              With faint tone
Thus ending, from her bed the queen arose,
And flung a robe around her. Pharaoh, too,
Silent with stroke of fear, rose hurriedly,
And robed himself; and both together then
Were passing from the chamber, when, behold!
Even in the palace a loud wail burst forth,
So hideous, that they started, and stepped back,
And looked each other in the face, and griped
Each on the arm of the other, and stood still,
Ghastly as death. But, nigh and nigher came
The outcry; every instant louder still,
And wilder waxing. Staggering, went the king;
Drew wide the door: and, close without, beheld
A throng of women, and men, with heads bent low,
Wringing their hands; weeping and wailing loud,
As each for a lost child. When him they saw,
At once they ceased their cry. He could not speak;
But with looks piteously questioned. On his knees
Then one, the favored servant of the prince,
Sank down before him. "Splendor of the Sun,
Slay me not for the tidings that I tell!
Thy first-born . . . ."
                    "Bring us to him instantly,"
With faint voice gasped the queen, outstepping quick:
"And some of you go swiftly; and the leech
Bid follow. Pharaoh, come."
                              With trembling hand,
His arm she seized, and gently drew him on;

Whispering of hope,—though in her was no hope.
Speechless,—with foot unsteady,—all strength lost,—
Jaw dropped,—eyes glaring,—his loose shaking hand
On her frail arm low hanging,—he crawled on,
Smitten at last to the dust. The attendant group,—
As though a corpse they followed to the grave,—
With streaming eyes, and bowed heads, sobbing aloud,
Behind them walked: but, when the chamber of death
Open before them stood, shuddering, drew back.
The father, and his queen, went in alone;
And the door closed upon them.
                              Hushed, and pale,
While those without awaited, momently
The king's wild cry expecting,—once again
Within the palace a great shriek arose;
Another—and another—and a fourth!
And while, all blank with terror, fixed they stood,
Each on his fellows staring, lo! like lead,
Even of themselves dropped one upon the floor;
Black, shrivelled, as a fly scorched in the flame!
All looked upon him,—screamed; and, screaming, fled,
As if, behind them, a grim Death they had seen,
With bony hand outstretched.
                            The king, meantime,
Tottering feebly,—for no hope he had,—
Went onward toward the bed. A snow-white sheet,
All covering up, with icy tongue spake plain,
Death underneath. He touched it,—shivered, shrank;
Dropped on his knees; with both palms pressed his head;
Bowed down, and a low piteous wailing made,
Even like a homeless dog. The weeping queen
Beside him kneeled; his left arm with both hands
Tremblingly grasped, and leaned thereon her cheek,
Lovingly pressing it,—yet no word spake.
All they who in the chamber were, looked on,
Silently weeping. But, when ceased at last
The father's piteous wail,—as from the clouds,
Came in a voice of lamentation dire,
From the whole city rising; then, anon,
The cries within the palace; and, more loud,

And close without the chamber, the great shriek
Of them who, horrified, fled. The attendants all
Looked each in the face of the other; but moved not,
Nor a word uttered. Once, with startled look,
The queen lift up her head; but soon again
Rested her loving cheek on Pharaoh's arm,
And low words 'gan to speak. Nought heard the king;
Deafened by sorrow.
     But a stroke, at length,
Came on the door; and, white and trembling with fear,
The aged physician entered: on the bed,
And on the kneeling king and queen, his eyes
Fixed, horror-stricken; and stood motionless,
Fearing, he knew not what. But, to the queen
A woman went, and whispered. To the king
Then whispered the fond wife. He shook the head;
But, aided by her weak arm, tottering, rose,
And stood, and turned him toward the leech, and said;
"Too late! too late! even power of magic now
Too late to save! . . . . Yet, look upon his face;
And say what slew him."
      Slowly moving then,
The aged physician, quaking, mute, advanced,
To look upon the corpse. Near to the head,
Arm locked in arm, stood Pharaoh and the queen;
Shrinking, yet eager-eyed,—on the white pall
Fixing their gaze,—expecting soon to see
The pale, calm face of death. But common death
To this had seemed as life: the shaking hand
Of the scared leech snatched hastily away
The ominous sheet; and lo!—a hideous thing,—
Shrunk as with fire; eyes open, mouth agape,
Tongue hanging out, all black as midnight,—glared
Like a foul demon on them! One dire shriek
The king sent up,—a moment, rigid as stone,
Stood staring; then fell heavily; and lay,
Struggling and foaming. One ear-piercing cry
The queen sent also; but, the piteous state
Of Pharaoh seeing, sank upon her knee
Beside him; and, with fond words, vainly strove

His sorrow to soothe.
                        But the physician now
Spake with authority; and submiss she rose :
With clasped hands then, and streaming eyes, stood still,
Waiting the issue.   Water on the face
Freely was cast : on brow, and temple, and breast,
Was pungent essence rubbed : and when, at length,
The eye-lids twinkled; the chest slowly heaved;
And deep sigh followed,—then, all hurriedly,
The leech commanded.   "With a careful hand,—
But on the instant,—lift ye up the king ;
And to his chamber bear him; and speak not."
Thus having ordered,—lest a second glance
Death-stroke should be,—with hasty step he went,
And covered up the corpse.
                           Soon on his bed
The king was laid; and gently, drop by drop,
Life-stirring draught was given; till, with full eye,
Upon his loving queen clear looks he cast;
Tokening of sense returned; but bitterest grief
Torturing the soul.   Then on her knees she sank,
Pressing his hand; and, with a trembling voice,
Implored him.
             "Oh, my Pharaoh, seest thou not
How vain, how wicked were it, more to strive
Against the God of Israel : for, be sure,
He is it, and not magic, that such things
Hath brought on thee, and Egypt.   The first-born
Throughout the land were threatened; and that wail
From all the city, telleth how the threat
Hath been fulfilled.   If longer thou persist
Israel to hold in bondage,—think, oh think
What *then* may be the punishment !   That same Power
Which smote the son, may, next, the father smite;
Nay, even the whole people !   Send thou, then,
I do beseech thee, lest even now should come
Worse evil,—for the sons of Amram send;
And beg of them implore their God to stay
This pestilence,—so all Israel may depart
Out of the land for ever."

                        While she spake,
Louder, and louder, close without the door,
Was heard a moaning, and a mingled sound
Of many voices talking earnestly;
Like men in grief, and terror. Soon there came
Within the chamber Pharaoh's younger sons:
Soter, the eldest now, and heir to the throne,
Drew nigh unto him; and, with tremulous voice,
Thus spake.
            "Oh send, my father, quickly send
For Moses: bid him stay this plague; then go,
He, and his people with him, from the land;
Else shall we perish all. Thy priests and lords
Are gathered at the door; and call on thee
To send the Hebrews forth; yea, this same night,
To bid them hence; even though with silver and gold
Need be to urge them: for, with one accord,
All people cry,—' our first-born hath been slain!'
And death on the whole nation soon may fall,
If Israel go not quickly."
                        "I will send,"
With weak voice Pharaoh said; "but, will he come?
For, when, in my great wrath,—in sight of all
The princes, priests, and rulers,—from the court
I drove him,—cried I not to him aloud,
'See thou my face no more; for in that day
Thou darest to see it, surely shalt thou die'? . . . .
Yet, haply, when I send, he may forgive;
And come before me. Haste ye then away;
Ye, and the priests and lords who are at hand:
Go on the instant; stay not to speak word;
But go: and, if the Hebrews slumber, strike
Loudly upon the door, till they arise.
And, when ye shall behold them, then cry out,
Even all together, imploring them, once more
To come before me; for, in verity, now,
Shall their whole wish be granted. In your hands
Take with you jewels of silver, and jewels of gold;
All that ye have upon you:—and of mine,—
There, on the porphyry table—take them quick,—

Rings, chains, necklaces, armlets,—take them all,—
All save the ruby alone: and, when ye see
That they have both set forth,—then, in the house
Of Aaron enter; and, to them within,
Give freely, saying,—'get ye out with speed
From Egypt, all ye Hebrews,—even this night
Get ye all forth. Your young, your old, your flocks,
Your herds, your cattle,—whatsoe'er is yours,
Take with you, and depart,—for thus the king
His will hath spoken. When the sun shall rise,
In the desert let him see you. Unto all
Your people this make known; and bid them ask,
Each of Egyptian neighbour, jewels of gold,
And jewels of silver,—as the custom is
Of guests departing,—for the king will send
Command that such be given you, with free hand,
Even as *we* now have given.'
"So unto them
Speak ye, and earnestly: then, afterward,
See ye that messengers and criers go
Throughout the city, and the lands around,
Proclaiming so my will. Now speed ye—speed:
Life, death, are on your steps. Away! away!"

Not tarrying to say word,—terror, and joy,
Contending in them,—in their tremulous hands,
From off the porphyry table, the rich gems
The princes eagerly snatched, and hurried forth;
And, to the priests and lords without, declared
The will of Pharaoh. With one impulse then,
At speed went all together to the house
Of Aaron; and on him, and Moses, cried,
Beseeching them before the king to go,
And stay the Plague.
"Even I, O Moses, I,
Thamusin, thy stern enemy of old,
Implore thee lift the curse. Mine eldest born
Hath fallen before it; and my second child
Suddenly lieth sick. Be merciful,
And take away the scourge!"

                            And even as he,
The stern High-priest,—so, with uplifted hands,
And tearful eyes, prayed all the priests and lords,—
Each mourning his first-born.
                            No word replied
The sons of Amram; but,—for well they knew
Summons would come; and ready stood prepared,—
Straight toward the palace sped.
                            The princes, priests,
And lords, meantime,—as the command had been,—
To the house of Aaron hastened,—jewels of gold,
And jewels of silver,—all that on them were,
And all the king had sent,—with eager hand
Unto the people giving. Nor refused
Any of these, when richest jewel of gold,
Or silver, was thrust on him; "for great debt
Ye owe to Israel,"—said they; "and the Lord
Willeth that thus ye do."
                            "Yea, and the *king*
So willeth," cried the prince; "and this the word
He sendeth to you. 'Get ye out with speed
From Egypt, all ye Hebrews;—even this night
Get ye all forth. Your young, your old, your flocks,
Your herds, your cattle,—whatsoe'er is yours,
Take with you, and depart. Now unto all
Your people this make known: and bid them ask,
Each of Egyptian neighbour, jewels of gold,
And jewels of silver,—as old custom is
Of guests departing,—for the king doth send
Command that such be given you, with free hand,
Even as we now have given.'
                            "So unto you,
Through me, saith Pharaoh. And we hasten now
Throughout the city, and the lands about,
Criers to send, and messengers,—who his will,
To all of Egypt, and of Israel, too,
Loudly shall trumpet forth. Lose not the hour,
Ye Hebrews; but, when next the sun shall rise,
In the desert let him see you."
                            "As thou say'st,"

2 E

Calmly a priest replied, "so do we mean;
So meant; for, wilt thou look upon us, prince,
Thou may behold the shoes upon our feet;
Our loins up-girt; the staffs within our hands;
All ready to set forth: our flocks, and herds,
And cattle, too, are ready; and, of food
For a long journey, such as may suffice:
And, ere the night shall pass, be sure we go;
For thus hath God commanded."
                              All this while,
Tremblingly Pharaoh waited; a great fear
Shaking him, lest no more should Moses trust
The tongue that four times to his God had lied;
But, in a righteous anger, should hound on
The Black Death; till all people it should strike,
And Egypt make one charnel-house. Distraught,
This way, and that, he looked, as rose the cries,—
Now, in the palace,—in the city, now,—
Now, shrieks of women; now, hoarse wails of men;
Now, all together rising, like the howl
Of a whole nation perishing. On the face
Of those about him,—on his own pale hands—
Anxiously stared he oft,—dreading to see
Death-shadow on them; and impatiently,
Still muttered; "Wherefore come they not? long since
Here had they been, so willed. Ah! bent are they
On vengeance; and will have it. Fool! fool! fool!
To hope that yet the fifth time would they trust
Who four times lies had spoken. Send ye forth,"—
At length aloud he cried,—"or haste yourselves,
Some of ye,—to the house of Aaron haste,
And hither bring them. No refusal hear;
But tell them . . . . . . Ha! they come."
                                    With staggering foot,
All pride o'erthrown, thus speaking, he went on;
And, half-way meeting them, with lifted hands,
Cried piteously: "Have mercy! stay this plague!
And by all gods of Egypt do I swear
Never to cross you more! But now, now, now,—
This instant stay it: for, like other plagues,

If three days, or but one, it ravage us,
Dead are we all! Already have I sent
Full word unto your people; and again
Thus do I speak it. Hasten, and get forth;
Both ye, and all of Israel, from the land.
Go—serve the Lord as ye have said: go all:
Horse, camel, mule, flocks, herds,—all that ye have,—
Take quickly, and be gone. . . . . . . And bless me too."

Upon the haggard face, and quivering limbs,
Silent awhile, the sons of Amram looked;
Noting the mortal terror; the hard heart,
Soft as an infant's; the great pride laid low;
The tongue, at last, truth speaking. But, even yet,
Misdoubted Moses, lest, what now firm fixed
As earth appeared,—might, under passion's blast,
Sway to and fro like water. Pondering thus,
Came back on him that vision terrible,
Erewhile in spirit seen,—an ocean depth,—
A host engulfed,—gone utterly, as stones,
In deep sea cast! . . . . . Had all illusion been?
A daylight dream,—sense wandering?—or, alas!
A flash from that great mirror, which on eye
Of prophet flings the future;—a thing fixed
As the hills, though unexistent? . . . . . Or, perchance,
A token had it been of what *would* be,—
Pharaoh repenting not, obeying not?
And, now,—repentant, and obedient,—
The doom might he not 'scape? . . . . . But, what if sin
Again he should commit? Again call back
The God-pledged word,—aiming again to gyve
The limbs of once freed Israel?—Verily, then,
Might the dread hand fall on them; yea, even so
As in the vision shadowed,—utterly
Overwhelming him, and all! With look awe-filled,
Voice solemn as low thunder at dead night,
And eyes that, like to fires on sea-cliff fixed,
Calm warning gave of peril,—thus, at length,
Lifting the hand, he spake.
                    "Thy words, O king,

Not by the tongue alone, as heretofore,
But from thy soul are spoken. What thou say'st,
That, truly, dost thou mean. Thy stony heart,—
As I foretold would be,—soft hath become,
Even as wax: thy stubborn oak of pride,
As a weak sapling. By power greater far
Than thine, subdued thou feelest; and dost bow
From topmost leaf to root; knowing how vain
Longer to stand resisting. But, the thoughts
Of man are foolish oft: though firmest set
On the right path to go,—yet, urged by pride,
By error led, too easily his feet
Turn off into the wrong; and to the pit,
Or quagmire bring him. If indeed thou seest
That by the veritable hand of God
Thou hast been smitten,—never more will pride,
Or hate, or lust of wealth, so blind thine eye,
That thou may think to oppose it. Well for thee,
If surely, then, thou knowest that God alone
All these great things hath done: but, if, alas!
Again, as heretofore, the power of spells,
Solely, thou deem thy vanquisher; if pride,
Wrath, hate, revenge, and hope of victory yet,
Again should madden thee to make a lie
Of promise to God spoken,—then, O king,
Cometh the end! Let not thy finger stir;
Speak thou not word,—make sign,—give look,—think
    thought,—
Aiming to bring back Israel, once gone forth;
Or, as the earth by deluge overwhelmed,
Beneath destruction infinite wilt thou lie,
Buried for ever! When the sun hath set,
Couldst thou recall him? bid him backward rise?
As little when, God-led, hath Israel passed
From out this Egypt,—may thou *him* bring back.
Here, face to face, stand we, who never more
Shall on each other look! word never more
Shall to each other speak! Be, then, thy last,
The words of truth: lie not again to God! . . . . .
As for this plague, already hath it ceased;

Your first-born all are dead. On them alone,—
Even as I said to thee,—the doom was sent.
It is accomplished. For thy sin 'twas sent:
Thou hast repented; and the firm word given
That Israel shall go forth. The rising sun
Will see him in the wilderness. Now, farewell.
My voice thou'lt hear no more : oh! on thy heart
Lettered for aye, as if on granite rock
Deep cut,—keep thou its warning! Haply, then,
The blessing which from me thou hast besought,
Even from the God of Israel may descend."

   Thus having spoken, Moses paused awhile,
Awaiting if the king might answer him.
But all distraught stood Pharaoh; haggard, and pale,
Confused, and trembling; a great terror, and grief,
Still racking him; and no word could he speak.
This when he saw,—to him, and to the queen,—
Who, at a distance standing, with moist eyes,
And hands hard pressed, looked on him anxiously,—
Moses, with pity filled, inclined the head,
Obeisance rendering. Aaron, too, bent low;
Then, with slow foot, together they went forth.

   On the instant, Sirois hurried to the king,—
By the hand caught him; and, with loving tone,
And brightening face, thus spake. "Oh Pharaoh dear!
At last thou hast done well; and never more,
Oh never more to folly wilt return!
Clear as in sunshine seest thou now, that God,
Jehovah, Israel's God, those fearful plagues
On thee, and Egypt, sent. For magic spells,
Think thou of them no more : nor let thy priests,
And sorcerers, as too oft, thy clearer thoughts
With their poor madness darken. Israel gone,
And gone for ever, Egypt will arise
Like a strong man whom sickness had bowed down,
When new health comes upon him as a flood,
And he goes forth rejoicing. Thank the gods
That now our night is gone, and daybreak come.

The past is past. If thou much evil mourn,
Think how much good remaineth: that the worst,
Worse tenfold might have been. Two sons thou hast;
Two daughters; and they love thee; thou lov'st them:
Oh Pharaoh! if that plague had smitten all!
Think, think; and be thou grateful to the God
Who, though incensed to the utmost, took but one!
Ponder on this; and let it comfort be;
But, oh, a warning too! Those terrible words
Forget thou never: think not even a thought
Of touching Israel more! . . . . . But, to thy bed
Return thou now, my Pharaoh; for yet night
Hath much to run; and oh, may gentle sleep,
Like a soft rain, fall on thee; and thy leaves
And flowers, now parched, to new life raise again;
That, as in spring's first freshness, they may bloom;
And once more all this land with fragrance fill."

ISRAEL IN EGYPT.

BOOK TWENTY-FIFTH.

STILL, of her course, two hours had night to run;
Yet, for departure so had all prepared;
So the Egyptians, fearing worse might come,
With prayers, and costliest gifts, had urged them on,—
That every Hebrew who in Zoan dwelled,
And round about, already had set forth
Toward Succoth: for, while yet the month was young,
From Moses had the strict command been sent,
That, on the evening of the fifteenth day,
There should all Israel gather. With glad hearts
Then journeyed they: on horse, mule, camel, or ass,
Some riding; but the multitude on foot;
Men, women, youths, and girls; all staff in hand;
Food, raiment, at their backs; within their vests,
The jewels of silver, and gold, cups, armlets, rings;
And every thing of cost, by Egypt given;
Even such in value as had been the spoil
Of a rich city conquered.
                          In light carts,
And wagons, drawn by oxen, or by mules,—
The aged, the sick, the infants, and the lame,
By women tended lovingly, were borne:
Also their household things, most needed; tools
Of iron, and of wood, which, on the way,

Chiefly would stead them,—hammer, spade, and saw,
Pickaxe, and iron bar; and spacious tents
For all the host of Israel.
                        Loosely ranked,
Yet not confused, went on the multitude:
But, in the midst, one band of vigorous men,—
From those select who in the Ethiop wars,
For Egypt, under Moses had drawn sword,—
In firm array, with warrior step marched on,
As if for battle; though nor sword, nor shield,
Nor any arms at all they had; but staffs
For travel only: their sole duty, now,
The bones of the great Patriarch to guard.
For, ere he died, had Joseph straightly sworn
The children of Israel, saying: "Surely God
Will visit you; and ye shall take my bones
Away hence with you." Therefore, that same night,
While yet 'twas early, Moses from the ground,
Wherein it lay, the hallowed chest had raised:
And now, with all meet pomp funereal
Attended; in an ark-like car, mule-drawn,
The holy relics went.
                      Clear moonlight shone
On the great multitude; and, from their walls
As the Egyptians looked,—vast as the sound
Of far-off sea, came to them the deep hum
Of countless voices; the thick tramp of feet;
The roll of wheels; the bleating of the sheep;
The neigh of horses, and the oxen's·low:
And, as they gazing stood, some, curses sent
Upon the Israelites; some, blessings prayed;
But all, as yet, were glad, that from the land,
At length they were departing: for a fear
On many had been that, even at the last,
As oft before, the proud king might recall
The promised grace; and, in return, might come
Plague even more horrible yet.
                           Morning drew near;
Pale waxèd the moonlight; and the eastern sky
Its fires 'gan kindle. Louder and louder then

Arose glad voices; for all hearts rejoiced;
Feeling that bondage was behind them now;
Before them, freedom, and hope. While on they sped,—
From north, and south, joined with them multitudes;
And, as they drew together, still went up
Long peals of exultation.
      Toward the land
Of Goshen not yet half-way had they reached,
When, underneath a canopy of cloud,
Splendid, and many-hued as sea of gems,
Upsoared the lord of day; for weary years,
The first sun that on Israel had arisen,
Not seeing him a slave. And ne'er before
On him had Israel looked, and glory such,
Felt in his rising. Over all the sky,
Seemed that his rays, in letters of golden light,
Had written "FREEDOM:" in the air it was,
Like an ethereal wine; at every step,
Earth thrilled it through them; in the song of birds,
They heard it carolled; the leaves whispered it;
The streamlets hummed; the hill-tops sang aloud:
All earth, and the great arch of heaven, at once,
As with loud voice, the proclamation made,
" FREEDOM TO ISRAEL!" Not one soul there was,—
Even of the sick, the aged, the suffering most,—
In which joy, like an inner sun, shone not.
Behind them was thick blackness; but, before,
Visions of glory for all life to come.

Thus on, yet slowly, went they; till, at length,
Nigh to the land of Goshen as they drew,—
Behold, descending from the mound, a host
Even as the stars in number! At that sight,
Joyfully shouted they; and, in reply,
Such clamor rose, that, with the double roar,
Air quivered; and the birds affrighted fled;
And, in the far off desert, the wild beast
Sprang up, and hearkened. Who in Zoan walked,
Stopped, and looked round, and marvelled at the din:
And even Pharaoh, from hot slumber waked,

Sprang up, and listened. Dark then grew his brow,
And his heart throbbed: for, as in maddening dreams,
His pride and wrath to inflame, had Satan wrought,
Picturing of Israel's glory, his own shame,—
So now, though broad awake, and quick to hear,
Sense so the demon ruled, that, in the acclaim
Of meeting brethren,—love and joy alone
All speaking unto all,—the voice he heard
Of triumph, and of mockery. Laughter, too,
Distinct he heard,—the vast uproarious laugh
Of Israel's insolent myriads: over him,
Even him, the Splendor of the Sun, that dross
Daring to triumph!
      Like the first small cloud
Above the horizon, telling storm at hand,—
Loomed on his soul the black thought that, even still,
Vengeance might seize them! But, as yet, worst rage,
By fear was mastered. "What if that same Power
Which, as with lightning, had the son shrunk up,—
Incensed anew, the father next should strike!"
Thought horrible! He shuddered; with both hands
His ears pressed closely,—the detested sound
All to shut out; then on the pillow sank,
Muttering; and waited till the din should cease.

  Meantime, with swifter foot, as they drew nigh,
Both hosts of Israel moved; in van of each,
Elders, and priests, with all their families.
On a fleet steed, gift of Egyptian lord,
Rode Moses: and when, coming on, he saw,
'Mong other friends of old, those chosen ones,
Rachel, and Reuben, Kohath, Malachi,
And timid Sarah, now with joy all bright,—
Forth rode he cheerfully; and from his steed
Alighted: they, too, from their beasts sprang down;
With others, on both sides; and eagerly
Met in the midst, embracing, and embraced:
All blessing, by all blest. But, on that pair,
The maid and youth, chiefly were blessings poured;
And them, and all their kindred, Moses prayed

Near to himself to journey,—so his eye
Ever might be upon them; from all harm,—
If possible harm were,—to guard them still.
Gladly consented they, and with him went:
And soon, though with slight order,—in one stream
The two great rivers mingled, and flowed on.

At eve, to Succoth came they; and new hosts
There waiting found: and still again went up
The peals of exultation. But, though great
That city, for one tenth of Israel
Room had it not. Of men for battle fit,
Six hundred thousand were they; of the rest,—
Old men, and youths, women, and girls, and babes,—
Four times that number: therefore on the plain,
All round the city, under tents they camped:
Their simple food took cheerfully: thanks, prayer,
And praise to God, with glowing hearts sent up:
Then, stretched on earth,—first free bed they had known;
Hard, yet more soft than down, with slavery,—
In happy slumber lay.
                     But, ere the sun
On the next morrow rose, all were astir,
Their journey to renew. Around him then,
From every tribe, the chief men Moses called,
And well instructed them, in fashion best
How such great host should move: confusion else
Must come upon them. After they had heard,
And well had understood,—each to his tribe
Swiftly returned. But, ere in order meet
For travel, all those myriads could be ranged,
The sun, high mounted, from a cloudless sky
Shone hotly on them; and their course was slow.

Toward Etham,—for a young and vigorous foot,
Not three hours' travel,—marched they; but, such toil
To women, to the young, and weak, it was,
That, ere they reached it, eve was drawing nigh.
Again upon the plain, each tribe apart,
As they had journeyed, joyfully they camped:

Again their light food took; praise, prayer, again
To heaven sent up; and soon in sleep were wrapped.

Early at morning, once more summons went,—
The Elders, priests, and chief men of each tribe,
Calling together. When they all had met,—
Standing before them, Aaron at his side,
Thus Moses spake. "To Canaan, as ye know,
Finally go we: but, by way direct,
Permitted not: for, when at night I stood
On Horeb; and the voice of God had heard,
Commanding how to Pharaoh I should go,
And out of Egypt bring forth Israel,—
Then also thus it spake: 'When thou hast brought
The people out of Egypt, on this mount
Shall ye serve God; and this a token shall be
That I have sent thee.' Toward the holy hill
Therefore I led you,—not the nearer way
To promised Canaan, through Philistine land;
Wherein, moreover, enemies had we found,
Prompt to withstand us. But again the voice
Of the Lord God, even in the night just passed,
Hath come unto me, saying; 'At morn speak thou
Unto the children of Israel, that they turn
Toward Pi-hahiroth, and before it camp,
'Twixt Migdol and the sea; right opposite
To Baal-zephon: by the sea-shore there,
Before it shall ye camp.' . . . . . What more was said,
I tell not now: but ye shall see how God
Will His great Hand Omnipotent put forth
For full deliverance. Quickly, then, return;
And speak unto the people; that with haste
They get them ready: for the way is long;
And if, while day is young, they set not forth,
Within the wilderness of the Red Sea
Night will entangle them."
                         Thus having said,
The assembly he dismissed: and, in brief time,
Throughout the host of Israel was it known
How God their course had ordered. With great joy

Then made they ready; and, ere second hour
Of day had wasted,—in ten separate bands,
Each broad as a great river, they marched on.
The hum of their glad voices, and the tread
Of that vast multitude, was like the sound
Of storm amid the forest.
                     But, anon,
Fell on them a dead silence: for, behold!
A tower-like pillar, dark as thundercloud;
Higher than loftiest pine; solid as rock
Appearing,—yet foundationed not on earth,—
Suddenly stood before them! Every eye
In the same moment saw it; every foot
Hurriedly stopped; and every heart beat loud,
For marvel, and fear. But, heaven-taught, Moses knew
Therein a sign from Heaven; and, turning round,
His voice uplifted.
                  "Be ye not afraid,
Children of Israel; for, what ye behold,
A token is from God that His ye are,
And that He guideth you. Within yon cloud
God's angel is; and, wheresoe'er it move,
There must we follow; asking not of man
Whereto it leadeth; fearing not, though rock,
Or gulf, or roaring sea, lie in the way:
For, Him obeying, through the deep, unwet;
Through fire, unsinged; through pestilence, and sword,
Unharmed shall we go on. Bow therefore down,
And worship God: and, after ye have prayed,
Arise; and let all voices send to Heaven
Our chorus of thanksgiving."
                         When he thus,
And with great voice, by thousands clearly heard,
Had spoken,—lighting from his horse, he kneeled,
Covered his face, and prayed. As he, so all:
And, like the moaning of a troubled sea,
Went up the sound of myriads,—with low voice,
Fervently worshipping. When they had risen,
And silent stood again—lifting his arm,
Moses began the song.

                        Even from the time
Of Abraham, to all Israel had that hymn
Been as a heart-voice,—glory unto God,
Praise and thanksgiving rendering. Every soul,
At the first word, caught fervor; every voice
Outpoured it; the weak pipe of trembling age;
Manhood's deep organ, and the clarion breath
Of fiery-blooded youth; heart-thrilling tones
Of woman in her summer, and clear ring
Of maidens, and young boys; while, over all,—
Like a bright spray above that sea of sound,—
Went up, from tens of myriads, the sweet song
Of childhood innocent. Every quivering hand
Was lifted; every gleaming eye, tear-filled,
Heavenward was turned. As, to the eagle aloft,
Ascends the roar of ocean, tempest-torn,
So, unto listening angels, in mid sky,
Pealed up the hymn of that vast multitude.

    The chorus ended: and, for little while,
Again all silent stood; tears wiping off,
Strength gathering; for, with that great ecstacy,
Even *soul* had seemed exhaling. Soon again
Was every head uplifted; every face
With a great joy was bright. Upon his beast
Sprang every rider; every foot moved on;
But every tongue was mute,—in such deep awe,
On the vast pillar of cloud all eyes were fixed,
Feeling God's angel there. Invisible
Its motion, yet before them still it went;
And, where it led, they followed.
                                    At high noon,
Steadfast it stood. Moses the meaning knew,
And bade the trumpets sound. Joyfully all
The signal heard,—for weary and faint they were,—
Then took forth food, and drink; and on the ground,
Panting, yet cheerful, sat, and were refreshed;
And talked together of that wondrous sign,
And all their God's great mercies: then, at last,
Covering their heads, at full length lay them down:

And soon o'er all that mighty multitude
A heavy slumber fell.
                    Three hours they slept;
But, by command of Moses summoned then,
'Gan waken: in a great amazement most,
Where they might be: yet, in a little while,
All to their feet arose; and eagerly
For the tower-pillar looked. There stood it still,
Sign of a present God, to guide and guard.
Unbidden, to the knee they sank, and prayed;
Then rose, and, waiting, stood; all in high hope;
By slumber sound refreshed; and in good heart
Their journey to renew: for now the sun,
By thick clouds mantled, poured no longer down
His withering fervor; and a fresh north wind
Brought lightness to their limbs. At length was heard
The silver trumpet's sound, signal of march;
And the vast host moved on.
                            Before them far,
Mountains, and rocks, they spied: and when, toward eve,
Nearer they drew, all marvelled; for, straight on,
As if to o'erclimb them, went the pillar of cloud;
And how might mortal follow! Silently,
And in deep awe, moved on the multitude:
Till, nigh the base of the hill-range arrived,
Rocks so precipitous saw they,—wings alone,
It seemed, might scale them. Still the cloud went on:
But, 'twixt the roots of two great hills, at last,
Pausing, wide passage showed. Prompt order then
Sent Moses, in what manner every tribe
Should enter; so, for easy march, might be
Free space to all. The tribe of Levi first,
In fit array went forward; and the cloud,
Which in the entrance of the gorge, till then,
Like a huge tower to bar the way, had stood,
Moved on before them. Tribe by tribe was formed;
Confused awhile, but orderly at last;
And, as commanded, marched. A wondrous length
Stretched out that human river,—flowing slow,
Yet not in silence; for the tread of man;

The tramp of beasts; the roll and jar of wheels;
The voices of the myriads,—mid high rocks
Echoing, and echoed back,—loud seemed as roar
And boiling of great billows.
                              Ere one half
Had entered in the gorge, the sun went down;
And darkness quickly fell. But, then, behold,
Wonder of wonders! what, by day, had been
A pillar of cloud to marshal them the way,—
Suddenly, now, a pillar of fire became,
To guide them through the night! Like new-risen sun
It flamed; and on the low-hung vault of cloud
Cast crimson; that the mountain-tops shone out;
And the deep pass,—else steeped in blackest gloom,—
Lay clear for the free footstep. Wondering, paused
The myriads; and the hand of God, again
Put forth to aid them, saw. Even as one man,
In the same moment the whole multitude
Bent down the head, and worshipped.
                                    The mid hour
Of night had come, ere; from the long defile,
The rearmost tribe had issued. Vanished then
The pillar of fire; and heavy darkness fell,
Earth and sea hiding. But, in little while,
As sight recovered, the clear-shining moon,
And glittering stars they saw; and, with glad hearts,
Their labors plied. Already on the plain
Myriads of tents stood pitched, ere from the pass
The rear had come; for still, as they arrived,
By Moses ordered, every tribe its place
In quiet took; and preparation made
To camp them for the night.
                            Soon, all was done:
Hunger and thirst were stayed; thanksgiving, prayer,
To God sent up; then, stretched upon the ground,
In the great fulness of their happiness,
To sleep serene they sank. On the vast plain
Near Pi-hahiroth, close unto the shore,
'Twixt Migdol and the sea; right opposite
To Baal-zephon, Israel lay encamped.

No foot was now astir; no voice was heard;
No sound, save of the low, deep breath of sleep,
From all those numberless,—like the steady moan
Of night-wind mid some antique forest afar;
Or, sometimes, the faint plash of slow-paced wave,
Washing the pebbly shore; or distant howl
Of wild beast mid the mountains. Fear was none
In any soul of Israel: not one eye
Waked to behold the hills that shut them in
On every side; save where, worse barrier, lay
The impassable sea. None doubtful was, how thence
Might they depart; none of pursuit had dread:
Beneath a sky serene, and glorious,
With moon, and sun-like stars all burning bright,
Soundly they slept; and knew not that, even then,
The chariots of all Egypt, and the horse,
Hotly were gathering; that, like thunderbolts,
They might fall on them, and slay utterly;
Or to yet worse captivity drive back.

ISRAEL IN EGYPT.

BOOK TWENTY-SIXTH.

FOR, day and night, by restless demons stirred,—
Like many fires in one combustion joined,—
King, sorcerers, priests, rulers, and captains all,
One monstrous yell of wrath and hate sent up,
'Gainst Israel, 'scaped at last! "Ah infamous!"
Roared out the king: "poison, or spells alone,
Those murders did,—no god: ye have no god,—
Yours only: nay, a veritable god
Such deed had scorned. Reptiles detestable!
I will fall on you: I will root you out;
Destroy you to the last,—man, woman, and child:
Or bring you back, with cord, and whip, and chain,
To your old slavery. Ho! send instantly;
And summon all my chariots, and my horse.
I will pursue. Haply in Goshen still
Some days they'll tarry. As the ox the corn,
So will I trample them. Send out,—send out.
Who knoweth of them,—by what way they went,
And whither bound?"
     Promptly a voice replied:
"Toward Goshen went they, Splendor of the Sun;
Bound, as they said, to Canaan; by the land

Of the Philistines. Swords will strike them there;
And save our labor."
                              "Nay, nay," stormed the king;
" With my own sword I'll strike them,—I alone:
Vengeance is mine, not the Philistines. Scum!
I'll sweep them from the earth. Even stay they not
One day in Goshen,—yet, ere the dull snake
To Gaza creep, our lion shall spring on,
And seize it, fang and claw."
                              While yet he spake,
Entered in haste two men; and toward the throne
Advanced, and bowed, and stood as they would speak.
Faces like flame they had; and from their brows
Sweat like great rain-drops fell: from head to foot,
Mere dust their raiment seemed. With eyes fire-bright,
And quivering lips, upon the king they looked,
Anxiously waiting. Their disordered state
Told plainly, that of some momentous thing
Came they to speak: therefore at once the sign
Permissive gave he; and at once bowed both;
Both in quick speech began: but then the one,
Frowning, his comrade silenced; and, again
Toward Pharaoh looking, spake. " O, Light of Day,—
Surely the gods of Egypt have at last
Arisen, to lift thee up, and strike to earth
The miscreants who have plagued us! Mad, or blind,
Of their own will into a net they go,
Where easily every man, woman, and child,
Horse, ox, mule, camel; all the silver, and gold,
And precious stones,—yea, all that they have begged,
Or stolen, may thou seize! Wilt thou believe,
O Pharaoh, that the cunning sorcerer
Such folly could do? Yet, as I live, 'tis so!
South, toward the Red Sea, hath he led them on:
And even this night, 'twixt Migdol and the shore,
Near Pi-hahiroth, and right opposite
To Baal-zephon, will all Israel camp."

" How know ye this?" with hurried speech, and eyes
Eager and flashing, cried the impatient king.

"Light of the Sun," came forth the quick reply,
"With our own ears we heard it; and by mouth
Even of Moses spoken. Through report
Had it come to us, we had shut the sense,
As 'gainst a lie; for the mere fool alone,
Or madman, so could stumble. Dullest beast
Would not walk open-eyed into the trap:
Yet so doth Moses: for, throughout the earth,
Had he searched for it, spot he had not found,
Wherein so utterly, as in a net,
All Israel might be taken. Rock, and hill,
Impassable even to goat, or wilder thing,
On three sides gird that plain,—and, on the fourth,
The waters of the sea. By one sole pass
Can it be reached; by that alone be left.
If, therefore, when the slaves therein are trapped,
Thou wouldst destroy them, needeth but few spears,
To bar escape,—and famine will slay all.
If, rather, to just servitude again
Thou'dst force them,—when for hunger they shall howl,—
On hand and knee crawling, let them come forth,
And lick the dust before thee. They are thine,
O Pharaoh, body and soul; to slay, or take.
But, as the lightning must thy vengeance fly,
Or they will 'scape thee: for, tomorrow's sun
Quickly will show them in what pit they have fallen:
And, verily, far swifter than they went,
Will they speed back: and if, on the open plain,
At distance first they see thy coming on,—
Like small birds, when the eagle's shadow falls,
Wide scattering they'll fly off; and leave behind
The old and feeble only; then . . . ."
                                        "Stay, stay,"
Cried Pharaoh, frowning;—"what the king should do,
Needeth he not be taught. But tell me now,
And briefly,—where was Moses, when these words
Ye heard him speak? Moreover, by what chance,
Among the Hebrews were ye?"
                                        "Light of Day,"
Quick was the answer; "curious to behold

How they would fare, and whither they would go,
We with the Israelites journeyed. The first night,
At Succoth camped they: on the second night,
At Etham: on the third,—even this day's night—
Near to Azotus purposed they to lie.
But other course, meantime, had been resolved.
Ere yet 'twas sunrise, the whole camp was up:
For all the priests, and Elders, and chief men,
To Moses had been summoned. Following them,
Went we; and, on the outskirts of the throng,
Unnoted stood, and heard. Of slight account
The things that first were spoken; but, at length,
Mountain-high grew they; and on memory pressed,
Like horse-foot on soft clay: and, word for word,
O king, thus Moses spake. 'Again the voice
Of the Lord God, even in the night just gone,
Hath come unto me, saying; At morn speak thou
Unto the children of Israel, that they turn
Toward Pi-hahiroth; and before it camp,
'Twixt Migdol and the sea; right opposite
To Baal-zephon: by the seashore there
Before it shall ye camp.'
"Needed no more
That we should listen; for the place we knew,
Well as this Zoan: natives thereof, both;
And therein dwellers till these ten years past;
And knew that, entered, 'twould a prison be,
Stronger than walls of stone, and fetters of steel,—
Barred thou the outlet. Not a moment more
Tarried we then; but, at our swiftest, sped;
Sprang on our steeds; and never bridle drew
Till nigh unto the gate. Our own feet then
Deeming the swifter,—so the wearied beasts
Stumbled, and reeled,—down leaped we, and ran on;
Of our soiled garments heedless,—even though here
Into thy presence coming,—when the thing
We had to tell, must be as life, or death,
Unto thine enemies."
"Rightly have ye done;
And shall have honor," said the king, well pleased.

"But tell me truly now. The whole way hence
To yonder pass, and through it to their camp,
So surely know ye, that your lives ye'll gage,
Down on them suddenly to bring us all,
Both horse and chariots?"
                              "Come not second plague
Of hail, or darkness, or like sorcery,—
Though ten lives had we, Splendor of the Sun,
All would we peril. Every brook, and hill,
And landmark by the way, to Migdol hence,
Well as this city know we."
                              "Then at dawn
Be ye at hand. With chariot near the king's
Shall ye be honored: and, ere set of sun,
If ye bring Pharaoh on them,—all your lives
Shall be a summer. Lords, and rulers, hence.
Wherever they may lie, send ye the word;
Commanding every chariot, every horse,—
This day, or in the night, or by grey dawn,—
To the plain east of Zoan. Long ere sun
Touch point of pyramid, will the king appear,
To lead them on."
                    That said, down from the throne
He hurried. Lords, priests, captains, sorcerers, then,
All talking loud, all mad with joy, rushed forth.

Soon flew command; and proclamation went
Throughout the city, and the lands around;
Till, with the din of gathering,—like a camp
For battle arming in haste,—half Egypt rang.

But, these sad tidings when the queen had heard,
Terror, yea even a quaking of the soul,
Came on her,—as though voice from heaven itself
Pharaoh's death-doom had spoken! Trembling, pale,
She hastened; on her knees before him fell;
Wept, prayed, nay shrieked in her great agony:
"Oh Pharaoh, Pharaoh, hear me! If again
Thou mock the God of Israel, never more
These eyes shall see thee; never more thine eyes

Will on thy children look, thy once loved wife!
The grave will swallow thee! I see black Death
Standing to smite! Loved Pharaoh, go not hence!
Remember how the threats of Israel's God
All were fulfilled: and that last terrible threat,—
Last, and most terrible,—sure as stroke of fate
Will fall upon thee, if again thou sin!
Hearken the words, O Pharaoh; as with fire,
They are burnt in me: 'Let not thy finger stir;
Speak thou not word,—make sign,—give look,—think
    thought,—
Aiming to bring back Israel, once gone forth;
Or, as the earth by deluge overwhelmed,
Beneath destruction infinite wilt thou lie,
Buried for ever!'"
                    Roughly from his knees
Pharaoh her hands shook off,—then backward drew,
And with stern voice exclaimed; "A fool thou art;
Vex me no more: if god the Hebrews had,
Here was his power: elsewhere as nought it is.
But, over those vile slaves, here, everywhere,
My power shall be. No! finger I'll not stir;
Make sign, think thought against them; but I'll take
Chariots, and horse, and trample them to dust.
Then let their god destruction infinite
Send on me, if he can! Away, away:
Plead thou no longer: see my face no more,
Till, victor, I come back. I hear thee not:
I will not hear: farewell."
                    With hurried step,
Thus speaking, from the chamber he went forth:
And the queen fell upon the floor, and wept.
Throughout the day sternly did he refuse,
When messenger she sent, with humble prayer,
That she might visit him: his loved daughters, too,—
Urged by the queen to implore him,—with harsh words,
Drove he away: for, demon-fired he was,
And rushing on destruction.
                    Through that night,
Round Zoan was the sound of gathering war;

Voices of men; the neigh and tramp of steeds;
The roll of wheels: and, with first grey of dawn,
All the eastern plain was thronged; in panoply
Of battle bright stood so great armament.
Six hundred chosen chariots; and, with them
The chariots of all Egypt; and the horse,
Five times ten thousand,—such the number was,—
All men of war, and thirsting for their blood,
Whom now, against defenceless Israel,
The mad, doomed monarch led.
                                Like to the sound
Of flooded cataract was their setting forth.

   Crowding the eastern wall, women and men,
With anxious looks,—silent, or talking low,
Gazed after them; some, hoping vengeance sharp
Would fall on guileful Israel; many, in doubt
Lest on all Egypt even worse plagues might come;
And many, pale with terror, lest some ill,—
They knew not what,—but horrible and strange
Beyond all else,—on Pharaoh, and his host,—
Through sorcery, or from Israel's wrathful God—
Destruction utter should bring. Till from their sight
The rearmost rank had vanished, thus they stood;
Then hurried from the wall: and in the streets,
And public places, gathering into groups,
Their thoughts spake one to the other. Voices loud,
And rough, at times were heard; but, more and more,
As the day waned, they sank: and when, at length,
The sun went down, and men 'gan homeward walk,—
So dark a terror crept upon them all,
That through the city was one sound alone;
A low deep murmur, as of voices hushed
In chamber of the dead.

ISRAEL IN EGYPT.

BOOK TWENTY-SEVENTH.

HASTY, and fierce,—
Though like a shower of fire the sunbeams poured,—
Pharaoh drove onward, till both horse and man
With toil were faint, panting, and bathed with sweat;
With thirst nigh frenzied. But yet onward—on,
Pointed the guides,—still on,—till gleamed, at length,
Nor distant, a broad stream; and, nigh its banks,
Fresh grass, trees overhanging, and thick groves,
Where night seemed hiding. To the cool shade come,—
They slacked the armour,—laid aside the helm,—
With food, and drink, themselves and steeds refreshed—
Sank on the ground, and slept. Four hours they slept;
Then, with new strength, set forth. Once more, at foot
Of the great mountain barrier, they made pause;
Again took food, and rest,—that man, and horse,
With full force might fall on; then, while the sun
Yet two hours had to travel,—at high speed,
Burning to slay, or capture, through the pass
Began to thunder. Meantime, all that day,
Till toward the evening, in calm confidence,
And full content,—still trusting in their God,
Israel had rested. From that rock-girt plain,
Toward Horeb journeying, how they might go out,

Curious to know,—many at morn had sped;
And every rock, and hill, from end to end,
Heedfully searched: but, that one pass except,
Through which by night they had entered, none had found.
To all the people soon had this been told:
Yet, for awhile, mere wonder did it raise,
And busy talk: for, of pursuit, no fear
Now had they; and in Moses put firm trust:
Nay, willingly, in that sweet solitude,
Weeks would have passed; clambering the rocks for flowers,
Unknown before; or, newer pleasure still,
Along the sea beach wandering.
      But, at length,
A faithless few, who rather in the gods
Of Egypt had believed,—from infancy
Instructed so,—than in the one sole God,—
Doubts and fears raised among them. "Wherefore here
Hath Moses brought us?" said they: "If the king,—
As oft before,—repent him, and pursue,
Escape for us is none. Through that same pass.
Whereby we entered, 'gainst us will he come:
And, like pent sheep, here must we wait the knife;
Or, as a flock, driven by his dogs of war,
Go back to bondage. If, as Moses said,
To Horeb are we bound,—wherefore, we ask,
To this mere cage conduct us,—this rock-net,—
This trap for a whole people,—this broad pit,
Leading to nothing? Why, no foot of way
Toward Horeb can we go, till, step by step,
We tread back all the march of yesterday.
Plain 'tis that, of himself, he knoweth not
Aright to guide us; and that marvellous voice,—
God's, as he thought,—which hither bade us come,
Perchance a dream was, only. Fit it were
He should be questioned, wherefore to this den
He hath brought us; how long here shall we sojourn
And by what way depart."
      With words like these,

Much discontent, and doubt, and dread, they raised;
And, gathering round them soon a multitude,
To seek him hastened.   Close unto the shore
Had Levi, first arriving, pitched their tents:
And Moses, at that hour, on the steep beach
Seated at ease,—to Zipporah his wife,
And his two sons; to Kohath, Malachi,
Sarah, and Rachel, and Reuben, held discourse
On the great wonders of the sea; and, chief,
Of the vast ocean deeps; to which compared,
That Red Sea were a streamlet: but, through all,
Still pointing out the wisdom, and the might
Of Him who all created.   While he spake,
Came one who said, " The people ask for thee,
O Moses; wilt thou come, and speak with them?"

Then the great leader rose; and, without word
Of question, followed.   To the open space,
'Twixt tribes of Levi, and of Benjamin,
When he had come,—behold, a concourse great,
Restless, and noisy; hundreds of quick tongues
Talking together.   But, as he drew nigh,
The hubbub ceased; and when, with gentle tone,
He spake; enquiring wherefore him they sought,—
So, by the majesty of mien, and voice,
O'erawed were they, that, for awhile, none there
The offensive word dared speak.   At length stood forth
Pildash,—a headstrong, discontented man;
Ever the first, against authority,
To wag the tongue: and, with what face he might,
That nobleness confronting, sourly thus.

" Our thoughts are troubled, Moses; for much doubt
Is come among the people, lest, perplexed,
Or ignorant of the way, into a trap
Thou have misled us.   If to Horeb bound,
Ere Canaan entering,—as thyself didst say,—
Why hither are we brought; from our straight course
So wandering; and by long, and weary way,

Which all must be retrodden, ere again
To the right path we come; and where, meanwhile,
If Pharaoh fall upon us, we must die
As cattle in the shambles. Furthermore,
The people murmur,—asking how long here
They shall be prisoned: and by what way hence
They may escape, if through that one sole pass,
Known to us all, the enemy should come.
Surely, though none else know it, *thou* must know
Some way of safety for us! Madness, else,
Stark madness only, to a pit like this
Could have led Israel; to a very trap,
Wherein, if Pharaoh find us, every soul
He may smite dead; or scourge with whips of steel,
And drive back to yet heavier slavery.
So in their trouble do the people talk:
And now they call upon thee, to expound
Wherefore it thus hath been; and what the next
Thou dost design for them."
                              With solemn voice,
And look severe, then Moses made reply.
" Not Israel speaketh thus, but thou thyself,
And some few like to thee,—infirm of faith,
Of spirit fractious: ever, in the best,
The worst espying: honey into gall
Eager to turn; sunshine to stormy night.
To you I speak no more ; or not as yet,
Till the dark spirit leave you; and your eyes
Be opened, and your turbulent hearts be stilled.
But, to *you*, men of Israel, half seduced
By these bold impious into discontent,
And fear, now speak I. Wherefore cry ye out,
Echoing these reasonless, that ye are brought
Into a snare? BY CLEAR COMMAND OF GOD,
Here are we camped! How long we shall remain,—
Whither we next shall go,—and by what way,—
Leave we to Him; who, when the hour hath come,
The word will send unto us; and the sign
To lead us on. By day, a pillar of cloud,
By night, a pillar of fire, before us went,

Hither to bring us;—and that sign again,
Doubt not, when He so ordereth, will appear,
Hence to conduct us. And, where'er it guide,—
Though over mountains, must we follow it;
Though o'er the waters of the sea it go,—
Even on the waters must we plant the foot,
Fearless; for, wheresoe'er it leadeth,—there,
Be sure, God will uphold us. Rest ye then,
In quietness of soul; and humbly wait
What things soever He may do for us.
Care for your women, and your little ones,
That they lack nothing: and yourselves take rest;
And be in all things ready; for the hour
No man can tell, when hence we must depart;
Or if in peace, or if before the sword;
Nor what may be the labor of the way.
List not again to words of discontent,
From unbelieving lips; but worship God;
In Him place all your trust: for, be assured,
Though ye the way see not, His gracious hand
Is over us, our deliverance working out.
Now, all who hear me, go among the rest,
And bid their hearts be still."
       These gentle words,
With a mild dignity spoken, struck with shame
The discontented; and the weak made strong;
The doubtful made assured. Forthwith they went,
And mingled with their brethren; and spake out
The words of Moses: and, in little while,
All were again at peace.
      But, brief the calm!
While in their tents at evening-meal they sat,
Quiet, and happy,—suddenly, a dread shout,
Wild, horrible,—for demons swelled the cry,—
Tore through the air. Upstarting, pale with dread,
Forth hurried they; and lo! on a great height
Midway the pass,—red in the westering sun,
Like hurricane of flame,—the shining cars
And steel-clad horse of Egypt rushing on!
Spears and swords shaking aloft, exultingly

On came they; mad for vengeance; yelling aloud:
For, though in shadow of the mountains lay,
The myriad tents, yet the keen vulture eyes,
Outpeering, had beheld; the iron beaks,
The wide-spread talons, longed to clutch, and rend.

   As though by palsy stricken,—a brief while,
Speechless, and trembling, Israel stood, and gazed;
Then a great wail sent up,—for all saw death
Immediate coming on them. To the ground
Some cast themselves; some beat upon their breasts,
And tore their hair, and gnashed their teeth, and cursed;
Some rent their garments, running here and there;
Women and children shrieked out franticly;
And the whole multitude swayed to and fro,
Like forest in the storm.
                    Soon rose again,
But louder far, clamors of discontent
'Gainst Moses; "who to that perdition had brought
The foolish, credulous people;" "Let us go
And curse him," cried out some, "for he alone
Hath led us to this death; trusting in dreams,
And voices, madness-gendered."
                          "Let us run
And stone him," Pildash bellowed.
                              "Hear him first,"
Cried others; "for a way he yet may know
To lead us hence."
                 "Then must he bore the hills,
Or float us o'er the waters," came reply;
"For other way is none."
                       "Still trust in God,"
Spake out aloud one voice; "in God still trust,
And in His servant Moses. Hearken not,
Children of Israel, to the wicked tongues;
For they are stings of scorpions. Be ye men;
And have good heart,—whether to live, or die.
Be silent, and be firm; and, orderly,
Let us go on, and hear what shall be said
By Moses, and by Aaron: better they

Will teach us, than these ignorant, and mad,
Spiteful, and full of lies."
"He speaketh well,"
Cried many.
"Nay, he speaketh like a fool,"
Pildash called out, "a poor deluded fool;
And fools ye, if ye hearken. But, away;
Let us find Moses,—talk if ye must have,—
And hear what he can say: rare comfort now!"

Thousands of voices clamoring eagerly,
Then went the people on. Throughout the camp,
In like way, toward the tents of Levi pressed
The strong men; but the agëd, and the weak,
The women, and the children, stayed behind,
Weeping and wailing,—all eyes terror-fixed
On the great living cataract of war,
Speeding to bury them.
To the open place
Where stood the car which bore the honored bones
Of the great patriarch, hastily had sped
Moses, and Aaron, with the Elders, and priests
Of Levi; and, of other tribes at hand,
Elders, and priests, no few: and, from the rest,
Still came they in; and multitudes besides,
With a great clamor running; crying aloud
On Moses; some, imploring,—cursing, some;
All thrusting, struggling, who should nighest stand,
That they might hear him speak. Tents were o'erthrown
By the fast swelling flood, and trampled on:
Women, and children, shrieked, and wildly ran,
As from the sword. Confusion, and dismay,
Worse than of Babel was. But, mid the storm,
On a low mount,—far seeing,—seen from far,
Serenely still stood Moses: at his side,
Aaron alone; and, 'neath them, round the base,—
In silence, but with troubled countenance,
A throng of priests, and Elders. Bitter words
Flew from the multitude,—"traitor, dreamer, fool!"
Some bellowed; "Israel's blood is on thy head!
Thou hast betrayed us!"

"Stone him!" Pildash yelled:
"He hath slain us all,—let him the first be slain!"

"Were there no graves in Egypt?" others cried,
"That in the wilderness we are brought to die?"

"Why hast thou thus dealt with us?"
"Said we not,
Let us alone, that we in Egypt may serve?"

"And better far for Israel had it been,
To serve the Egyptians, than that we should come
To perish in the wilderness."
But then
Rose other voices. "Moses, speak to us;
For yet we trust in thee, and in our God."

"Be silent, men of Israel; and stand still,
That we may hear."
Then Moses stretched his arms,
Attention asking: but, when yet the din
Abated not, toward heaven his face he raised,
And clasped hands, as in prayer. The sun had set;
Twilight to dusk was hasting; yet, distinct
As though a beam from heaven had kindled it,
Brightly his countenance shone. When that they saw,
Silence fell on the people. Moses then,
Pointing toward heaven, with power spake out, and said.

"Know ye who made the sun, the stars, the moon,
All yon vast arch of Heaven? Know ye the hand
That fashioned earth; and with his waters filled
The beds of the deep seas? . . . . Is He not God,
Yea God of Israel? . . . . Think ye that yon king
Is greater yet than He? . . . . A thousand years
The might of all the Pharaohs, first, and last,—
To the full put forth,—hath but few pyramids, towers,
And cities built: but the sole word of God,
In six days made the heavens, the earth, the sea,
Sun, moon, and stars; and every thing that is.

Can, then, *one* Pharaoh do, *against* you, more
Than, *for* you, God? . . . 'But, *will* God help?'—-ye ask.
Ah! men of little faith! have ye not seen
The wondrous things already for us done?
Ten plagues,—the like of which, through all the earth,
Never were known before, hath He not sent
On Egypt, to force Pharaoh let us go?
When all the waters of the land were blood,—
Egypt even mad for thirst,—gave He not us
Of crystal springs to drink? When frogs, lice, flies,
Tormented them,—touched they one Israelite?
Of murrain when their beasts by thousands died,—
Fell there of ours even one? When Egypt burned
With ulcerous blotches,—was one Hebrew foul?
When the hail slew its thousands, men and beasts
Of Egypt,—harmed it one of Israel?
Mid the thick darkness over all the land,
When Pharaoh and his people were as blind,—
Had ye not in your houses pleasant light?
And, when the angel of God the first-born smote
Of all the Egyptians,—of yours died there one? . . .
Such marvellous things beholding, can ye ask,
Will God give help to us? *Hath* He not given?
Who, think ye, save Jehovah, these things did?
And, having so far wrought, can ye believe
He would forsake us,—lacking strength, or will,
All to accomplish? Can ye think that God
Like man is,—weak in counsel,—changeable
In purpose,—one day willing; and, the next,
Unwilling,—doubtful, or irresolute,
Or fearful to perform? Nay,—for, with Him,
To will,—to do,—are one. That which He bids,
Is done in the bidding; though a thousand years
Lie 'twixt the word, and act. When first the voice
Of the Lord God on Horeb spake to me,
Commanding that to Pharaoh I should go,
And out of Egypt bring forth Israel,—
EVEN IN THAT MOMENT ISRAEL WAS BROUGHT FORTH!
Ye see it not as yet; for, bit by bit,
Man's weak eye noteth,—even as, foot by foot,

Distance he measureth. Long, to us, the path
From Zoan hither,—trodden step by step;—
But, had the lightning that way travelled, lo,
Here, and in Zoan, at same point of time,
Men had cried out, 'it lightens!' So, with God,
Present, and future, as one moment are:
With HIM, a thousand years, as but one day;
One day as a thousand years. What is begun,—
With HIM, is finished. Our deliverance, then,
Assured is as the thing done ages back.
God sees all things complete,—in progress, man:
And, in that progress, now, such fearful thing
Do ye behold, that all the wonders past
Seem blotted from your sight; as if the spears,
The arrows, swords, the chariots and the horse
Of Pharaoh, mightier than Jehovah were;
And all that He hath done, must be as nought! ......
Ay——ye hear now the thunder of their wheels,
And their horse-trampling: with one ear, to me,
Speaking of Him Omnipotent, ye list;
But, with the other,—as though God were none,
Or impotent to save,—ye drink in dread
From a poor mortal clamor! Be ye sure,
That for Jehovah's purpose, not their own,
Hither they come against us. Factious men,
And unbelieving,—with the words of scorn,
And bitter malice, have cried out on me,
'Why hast thou hither brought us? to this place,
Wherefrom is no escape: on three sides, rocks
Impassable; and, on the fourth, the sea;
And, now, behind us, Pharaoh and his host?'
Not *I* have brought you, men of Israel,
But THE LORD GOD! For, both to me He spake,
Commanding us the way; and His own sign,—
A pillar of cloud by day, of fire by night,—
Sent to conduct us. Is there of you one,
Who this great marvel saw not? Yet, alas!
Though clear as noonday sun ye must behold
That God is for us,—let but Egypt's king
Rattle the sword against you,—and ye sink,
Fear-palsied, and the Omnipotent forget!

Ah! murmuring that hither are ye brought,
Not against *me* ye rail, but 'gainst your God!
Had my poor wisdom ruled,—to any place,
Rather than this, had I conducted you:
For well, of yore, I knew it, as a pit
Wherein, defenceless as a flock of sheep
Penned up for slaughter, verily must they lie,
'Gainst whom should come the enemy.—But, think not
That therefore do I fear; or doubt the end;
Or, if I could, would fly; or, if my word
Could rend the rocks, and leave you passage free,—
That I would speak it! No. Though Pharaoh's might
Could dash this Red Sea over Sinai's brow,—
Yet, trusting in the promise of our God,
Nought would I fear him! To this perilous spot,—
Of all within the realm *most* perilous,—
By the plain hand of God have we been brought:
And here, then, be ye certain, greatest is
Our safety; greatest, too, will be the victory!

" Even yet hangs terror o'er you, like thick night:
But the day cometh. Have ye never heard,
How, when this earth was without form and void;
And darkness on the face of the great deep,—
God said, 'Let there be light,'—and there *was* light?
Even so on your thick darkness a great light
Soon will burst forth. In whatsoever way
His will may work,—sure as yon heaven above,
This earth beneath,—deliverance draweth near;
Yea, a complete deliverance. From the sky,
Chariots innumerable, and horses winged,
May come to bear us hence:—mountains may sink,
And leave us level way:—deep into earth
The sea may dive; or be dried up like dew,
That we may pass:—on Pharaoh, and his host,
Hills may come down,—earthquake may swallow them,—
The deep may leave its bed, and cover them:—
Work howsoe'er He may,—deliverance swift,—
Yea, even this night,—God will to Israel bring!
Lift then . . ."

With more than prophet's ardor, and tone
Thrilling as victory-trumpet, speaking thus,—
Suddenly mute, he sank; and, face to earth,
Lay prostrate: for, from highest heaven, again
Came down to him the Voice.
"Why unto me
Thus criest thou? To the children of Israel speak,
That they go forward. But, lift thou thy rod,
And stretch thine hand out, and divide the sea;
And through the midst thereof, upon dry ground,
My people shall pass on. Hard are the hearts
Of the Egyptians: they will follow quick,
To slay them. Then, on Pharaoh, and his host,
His chariots, and his horsemen, will the hand
Of God fall heavily! So all men may know,
That, before Him, the mightiest are as dust."

Save Moses, no man heard: but, in great awe
Stood all the people;—for, while spake the Voice,
Earth, and air, trembled. In the silence deep,
Louder, and nearer, heard they the horse-clang,—
The thunder of the chariots, hurrying on,—
The uproar of fierce voices: yet no eye,
Turned toward them now: astonished, motionless,
As in a trance seemed all,—their heads bowed down,
Their clasped hands quivering.
But, in little while,
Moses stood up; his countenance yet more bright;
His voice loud, and exultant; and thus cried.
"Fear ye not, children of Israel; but stand still;
And the salvation of the Lord behold,
Which even this day will He show unto you:
For the Egyptians whom ye have seen today,
Them shall ye see again no more for ever.
God will fight for you; ye shall hold your peace.
Now, all ye people, to your tribes go back:
Strike every tent: in order set yourselves;
Your flocks, and herds, your camels, oxen, wains;
And toward the seashore march: then shall ye see
How God will lead us forth."

                        Like men from sleep,
And fearful dreams awaked; and, with new hope,
And strength, on some bold enterprise intent,—
Those great words having heard, each to his task,
The people hasted. Since the noon, had blown
A mighty strong east wind; but not a cloud
As yet had come; and, with unwonted light,
Blazed out the stars; so that, with ease, and speed,
Their work was done. Then, all along the shore,
Tribe behind tribe, in orderly array,
They gathered; and stood still.
                            With long, sharp slope,
The lofty plain down to the sea-marge fell;
So, with clear view, rank over rank might look
On the vexed deep beneath. With heavy roll,
Wave after wave,—jet black, or smeared with gleams
Of glittering starlight,—on the sandy beach
Broke, foaming; and dragged back; and burst again,
With noise like far-off thunder. Thus stood they,
Mute, and prepared; waiting some marvel to come.

   But, suddenly, from the whole multitude burst
Cries of amazement; for, as from the depths
It had upstarted,—the great pillar of fire
Stood blazing on the waters! Every eye
Shut, as at lightning-flash. Man, woman, child,
Throughout the host had seen it: yet again,
Lids quivering, all looked out,—eager to see
If aright they had seen, — though plain as mid-day sun,
Before them had it stood; as if to sign
Their path across the deep!—a miracle,
Could it be done, beyond all miracles else.
Yea,—rightly had they seen,—there stood it still,
Dashing the billows with fire; and all the air
Flooding with glory!
                     But great terror then
On thousands came; for, looking back, they saw
Mountain, and rock, as to a new-risen sun,
Radiantly glowing: and full surely, now

Pharaoh, they thought, would waken, and leap up;
And see their plight; and fall upon them yet.

But nought feared Moses. Clear had been command
What he should do: and, for the rest, to God,
Unquestioning, all he left. But, when he saw
That in deep silence paused the multitude,
Gazing upon him, waiting what should come,—
To a low rock above the waves he walked:
Stood, looked to heaven, and lifted up his rod,
And stretched it o'er the sea.
      As though a plough,
Titanic, lightning-swift, from shore to shore,
To its bed had ploughed the deep,—leaving agape
The monstrous furrow; and the white sea sands,
All glistening——so, at falling of the rod,
Rent were the waters, and the depths were bared!
Thundering, to right and left the billows ran;
Reared up, and stood like walls; like ice-cliffs stood:
And lo! betwixt them, far as eye could reach,—
Down in the heart of the sea, a broad bright path;
A highway for a nation! But, behold!
Again a marvel: for, while yet they gazed,—
Deep in the chasm,—as with a voice from heaven
Calling them on,—blazed out the pillar of fire!

As earth had opened, or heaven's arch come down,
Astounded stood the people; motionless;
Almost of sense bereft.
     A maiden first,
Upon a milk-white mule, before the rest
A few steps moved, and paused: toward Moses looked;
Then heavenward, as in prayer; bowed her meek head,
And down the steep bank rode. Close after her,
On a hot steed, a youth; two aged men,
And one weak woman, followed. Burst out then
From the whole multitude, a voice of joy;
And, forward pressing, every head bent low,
Down the steep shore they went. 'Twixt wall, and wall,
Thousands abreast, on the bright glistening road,

Down went they; horsemen first; the cattle then;
The laden camels, and wains; then those on foot:
Tribe after-tribe, all orderly, all mute,
All worshipping their God,—to the sea-depths
Fearlessly down they went.
      Their children and wives
With Levi having sent, that, unperplexed,
Themselves might all direct,—last of the host,
Moses and Aaron, with their heads bent low,
And glad hearts praising God, together rode.
Thus, all in silence, as through dell profound
Amid the mountains, Israel went on,
Treading the shining bottom of the deep!

 Meantime, the Egyptians slumbered. From the pass
Ere half could issue, darkness had come down:
And word from Pharaoh, therefore, had been sent,
That, till the dawn, the sword should be at peace:
In Migdol, and in Pi-hahiroth, some
Couched for the night: but on the dewy grass,
Sore wearied, sank the rest; even than revenge,
Sleep deeming sweeter.
      But the unwearied ones,
The Spirits of Evil, slept not. On the camp
Of Israel, till night-fell, had they looked down,—
Seeing the mortal terror; all athirst
For the great consummation,—Israel swept
From off the face of earth; or backward led
To old captivity,—and God so foiled.
But, suddenly, when came the Voice Divine,
To Moses speaking,—unendurable all
They felt that Presence;—and, as darkness flies
From sunbeams, so fled they: nor, till by Heaven
Permitted, could return; or, through the gloom
'Twixt them and Israel, pierce.
      But power, at length,
Restored they felt; and toward the camp looked out.
Lo! the vast plain was empty!—to its bed,
The stormy sea rent open!—far away,
A great light in its depths;—and all the host

Of Israel marching on!
                    Satan himself,
In that same instant, stood beside the king,—
In form, and voice, a captain of his guard,—
And cried aloud; "O Splendor of the Sun,
Awake, awake! Thy chariots, and thy horse,
Call up; and thunder on false Israel!
The sorcerer hath channelled the deep sea;
And the slaves go onward dry-shod!"
                              Like a shaft
Loosed from the bow, sprang Pharaoh. "Haste," he
    cried;
"Bid sound the trumpets: run throughout the camp:
Cry, 'Up! The slaves escape! To the sea, the sea!'"

   Speaking, himself ran out, and called aloud.
But Satan, where most numerous lay the host,
Flew; and, tower-statured, stood; and sent abroad
Voice so terrific, that, from cloud to earth,
The air was shattered; and the very ground,
As with great blows was shaken. "Wake! awake!
Up, every horse, and chariot, and pursue!
The sea-bed is laid bare, and Israel flies!
Up, Up; pursue, and slay!"
                        Down in the depths,—
Like to articulate thunder over head,—
Even to the van of Israel reached the cry!
Sound so tremendous never ear had heard;
And, of the horsemen, many from the rest
Dashed onward, terror-struck. But that gentle maid,
Still with the foremost riding fearlessly,
Though silent, and awe-filled,—the secret bed
Of the deep beholding, and the watery cliffs
By Power Divine upheld,—upon the youth
At her left hand smiled lovingly, and said;
"Call out unto them—'Be ye not afraid:
Is not God with us?'"
                    Her encouraging words
With loud voice Reuben echoed: and, as *he*,
So cried out thousands aloud; that, to the rank,

Rode back the flyers, ashamed. With steady pace,
Again then all went on.
                                    But, while to these,
At distance, such the terror of that shout
Demoniac,—to the Egyptians, underneath
The living crater, terrible more than roar
Of battling thunders was it. Man, and horse,
In a moment sprang to their feet; the heaviest sleep
Gone,—even as darkness, at the opening lid.
No trumpet needed now,—like hounds let loose,
Away to the chase they flew. Each, as to horse,
Or car he sprang,—untarrying rank to take,
Or hear command,—captains and soldiers mixed,—
Headlong urged onward. Even for the king
None waited: and, of horsemen, many there were
Who, ere into his chariot he could mount,
Far on the plain were flying. But, erelong,
Borne by his wind-swift steeds, in midst of them
Flashed he; burning with fury; clamoring loud:
And, of his chosen chariots, after him
Soon came on many; all at tempest speed
Battering the ground; the scourges whirling high;
Cries going up, and curses terrible
Against perfidious Israel. In brief time,
With noise as of a hurricane, all the horse
And chariots tore the plain. But, foremost far,
Flew Pharaoh now; and, soon above the brink
Of the steep shore arriving,—hurriedly stopped;
And looked down on the troubled sea; and saw
A wide road therein; and, to either hand,
The billows sharply curbed; and like huge cliffs
Upstanding: and, far onward, and deep down
Within the chasm,—as in a very blaze
Of sunshine all distinct,—the countless host
Of Israel wending on! Amazement great
Fell on him. With wide-opened eyes, he stood,—
As doubting what he saw: such wonderment
Of magic seemed it: for, of God's own hand
Therein displayed, even yet believed he not;
Blind to the last. With fiery speed, came soon

Chariots, and horse ; and close upon the brink
Stopped also ; and looked down, in wonder and fear :
The void so awful ; so death-threatening
The watery heights ; held up, in that vexed sea,—
They doubted not,—by sorcery alone ;
And, by same terrible power, to be let loose,
At the dread sorcerer's will.
      "Hold, Pharaoh, hold!"
Cried Hophra ; from his chariot leaping down,
And running toward the king : "I like it not.
Magic most damnable this, in one great trap
To catch all Egypt ! Fling not life away
On this false road ; but let the Hebrews go !
We cannot match yon wizard. All our art
Not for a moment could hold back those deeps,
If he would hurl them on us ! To leave pass
For Israel only, hath he scooped the sea,
And piled its waters. If thou enter in,
Oh Pharaoh, thou art lost !"
      Like one long shriek
Sounded his warning cry. But, demon-fired,
Cared not the king. "Down, down!" madly he cried ;
"They crawl on foot : with horse, and chariots, we
May sweep on them like wind ! Away, away !
Down on them, every chariot, every horse !
On, on ! smite, trample, and slay !"
      Thus calling out,
In his own hands the reins and scourge he caught ;
And whirled on high the thong, and smote the steeds,
And drove them thundering down into the depth !
Fired by the sight, and by the maniac cry,—
The charioteers, and horsemen, yelling aloud,
Rushed after him headlong down to the bed of the sea !

 In line direct as if by sunbeam drawn,
Before them lay the road ; and, far thereon,
The Israelites : yet not a doubt had they
Soon to o'ertake, and slay them. With wild cries,
As at the hunt of beasts, they rent the air ;
Breasting the strong east wind ; and through the sands,

That sank beneath the wheel, and stamping hoof,
Urging their panting horses.
                            But, erelong,
Yet other hindrance found they: ponderous clouds
Suddenly filled the air; the steady blast,
Like a struck lion, roared out angrily:
Sharp sloping from the sky, came down large rain:
The clouds hailed lightnings; thunders rocked the air:
Yet still, all demon-maddened, drove they on,
Down, down to the deep; for still, in every pause
Of wind and thunder, Pharaoh's voice was heard,
Calling them onward: and,—in outward form
Of charioteer, and horseman,—demons, too,
Soul-maddening yells sent up.
                            But, more and more
Heavily dragged the wheels: deeper the hoofs
Sank in the sand: louder the pantings rose.
The tempest also, through the great sea-gorge,
As through a deep defile among the hills,
Fiercer and fiercer smote them. In the roar
Of wind, and thunder, at length, and dash of rain,
The mad king's shriekings,—even the demon-cries,—
By few were heard at all: and a dark fear
Crept over them, when,—lower going down
Into the depth,—quick glances they cast up,
And saw the o'erhanging waters, higher and higher
Still towering; in the lightning, and the glare
Of the fire-pillar, like to cliffs of flame.
Nathless, still urged they on the terrible chase;
Still on the Israelites gaining rapidly:
Till, toward the middle of the midnight watch,—
Within few bow-shots come; and confident now
That in the very midst soon should they be,
Smiting, and trampling,—such wild yell they raised,
That, through the thunder, wind, and roar of wave,
To the foremost of the Israelites it reached;
And with cold terror smote them, that their hearts
Sank, as at death-touch; and, for flight itself,
Strength had they none.
                        But still that gentle maid,—

Alway in foremost rank,—looking around,
Spake cheeringly. "Father, lift up thy voice,—
And thou, too, Reuben,—cry unto the men,
'Be not afraid; put all your trust in God.
Hath He not opened for you the sea-depths,
That ye may pass? and shall *man* hinder Him?'"

Her stirring words from rank to rank flew quick,
And many a heart made joyful. In like way,
Unto the rear, on whom worse terror was,
Spake Moses, and Aaron, riding rapidly
To right, and left; and, with a voice of power,
Bidding them fear not. Still the maniac cries
Louder they heard,—nearer, and nearer yet;—
The wheels harsh grinding, and the tramp of horse;—
Yet, in protection of Jehovah's might
Confiding, and fulfilment of His word,
Nought feared at all; but, with untroubled soul,
The end awaited.
     Within bow-shot now
Of Israel drove the Egyptian thunder-cloud;
And from the king, and all his men of war,
Louder and louder came the savage yells,
Curses and threats,—when, suddenly, behold!
Darkness, like a thick pall, dropped over them!
Their clamor ceased on the instant: every horse
Stood fixed; and every man for terror gasped;
And not a tongue could speak!
       On Israel, too,
Came darkness: for, behold! the pillar of fire,
Which still before them, as their guide, had gone,—
Even in the twinkling of an eye, removed,
And went behind them! so that blackest night
Awhile encompassed them; and mortal dread
O'ershadowed. "God hath left us!" they shrieked out;
"We are delivered up unto the sword!"

"God is aye with us,"—in triumphant tone
Cried Rachel,—"our salvation is at hand!"

"God is aye with us,"—shouted Reuben then;
"Salvation is at hand!" Then Kohath, too,
And Malachi, and others who had heard,
Lift up their voices: rank to rank called out
The inspiring words: and, even while yet they cried,—
Sight gathering strength,—from the great glory behind,
Soon, as in sunrise, seemed they; and went on
Rejoicing; for Jehovah's outstretched hand
They saw, deliverance bringing.
                                From first step
Of that night's wondrous march, strength had all felt,
Unknown till then; lightness of heart, and limb,
That bore them swiftly on: but, now, even more
Uplifted felt they; and, with rapid strides,
Swept o'er the sands; which sank not to their tread,
But, rather, seemed, as with a living power,
To raise, and press them onward.
                                Wherefore thus
The fiery pillar had behind them gone,
Reasoned as yet but few: for most, enough,
That surely had God ordained it; and that, so,
Best must it be. But instantly knew they,
The sons of Amram,—when, like new-risen sun,
Close in the rear it shone,—that, to divide
Egypt from Israel, had the angel of God
The pillar of fire removed; thus to keep back,
As with a wall of flame, their enemies.
But evën they knew not that, while great light
It gave to Israel,—from its face of cloud,
On Egypt it poured blackness; and brought down
Fear, and confusion.
                    As in sunshine, then,
Lightly and swiftly went the Hebrews on;
Hearing, indeed, the thunder, and the roar
Of waters overhead; yet, by no stroke
Of lightning troubled, nor one drop of rain.
But,—for the host of Egypt,—tempest, and rain,
And thunder staggered them; and darkness thick,
By lightnings only kindled. Mortal fear

Sank every heart: their blowing horses reeled;
Their chariots dragged on heavily: yet still
Forward they pressed; unknowing that in light,
As of the morn, went Israel; and full sure,
Even with their out-worn steeds, soon to o'ertake
Men slowly toiling on foot.
      But now no more
Clamors of hate and vengeance were sent up:
In gloomy silence they all labored on;
Staring aghast,—as deep, and deeper yet,
Down went they,—to behold the watery cliffs,
Higher, and higher, towering, right, and left;
Pitch-black, or lightning-fired; but evermore
Looking down death upon them.
      By command,
In chariots nigh the king his sorcerers rode;
And, in brief silence of the thunder, thus,
Lifting his voice to the height, he questioned them.
"Where be the slaves? But now, as in broad day,
Clearly we saw them, scarce a bow-shot off,—
Yet, now, with keenest out-look, not one man
Or beast we see; but, in their place, thick cloud;
A blackness solid as earth; ay, even like that
Which three days tombed all Egypt. Can ye not
One ray of light call up to kindle it,
And show the bondsmen? Why, a very sun,
To guide them, Moses called: not even the light
Of one poor torch can all your art bid forth?
Heard I not clearly, at times, the neigh of horse,
And even but now the outcry of the men,
Verily should I doubt if magic power
Had not their whole host carried through the air;
Or underneath the earth. . . . . What! not one word
Have ye in answer? . . . . Hophra, speak out thou.
Thou, who to life couldst summon back the dead,
Surely on darkness mayst bring light enough
To pierce yon cloud; and let us see the slaves."

With stern and solemn voice, to Pharaoh then
Hophra made answer.

"King—thy slaves are free!
Are lost to thee for aye! Crown, sceptre, throne,
Kingdom, and life are lost! Ah,—cried I not
In anguish to thee, from this fatal trap
To keep thy foot; and let the Hebrews flee?
Were't not that, surely, more than half-way o'er
We have journeyed,—lived there but a shadow of hope,
Even yet might I implore thee to turn back,
And let the Israelites go. But, ah! O king!
Do now whatso' thou wilt! Go on,—go back,—
Stay where thou art,—alike must be the end!
Look to the watery mountains overhead;
And think what 'tis upholds them; what will loose!
See the foam quivering on their angry lips!
They roar,—they gnash the teeth, and spit at us:
They know us for their prey: they long to leap!
Could we outspeed the hurricane,—neither shore
Now might we reach! their jaws would swallow us!"

"Coward, and fool!" cried Pharaoh: "On, press on:
Perchance even now, though we behold them not,
Our horses graze their heels. Ply scourge, drive spur;
Away, away! Yet look forth heedfully:
And who first sees them,—loudly on the king
Let him cry out; then come before his face,
For thanks, and guerdon; even the richest gem
On Pharaoh's finger." Of the charioteers,
And horsemen, at these words, went out no few,
Spurring, and scourging: but, in thickest night
Quickly bewildered,—stopped, and stirred no more,
Till the dread cloud had passed; and, close at hand,
They spied the horse, and chariots. With them then
They mingled; and not one again went forth.

Thus, till the morning watch, through tempest, and
    rain,
Lightning, and thunder, did they labor on;
Awe-struck, and silent; save when, man to man,
Desponding spake they, wondering what should come.

But heavier, now, and heavier dragged the wheels:
Deeper, and deeper in the sand 'gan sink
The straining horses; and, like second storm,
Sounded their pantings; for, up hill, at length,
Nearing the land, they clomb; and harder toiled,
And slower still made way.
                        With boastful voice,
At length cried Pharaoh, "We shall smite them yet:
Nigh to the shore we draw. Once on firm ground,
Soon shall we be among them. At the most,
One hour can we hold onward. . . . . Hark!—Ye gods!
We are upon them *now!* Hear ye not plain
The lowing of their oxen? On! away!
Heed not the darkness! plunge into it deep.
'Tis but the trick of magic,—a false cloud,—
Burst through it, and fall on. Once with them mixed,
The sorcerer will not dare call down the waves,
Lest Israel, too, should perish. Lift now up
Your voices all together in a shout
Shall loose their joints. Spur then, and smite your steeds,
And drive into the blackness; and stop not
Till in the midst ye come, and trample them."

So Pharaoh, by the Arch-Fiend to frenzy fired:
And, by a legion possessed,—both men, and steeds—
Chariots, and horse, in a moment thundered on,
Tearing the sands; men yelling like wild beasts;
The horses madly shrieking. But, behold!
Even in a moment,—as a heavy weight
Drops on the ground,—so, a dead silence fell,
And the wild hurly crushed. The demons fled:
In full career, trembling, the horses stopped:
Men shrank back, shuddering: rain, and roaring wind,
Stayed in mid blast: the billows overhead
Sank voiceless: half-way down from heaven,
Died out the bolts: a stillness of the grave,
And darkness, shadowed earth, and sea, and sky:
And, lo! from out the cloud,—lightning his eyes,
His brow piled thunders,—the great angel of God
Looked down upon the host!

                         Breath, motion, stopped:
The men became as stones! The very steeds
Felt Supernatural Presence; and recoiled,
Staring, and trembling.
                         But, anon, went up
A cry that shivered the air,—"Turn back! turn back!
Let us flee from the face of Israel! The Lord
Fighteth for them against the Egyptians! Turn,
Turn back, and flee!"
                         At that terrific cry,
Sharply the horses were turned,—horse against horse
Dashing, and casting down! Wheel inside wheel
Entangling, grinding horribly, was torn off:
Axles were snapped, and chariots flung to the ground;
Yet on flew the horses still. In one dense mass,—
Confusion infinite,—down to the deep—down—down—
They tore along the sands. But, heavier soon
The chariots dragged; deeper sank hoof, and wheel:
The panting coursers staggered, stopped, and groaned.
Vain were the driver's curse, the stamping foot,
The prick of spear, the sharply hissing scourge.
One car except, all at the last stood still,—
Steeds fallen, and dying; or, with vain attempt,
Struggling a step to move. In wild despair,
Men cried aloud; and lifted up their hands,
Calling on Egypt's gods: some, to the ground
Headforemost leaped; with mad hope, even on foot,
To path the sea-depths: but, at every step,
Deeper and deeper they sank,—as though the sands
Knew them, and clutched their prey. Then did they
    howl,
And curse themselves, and Pharaoh, and Israel,
And their own gods, who saw, and would not help;
And call upon the lightnings to come down,
And blast them. But the curse, and prayer, alike,
In wind and thunder were lost.
                         Pharaoh, meantime,
Alone within his chariot, labored on,
Frenzied with terror. But, still more and more,
The wheels sank, and the horse-feet,—till, at last,

To the axles buried,—as in rock hard fixed,
Stood the car, motionless. On the cavalry, then,
Short space before him,—crowded, and confused;
Driving the spur, but deep, and deeper still,
Sinking at every step, and floundering,—
In pauses of the thunder, and the wind,
Cried he incessantly; "A horse, a horse,—
It is the king who calls. A horse—The king—
A horse for Pharaoh!"—But they heard him not;
Or did not heed. For his own life alone
Cared each man now: to right and left they glared
On the death-boding waters; and not one,
The king of kings to save, would backward look.

Meantime, with vigorous limb, and cheerful heart,
Still pressing onward,—Israel the steep shore
Had mounted; every man, and woman, and child,
And every beast. Fled then the pillar of fire,
And the grey dawn appeared. The cattle first
Driven forward,—all along the edge of the sea,
Crowding the high steep land, the people stood,
Silent, and pale, awaiting what should come:
For, that the Hand Omnipotent, in that hour,
A mighty work to accomplish, was put forth,
Doubt had they none. On Egypt, punishment,
Sudden and fearful, looked they to behold:
But, unto Israel, as the promise had been,
Salvation brought; yea, full deliverance.

Silently then they stood; down the great chasm
With strained eyes looking. In that depth, as yet,
The grey light pierced not; and dusk horror filled
The fearful void; save when a lingering bolt
For a moment fired the darkness, and flashed back
From arms and chariots. In the brief gleam, then,
They saw that, not pursuing, but in flight,
The Egyptians toiled, and fear-struck; for, like howl
Of wintry tempest, hideous wailings rose;
Outcries of uttermost horror and despair,
As when the drowning sink. All shuddering,

Pallid, and speechless, gazed the Israelites:
For the great billows,—to the very brink
Of the dread sea-chasm rushing, leaning o'er,—
At every heave, seemed frantic to break loose
From the Power that held them back; and the piled deeps
Hurl down into the void.   But, rapidly
Day brightened: and, when rose the sun, and shot
Right in the depth of the gorge his level rays,—
Clearly then saw they the Egyptian host,—
So terrible once,—in dire confusion now,
And horror infinite; with vain attempt,
Struggling to fly: their chariots all firm fixed;
Their horsemen, as through quagmires, laboring;
Their men on foot, nigh to the knee sunk down;
And all with arms and faces lifted up
To the overhanging deeps. With hands hard clasped,
White lips, strained eyeballs, — shuddering, breathing quick,
Long stood they gazing; listening the wild shrieks;
Beholding the death-struggle.   But, at length,
Face to the ground sank Moses,—for the Voice
Again came down to him,—to him alone,
Thus saying; "Stretch out thine hand over the sea;
That on the Egyptians may the waters come,
Upon their chariots, and upon their horse."

O'erawed awhile he lay; then slowly rose,
Pallid, and trembling. A brief time he stood,
On the depth gazing, and the agonized host;
Then looked to heaven, and lifted up the rod,
And stretched it o'er the sea.   The piled-up waves
Expecting stood: they knew the sign, and sank!
Headlong on both sides of the chasm at once,
Like a thousand hurricanes roaring, down they sank:
Fierce as destroying demons met in the midst:
Clashed, — leaped, — swept back;—in mountain ridges again

Upgathered, foam-crowned as high cliffs with snow:
Again plunged down,—shocked,—broke,—arose anew,
Hill lashing hill;—roared, reeled, and rocked, and
    boiled;—
All the great deep shaking in every limb,
Like maniac in his frenzy's agony!

At their first stamp, the mighty armament
Of Egypt, like a spark, was trodden out!
The dust of their great battle reached the clouds;—
Their shouts were as thronging thunders: with their
    crash,
All the shores trembled, and the eternal hills!

Shuddering, and faint, and heart-sick; with raised
    hands,
Faces like death, eyes gleaming, shaking knees,
The Hebrews gazing stood. A wonderment
Beyond all wonders past had they beheld:
The might of God, as though with visible arm
From heaven put forth, smiting their enemies:
Pharaoh, his men of war, chariots, and horse,
Buried for ever; and, above their grave,
The enormous waves exulting: the whole sea,
Far as the eye could reach, a battle-field
For clashing mountains!
                         Gazing, long they stood,
Bewildered, mute with awe: but, when, at length,
The uproar slackened, man to man cried out,
In words of joy and thankfulness; "Our God,
Hath now indeed His mighty hand put forth,
To strike the oppressor, and His people save!
Glory and praise to Him for evermore!"

Then Moses spake aloud; "Call hither now
The priests, and Elders; the musicians all,
And singers; for a great song will we sing
To God for our deliverance."
                              Soon came they:
And, when he saw that all awaited him,—

With sudden inspiration filled, his voice
He lifted up, and sang: and all the rest,
Like inspiration catching, mightily
Sent forth the voice; that, as at trumpet-blast,
Leaped every heart of Israel. Thus they sang.

"I will sing unto the Lord,
For He hath triumphed gloriously;
The horse and his rider hath He thrown into the sea!
Pharaoh's chariots and his horse
Hath he cast into the sea;
His chosen captains hath He drownëd.

"The depths have covered them!
They sank into the bottom as a stone!
They sank as lead in the mighty waters!
The floods stood upright as a heap;
The depths were congealed in the heart of the sea!

" Who is like unto Thee, O Lord,
Who is like Thee, glorious in holiness,
Fearful in praises, doing wonders!
The Lord shall reign for ever and ever!"

Then Miriam the prophetess, sister of Aaron, took
A timbrel in her hand; and, after her,
The women all, with timbrels and dances went;
And Miriam sang aloud, and answered them:
"Sing ye unto the Lord,
For He hath triumphed gloriously;
The horse and his rider hath He thrown into the sea!"

Then, when the song had ended, once again
With clear voice Moses spake.
                    "Pitch now your tents,
Ye men of Israel; and take food, and rest:
Even till the ninth hour rest. But gather then,
That all our voices may go up in prayer,
And praise, and glory unto God, who thus
Hath smitten the oppressor, and brought forth

His people out of bondage. Two days more
Here will we rest; that, all in health and strength,
Into the desert of Shur we may go on,
Toward Horeb;—for, as ye before have heard,—
Upon that holy mountain while by night
I watched my father's flocks,—from the burning bush
Thus the Lord spake to me: 'When thou hast brought
The people out of Egypt, on this hill,
Shall ye serve God.' Toward Horeb, therefore, first,
Our way is: onward thence to that fair land,
Flowing with milk and honey,—wherein, at length,
As in their home, after long exile past,
The bones of our loved Joseph may be tombed;
In peace for ever to sleep;—that Canaan,
Whence into Egypt holy Abraham came;
Wherein,—so was it promised him—should dwell
His sons, a numerous people. . . . . And, behold!
Even now begins fulfilment of that word!
Here we, his sons, and daughters, a great host,
By God Himself conducted, ready stand
Thither to journey! . . . . Perils may we meet;
Hunger, and thirst, the pestilence, and the sword:
Even our own sins, of enemies the worst,
May fight against us: none the end can see. . . . .
Who shall arrive,—who perish by the way,
God only knoweth! . . . . But, great things indeed,
For us, His favored children, hath He done;
And will not, like to changeful man, his face
Turn from us, if from Him ourselves turn not.
Our God He hath been,—is,—and aye will be,
While we His people.—Glory, honor, and power,
In Heaven, and earth, to Him for evermore!"

THE END.

www.ingramcontent.com/pod-product-compliance
Lightning Source LLC
Chambersburg PA
CBHW040326300426
44113CB00020B/2668